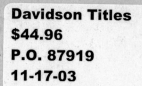

PROJECT
MANAGEMENT

PROJECT MANAGEMENT
Achieving Project Bottom-Line Succe$$

WILLIAM J. PINKERTON

McGraw-Hill
New York • Chicago • San Francisco • Lisbon • London • Madrid
Mexico City • Milan • New Delhi • San Juan • Seoul
Singapore • Sydney • Toronto

The McGraw·Hill Companies

Library of Congress Cataloging-in-Publication Data

Pinkerton, William J.
    Project management : achieving project bottom-line succe$$ /
William J. Pinkerton.
        p.   cm.
    The word 'success' in the subtitle is written with two dollar signs.
    Includes index.
    ISBN 0-07-141281-6 (alk. paper)
    1. Project management.   I. Title.
HD69.P75P547   2003
658.4'04—dc21   2002044873

1 2 3 4 5 6 7 8 9 0   DOC/DOC   0 9 8 7 6 5 4 3

ISBN 0-07-141281-6

*The sponsoring editor for this book was Larry S. Hager, the editing
supervisor was Stephen M. Smith, and the production supervisor was
Pamela A. Pelton. It was set in Fairfield Medium by Joanne Morbit of
McGraw-Hill Professional's Hightstown, N.J., composition unit.*

Printed and bound by RR Donnelley.

This book is printed on recycled, acid-free paper containing a
minimum of 50% recycled, de-inked fiber.

McGraw-Hill books are available at special quantity discounts to use as
premiums and sales promotions, or for use in corporate training programs.
For more information, please write to the Director of Special Sales,
McGraw-Hill Professional, Two Penn Plaza, New York, NY 10121-2298.
Or contact your local bookstore.

CONTENTS

CHAPTER EIGHT. PROJECT EXECUTION— CONSTRUCTION AND INSTALLATION

CHAPTER NINE. ON-SITE (PREOPERATIONAL) TESTING

CHAPTER TEN. COMMISSIONING!

CHAPTER ELEVEN. PROJECT-RELATED TRAINING

CHAPTER TWELVE. THE SMALLER PROJECTS   267

CHAPTER THIRTEEN. THE ENVIRONMENTAL PROJECT   281

FOREWORD

One of the biggest challenges facing today's major industrial corporations is the manner in which capital improvement projects are handled. So much depends on it. Not only are capital improvement projects expensive (some in the hundreds of millions of dollars), but a wrong strategic decision can cost a company its place in the market. The result can be disastrous, to say the least.

In this book, William J. Pinkerton offers a candid look not only at the origins, planning, and execution of these projects but also at the strategic thinking that should be taking place from the outset. I say "should be" because, unfortunately, too often this strategic thinking isn't taking place. In over 35 years of observing and taking part in some of the largest capital improvement projects in the world, I can state unequivocally that this book has hit the nail square on the head; that is, one must think and plan strategically with but one overriding priority in mind—all activities must take direct aim at positive contribution to the corporate bottom line. Nothing else matters!

Now I know that almost every CEO, every general manager, every project manager will say that this is exactly what he or she does. But it isn't true! Many, many projects shouldn't go forward at all. They are products of emotionalism, ego, short-term gain, and illogical or "sideways" thinking that are usually brought about by insufficient front-end planning. Most of these projects will fail; and by *fail* I mean they will either return less than they should to the bottom line or, in the worst cases, seriously damage the corporate entity. Only rarely will a failed project lead a company into total failure; a *series* of these projects can, however, lead to corporate demise over an extended period of time.

One of the points made dramatically in this book is the widespread misunderstanding by many project teams of the term *bottom-line dollar*. The million-, multimillion-, and, yes, even *billion*-dollar project cost terms are thrown about so easily by corporate project planners and teams that the impact of the origin of these huge sums of capital becomes obscured. These are not *sales* dollars; these are dollars that collectively make up the "bottom line." These are corporate *profits* that are being spent! It takes a tremendous amount of product sales to produce these dollars. This, then, is the reason that the message put forward by this book is so important.

We are now operating in a global economy and, although most managers have the best interests of the company at heart, many of the decisions we have seen indicate that they are triggered by interests that are in reality short-term solutions, solutions that may not be in the best long-term interests of the corporation, venture, or other entity.

The term *Project <u>Bottom-Line</u> Success!* is not just another empty corporate phrase; it's a philosophy, a philosophy that can help guide our thinking as we consider the impact on the venture of these decisions affecting capital improvement projects.

The decisions that we make may not only affect the project at hand, but the long-term competitiveness of our respective companies. It is after all a *global* economy and the competition is fierce.

Project <u>Bottom-Line</u> Success!, or *PBLS*, is a model for first assessing the need and then making the proper decisions in the execution of a project. It addresses not just the aspects of design, procurement, and construction activities, but, more important, the effect of the project on the corporate bottom line and the long-term strategic interests of the company.

The use of a structured methodology leading to successful project selection, execution, and start-up is absolutely essential because the project costs, although sometimes high, pale in comparison to the operating costs and loss of revenues and profits if the project is a failure, from the standpoint of either selection or execution.

When operating revenues are in the many thousands of dollars per minute, we cannot afford the mistake of either an unneeded project or a poorly executed one. The costs can be catastrophic not only to the company's bottom line, but also to its position in the marketplace relative to its competitors.

Good project management and start-ups are absolutely paramount to the success of any company. The cost of poorly planned and executed projects often exceeds the cost of the capital investment, effectively forcing the stockholders to pay in many cases double what they should for their investment. This is not only unfair to the stockholders, it could even lead to the demise of the venture. Investors don't back losing propositions for long.

A successful project starts with the germ of an idea. The idea must be good, and it must fit in with corporate strategy. There is no room in the *Project Bottom-Line Success!* methodology for what we might call emotionally driven projects. Emotionally driven projects almost invariably end up with a less-than-desired outcome, and can certainly inflict harm on the corporate bottom line.

For this philosophy to be successful, the client company must also lean on its suppliers and contractors to adopt the same approach. The effort cannot be one sided. *PBLS* language and philosophy should be written into the inquiries and specifications furnished to any prospective bidder or supplier. If a proposed supplier or contractor doesn't wish to comply with this type of approach to project planning and execution, it should be dropped from consideration.

We are asked sometimes, "What is the most important phase of a project?" Although all phases are critically important, we would have to say that, first, defining the need through strategic planning (to avoid the waste of huge sums of bottom-line dollars) and, second, proper and detailed preproject planning are probably the most important. Get these two areas right and the capital improvement project has a much better chance of succeeding.

It is my contention that a project that has suffered through poor execution and start-up will never, ever achieve its fully intended benefits and will therefore return less than it should to the bottom line of the venture or company. Put several of these together and the corporation itself may be in jeopardy.

There is no, repeat no, guarantee of success for any major project. However, the adoption of this *PBLS* methodology can produce the highest degree of probability of success that I have come across in my 30-odd years of experience with large capital-improvement undertakings.

This is a rapidly changing world. We are in the midst of a changeover from the machine age to the information age. Corporations must change not only the way they have been doing things, but also the way they *think* things. Sometimes the project that is *not* undertaken is the most profitable business decision of the year! The very first *PBLS* "principle," as defined in this book, is profound in its simplicity:

> If project need cannot be justified on the basis of a realistically and sufficiently positive contribution to the venture *bottom line*, legal mandates, or safety considerations, then the project should not go forward.

Strategic planning, as an integral part of the PBLS philosophy, is paramount to success. If the capital improvement project is fatally flawed through a failure on the part of executives to think beyond the next two or three quarters, then no amount of solid project management will help. This is why we say that, in the final analysis, *PBLS* is a top-down philosophy.

This book is excellent reading, *must* reading, for anyone— corporate executive or project manager, engineer or operator, business systems analyst or consultant—who seriously wants to see the capital improvement projects he or she is concerned with take a turn for the better. In fact, it just may be the ticket your company needs to remain in the chase!

G. Brian Jones
General Manager, Systems and Process Control
U.S. Steel Corporation

PREFACE

Down through the pages of history, we read of great projects planned, initiated, and executed by those who have gone before. Some of these projects are only myths filtered through the haze of centuries past, leaving scant, if any, trace; other projects are tangible and lasting, monuments to past people and present sources of inspiration.

We read of the Colossus of Rhodes—what an engineering feat that must have been! We read in the biblical record of the ancient Tower of Babel, reaching to the heavens. But did it really exist? What of the Hanging Gardens of Babylon or of the Library of Alexandria, holding all the knowledge of mankind to that point? Were those projects actually executed? How did they go? Did they achieve the goals that their planners, their engineers, their builders had set for them? The answer is that no one really knows. Although evidence has recently come to light that supports their existence, the facts are still shrouded in the mystery of the ages.

But let's assume that those projects were real and explore that last question for a moment. Should we not say that the answer depends on just what those goals were? If, for example, the ancient client's goal was *to be remembered,* then, to a certain degree, the goal was accomplished. These projects were so magnificent that people have remembered them and those they honored down through the ages.

If, on the other hand, the goal was to build a lasting edifice and we are left with only a myth, the goal may not have been accomplished; the project may have been a needless waste of an ancient people's treasury—an ancient boondoggle.

Ah, but we do, indeed, know of one series of projects that meet both goal criteria!

THE PYRAMIDS

The Pyramids—those ancient wonders whose purpose was not only to proclaim the power and the glory of their builders, but also to provide the future with a lasting memorial to their culture. Although the Pyramids have long been wrapped in mystery and lore, they were actually projects about which we do know something.

We know, for example, the name of the architect/engineer who designed and oversaw the building of the first great pyramid, the "step pyramid" of King Joser. The architect's name, frozen forever in hieroglyphic writings, was Imhotep. Both his name and his accomplishments as an architect and engineer were revered, not only by the Egyptian pharaoh for whom he worked, but also by the ancient Athenians, who knew something of architecture themselves.

We also know a good deal about one of the most interesting of the ancient projects, the Great Pyramid of Khufu. As with most projects, the construction phase of the Khufu Pyramid had problems. For one thing, the wheel had not yet been introduced into Egypt, at least not as a method of conveyance. Therefore, all stones had to be laboriously dragged on skids or on a slick mud surface to their destination. And how did Pharaoh Khufu's engineer raise these heavy stones to their ever-increasing resting height? No, not by antigravity ray machines from alien spacecraft, not by forces known only to the Ancients, but simply by continuing the drag up long and gradual earthen inclines by a more mundane source of power—manpower.

We can only imagine some of the labor force problems: sickness, malcontents, the feeding of thousands. (Although nonpaid conscripts or, in some instances, low-paid soldiers made up the majority of the work force, very few actual slaves were used, contrary to the Hollywood view of this great project.) However, we can imagine that after several years of backbreaking drudgery, the concept of "for king and country" wore very thin, leading to mounting labor problems.

And talk about scope creep! The client (Pharaoh Khufu) changed his mind not just once, but twice during the construction phase, as to just how high in the structure he desired his burial chamber. These changes, coming in the middle of the project, created structural changes that resulted in broadening the monument's base and height. Obviously, much work had to be redone in order to make the required changes. Budget and schedule were severely overrun, as they almost invariably are when the scope of the project is ill-defined from the very beginning.

But much was learned from these early projects. We still recognize the pyramid as a basic shape, a shape of extraordinary strength. These builders had a profound influence on the continuing efforts in architecture, engineering, and, oh yes, project management!

Let's now shift forward a few millennia to a series of projects that not only were awesome in their scope, but also led the way to new project management concepts, precepts, and principles.

THE APOLLO PROGRAM

We had to use both research and some imagination in exploring the great Pyramid projects, but we have no such problem when it comes to Apollo. Never was a project more planned, more documented, or more witnessed than our journeys to the moon and, in contemporary programs, beyond.

This writer was fortunate in that, for 10 years, I took part in those historic projects at the Cape Kennedy Space Center in Florida, from the Gemini launches, through the Apollo moon missions, and on through to the conclusion of the Skylab program.

As we studied case upon case of actual project execution in preparation and development of the seminar and workshop series entitled "Design for Start-up," we saw that the principles and tenets upon which we had built this series were strikingly similar to the project management methodology that drove the Apollo program almost 30 years before. In Apollo, the buzzwords may have been a little different, but the principles and tenets of teamwork, the preplanning, the clearly defined objectives, and a recognition of the risks involved were obviously the same.

The Apollo program was, indisputably, a gigantic success. It scored success after success in a series of individual steps, or projects, culminating in Apollo 11 and subsequent manned landings and safe returns to earth. America soared with Apollo. If ever there was a doubt that the United States led the world in technological development, it was put to rest on the Mares and the Laurentian Highlands of the Moon.

In retrospect, each of the program's many, many glittering successes was brought about by an almost religious adherence of the entire project team of hundreds, if not thousands, of people to the principles and tenets we shall be considering in this book.

But there were stumbles along the way. Tragic failures. Likewise, in retrospect, with *every failure,* the trail of evidence bright as a Saturn rocket's fiery tail points unerringly to the omission or blatant disregard of these same principles and tenets. Let's look briefly at a few examples.

APOLLO 11

The Apollo 11 mission was a mind-boggling success. The hundreds of thousands of individual parts, pieces, and systems that made up the awesome Saturn V rocket performed flawlessly through the long countdown procedure, the launch, the lunar landing, and the historic "one small step" statement. Then, through lunar lift-off, return, and successful landing it all looked so, well...rehearsed. And rehearsed it was. The launch team, from pad technician to astronaut, had planned, planned, and replanned, had trained, trained, and retrained. In the words of the NASA Launch Director Gene Kranz, "We make our mistakes in training, so as not to make them in the real game."

But a price had been paid to learn these basic principles of project management. A terrible price.

APOLLO 1

On a beautiful day in January 1967, in the early evening hours, a critical dress rehearsal in preparation for the first Apollo flight came to a sudden end in a white-hot glow of oxygen-fed fire at the 220-foot level of pad 34. In a few, brief seconds the program had lost three of its finest astronauts. Virgil "Gus" Grissom, Ed White, and Roger Chaffee were gone.

The investigations continued for months. The program came to an abrupt standstill. The immediate cause of the spark that set off the conflagration was almost impossible to discern, although some said it was a small tool lodged between wiring bundles, indicating a slip in quality procedures. But regardless of the immediate cause, investigators were looking for the root cause. And it was not too hard to find.

Here was a spacecraft, jammed with both flammables and electronic circuits, operating in a *pressurized, pure oxygen atmosphere.* It was a bomb just waiting to go off. These were bright and intelligent design engineers. Why would they design such a craft? *Expediency.* An unrealistic schedule. It's easier and quicker to design a single-gas system using oxygen than to design a two-gas system using oxygen and nitrogen. And America was in a race to the moon! Whatever would get us there quicker than the Russians was pretty much the rule of the day. However, even the Russians knew better than to design a single-gas system; their spacecraft was designed with an N_2O_2 system from the beginning.

Learning this lesson, the lesson of avoiding unrealistic schedules, was costly, both in the tragic loss of a fine crew and in the ensuing delays and extra costs caused by the necessity of spacecraft redesign. Unfortunately, memories are short; it would not be the last time that this and ensuing programs would be plagued by unrealistic schedules and emotional or ego-dominated decisions. The Challenger tragedy is a case in point.

CHALLENGER

The Challenger event appears to have been a tragic case of a project launch decision dominated, at least to some degree, by emotion and peripheral, or outside, pressures. (Be aware that much of what we say here is conjecture based only upon newspaper and television accounts of this event; we were not personally involved.)

It appears, however, that Challenger was launched on a cold (very cold for Florida) morning, in a continuing series of "scientific" missions. Although the mission did, indeed, allow for some scientific experiments, it was apparent to even a casual observer that the real aim was centered in public relations concerns, i.e., to show the world that American space travel was now commonplace enough to send a grade-school teacher into earth orbit.

Apparently, a known potential problem had existed for some time with a large sealing O ring on the booster. According to some, low ambient temperatures at launch time could impede the flow of O-ring material into its seating grooves. It was later reported that at least some engineers from the booster contractor's offices had attempted to warn the launch team to delay until weather conditions improved.

But there were many "important people" on hand to witness this launch, and their presence undoubtedly increased the pressure on the launch team to go with the schedule.

We, most of us, saw the terrible results. The entire crew was lost in the ensuing fiery explosion. There was such excellent coverage by the media, owing to the fact that a beautiful, young school teacher was going into space, that the entire nation witnessed, close up, the Challenger mission's destruction.

We cannot, and will not, say for certain that the decision to launch was based on anything other than good engineering practice. However, we do know that in many similar situations, where emotional issues and egos have either taken control or played a part in the decision-making process, other projects have also suffered catastrophic losses. But perhaps none so poignant and sad as the fate that befell Challenger.

Overall, however, both the Apollo and ensuing programs were tremendously successful, leaving a legacy of technological advancement unmatched in history for such a short period of time. We continue to reap the benefits of these ventures today through our computers, increased knowledge of our own planet, and in new products and methods such as the microchip and miniaturization; the list could go on and on.

But for those of us who strive to execute projects better and better, the knowledge gained is *the project management methodology* that led us to the moon and beyond.

As we delve into the principles, the tenets, the *methodology* of project management, we think you will see their correlation to those great projects of the past. Experience is, after all, the best teacher.

GUARDING THE BOTTOM LINE—THROUGH BETTER PROJECT MANAGEMENT

In this book we will refer repeatedly to the term *Project Bottom-Line Success!*, or *PBLS*. This term simply refers to the structured methodology that we feel is essential to the achievement of a successful outcome in the practice of project management. Why *Bottom-Line*? Because we feel very strongly that the contribution to the venture or corporate bottom line is the most important consideration of project management teams, and that this fact is sometimes lost in the clamor of project execution. (If a project is perfectly executed but adds little or nothing to the bottom line, then why was it done?)

Let us state right here, at the outset, that this book contains no secrets: no new gimmicks or fads, no motivational buzzwords (unless you wish to call our methodology, *Project Bottom-Line Success!*, a buzzword), no bombshells. All we're going to do is lay out basic management techniques and practices that you have probably known all along—just good, commonsense practices. In the press of budget, schedule, or other demands, you may not have always implemented these techniques and practices to the fullest extent possible. No one *sets out* to execute projects in any other way than in a logically laid out manner, with planning being accomplished in orderly, detailed sequences. However, budget, schedule, boss, and client pressures often result in project team decisions that may appear justifiable at the time, but are disastrous in retrospect.

In the following pages we will attempt to assist you in bringing your current or future capital improvement project to a more successful conclusion, at least perhaps more successfully than you have been able to in the past.

We will do this by introducing you to the principles and tenets upon which almost all successful projects are based. Some of these principles, when stated in their simplest form, are nothing more than an application of common sense. I'm sure you're going to be saying, "But I knew that already" or, "Everybody knows that!" And we will say, "Ah yes—but did you *do* it that way?"

As we make this journey, we will lead you logically, step by step, through the required planning and the options and then will try to help you avoid the pitfalls and potentially disastrous, although common, judgment and decision-making errors you will almost certainly face on any capital project.

Scrupulous implementation of *Project <u>Bottom-Line</u> Success!* principles and techniques will help ensure that project teams make the right decisions at the right times, resulting in more project start-ups that are "nonevents" rather than the madhouse, three-ring circuses that they often become.

As a reinforcement to the *PBLS* philosophy, we will explore numerous case studies of actual projects to see where and why they broke down or, on the other hand, what made them successful. We think you'll agree—it simply takes a commonsense, *Project <u>Bottom-Line</u> Success!* approach to make any project a real winner, a project that contributes substantially, and quickly, to your company's bottom line.

Let us begin.

William J. Pinkerton

ACKNOWLEDGMENTS

Much of the material, most of the case studies, and certainly a good deal of the structure and organization of the project management philosophy set down on the following pages have come from the American steel industry.

Although the roots of the *Project Bottom-Line Success!* (*PBLS*) methodology reach back to the early days of the U.S. manned space program (Mercury, Gemini, Apollo, and Skylab), it was U.S. Steel Engineering that recognized the need for a more structured approach to the management of industrial capital-improvement projects. With foresight and a considerable number of planning sessions a program entitled "Design for Start-up," or DFSU, was initiated.

This precursor to what we now call *Project Bottom-Line Success!* indoctrinated U.S. Steel engineers and project management teams with a more structured approach to the management of projects both large and small. DFSU also imbued most participants in the program with a newly found confidence that facility start-up could, in fact, be accomplished smoothly and without the long, costly delays experienced on some past projects.

The driving force behind the Design for Start-up program was, and remains, Bernard J. Fedak, General Manager, Engineering, at U.S. Steel, and G. Brian Jones, General Manager, Systems and Process Control, U.S. Steel. To these two fine engineers and managers go a world of thanks. The impact of their assistance and support in the development and implementation of the Design for Start-up program at U.S. Steel, and its subsequent influence on both the *Project Bottom-Line Success!* methodology and this book, cannot be overstated.

My thanks and appreciation also go to John L. Davis, Director of Engineering at National Steel Corporation, for his help and encouragement both in the development of the *PBLS* workshop series and in the writing of this book. And while mentioning National Steel, I certainly don't want to overlook Rich Baranowski, Director of Information Systems, with whom I have spent many hours discussing the finer points of project management, especially as it applies to information systems projects. It's not hard to see why both of these excellent engineers and managers are held in such high esteem by their company.

Many thanks, also, are given to Dave Davis, our talented writer and editor at Project Services International in the "DFSU days." Dave's efforts in the development of Design for Start-up were of huge significance, to say the least. Many of the case studies used in this book were initially compiled by Dave.

Much of the final editing for this book was accomplished by Joyce Hall, a lady of exceptional editing skills. Thanks a million, Joyce, for untangling some of my writing idiosyncrasies.

And to Robert A. Hall, our computer and software guru, thanks, and thanks again, for bailing me out whenever the computer seemed to be winning in my struggle to master its mysteries. With your help, I was always able to come out on top.

To Dawn Hughes, our graphics designer, and to everyone on the Project Services International staff who had a hand in bringing this book to fruition, thank you very, very much. Your help is deeply appreciated.

And to my greatest supporter, my lovely wife Rita, a very special thanks not only for encouraging me to keep writing, but also for enduring many evenings in silence, while I tapped away on my laptop. Thanks, honey.

Another area of special significance in the development of material for this book, and one I would be remiss not to acknowledge, is the input of the hundreds of engineers, managers, operators and maintenance personnel, purchasing agents and buyers, equipment suppliers, and contractors who have attended our many lectures, seminars, and workshops. In our effort to fine tune the project management process, we have continually queried our attendees (to date, over 3500) and project management acquaintances in regard to project problems, solutions, and eventual outcomes. In some instances, the problems and solutions that have been related have resulted in case studies, the case studies we share with you in this book. (By the way, as you will soon notice, we have altered the names of the companies involved in the case studies we have included; we care only about lessons learned, not who paid the price for our learning.)

The one thing that has been apparent throughout these project management discussions is the sincere interest and desire on the part of all these people to share their experiences with others, to try to make the next project team's job just a little easier.

For this, I thank all of you from the bottom of my heart.

All of the above, however, would have been for naught without the very patient and considerate help of McGraw-Hill's staff in general, and Larry Hager and Stephen Smith in particular. Any writer who is fortunate enough to find these two fine editors in his or her corner will have come a long way in realizing the goal of getting a book to market. Thank you both very, very much.

Our Mission: To teach project teams to execute capital projects more successfully by focusing not only on achievement of the promised benefits, but also on corporate and venture *bottom-line* improvement. This stated mission recognizes that the ultimate goal can be accomplished only by convincing project-associated personnel of the critical importance of maintaining a constant awareness of the potential long-term effects of project decisions, of teamwork, and of the importance of the stakeholder approach. The fundamental precepts of this methodology are:

- Clearly defined objectives
- Recognition of risks
- Teamwork
- Preproject planning
- Detailed definition of scope

PROJECT MANAGEMENT

VENTURES, PROJECTS, AND THE BOTTOM LINE

VENTURES

ven·ture (ven'cher) *n* **1**: a business enterprise in which there is danger of loss as well as chance for profit

As stated in *Webster's New World Dictionary,* a venture is a business enterprise that not only holds the expectation of profit, but also holds a certain degree of risk of loss, even to the point of total failure.

THE CONCEPT

The life cycle of a venture begins with a concept, emanating from an idea, which has in turn probably been derived from an observation. The observation may have been the appearance of a market opportunity, a change in trends, newly discovered technology, or perhaps a combination of what seems to the observer to be favorable conditions. To get to the venture stage, this concept must usually survive the scrutiny of an investment analysis that will undoubtedly consist of market and feasibility studies, preliminary business plan development, and a search for capital or financial backing (see Fig. 1).

The budding venture will then enter a firming up, or formative, phase. Interested stakeholders will step forward and commit to the venture. The business plan will be finalized;

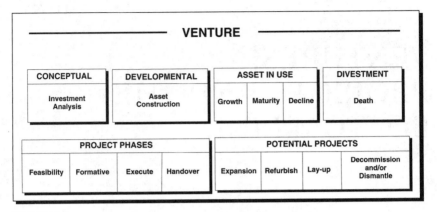

FIGURE 1

major equipment suppliers will be identified; a project manager will be selected; and a project team will be brought together. An architectural/engineering company will, in many instances, be brought aboard and engineering will commence. Specifications and drawings will be produced, price quotes will be received, and the venture's initial project concept will graduate to the next stage, the developmental stage.

THE DEVELOPMENT

The developmental stage of the venture consists primarily of what we will call *asset construction.* This stage will encompass both the execution phase of the project, i.e., procurement, construction, testing, training of personnel, and commissioning, followed by handover to permanent operating forces and subsequent initial operations. If the original premise of venture need was correct, if the project was handled properly in each of the described phases, and if sound project management principles were employed, then the venture should be off to a good start and should soon be returning a profit to the investors through a healthy bottom line.

The new facility may comprise the entire company or corporate entity. On the other hand, the new facility may be but one operating unit of a large company or corporate entity having several separate facilities producing the same, or different, products. Therefore, the *venture* may be a company *or* a facility. Regardless of which it might be, it will now enter the next of several phases in its life cycle.

THE ASSET IN USE

Most facilities, after they have proved themselves, will enter a growth phase; they will tend to expand. This expansion will be in response not only to normal market pressures but also to the innate desire of people, both investors and plant management, to take the venture to its limits. New markets will be sought, better product quality will be pursued, and the state of the art will become a goal. Any of these forces can trigger expansion projects. Some of these expansions may be large capital projects, larger possibly than the original facility project. We shall discuss later, and in more detail, some of those forces that bring about expansion projects.

As the venture continues through its life cycle, it will at some point enter into its *mature* stage. Equipment will begin to show its age, begin to wear out, and need replacement. These occurrences will certainly bring about another and even more compelling set of projects, the refurbishment projects. Of course, some refurbishment will be ongoing by the maintenance forces, but only up to a point; after that, and in conjunction with upgrades in technology, refurbishment will become capital improvement.

Finally, at some point in time, a general decline of the facility will begin to take place. Large systems will have reached their repairable limits; i.e., they will get to a point where it is not economically feasible to continue to refurbish. Technology will have advanced; newer and more economical methods will have been developed, either in the making of the product the facility was built to produce or in another product that has been found to more economically address the market demand. Different areas or sections of the facility will no longer be producing. However, since the equipment contained

in these sections or systems may still have, in some cases, considerable value, *lay-up* projects will be the order of the day.
Some call this "mothballing," but regardless of the terminology used, it is simply the process of protecting and preserving
the current condition of equipment and materials.

THE DIVESTMENT

And finally, all things come to an end. Out there in the future
somewhere, hopefully far in the future, lies the end of the
venture. As the sailing industry gave way to steamships, as
horse and carriage gave way to automobiles, so too will our
facilities of today give way to the facilities of tomorrow. And
when that happens, another type project will begin: decommissioning, dismantling projects. The remaining equipment
will have at least some value, if only scrap value; the land
itself will need to be cleared, possibly decontaminated, so that
it can be a marketable asset to its owners.

So, as can be seen, a venture is an entity with a definite
life cycle. The venture is also only as healthy as the stream of
projects that support it. A series of poorly executed projects
with long, drawn-out start-ups can seriously weaken a venture, and even lead to its demise. If a venture is unprofitable
and shows little sign of righting itself, investors will no
longer back it. They will find better, more profitable places to
invest. The entire impetus of this book and the *Project
Bottom-Line Success!* (PBLS) methodology is to keep the
venture's bottom line as healthy as possible for as long as
possible. This goal is, obviously, in the best interests of all
concerned parties.

PROJECTS

pro·ject (präj′ekt) *n* 1: a plan; scheme; an organized undertaking

Projects come in all sizes and types, with price tags ranging
from a few thousand dollars to many millions. Regardless of

size, type, or cost, a project is an investment in a company's future and each project impacts, either negatively or positively, the company's ability to produce a profit. Ill-conceived and/or poorly managed projects will almost certainly have a negative impact on the company; a succession of such projects may result in the failure of the company itself. Projects that are well managed will enhance the company's profit-making and competitive abilities.

> Personnel charged with the responsibility of conducting projects should try to put themselves in the shoes of the *investors* of corporate working capital.

An *investor*, by definition, is one who puts money to a use expected to yield a profit or income. Investors naturally desire that their investment be spent wisely and that their return, or profit, on that investment be realized as soon as possible. *Investment return*, profit generated by the sale of products and services, is the life's blood of any commercial undertaking. Project teams that squander the venture's investment capital by poor project planning and execution are, in effect, bleeding that venture—perhaps even to an early demise.

THE GLOBAL VIEW

Like it or not, we are all engaged in competition that is increasingly global in nature. Regardless of the industry we are in or the clientele that we serve, we must be aware that there are others out there who are constantly trying to take our place in the market. All they must do is find a way to produce *our* product at a lower price. Sometimes that price differential is very small. We must continually look for ways to lower our costs in order to remain competitive.

The methods open to us in the battle to remain cost competitive are shrinking. For the most part, downsizing has run its course. Further cuts, in most industries, would be counterproductive; i.e., the actual viability of maintaining the business and the client base would be put at risk. Labor costs are more or less fixed; concessions are becoming a very difficult sell. Material and equipment costs are also fixed for the most part. We are left with very few areas where we can effectively fight in the global marketplace.

There is one area, however, where we can make a difference, and that is in the manner in which we conduct our capital projects. Even our competitors must execute capital projects to remain in the game. Large capital projects can have a swing of many millions of bottom-line dollars. Swing these projects positively, comparatively speaking, and you will be giving your venture or your company a competitive edge in pricing its product. Swing it negatively, on the other hand, and you just may find yourself on the outside, looking in!

THE *Project Bottom-Line Success!* PHILOSOPHY

The dictionary defines *bottom line* as (1) net profit or loss and (2) the primary or most important consideration. In the *PBLS* philosophy of project management, the project's impact on the venture's bottom line is *the* most important consideration. Although usually mutually inclusive or synonymous, venture success and project success may sometimes be at odds within this philosophy. This seemingly anomalous statement will become more clear as we probe project justification and motive.

A *principle* is a tenet by which a person chooses to conduct his or her actions. The *PBLS* philosophy is founded on several fundamental principles aimed at sustaining long-term venture success, rather than simply achieve short-term project success.

PBLS principles are tenets of project management having positive venture contribution as their primary concern. To be successfully applied to project management, the principles of this philosophy must govern not only the conduct of the project team itself but, prior to that, the thinking of the corporate decision makers.

A wide variety of projects will occur within the life cycle of a venture, bringing with them new technology, processes, and equipment. The long-term health and success of the venture depends on the bottom-line success of these projects. This book, and the principles and practices contained in the description and discussion of each project element, is intended as a guide to accomplishing that success. The *PBLS* philosophy is applicable to any size project (with certain caveats that we will explore later), regardless of the nature of the venture.

THE PROJECT ELEMENTS

Although there are many different perspectives from which to view a capital project, we have found that, in general, almost all capital projects can be considered to be composed of eight prime elements. These eight elements are:

1. Project origination and definition
2. Preproject planning and organization
3. Design, procurement, and pretesting
4. Construction and installation
5. Training
6. Preoperational testing
7. Start-up (commissioning) and initial operations
8. Closeout and make-good analysis

In the following chapters we shall discuss these elements in some detail, while providing proved techniques and methods you might wish to consider as you plan and execute your current or upcoming project. Additionally, we will take a look at some of the "not so usual" projects such as re-engineering, environmental, and upgrade projects. We'll also reinforce certain points with actual case studies taken from the field. (In all cases we have changed project names, locations, and companies involved for the obvious reasons; i.e., we don't wish to embarrass anyone or reveal any particular organizational weakness.)

Again, our goal is to zero in on protecting and enhancing the venture or corporate bottom line through practical, commonsense project management. Therefore, before delving into the nuts and bolts of project phases, it might be instructive to examine projects from a financial perspective.

THE BOTTOM LINE—FINANCIALLY SPEAKING

Let's take the time, right here at the outset, to look at an example of just how easily a few small, seemingly insignificant errors in judgment can impact the best-laid plans of a project team. Two financial scenarios are presented for analysis. The first scenario examines the financial implications to the project and venture that result from sound planning and application of *PBLS* principles. The second scenario examines the financial implications to the project and venture when sound planning and *PBLS* principles are not followed.

As we look at other cases in the following chapters, it might be interesting to see how many of them have made the same decisions that we see here, and how many of them have suffered the same results.

C A S E   S T U D Y   **1**

The Financial Impact of Project Decisions

PROJECT NEED

Blastech, Inc. operates two hazardous waste reactor facilities in a large industrial park complex. Wastewater from the two reactor facilities is routed to two competing wastewater treatment companies, one of which is located in the industrial park, the other outside. These companies are Clearwater Company and the BioTreat Corporation. Both facilities have approximately the same treatment capacity. Although water used by the reactor facilities can be routed to either

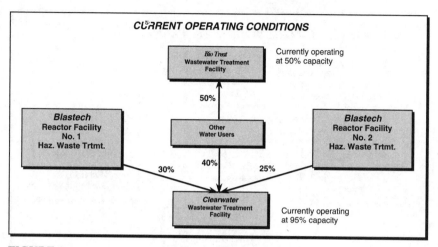

FIGURE 2

treatment plant, discharges are typically routed to Clearwater, which is located in the industrial park and considerably closer than BioTreat.

The Clearwater treatment facility has seen a 25 percent increase in incoming wastewater in the last 5 years. The facility is 12 years old and uses an outdated "relay logic" control system.

Currently, the Clearwater facility operates at 95 percent of its design capacity, with approximately 55 percent of this capacity being fed from the two Blastech facilities and the remaining 40 percent coming from other industrial customers in the area. (See Fig. 2.) This means that Clearwater must operate at near-perfect levels to maintain EPA effluent standards. Coupled with a projected 50 percent increase in incoming wastewater over the next 1 to 4 years, the need for a renovation and expansion project is obvious.

Clearwater expects the major portion of the increased demand for services to come from Blastech reactor 1 as a result of the upcoming outage work and expansion of that facility. It is expected that additional demands will come from "other" water users in the area who are prohibited by law from sending their wastewater back to the surrounding watershed and aquifer without considerable treatment.

If Clearwater is to continue to compete with BioTreat it must be prepared to meet projected influent increases and EPA effluent standards. For this reason, Clearwater has planned an improvement project to increase process capacity, but without interrupting service to its clients, particularly the two Blastech reactor facilities.

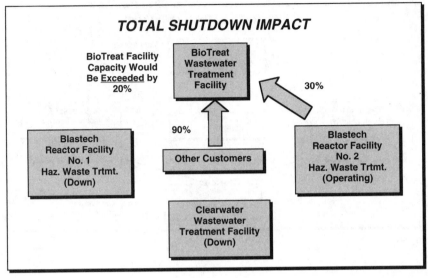

FIGURE 3

To accomplish the facility upgrade without service interruption, Clearwater has planned the execution of the project to coincide with Blastech's extended shutdown of its no. 1 hazardous waste treatment reactor facility for major modifications and maintenance. The Blastech no. 1 facility outage was scheduled to occur 8 to 9 months from the time Clearwater initiated project planning. But this plan has serious drawbacks. Let's look at Fig. 3.

As can be clearly seen in Fig. 3, a total shutdown of the Clearwater facility would result in an undesirable impact on other industrial park users because the BioTreat facility does not have the capacity to handle total treatment demand. Therefore, the Clearwater facility *must find a way to continue to operate at or near 50 percent capacity at all times in order to accommodate all industrial park users.*

PRIMARY PROJECT OBJECTIVES

To meet both projected influent increases and EPA effluent standards, it was obvious to management that there existed an absolute necessity to increase the Clearwater facility's process capacity and efficiency without interrupting plant operations or compromising current effluent quality. This objective was also driven by recently signed contracts with the Blastech Corporation that assured levels of feedwater from the reactor facilities sufficient to justify the expansion investment. (Bear in mind however, that on the other side of the coin Clearwater was also contractually obligated to handle that amount of contaminated wastewater!)

THE ENGINEERING STUDY

An engineering company was contracted to perform a cursory study, and the results were used to prepare an appropriation request. The study identified and recommended improvements to increase the efficiency and maximum capacity of the Clearwater Wastewater Treatment Facility.

The study recommended that Clearwater construct a parallel treatment plant *prior to the outage of the Blastech no. 1 reactor facility* (see Fig. 4).

THE PROJECT SCOPE

The parallel facility would be programmable logic controller (PLC)–controlled and operate at 50 percent of the capacity of the existing facility. After completion and start-up of the expansion facility, the modernization of the existing facility would be initiated and completed during Blastech's no. 1 reactor facility outage. As can be seen in Fig. 4, this plan would permit Clearwater to process wastewater and generate revenue throughout the duration of the project. It is this type planning that leads to a healthy bottom line. Even more important, this plan allows Clearwater to maintain full service to Blastech, its primary customer.

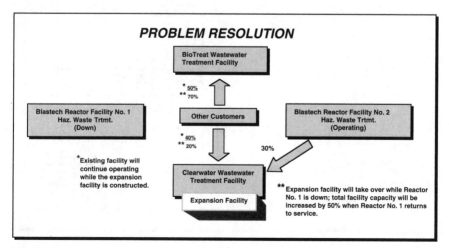

FIGURE 4

However, what has been ascertained here is the project *strategy*, not the project scope. On the basis of this strategy, the scope must be identified in as much detail as possible in the short time remaining of this window of opportunity. It is here that many projects break down. In the effort to fast-track a project that must get off to a quick start, many project teams tend to forego the detailed planning and project organization that will lead to a successful conclusion. They seem to be saying "Damn the torpedoes—full speed ahead!" (The problem is, those "torpedoes" are very risky.)

PRELIMINARY PROJECT SCHEDULE AND COST

A 12-month preliminary project schedule was developed. Since time was of the essence (Blastech reactor no. 1 would be taken down for maintenance and upgrades on September 1), a project design starting date of February 1 was recommended with fast-track construction scheduled to begin in early March (see Fig. 5).

Initial operation of the expansion facility would commence on September 1, to coincide with and support the Blastech outage. Modernization of the existing facility would begin at that time and come back on line by January 1 of the next year. This project schedule included all work for both the expansion facility and modernization of the existing facility. For the purpose of this discussion, the

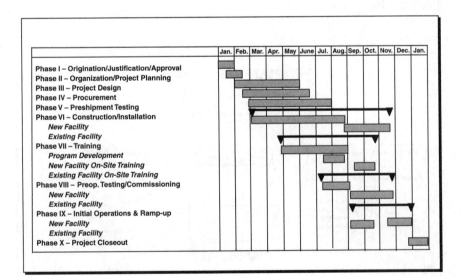

FIGURE 5

project schedule covers year 1. Years 2 and 3 are time required for the facility to come to full design capacity, earn back the cost of the project, and again become profitable.

THE BUDGET

The preliminary project cost estimate came in at about $10,360,100 (see Fig. 6). This estimate did not include the cost of money, as the Clearwater accounting department preferred to view borrowed funds separately. However, the project team was well aware that the cost of funding was being carefully monitored.

The budget carefully considered the risks that had been noted in the engineering study and took steps to fund alleviation efforts where it was felt the risks were too great. For example, a considerable amount was earmarked for off-site testing and vendor shop inspection of equipment and materials. Another area of concern was the training of personnel, since a completely new system of control was to be introduced, along with some equipment that would be unfamiliar to the workforce.

Description: Wastewater Treatment Facility		Appropriation Requested: $10,360,100	
Time Schedule for Completion: 12 months		Cost of Money (Loan): 1% per month	

Phase No.	Project Phase Descriptions	Time Required	Money Allotted
Phase I	Project Origination/Justification/Approval	1 month	$ 49,500
Phase II	Organization/Project Management	1 month	$ 49,500
Phase III	Project Design	4 months	$ 390,000
Phase IV	Procurement	6 months	$4,462,000
Phase V	Preshipment Testing	5 months	$ 473,000
Phase VI	Construction/Installation New Expansion Facility Modernize Existing Facility	9 months 6 months 3 months	$3,386,000 $2,540,000 $ 846,000
Phase VII	Training	6 months	$ 294,900
Phase VIII	Preoperational Testing and Commissioning New Expansion Facility Modernize Existing Facility	4 months 2 months 2 months	$ 523,200 $ 392,400 $ 130,800
Phase IX	Initial Operations New Expansion Facility Modernize Existing Facility	3 months 2 months 1 month	$ 682,000 $ 506,000 $ 176,000
Phase X	Project Closeout	indef	$ 50,000

FIGURE 6

The study had also provided preliminary information to address the following appropriation request sections:

- Project Risks
- Technical Feasibility of the Project
- Economic Feasibility of the Project
- Project Impact on Existing Facilities

APPROPRIATION REQUEST PREPARATION

Clearwater facility management assigned a plant engineer to begin preparing detailed labor and cost estimates for each phase of the project based on the study results. The appropriation request was to be completed and submitted for approval. The plant engineer was named project manager (PM) and began the detailed planning which would be required for execution of the project.

PROJECT LABOR AND COST ESTIMATES

The PM itemized and expanded the sequential tasks required for each phase of the project. Labor estimates in worker-days were assigned to each task. Estimated costs for each task were calculated, based on an average labor rate of $400 per worker-day. The resulting cost estimates for each project phase were distributed throughout the life of the project, and monthly project expenses were charted (see Fig. 7).

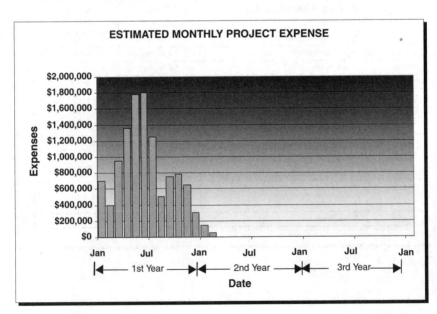

FIGURE 7

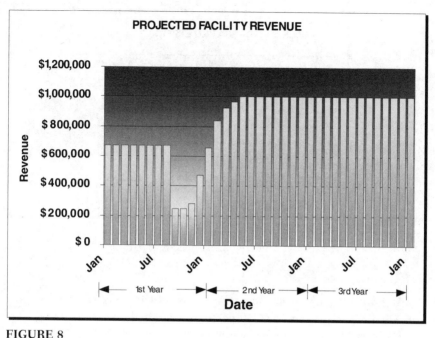

FIGURE 8

Projected Facility Revenues

Facility revenues were estimated by using the already negotiated commercial rate for processing hazardous waste facility wastewater. According to the scope of work, Clearwater facility revenue should continue at current levels until the expansion facility is completed (see Fig. 8). At that time, the facility capacity decreases by more than 50 percent with revenue following suit. At project completion, that is, after the existing facility up-grade is complete, capacity will increase to approximately 150 percent of its original capacity (following a start-up period) and revenue will follow.

Projected Operating Expenses

Operating costs are the costs incurred to operate and maintain the facility. For the purpose of this discussion, operating costs are divided into fixed costs (e.g., operator and maintenance personnel wages and spare parts) and variable costs (e.g., electricity and treatment chemicals and materials). Operating costs will remain stable throughout the project because either the existing facility or the expansion facility will always be operating (see Fig. 9).

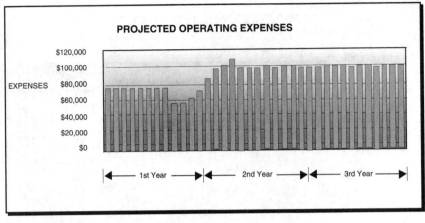

FIGURE 9

At project completion, operating costs will increase gradually (following capacity) to about 130 percent of original operating costs. The facility will still require six operators, two per shift. Maintenance costs will increase because of more equipment in the facility; however, improved reliability will moderate the increase.

THE COST OF MONEY

Time value of money.   Invested or banked currency, as with any medium of exchange, has an inherent ability to appreciate in value over time, and the diversion of capital to any other use interrupts this potential appreciation. Thus, the time value of money in a capital appropriation is a real and actual expense to the venture.

From whence does the money to fund a project originate? Money can be borrowed from a financial institution, it can be received from investors by issuing corporate bonds, or it can be set aside from company assets. In all cases, there is a cost associated with the use of these funds. When borrowed, the cost is associated with the interest charged by the financial institution. When received from investors, the cost is associated with the interest paid to the bondholders. When the funds are set aside from company assets, the cost is associated with the loss of interest or dividends that the company assets would have earned had they remained as investment funds or been invested in an alternative project.

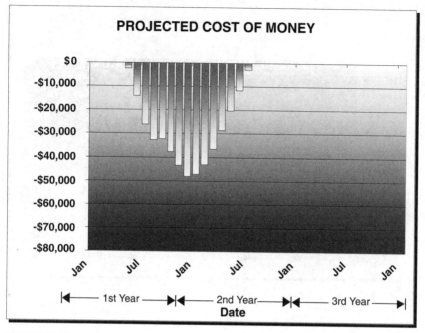

FIGURE 10

The cost of money is usually determined by multiplying the cumulative amount of outstanding funds by the current interest rate. For our purposes, the cumulative amount of outstanding funds will be determined by subtracting monthly project expenses and operating expenses from monthly facility revenue.

The current interest rate for this exercise is 12 percent per year, or roughly 1 percent per month. As stated previously, the monthly cost of money is the product of the current interest rate and the cumulative amount of outstanding funds. Figure 10 plots this projected cost across the course of the project.

THE BOTTOM LINE

Profit is the amount of monthly funds remaining after the cost of money is added to the cumulative amount of outstanding funds. A positive number indicates a profit and a negative number indicates a loss. For our purposes, profit/loss will be determined by including the monthly cost of money in the monthly revenue calculation. (As stated, this calculation is based on revenue less project and operating expense.)

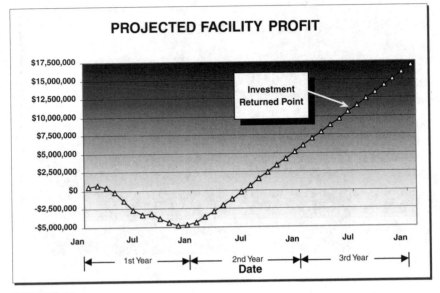

FIGURE 11

From the projected facility profits graph (Fig. 11), we can see that projected facility profit becomes positive in July of the second year, with a 100 percent return on the investment in August of the third year.

This project is well planned and, barring any highly unusual catastrophic event, should conclude successfully with just slightly over a $2^1/2$-year return on investment (ROI) period. Although all projects hold risk, this project team has taken steps to alleviate those risks most likely to occur.

BUT THE SCENE CHANGES

Unfortunately, the foregoing scenario was not allowed to stand. As happens too many times, some of the risk elements were "managed" back into the mix. When the carefully considered budget was placed before a senior executive, it was turned back with the admonition, "You'll have to get that number below 10 million before I'll take it to the board." No real reason—just an arbitrary number that seemed to the senior executive to be within the context of a reasonable edict. After all, the budget reduction called for was less than $3^1/2$ percent of the budget that had been presented. To this executive, he was simply challenging his project team to "tighten their belts."

Also, as too often happens, this project team responded in a totally predictable manner. In their search for areas to cut, they gravitated immediately to the areas where risk had been alleviated, that is, the off-site testing and inspection of equipment and materials and the training of personnel. Why cut here? Because these items hold *intangible* benefits, as opposed to changes that show up as finite changes to drawings and equipment. Nobody wants to give up any "bells or whistles" in the new design. After all, a cut in a risk alleviation factor may not hurt—it probably won't happen anyway. (Or so the rationalization goes.)

As can be seen from the budget depicted in Fig. 6, $473,600 had been allocated to the off-site, or vendor shop, testing and inspection of equipment and materials. This was to be done in order to prevent defective equipment or materials from arriving at site where the late discovery of a defect or malfunctioning equipment would almost certainly result in delay to the project schedule.

In their effort to produce the required reduction in project budget, the project team elected to reduce the allocated amount for off-site inspection by 50 percent, or $236,800. The team rationalized this decision by going over the equipment list and ensuring that the most critical items would remain in the off-site testing program.

The next area to come under the budget knife was the personnel training program. In addition to the training customarily supplied by the equipment suppliers, the project team had planned to include the services of a professional training company to perform a training needs assessment and skills inventory, to develop an in-depth training program, and to coordinate the entire training effort. It had been felt that this step was necessary to ensure that the Clearwater operators and maintenance personnel were sufficiently trained to bring the expanded and upgraded facility on-line in the shortest possible time and then to be able to operate and maintain it with a high degree of capability.

However, with the overriding need to reduce the budget, it was decided to forego the professional training efforts and to limit the training effort to the equipment-supplier training. This allowed the project team to reduce the training allocation from $294,900 to $147,450.

As can readily be seen in Fig. 12, the effect of these cuts, totaling $384,250, gave the senior executive the sub-$10,000,000 budget called for.

RISK AND EFFECT

What risks have been assumed by arbitrarily reducing the training budget? The greatest risk is that the learning curve will be extended.

Budget Reduction Plan

Actions: Savings:

Cut Training Budget by 50% $294,900 ÷ 2 = $147,450
Cut Preshipment Testing and Inspections by 50% $473,600 ÷ 2 = $236,800

                                              Total Savings $384,250

                              Original Project Budget $10,360,100
                              Budget Reduction Plan $384,250

                              New Project Budget $ 9,975,850

FIGURE 12

This means that it will take longer for the workforce to attain the required job proficiency and productivity. In this case, it took much longer to reach the projected revenue and resulted in a corresponding increase in the operating costs.

What were the consequences of reducing the preshipment testing budget? First of all, discrepant equipment and materials found their way to the construction site; they always do. This increased the duration and subsequent cost of the construction phase of the project. In this case, the construction phase was extended by 3 months with a consequent cost increase of 15 percent. The delays encountered in the construction phase have a domino effect; i.e., extending the construction phase forces a slip in the preoperational testing phase and the initial operations phase. Both of these phases slipped by 3 months. The cost of the preoperational testing phase increased 25 percent and initial operations costs increased 5 percent. The cost increases noted here are a result of increased labor costs incurred by retaining project personnel beyond the planned completion date.

Also, when the operating forces attempted to start up the facility, their training had not covered a sufficient number of operating situations. Poor response to one situation resulted in the destruction of a critical piece of equipment for which no spare was immediately available. The consequences included additional costs of $225,000 and a 1-month additional delay for replacement and installation.

As can be seen in Fig. 13, the difference between the amount saved in budget cuts and the amount expended in schedule delays

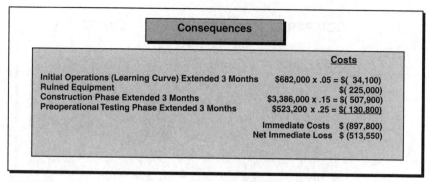

FIGURE 13

and ruined equipment is a *negative* $513,550. However, as we shall soon see, this loss, as bad as it is, is only the tip of the iceberg.

THE "ICEBERG"

The combined effects of the extended learning curve, construction delays, and equipment problem delays also affect the cost of money and facility profits. The cost of money is calculated on the outstanding balance of venture funds. The longer the facility has funds outstanding, the higher the cost of that funding.

Furthermore, the inability of the facility to treat the required amount of contaminated water when Blastech 1 came back on-line brought about penalties because the facility could not meet its treatment commitments.

All of these problems, therefore, delayed the facility profit breakeven point. In this scenario, revenue and operating costs did not reach their projected monthly levels ($1,000,000 and $100,000, respectively) until January of the third year. This increased the cost of money and extended the facility profit breakeven point to January of the third year. Superimposing the actual graphed results over the original plan graphs we have already seen clearly demonstrates the dramatic effects of the schedule overrun. The magnitude of the losses may be surprising.

PROJECT EXPENSES

This one is simple. Here, in Fig. 14, we're seeing the immediate costs of approximately $513,000 that were caused simply by keeping people on the project site longer than planned, by ruined equipment, etc.

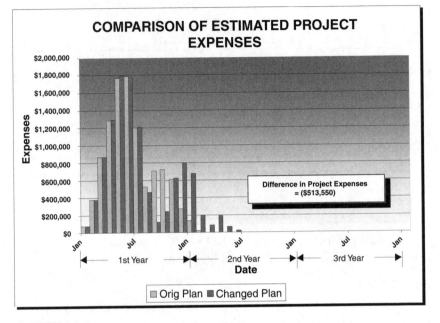

COMPARISON OF ESTIMATED PROJECT EXPENSES

Difference in Project Expenses = ($513,550)

☐ Orig Plan ■ Changed Plan

FIGURE 14

FACILITY REVENUES

But now we get to the iceberg itself—the revenue that was left behind when the facility did not start up as planned. As we saw earlier, the planning included dropping revenues by approximately 50 percent, then operating via the expansion facility while the Blastech reactor was down for planned maintenance and improvements. During this period the plan had been to improve and upgrade the existing facility and then bring up all units as Blastech no. 1 came back on-line. However, the problems encountered caused delays and the facility was not ready when needed. We can see the devastating financial effects in Fig. 15.

The start-up dragged on and on for 7 long months before the facility could operate at design capacity. The difference in the two curves is dramatic and, when the curves are viewed in this manner, dollars can be applied to the bars. The amount of revenue "left behind" is a staggering $3,236,306.

When will the company get this money back? The answer is— never! This is revenue that should have gone to the bottom line over that 7-month period, but failed to show up. This is where the real losses are; the original immediate losses pale by comparison.

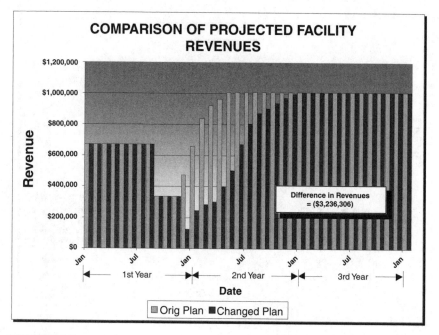

FIGURE 15

And there are other potentially disastrous consequences, i.e., angry customers (possibly even the loss of major accounts), fines, morale problems, damaged careers, etc.

FACILITY OPERATING EXPENSE

In Fig. 16, we see a strange result of the project delays. Earlier we saw that facility operating expenses were pretty cut and dried: monthly expenses of approximately $80,000 before the expansion and upgrade project, approximately $100,000 after the change with a short ramp-up in between.

However, the start-up delay bites operations as well as engineering. The unusual spikes we see in Fig. 16 are the results of approximately $500,000 in EPA fines against the facility for the dumping of out-of-spec water when Blastech no. 1 came on-line and the Clearwater facility was unable to sufficiently respond. (Remember that Clearwater was contractually obligated.)

There were, of course, other facilities expenses that were also higher than anticipated during this period of time (approximately $238,000 higher), but you can bet that the biggest growl from the operating forces was the one in response to the ignominy of those fines!

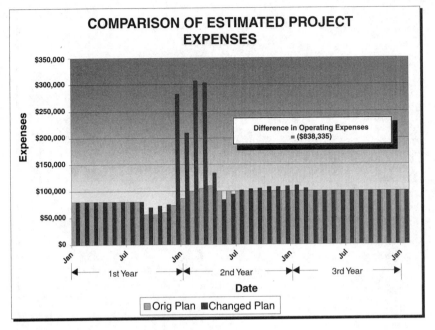

FIGURE 16

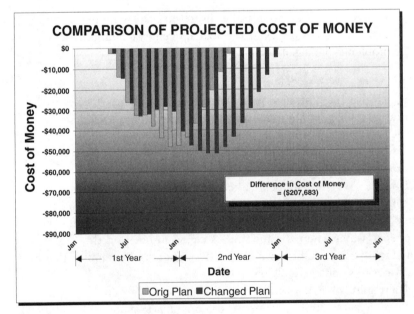

FIGURE 17

The Cost of Money

Since the project turned out not only to be more expensive than planned, but also went on for a longer period of time than planned, the funding requirements were also affected. The chart in Fig. 17 speaks for itself, and should serve to convince anybody that money is never free.

And, finally, we get to that all-important *bottom line*. What has happened to facility profits during this problem-plagued, delayed start-up? Obviously, the bottom line took a hit, so to speak, but many will be surprised at the magnitude of that hit. Add all the fines, the cost of ruined equipment, higher construction and start-up costs, the added cost of money, and the revenue left behind by the delay, and the total loss to the bottom line is a staggering $4,800,000 (see Fig. 18).

Of course, we will never know for sure that the budget cuts made were the sole reasons for this fiasco. However, we do know that this corporate manager, this project team, elected to roll the dice in some risky areas—and they came up losers.

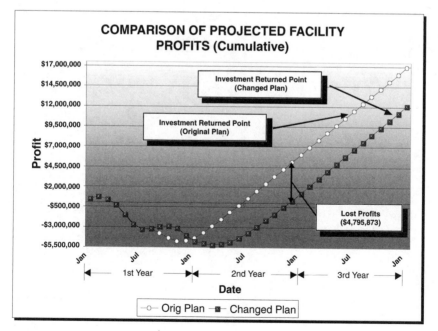

FIGURE 18

CONCLUSIONS

By circumventing the application of sound, commonsense, bottom-line principles associated with the training of personnel and the pre-shipment testing of equipment, the facility profit breakeven point was delayed 7 months. This may not make the venture unsuccessful, but it does defer facility profits for 7 months, making the project unnecessarily expensive and placing unnecessary risk on the venture. It also provides an incentive to Blastech to increase its utilization of the BioTreat facility.

This 7-month delay in profitability results in a loss of revenue and profit of over $4.8 million. These are untaxed *bottom-line* dollars! What if *you* were an investor?

PROJECT ORIGINATION— DEFINING THE NEED

PROJECT ORIGINS—DETERMINING NEED

Capital projects can originate from several places or perceived needs. The need for a new, or "greenfield," facility will usually be pretty well defined before investor institutions will agree to provide the capital needed to build. Occasionally, of course, even hard-eyed lenders will get carried away with the rhetoric of a good salesperson who successfully sells blue-sky returns on investment. These are projects that are usually destined to become the white elephants we hear about or read of in the business pages from time to time.

The need for investment in a capital project, however, generally arises from one of three sources:

- *Market demand,* which includes the development of new products, seizing opportunities to increase market share of current products, or moving to retain current business.
- *Governmental or company mandate,* which includes responding to health, safety, or environmental concerns.
- *Cost reduction strategies,* which include projects to improve efficiency, such as decreasing maintenance or operating costs, or increasing production while holding costs stable.

Determining the need for a project is relatively easy if the purpose of the project is to comply with a government or company mandate or to meet a known and continuing market demand. For example, a chemical manufacturer may define a need to upgrade a process line to comply with new air quality regulations or to upgrade its product quality to meet known customer requirements. These needs are defined by knowledge, not by assumption.

However, if the need is perceived (as opposed to known), defining the need is more difficult because strategic planners must predict customer demands, market trends, and future economic conditions. For example, corporate planners may anticipate a gradual increase in the use of composite materials in automaking over the next 20 years. Planners decide that a new, state-of-the-art facility for producing composites will help the company secure and maintain a profitable market share of the auto industry's demand for these materials. This need is defined not by exact knowledge, but by informed assumption. Care must be taken, however, that an "informed assumption" based on credible supporting trends isn't a mask for an emotional desire for a new facility.

Another area where actual need sometimes appears to be based on exact knowledge, but may, in fact, be an assumption, is the area of cost reduction strategies, i.e., projects that are intended to improve efficiency or decrease operating costs.

It is in these areas where many managers and project teams run into trouble. These projects are almost always undertaken in an operating facility and are usually the result of one person's idea of how best to solve a perceived problem or of how the operation might be run, in his or her opinion, more smoothly or efficiently.

The problem arises when the person, the team, or whoever is the driving force becomes so convinced that this great idea is the answer to the perceived problem that they refuse to impartially analyze the proposed solution or consider alternative solutions. The drive for the project suddenly assumes a life of its own, and the end result may be a delayed, perhaps even failed, project. This scenario develops even more readily when the driving force or the one with the "great idea" is in a position of power or authority.

It is sometimes so difficult in such a situation to comment realistically to a strong personality that everyone finally becomes caught up in the drive to justify the project. In this manner many projects are started that cause later observers to ask, in wonderment, "How did we ever get ourselves into this mess?" We have seen projects that have originated this way end up costing millions in overruns or in otherwise unneeded bleeding from the corporate bottom line.

STRATEGIC PLAN LINKAGE

Carefully considered strategic planning should, in all instances, drive capital improvement projects. Even projects that look good from a return on investment (ROI) standpoint on a short-term basis may not look so good when viewed as long-term strategy. Corporate capital budgets are not a bottomless pit of money, and funding for a short-term gain may consume funding better spent on a more strategically oriented project—penetration of a new market, perhaps!

Some companies, however, fail to recognize or to fully appreciate the value of long-range, strategic planning. In fact, all too often positions in the "strategic-planning group" are relegated to upper-level managers in the twilight of their careers with the company and no longer are on track for the top job. To many, long-range strategic planning is out there so far in the future, i.e., 5, 10, perhaps even more years, that it tends to lose its significance. In actuality, strategic planning is vitally important and should be addressed by the best minds in the company.

It is here, also, where many companies, even some large corporations have great difficulty. To be truly successful in today's highly charged and highly competitive market, the decision makers must not only have a good grasp on project requirements limits, causes and effects, but also have a keen awareness of business trends, market analyses, and customer relations. Unfortunately, many companies are weak in both areas.

Key managers and executives should be part and parcel of the strategic planning group, and in meetings should set strategies, goals, and priorities. Markets should be studied, as well as global trends. Successful companies will be flexible in the coming years. Within the most successful of these companies, the strategic plan will be common knowledge. When the plan is good, and everyone in the company actively supports it, it can hardly fail!

> Hindsight is, certainly, 20/20; however, just think about it for a moment—if you had known 5 or 10 years ago what you do today, you would probably have made some drastically different decisions. Why should we think the *next* 5 or 10 years will be any different? This is why strategic planning, and the linkage of project decisions to strategic planning, is so important.

In the "visioning process," undertaken by so many companies today, major projects and priorities are addressed, so that funding may ultimately be available for those projects that best fit into both the strategic plan and corporate funding capability. In each project consideration, the project must be first looked at with an eye to strategic business interests. When this tenet of management is ignored, disaster can sometimes result.

Most CEOs focus much more on the commercial, production, and "people" aspects of managing their companies than on the capital end of the business, that is, the strategic, longer-term facility issues. They fail to recognize the impact that the longer-term issues will have on the venture, that is, on those commercial, production, and people aspects.

There are forces at work in most industries that tend to exert control over those industries. In a tightly knit industry, most companies will fail to get outside the niche they have created for themselves. That niche will have them reacting to the immediate business pressures while ignoring building for the future. They will continue to look very much like their competitors. In the steel industry, for example, there are many forces at work that tend to prevent the steel producers from controlling their own destinies. For example, howsoever goes OPEC, so go pipe mill products. And as for flat-roll products, their destinies are ruled by giant customers, the automotive and appliance manufacturers. Also, this controlling influence is especially true when unions are involved heavily in the operations. (Unions are generally striving for parity within an industry, keeping wages and benefits very similar.)

The health of the home construction industry is greatly influenced by interest rates; the lumber and drywall industries are dependent on the home construction industry, and so on, and so on.

On the other hand, some companies in the large industrial markets are spending from 15 to 20 percent of their net worth *per year* on capital projects. In other words, these companies have a chance, every 5 years or so, to totally reinvent themselves. This means that a company has much more ability to control its own destiny if it spends this money wisely, not only by executing capital projects better, but also by looking to the future and *choosing wisely* which projects to undertake.

Compare the company that does these things well versus the company that does these things poorly, or at least not as well. Say they each spend $200 to $300 million per year on capital improvement projects; then look at their returns. The difference in their returns on investment may be as much as 10 percent per year. Now look at what that does to their respective bottom lines over an extended period; they grow further and further apart. Go out 2 years, 5 years, 7 years—the gap keeps getting wider and wider. The company that didn't carefully gauge its capital improvement projects to a well-considered strategic plan will be looking back and saying, "How could we have been that dumb? That facility is useless now." The wiser planner and spender will be looking back and saying, "Boy, was that ever a good idea!"

Look also at potential outcome; the better one will usually survive, while the one that is consistently less adept in its approach and execution of capital projects probably won't. This is true in most industries that are highly competitive, i.e., the oil and gas industry, the chemical industry, and so on.

It's a dog-eat-dog world; the ones who understand and consistently carry out the strategic plan, choose the right projects, consistently focus on "front-end loading" and then execute capital projects properly will at least have a higher probability of survival. This approach, these "competencies," however, must be continually worked on. As new engineers come into the workforce they must be trained, and then constantly refreshed, to avoid losing it.

SHORT-TERM GOALS

One of the problems, however, is that these attributes, the ones just mentioned, will never become "core competencies" in many companies. Unfortunately, this problem is exacerbated by those companies' own leadership. Many upper-echelon managers and executives don't consider these things *to be* core competencies and, in fact play them down in their zeal for short-term business goals. We see recently where many companies have reduced their engineering groups almost to nonexistence and are attempting to run large capital projects solely with contractors, overseeing these contractors with business-oriented managers. (It is our opinion that it is much easier to find project people who are business oriented than it is to find business people who are project oriented.) This may be why we have been seeing some of the capital project disasters we've been seeing lately.

Most companies don't really have a strategic plan; many don't even have a tactical plan. The executives of these companies are more concerned with the day-to-day operations, the worker on the plant floor, the weekly and quarterly reports. After all, in many cases their own annual bonuses are tied to these reporting periods. Immediate gain may be very high on their priority lists, and as a result, capital improvement projects are selected with short-term goals in mind. For these reasons they may not be thinking where they want to be (or where the company *needs* to be) 5 years from now.

LIVING IN THE FUTURE

Eminently successful companies, on the other hand, know *exactly* where they are going to be in 5 years. Take General

Electric, for example. G.E. executives *live* 5 years in the future! The Jack Welches, the Lee Iaccocas, the Bill Gateses always have a strategic plan. This type of executive closely watches the world scene, anticipating political, financial, and demographic changes, and then moves quickly to take advantage of evolving opportunity. Companies that are guided by forward-thinking, strategic planners will continue to thrive. Their stock will continue to be solid gold in the marketplace. *The others are just competing to see who will be the last dinosaur!*

The point we're really trying to make here is that, although the proper execution of the capital improvement program is the responsibility of the cognizant engineering group, the program itself must be well thought out and driven by an upper-management echelon that is looking to the future rather than to the short-term. The strategic planning must then be fed down to sales, operating, and engineering forces (see Fig. 19) so that their *preproject planning* efforts are headed in the right direction. By the same token, good, solid information must be

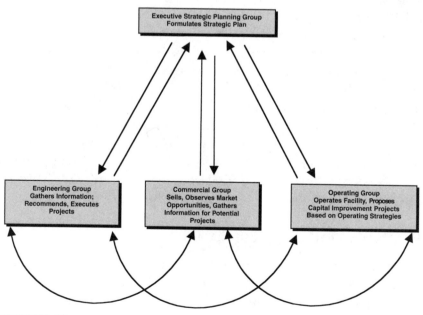

FIGURE 19

fed up the chain to assist those who are involved in the strategic planning effort.

What should trigger a decision to go forward with a capital project? The first question that should be asked is, "Is it a strategic fit?" If the answer is "No," or "I don't know," then that company should take a step back and decide just where it wants to be 5 years down the road. And does that particular product, as produced by the proposed capital project, fit in with that view?

Another mistake that we see so often in the decision-making process is a decision to go forward based on a simple spreadsheet analysis of costs and benefits, without a real risk analysis of the product's future performance in the marketplace. For example, if the spreadsheet analysis for a $150 million capital improvement project shows a 15 or 20 percent return on investment and the spreadsheet assumed a cookie-cutter repeat every year for 10 years, the project looks like a no-brainer—we forge ahead. But a solid, robust risk analysis, one that feeds in some good trending data of the potential ups and downs ahead might paint a completely different picture. This, coupled with a well-considered strategic plan, might stop this project dead in its tracks!

Another big, big problem that we see is the tendency to set the appropriation too soon, that is, before all the facts are known. In many cases, upper management sets "the number" first and then attempts to fit a project to the number. The problem is that, all too often, the number that has been set is Chevrolet; the project demanded is Cadillac!

Later, when the project team is attempting to get the real-world project back to the fantasy-world budget, critical project sequences are cut in an effort to save the budget. (*Nobody* wants to go back up the chain and ask for more funding!)

PLANNING *BEFORE* APPROPRIATING

What needs to be done? An initial funding should be approved for preproject planning. This funding should be sufficient to allow scope development to the degree that is required to enable a *sensible* project funding appropriation to be allocated.

Preliminary engineering, scope development, risk assessment and prioritization should all take place *before* the major portion of the appropriation is approved. (An obvious benefit here: a second opportunity to back out of a questionable project decision before significant capital is spent on what may begin to look like a losing proposition.)

Think about it for a moment; the more engineering that is done prior to appropriation, the more the alternatives that will be investigated. Just this one aspect can save a ton of money! This may not be the macho approach that some seem to prefer ("Damn the torpedoes, full speed ahead!"), but in a highly risk averse industry it's the sanest approach to take. However, this type thinking takes project-knowledgeable business people, and, as we've already stated, not all companies are blessed with this type leadership.

Another aspect to think about is what we might refer to as "paying the piper." When, usually after much study, a commercial decision is made—i.e., we stop making this product, we start (or stop) servicing that market, we get into or out of this or that business, etc.—the effects are immediate. However, when a major project decision is made, it may be 2, 3, or even more years before the full effects of that decision are felt, or recognized. The decision maker may bask in the euphoria of the "command decision" he or she has made for a long time before it is recognized that the decision was totally flawed. When we know that the "piper payment" is way out there in the future, we sometimes tend to make decisions without completely weighing the consequences as carefully as we would if the payment were immediate.

Most companies will fail to recognize this need for much more rigorous "front-end loading" on major capital improvement projects and will continue to commit major blunders costing millions of dollars (and in some cases, the company's survival). A savvy CEO will benchmark the project execution, costs and benefits against others to see how the company stacks up. If the company's projects are costing more and returning less, on average, than those of a similar nature by other companies, then changes should be made. (Maybe by not even *doing* some projects!) If this practice were more widespread, we would probably see fewer, but significantly more successful, capital projects.

Another notion that must be overcome is that money is somehow free. This notion derives from the annual setting of divisional capital improvement budgets, with the underlying connotation that this money is there to be spent, therefore it must be spent, ergo—it's free! This money is usually looked upon by the business units or divisions as an *entitlement*, put there to be spent, sometimes regardless of the comparative worth of the projects that consume the money. Suppose, for example, that you were to try to take away a portion of an operating unit's budget that is proposed for a capital improvement program, a program that has been estimated to yield 20 percent. Instead, you decide to assign that money to another operating unit that would use it for capital improvement projects yielding 40 percent. The first operating unit will usually fight tooth and nail to retain that money! Add to this the fact that most CEOs don't like to say no to their operating unit managers, and the stage has been set for another round of projects that either (1) return less than they should or (2) are completely unsuccessful in improving the corporate bottom line.

We have heard project-oriented people ask, time after time, how are these things ever going to be changed? The answer is that in some companies, some *large* companies, they never will. These companies stand a good chance, sooner or later, of joining that extinct dinosaur list. On the other hand, a few will correct these practices in time and will go on to become those forward-thinking companies to which we earlier referred.

REALITY CHECK

Everyone in the loop must take care that the need for a project is real, that it is not undertaken simply because it can be done or as an emotional answer to a perceived need or problem. Sometimes an operational change or further training will suffice. Decision makers should thoroughly evaluate and critically analyze the evidence supporting project need by actually conducting a reality check to verify that the need for a project does, in fact, exist. The reality check may involve the use of a third-party company and take the form of a feasibility study along with a "get-real" meeting consisting of both the facility engineers and facility operating management.

If a third-party company is used to conduct a feasibility study, the preproject planning group must ensure that study results are truly impartial. This can usually be accomplished by selecting a third-party agency that has no vested interest in the project, i.e., a company that will not function in any capacity on the ensuing project.

We observed a company, just recently, hire the front runner for the prime contractor position to perform a feasibility study for the proposed project. The study was not only intended to define the need for the project but also provide the preliminary cost numbers in order that a decision could be reached by upper management as go or no-go. Now, could anyone seriously believe that the front runner for the prime contractor position would say, "No—this project really shouldn't be done."? (It didn't.) Also, the very attractive preliminary cost numbers turned out later to be considerably understated—*after* the project had been budgeted at that estimate.

> Reality checks and feasibility studies must be carried out with complete neutrality; otherwise they will almost invariably produce only the results someone wants to hear.

The genesis of successful projects should be a clear justification of project need. This idea is expressed in the first *Project Bottom-Line Success!* (*PBLS*) principle:

> **If project need cannot be justified on the basis of a realistically and sufficiently positive contribution to the venture bottom line, or on the basis of legal mandates or safety considerations, then the project should not go forward.**

If It Isn't Needed

We can express this principle in even more simple terms: If a project isn't needed, don't do it! It would be better to keep the money in the bank and draw interest. Or, perhaps, spend it on another capital project that is truly needed. Whatever you do, just don't waste money. Remember, these are not "sales dollars" you will be spending; these are very precious, hard-to-get, bottom-line dollars! What do we mean by *bottom-line dollars?* Operations expenses, including the salaries of all workers, have already been taken out; the salaries of administration, of sales and marketing, your salary, taxes, rent, and on and on; all have already come out of these dollars that you are proposing to spend. They have become *bottom-line* dollars. Think of how much product must be sold, again, to replace them. The health of your company or venture, perhaps even its very survivability, depends on just how well you guard these dollars.

You may not have a choice in whether to do, or not to do, a project when that project is mandated by governmental or company regulations or requirements. These mandates usually result as a response to health, safety, or environmental concerns or agreements, and you, as a project team, have no recourse but to execute them. However, these projects should most certainly be executed in as economically frugal a manner as possible. Here you will be trying to hold the outflow of bottom-line dollars to the lowest possible level, since the end result of this type project is not usually associated with profit-making sales. However, we hasten to add, projects of this nature can certainly sometimes help protect the bottom line by helping avoid environmental sanctions, personnel lawsuits over safety issues, etc.

Perhaps a simple graphic might better explain the questions that sometime arise when considering the viability of a proposed project. As can be seen in Fig. 20, the problem isn't really at the extremes of the go/no-go arrows; rather, the problem is in the critical decision zone between. The no-go side holds much more risk than the go side, and we frequently see project protagonists painting the benefits, budgets, and schedules to a bit rosier hue when the decision to be made is in that middle twilight zone.

As far as is possible, define the project need by cold, hard facts based on detailed definition of the scope. While doing so will not ensure the success of a venture or project, it will *increase the likelihood* of success. Regardless of why the project is needed, companies must justify the investment by defining its specific nature and then comparing the installa-

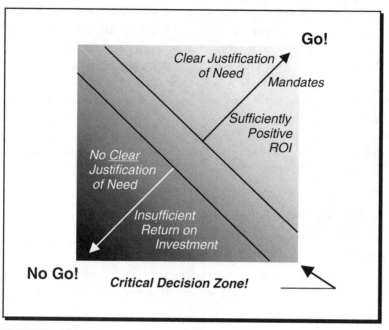

FIGURE 20

tion and life cycle costs with anticipated return. As we explore outcomes in more detail in a later chapter, we will see that project results are accountable to, and should be measured against both the business and strategic plan.

Let's look, for just a moment, at another example case where a reality check such as we have discussed might have saved a large steel producer some of its bottom-line dollars.

C A S E   S T U D Y   **2**

Exit-Shear Installation: "Pay Me Now—or Pay Me Later"

PROJECT BACKGROUND

In October of 1983, the Tandem Cold Mill (TCM) operators at Huron Steel's Shore Works requested that the plant Engineering Department install a new exit shear on the cold mill's no. 4 tandem mill.

Fourteen months later, in December of 1984, the Engineering Department estimated a total cost of $280,000 for the exit-shear installation and recommended that the project be placed in the Shore Works' 1986 budget. However, plant management continually deferred the request in favor of what they felt were more pressing project requirements and a decade passed. In February of 1993 the Cold Mill again requested the exit shear installation. Twenty-two more months passed. In December of 1994, plant management approved the request with a budget of $265,000. Work was to be started in January of 1995 and completed in August of the same year.

PROJECT APPROPRIATION

The appropriation request for exit shear installation identified the following benefits:

- Reduce initial reject rates for mill marks in order to provide customers with coils that meet their specifications for quality and delivery.

- Reduce delay time associated with the practice of hand shearing and increase ease and efficiency of strip inspection.

- Maintain a safe working environment by eliminating the practice of hand shearing.

The TCM's hand shearing practice involved manually and partially cutting the strip in the mill before tail-out and breaking the strip with reel tension on critical exposed material. The inspector would then inspect the strip. Hand shearing and breaking the strip with reel tension made inspection easier but was hazardous, time-consuming, and often disturbed critical tension reel characteristics.

Under hand shearing practices, the strip's tail end was usually dirty, oily, scratched, and sometimes cambered and telescoped, especially if the rolls were gapped at tailout. Inspectors were unable to roll the strip out beyond these conditions on the turnover rolls, making it difficult to detect mill marks during inspection. This resulted in less than desirable extremity coil conditions reaching Tandem Cold Mill customers. The reject rate from customers' inspectors was sometimes high.

To eliminate these conditions and achieve intended benefits, the scope of work called for the purchase and installation of an exit-end hydraulic shear that would cut the strip after the no. 5 stand.

Specific work items included the following:

- Remove existing apron, tensiometer rolls, and air sweeps.
- Modify existing movable x-ray guards and piping.
- Install exit shear unit, air sweeps on shear frame, and carryover roll on shear frame.
- Install hydraulic controls, valve stand, and piping.
- Install operator panel.
- Install conduit, wiring, and terminations.
- Modify digital microprocessor control (DMC) logic for safety interlocks.
- Modify pulpit operator's screen and level 1 control.

The new shear would utilize the existing hydraulic system and would include the installation of push buttons on the no. 5 stand's operator station with all required interlocks for maintenance and safety. Operation of the shear would be accomplished by using the no. 5 stand's operating pulpit screens.

Total cost for the installation was established at $265,000 with an anticipated annual savings of $225,000 realized from increased production and reduced rejects for mill marks. The appropriation also identified a 58.66 percent ROI and 1.46-year payback.

The budget for shear purchase and installation was based on the following assumptions:

- Plant forces would be used for construction/installation.
- Plant engineers would conduct installation testing and subsequent commissioning.
- Installation would require one 4-day outage.
- Delivery time for shear equipment would be 7 months.

The appropriation identified an 8-month schedule, with work beginning in January and shear installation and start-up in August of 1996. In order to meet this tight schedule, work commenced without benefit of any project preauthorization engineering.

PROJECT ORGANIZATION/MANAGEMENT

Although Cold Mill operations and maintenance personnel participated in the development of the scope for the exit shear appropriation, the project implementation team consisted of Shore Works' Engineering Department personnel and the primary supplier. Cold Mill operating and maintenance representatives were kept informed of the project's progress and were asked to provide advice and consultation only on an as-requested basis.

The core project team consisted of the following:

- A Shore Works project manager/engineer
- A Shore Works construction/installation engineer
- A Shore Works start-up engineer (to come on board later in the project)
- The primary supplier project manager
- The primary supplier project engineer

The makeup of the project team was dictated by project size, personnel availability, and the specific nature of the project.

PROJECT DESIGN, PROCUREMENT, AND PRETESTING

Exit-shear design was based on a similar installation at a nearby competitor's facility. In preparation for the design work, project team members visited the competitor's facility and made a visual inspection of the shear installation. Specifications called for the shear to be designed to fit in a limited space.

To make room for the shear, engineers planned to remove a fixed roll used for the shape control system. Critical path items identified for the shear installation were shear delivery and available mill downtime for installation. Start-up planning during project design consisted of a preliminary outage schedule identifying work responsibilities for vendors and plant forces.

The Shore Works project team, working in conjunction with the plant's purchasing department, identified three possible suppliers for shear installation and requested bids from each. Two of the vendors declined to quote the job because they felt that they could not design a new shear or revise an existing shear to accommodate the space limitations at the no. 5 stand.

The remaining supplier, Congruent Equipment Company, quoted a price of $150,000 and a 110-day delivery schedule. The quote consisted of complete design, fabrication, and delivery of the shear, including design, specification, and ordering of parts and equipment required for installation. The quote did not include installation, which Shore Works planned to accomplish with in-house forces. The quote did, however, include preshipment testing to verify proper shear design and operation, a 1-year warranty on parts, and delivery of spares prior to installation outage. The cost of spares was estimated at 5 percent of the capital cost (a common practice in appropriation request development at Shore Works). As it turned out, the cost of spares was greater than anticipated.

The project team, again with the consultation and advice of purchasing, awarded the job to Congruent as a single-source contract based on price, schedule, past performance, and the fact that Congruent had supplied the existing shear on which the design was based. Congruent selected three subcontractors to provide supporting work.

Congruent quickly mobilized its team and began design work under the supervision of the Shore Works' project manager and engineer. During detailed engineering, the project team discovered that the original scope of mill modifications would have to be expanded to accommodate the final configuration and location of the shear.

In addition to problems caused by these modifications, the project team realized that Congruent had failed to order a hydraulic control valve that was critical to shear installation and operation. Once the omission was discovered, the Shore Works' project engineer assumed personal responsibility for expediting ordering and delivery of the valve.

Preshipment testing of the shear was a condition of the purchase order. Procedures for testing the shear were developed by the manufacturer with the review and approval of the Shore Works' project team. The test itself consisted of actually shearing various pieces of metal to verify proper operation. The test was witnessed by Shore Works' engineers and correct fabrication and operation was verified.

The only drawback to the test was that the shear had to be operated mechanically because Congruent had failed to order the hydraulic control valve. However, this had no discernible impact on start-up. Upon successful completion of the test, Shore Works' engineers authorized the shear for shipment to site.

PROJECT CONSTRUCTION/INSTALLATION, PREOPERATIONAL TESTING, AND COMMISSIONING

The project team's original plan (and budget) called for the shear to be installed by plant forces during a single 4-day outage. However, because of the unanticipated mill modifications identified during detailed design, the project team requested that Congruent conduct the installation. Congruent accepted this responsibility but stated that it needed a full 7-day round-the-clock outage to install and place the shear into operation. The Shore Works' project team approved this approach and a 7-day outage was carefully planned for October of 1995.

One week prior to the outage, the Cold Mill Department decided to defer the outage until 1996 because of budget constraints. The outage plan was further complicated when Shore Works' management dictated that 7-day outages would no longer be allowed for the Cold Mill. This required that the project team revise the outage plan from a single 7-day outage to two 4-day outages. Thus, Shore Works incurred a cancellation fee for postponing the outage as well as extra costs to accommodate the two-outage approach.

In addition, extra cost was added to rent a mobile crane for Congruent's use during the outages. Originally, Shore Works' forces were going to use the building crane for equipment removal and installation. When the shear installation was awarded to the supplier, a dedicated mobile crane was required for installation to expedite construction work, minimize required mill downtime, and free the building crane for Cold Mill maintenance activities during the outage.

The first outage got underway at 7:00 A.M., March 18, 1996, and continued round the clock until 5:00 A.M., March 22. The outage proceeded generally as planned.

The only significant problems encountered during this outage were a small fire at the top of the mill and safety issues associated with the rental crane. The fire resulted in a 6-hour delay while the Plant Safety Department conducted an investigation. Arrangements were made to correct the safety issues with the crane, the lost time was made up, and the outage work was completed on schedule.

The second outage occurred from April 21 to April 24, 1996, and although it got a late start on the first day because of a generator motor failure, this outage also proceeded smoothly. Congruent completed its work 3 hours ahead of schedule on April 24, 1996, and the shear was successfully tested on production run coil. Installation and testing were accomplished according to procedures that had been developed by the project team. Only two relatively minor additional changes were made to the installation.

Following these changes and the development of a small punch list of final completion items, the Shore Works' project team declared the shear fully operational and ready for use. None of the punch list items impacted operation and Congruent was scheduled to complete the list at the Cold Mill's next regularly scheduled maintenance downturn.

Both outages accomplished their objectives with a minimum of trouble and delay. Extra costs, however, were incurred for the following reasons. Shore Works requested that Congruent's system electrical design engineer be on hand to assist with last-minute software changes required by the operating department. While this proved extremely helpful, it had not been a part of Congruent's installation quote. In addition, there were extra charges for preoutage work that Shore Works' forces were originally scheduled to complete but were handed over to Congruent in order to meet the schedule.

PROJECT TRAINING AND INITIAL OPERATIONS

Congruent and its subcontractors were prepared to provide operator and maintenance training to Shore Works' forces prior to the final outage. Training was to consist of 75 percent classroom and 25 percent hands-on operation covering all aspects of shear operation, maintenance, and safety.

Training was scheduled and materials prepared, but actual classes were postponed several times as a result of mill maintenance requirements. Although operation and maintenance forces participated in installation and start-up, they had not been formally trained prior to the second outage. The formal training program was rescheduled for the second week of May.

Initial operation of the shear was delayed because personnel had not been trained and because the Cold Mill had not developed safe operating procedures at the time of the second outage. Management decided to delay shear operation until these procedures were written and training had been conducted.

OVERVIEW EVALUATION

Like most projects, installation of the Cold Mill exit shear had a mixture of positive and negative aspects.

ON THE PLUS SIDE

Close, proactive management was key to the success of the design and installation of the exit shear. In retrospect, the Shore Works' project team made a wise decision in selecting Congruent as its single-source contractor. Over the course of the project, and especially during installation, Congruent justified Shore Works' confidence.

Project preshipment testing was also a critical factor contributing to the success of the installation. The project team specified preshipment testing in its purchase order for the shear, then followed through by witnessing and verifying that the shear was ready for shipment. This undoubtedly played a key role in the smooth on-site testing and start-up of the shear.

Another positive aspect of the project was the performance of the project team and the contractors during the outages. Both outages were well planned and organized and experienced minimal problems. Work was completed on schedule, and the shear was installed and tested with excellent results.

ON THE NEGATIVE SIDE

With an original budget of $265,000, this project experienced an overrun of approximately $180,000. Most of the overrun can be contributed to a lack of preauthorization engineering. Had the project team taken the time to closely study the shear installation at the competitor's facility, field modifications and contractor installation that were added as extra work could have been negotiated at the time of purchase, possibly resulting in a lower price for these services. Once the project was underway the project team held very little leverage in negotiating these changes.

In addition, plant and Cold Mill management contributed to cost overruns by postponing the original outage, and then by requiring that the work be conducted over two 4-day outages instead of a single 7-day outage.

Cold Mill management was also responsible for delaying training and for not having safe operating procedures ready at the time of start-up. This effectively delayed operation of the shear for several weeks, which, in turn, delayed the achievement of intended benefits as stated in the appropriation.

The bottom-line success or failure of this project can be counted not only in cost overruns, but also in postponed benefits that need not, should not, have been postponed.

This project begs a big, big question, and that is: If this project truly contained the benefits as stated in the request by the operators of the Tandem Cold Mill, *why was it allowed to languish for 12 years?* If it *truly* held the benefits as stated, then the amount "left behind" in lost revenue was approximately $2,700,000, and the stated overrun of $180,000 pales in comparison!

How then, do we justify the need for a project, the request for investment by our investors? Not, certainly, by a precipitous jump to an emotionally arrived at conclusion, but rather by a series of rationally considered analyses leading to proof of need.

JUSTIFYING PROJECT NEED

To justify the project investment, managers must first justify the project need. Even though there may be a perceived need based on one or more of the factors already mentioned, i.e., market demand, cost reduction, efficiency improvement, etc., it is still only a perceived need until several other factors are considered. These factors can be evaluated properly through a preliminary, or pro-forma, authorization, followed by a considerable amount of preproject planning, or preauthorization engineering, before the bulk of funding is actually approved and/or committed.

Let's take a brief look at each of these factors to see just why they are so important to project success. Some projects may come to successful conclusion by sidestepping or omitting one or two of these vital areas of consideration at the outset of a capital project, but I wouldn't bet on that project. Some investors have, to their later dismay.

PRO-FORMA AUTHORIZATION

First, perhaps we should explain what we mean by the term *pro-forma authorization*. The preparation of a full-blown project authorization document will take time, in some cases many hours of work and considerable expense, before enough information is in place to cause investors to agree to the bulk release of the funds necessary to actually start work on the project. Additionally, some of the information that will be required in order to obtain this funding must come from equipment suppliers or major service contractors. These folks may be hesitant to expend the required effort to prepare even budget numbers unless there is a fairly good indication that the project will, in fact, proceed.

Pro-forma authorization, then, is a quick-look approach taken by members of upper management to see if, in their scheme of thinking, the project holds enough merit to proceed with the expenditure of preauthorization funding. Enough merit, that is, that will later lead to a favorable decision for full funding by the board, or by lenders, or whomever the ultimate deciding authority might be.

The *pro-forma review* will encompass, among other things, the viability of the project; i.e., does the project fit in with the long-range (strategic) plans of the venture? Does it fit in with the reality of market conditions? Are sufficient funds available? The pro-forma look will also consider the return on investment (ROI), a term we shall be hearing more and more as we proceed, along with a review of the benefits promised. Are these promised benefits verifiable, for example? This is assuming, of course, that *viable* long-range and strategic planning has taken place.

Once this review is concluded positively, the green light is usually given to proceed with the development of a project authorization document, and preliminary funds are allocated to allow this work to proceed. The pro-forma method is good, but as with any process, it is only as good as the information that goes into it. Care must be taken that overzealous project proponents don't give upper management a distorted view of the measuring factors, in particular the benefits to be gained. (In the review of one such proposed project, we were told that if the facility had actually realized all the benefits from workforce reduction that project proposers had promised over the past decade there wouldn't be any workforce left! No wonder that their subsequent project proposal submittals were taken with a grain of salt.)

Once the pro-forma authorization to proceed has been given, preauthorization engineering can begin in earnest with the ultimate goal of gathering enough information to develop a strategic project plan. This strategic plan is (you guessed it) the project authorization document, sometimes referred to as the PAD, or the AR (appropriation request).

> What we're saying here is that a considerable amount of pre-project planning, or preauthorization engineering, should take place *before* the bulk of funding takes place, not after. In project after project, we see full project funding approved first, with the project team then being forced to fit a project into that funding plan, a plan that hasn't yet been fed the details. This almost inevitably leads to budget overruns or budgets that are too fat and ends up with projects costing more than necessary.

Preauthorization Engineering

Preauthorization, or "conceptual," engineering begins almost coincidentally with the idea stage of the project's birth. We have all heard of the projects that begin at the dinner table or over lunch, where the first rudimentary drawings or flow diagrams are produced on a napkin to put forward an idea that its protagonist believes will solve a problem, reduce cost, or in some way add millions to the bottom line. Actually, that scenario of project inception is rare, but it makes good lead-in material for books and movies.

In reality, the origin of most projects is gradual, and comes about as managers and plant personnel or sales and marketing representatives, responding to pressure from customers, see the need as a matter of sensible deduction. Capital improvement projects must start with a business idea that supports the business plan and that will result in better or more cost-competitive products.

There is, however, a need for those rudimentary drawings or flow diagrams regardless of the project idea's origin so that the first important steps in the project development can take place. Those steps are preliminary scope development and preproject planning.

Preauthorization engineering, when properly accomplished, should include

1. The gathering of basic information
2. Developing and comparing alternatives
3. Analyzing strengths, weaknesses, and risks of alternative solutions (including the various systems and equipment which might be used)
4. Development of flow diagrams and other conceptual drawings
5. Selection of the best possible solution based on the factors analyzed

Preauthorization engineering is a critical point in almost all projects and serves to give project planners a solid foundation for planning a project with appropriate cost, schedule, and return on investment. We will discuss this project phase in detail as we take up the subject of project definition in the next chapter.

DEFINING THE PROJECT—PROJECT RISK FACTORS

There are many factors that go into the "defining" of a project. We could probably fill the next several pages just listing them, and then we'd miss a hundred. However, a significant percentage of those factors can be listed under two columns: scope definition and project risk. Since almost everything a project team does throughout a project is tied in some manner to these two terms, we will be discussing these scope and risk interrelationships throughout this book.

Because of the import of these subjects to the remaining content, we will open the discussion here and begin to develop some of the *PBLS* principles associated with scope definition and risk management.

SCOPE DEFINITION AND DEVELOPMENT

The importance of scope definition before appropriation of project funding is expressed in the second principle of *PBLS*:

Detailed scope definition is the cornerstone of achieving Project *Bottom-Line* Success!

To identify the scope in detail, project team planners must first establish a conceptual design that meets the project's strategic goal. The team must then evaluate the design's technical feasibility. This evaluation requires an objective analysis by experienced engineering personnel to determine if the appropriate technology exists to do the job. If not, research and development personnel must be consulted to determine the cost and effort of developing new technology.

If the project scope is not clearly defined at the outset, each organization involved in the planning and designing of the project will tend to impose its own version of what the scope should be. Chaos is likely to follow, with a corresponding increase in project risks. A clearly defined scope provides a unity of vision to help ensure that the facility you construct is the facility you need.

The Construction Industry Institute (CII) defines scope very simply as "the amount of work to which a bidder will be invited to commit a price." However, the arrival at the level of scope definition that will hold scope creep, the bane of all project budgets, to a minimum level is not quite so simple. It takes a commitment on the part of the project team to identify scope in detail, that is, to bring specifications and drawings to a detail sufficient to prevent later add-ons in the field. (By the way, those add-ons have a name out in the field; the contractor calls them "extra work." If you've been in project management long, you've heard the term and know the connotations.)

Not only are there ways of avoiding scope creep, but also there are some other very, very important reasons why you should commit to detailed scope definition. First, let's look at ways of avoiding scope creep.

IDENTIFY SCOPE EARLY, AND IN DETAIL!

The earlier, the better. Early detailed scope identification not only lays the groundwork for subsequent planning, but also it allows potential suppliers of equipment and services to more closely structure their quotes.

And there is an added benefit here that you may never have thought of: Many of the items that come up later as extra work, and for which your project will pay a premium rate to have done, would not in many instances have affected the contractor's quote one iota! It may be hard to believe, but if you think about it for a moment, I'm fairly certain you'll agree. And for those of you who say, "We can't afford to do a detailed scope definition; our budget won't allow it," the recognition of this little fact of life should convince you otherwise. Detailed scope definition will usually pay for itself several times over.

Now there's another vitally important reason for developing a detailed scope definition, and that reason involves risk. In many instances, if scope is not sufficiently defined, an item of extreme risk to the project—or even to the venture—may not be discernible and thus not alleviated. If you don't know a risk is there, how can you handle it? We'll be discussing risk and risk management later in this chapter.

CLARIFY OBJECTIVES; AVOID AMBIGUITY!

As you may recall from our mission statement at the very beginning of this text, one of the four main criteria for *Project Bottom-Line Success!*, in fact the very first criterion, was to have clearly defined objectives. Many projects have failed, either partially or totally, because of the project team's failure to clearly define the objectives, the parameters, or the scope.

For an industrial facility, objectives are typically stated in both qualitative and quantitative terms related to production. A clear and precise statement of a project's objectives is fundamental to the project's success. If objectives are muddled, project design and implementation, and the facility itself, will eventually reflect this confusion and lack of specificity.

It is imperative that bidders know, as specifically as possible, what they are being asked to propose. The greater the specificity of bid documents, the more accurate the cost and schedule estimates and/or bids from suppliers of goods and services will be.

Remember, any ambiguities or unresolved issues will eventually impact the project. You might think they have vanished because you've ignored them but, like a swamp monster, they're still out there, circling, circling!

Once decision has been made to proceed with a project, assessment and analysis of project risks must begin in earnest. Risk assessment and scope development go hand-in-hand. A *PBLS* axiom holds that:

> The greater the detail of scope development, the greater the opportunity to identify project risks.

DEFINING THE DEGREE OF SCOPE DEVELOPMENT

As we have stated before, if the scope of the proposed project is vague there may be project risks involved that the project team won't have a shot at alleviating. They won't even know the risks are there. Thus, defining project risks is a direct by-product of pinpoint scope definition.

It only stands to reason, therefore, that the first step in risk reduction is to ascertain just how well defined the scope is. There are probably several different ways of doing this, but the best it has been my pleasure to come across recently is a pro-cedural-type tool developed by the Construction Industry Institute's Front-End Planning Research Team and called the *project definition rating index* (PDRI).

By using a weighted unit method of measuring the degree of scope development on industrial projects, the PDRI identifies and precisely defines each critical element in a scope definition package and allows a project team to quickly isolate factors impacting project risk. The completed PDRI then provides a jumping-off place from which to perform a risk analysis, a vital step that should be standard operating procedure at the outset of any project.

Let's take a quick peek at one small section of a completed PDRI form (Fig. 21). Assume that this category of the "Basis of Project Decision" section is rated by an observer on a scale of 1 to 5, where 1 = complete definition, 2 = minor deficiencies, 3 = some deficiencies, 4 = major deficiencies, and 5 = incomplete or poor definition.

The element that is being measured here is Manufacturing Objectives Criteria, and it includes reliability, maintenance, and operating philosophies. These are all critical factors that should be well considered and planned in advance if the project is to proceed with any real understanding of how it will impact the venture's bottom line.

As can be seen, the observer rated two of these subelements at the 4 level, indicating major deficiencies. However, the same observer felt that the operating philosophy required had been more completely defined. The total weighted unit category score of 23 is far above an acceptable score of, say, 10. To proceed with the project without further definition of reliability requirements, along with a better handle on how the facility will be maintained, will be to incur considerable risk. This type of analysis should be applied to every facet of the project to

SECTION 1 - BASIS OF PROJECT DECISION							
MASTER SCORING UNIT	0	1	2	3	4	5	SCORE
CATEGORY: A. MANUFACTURING OBJECTIVES CRITERIA (Maximum Score = 45)							
A1. Reliability Philosophy	0	1	2	3	(14)	20	14
A2. Maintenance Philosophy	0	1	2	3	(7)	9	7
A3. Operating Philosophy	0	1	(2)	3	12	16	2
CATAGORY A TOTAL							23

FIGURE 21

rate, first, the degree of scope definition and, second, the degree of risk associated with the defined scope or lack thereof.

PRIORITIZE!

As previously stated, while ignoring risk is foolhardy, eradication of all risk is impractical. Sooner or later you would reach the point of diminishing returns, to the point of negativity. So what do we do? We *prioritize*. Using the results of the risk analysis, the project team should rank items according to the magnitude of their potential impact, then rank them again according to the degree of probability of occurrence.

After looking at risk alleviation strategies that could be implemented, estimate the cost of reducing the risks to acceptable levels, beginning with the risk item rated highest potential impact, highest occurrence probability. By the way, this business of risk analysis, prioritizing, and selecting risk alleviation strategies is not a one-person, project manager show; it should be a unified project team effort, with input from all stakeholders. Project managers, of course, make final calls.

RISK ALLEVIATION

Webster provides the following definition:

> **risk** (risk) *n* **1**: the chance of injury, damage, or loss; dangerous chance; hazard **2**: **a**: the chance of loss **b**: the degree of probability of loss

We can't usually look at a risk, only at the conditions that have been set in place that could cause a detrimental effect. Risk is, after all, only an uncertainty, and may result in no detrimental effect. We do know, however, that risk sometimes does result in a detrimental effect, and we are able therefore to quantify the probability of a particular result.

If we were to look at the probability, for example, of achieving a desired ROI for a particular project, it might look something like Fig. 22.

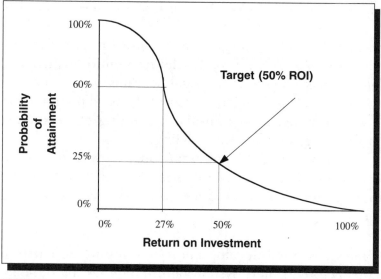

FIGURE 22

We can see that our analysis indicates a 60 to 70 percent probability that we will attain a 27 percent ROI. However, the same curve shows that, because of certain factors identified in our risk analysis, we can expect no more than a 25 percent probability of attaining our desired 50 percent ROI. Approval of our project authorization document may hinge on our ability to demonstrate a high degree of probability in attaining this return.

Obviously, something must change in order to increase the probability of attainment. The factors that contributed to the formation of this curve must change. Those factors may be in the area of lower budget, better/shorter start-up, quicker learning curve, etc. In some areas it may actually mean increasing the budget, short range, in order to realize bigger benefits long range. At any rate, changes should be made and the analysis run and rerun until the degree of confidence in the probability of attaining the desired return can be demonstrated. That is, of course, unless your board or your lenders are high-rollin' gamblers—and we doubt very much that they are.

The factors that affect this curve are uncertainties (risks). Risk uncertainty can be reduced in many ways. Changing from an unproved technology to one that has been proved to be successful is one way.

Another is to plan the project in more detail. Further develop the scope of the project; define requirements more completely. Look closely at the qualifications of the vendors' staffing. Increase the budget, if necessary, to allow for more testing of equipment, more in-depth training of personnel, more prototyping, simulating, modeling.

You can also reduce the potential consequences of a detrimental risk outcome. Some strategies you might wish to use in your ongoing effort to reduce those risk consequences could be:

- Parallel alternative development (developing concurrent backups before primary system failure *requires* the development of a backup).

- Decoupling related items, which means reducing dependencies. For example, if one person or unit is to complete two tasks in sequence and is behind in completing the first task, the project manager can assign the second task to someone else, or to a second unit.

- Tying vendor/contractor payments to milestone completion (protection against schedule slippage by vendors and contractors).

- Providing margins or reserves (contingency allowances). Contingencies should be provided not only for routine items such as budget and schedule, but also for:

    Estimate quality.   Contingency for errors or omissions in cost estimating.

    Adjustment contingency.   Contingency to bring an essentially completed project up to acceptable level.

    Price protection contingency.   To compensate for inflation of vendor-quoted purchased parts.

    Escalation contingency.   Required during periods of extreme inflation or price instability when vendors are unable or unwilling to quote a firm price and choose to protect their bids from uncertainty.

Specification or technical contingency. To deal with technical unknowns that may be encountered during project execution.

Risks can sometimes be avoided entirely or, perhaps, shared with another party or entity. To avoid risk entirely, don't do the project. (Of course as we have already seen, not doing the project may engender more risks of a different nature.) We could perhaps, however, reduce the scope of our response to the perceived need. Smaller responses sometimes can equate to smaller risks.

We can sometimes spread or share the risks associated with equipment delivery schedules and equipment performance by instituting contractual guarantees in our contract or purchase order awards. Be aware, however, that the provider or supplier of equipment and/or services will, in all probability, tailor the quote to cover its share of the risk.

Another stratagem that some client companies are now employing is known as *partnering*, whereby the risks, as well as some of the benefits, are shared. For example, the monetary benefits of budget underruns might be shared. A successful project might also mean that the vendor or contractor would become a *negotiated bidder* for the next project of a similar nature. (We shall discuss partnering arrangements in more detail a little later on.)

As stated, it is not practical to attempt to avoid or neutralize all risk associated with a capital project. However, we should always look for ways to reduce or alleviate individual risks, especially where the risk is high and/or the impact would be great.

Our third *Project Bottom-Line Success!* principle states:

> **The probability of project success increases proportionally to the degree of project risk reduction.**

What we mean here is that within any particular project's confines lies 100 percent of that particular project's risk. Given enough time and effort, we could probably identify about 95 percent of that project's block or ball of risk. Risk, being an uncertainty, carries with it some probability of detrimental outcome. If all the risk associated with the project were to result in detrimental outcome, the project would surely fail. The probability of failure, then, is inherently higher in a project where absolutely no alleviation measures are taken.

We can reduce this probability of an unsuccessful outcome by taking risk alleviation measures. If the probability of an unsuccessful outcome has been caused by risk factors, the reduction of those same risk factors will cause an immediate and equal increase in the *probability* of a successful outcome.

Probability curves and risk alleviation are sometimes a hard sell to a project team, primarily because, if you have alleviated a risk, it probably won't be recognized. Why? Because nothing happened. And, since risks are only probabilities and not sure things, the detrimental outcome might not have happened anyway! However, as stated earlier, there's a multibillion-dollar industry in Nevada that makes its very profitable living via the probability curve. Let's get back to our curve.

We can see the results of our risk reduction efforts only when we again perform the risk analysis and look at the resulting changes in the probability curve (Fig. 23).

After having effected some risk avoidance or risk alleviation stratagems and rerunning our risk analysis program, we can see a

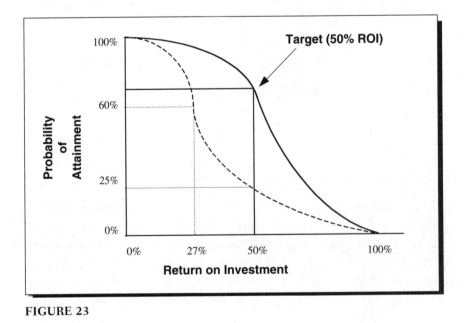

FIGURE 23

definite change in the ROI probability curve; we now have a 60 to 70 percent probability (not a certainty), that we will be successful in attaining a 50 percent ROI, our target. The probability can be pushed higher, depending on how much time and, certainly, budget we are willing to expend in risk alleviation efforts.

It might be helpful, at this point, to consider another case study to see where some of these principles and precepts might have helped a project team that suddenly found itself in the unenviable position of unexpected overrun on a major project. Again, although this case is placed in the steel industry, it could just as easily have taken place in any industry.

C A S E   S T U D Y   3

New Coating Line—"One-Stop Shop"

PROJECT BACKGROUND

In 1990, a well-known steel maker, Hartford Steel, embarked on a strategy to capture a greater share of the growing construction steel market. Encouraged by its recent success in a joint-venture coating line and spurred by burgeoning competition, Hartford's strategy depended on increasing its coating capacity for galvanized and aluminum-coated products.

There were several options open to Hartford, especially on the question of location, since Hartford operates from several different locations. Therefore, executive management invited each of Hartford's four major facilities to submit proposals for building a new line capable of producing 270,000 tons per year of galvanized and aluminum-coated material. In addition, a headquarters group was formed to weigh the pros and cons of constructing the coating line as a stand-alone facility at a greenfield site.

After careful consideration of the various proposals, executive management selected Hartford's Dover Cliffs plant as the best site for the new coating line. The project appropriation was approved in January 1991 and the project got underway in February with a 14-month completion schedule and a $64,000,000 budget.

PROJECT APPROPRIATION

The proposal for locating the coating line at the Dover Cliffs plant contained several persuasive arguments, one being that the Dover

Cliffs plant was already a major supplier of construction steel products and had been considering ways to differentiate its product line from that of its current competitors. Adding the new coating line to its existing facilities would make Dover Cliffs a full-line supplier to the construction market, offering a one-stop shop for construction products. Increased production resulting from the coating line would also redirect Dover's order book from a predominantly hot-rolled product to a value-added product.

Other strong points in the Dover Cliffs proposal included such things as accessibility to transport systems and a trained and well-educated workforce. Wary that executive management was predisposed to locating at a greenfield site, the Dover Cliffs team took great pains to convince the executive level that it could build the new line at its facility for at least $20 million dollars less. According to Dover Cliffs, this location would also allow the company to produce product at a $10-per-net-ton cost advantage over a greenfield-sited facility. And, as icing on the cake, the state and local government at the Dover Cliffs location weighed in with an enticing incentive package of tax rebates, training funds, low-cost bond financing, and infrastructure improvements.

On the basis of a $64 million project cost and a calculated ROI of 26 percent, Hartford management was sold, and the project got underway with the Dover Cliffs Engineering Department acting as its own general contractor, utilizing various vendors and suppliers to perform specific functions. The core project team consisted of the following:

- A Dover Cliffs project manager (who also doubled as lead mechanical engineer)
- A Dover Cliffs electrical project engineer
- A contract electrical engineer
- A Dover Cliffs operations manager
- A Dover Cliffs electrical maintenance manager

Subsequent additions to the project team included Dover Cliffs lead construction engineers (mechanical and electrical) and a commissioning manager, each of whom was brought on board to manage a particular portion of the project. Also, each of the equipment suppliers and the primary construction engineering firm had designated project managers who involved themselves in project planning and implementation of their individual work scopes as appropriate. Service suppliers were selected on the basis of Dover Cliffs' previous experience with these companies or on ties to the local economy. Equipment suppliers consisted of companies that had supplied the technology and systems for Hartford's existing coating facility.

Traditionally, the Dover Cliffs plant had divided project management implementation responsibilities according to project phases. The original project manager would lead the project from appropriation approval up to the construction phase. When construction began, a construction engineer assumed functional leadership of the team up to commissioning; at that point, the commissioning manager assumed control until turnover to operations for hot runs. This traditional management scheme was followed for the coating line project.

PROJECT PLANNING

Because little preplanning or preauthorization engineering was done for this project, the Dover Cliffs Engineering Department moved aggressively into project planning immediately following appropriation approval. The core project team was assembled and conducted a series of meetings to hammer out the project plan. The team reviewed basic design criteria, evaluated the general arrangement of the line, established lines of communication among the various core and adjunct team members, and addressed cost control issues. The team did not discuss project risks except in relation to specific areas such as schedule and equipment; no formal risk assessment or analysis was performed for the project. The project team attacked this project with a "can do" attitude, with little tolerance for those who questioned schedules, budgets, etc.

PROJECT DESIGN

Project design was based strictly on an existing Hartford coating line that had been constructed as a stand-alone facility in the mid-1980s. Specifications for process technology, systems, and equipment were duplicated from the existing coating line. The primary operating specification required that the new facility be capable of producing 270,000 tons per year of either galvanized or aluminum-coated product.

Process control specifications called for modern distributed control systems and computers to assist operators in running the line. However, the line was not designed to be fully automated. Current technology was to automate basic tasks and to provide operators with information needed to make sound decisions. To achieve critical surface and flatness parameters required by Dover Cliffs' customers, the process was to include a modern surface conditioning mill and a tension leveler.

PROJECT PROCUREMENT

Because Dover Cliffs was acting as its own general contractor, major contracts for equipment and engineering were handled in house. Virtually every major piece of equipment was purchased with no more than a one- or two-page performance specification based on duplicating existing equipment. The exception to this was the vertical furnace, which was required because of space limitations. Consequently, Dover Cliffs engineers based the selection of the furnace design and manufacturer on similar equipment at a competitor's facility.

Vendors were responsible for purchases required to manufacture their own equipment. Installation contractors placed the majority of construction material purchase orders (concrete, conduit, cable, pipe, etc.).

No quality assurance or quality control standards were included in equipment purchase orders.

The project team decided that quality assurance/quality control (QA/QC) standards were not necessary because equipment was being duplicated from an existing line. However, the project team thoroughly reviewed the existing installation to identify problem areas.

To meet the 14-month schedule, equipment had to be delivered on time and in the proper sequence for installation. Although the project team agreed that equipment delivery schedules were achievable, they also acknowledged that there was no schedule slack time to accommodate problems. Therefore, the team requested that Dover Cliffs' Purchasing Department provide full-time representation to ensure that order placement and equipment delivery would proceed smoothly. (However, the Purchasing Department was unable to provide full-time representation, and project team personnel spent considerable time and effort expediting equipment deliveries.)

At the time of order placement, specific time frames for equipment on-site testing and start-up had not been established. Rates for on-site testing and vendor assistance at start-up were negotiated at the time of equipment installation rather than as a part of the purchase orders. Materials and spares for start-up were incorporated in purchase orders on the basis of a review of items that had been supplied at the existing coating line.

PROJECT PRESHIPMENT TESTING

Dover Cliffs' planning for preshipment testing was concentrated on individual pieces of equipment and on the operation of the level 1, level 2, and distributive process control systems. Specific test standards were established for the level 1 software, and full line operation of the level 1 and distributive systems were conducted at the vendor shops. Minimal problems were encountered during preshipment testing of the control systems.

The project team adhered to its preshipment testing plan with few exceptions. However, some equipment was shipped without motors installed and aligned in order to maintain the construction schedule. While this situation had little effect on equipment start-up or operation, it did contribute to higher construction costs.

PROJECT CONSTRUCTION/INSTALLATION

The construction contractor and subcontractors were selected for their known capabilities and ties to the local area. While there was some consultation with the construction contractor during the early project stages, no in-depth review of construction requirements or planning was completed in conjunction with the contractor. The project team factored start-up requirements relative to construction into the overall plan, and a construction QA/QC program was established and implemented.

Fluctuations in equipment delivery hampered detailed construction scheduling. Additionally, the overall schedule had to be constantly modified to react to slippage in fabrication schedules caused by modifications requested by the project team. Eventually, the testing and commissioning requirements drove the construction schedule so that complete units of equipment could be turned over for commissioning.

As construction progressed, the project team realized that construction costs would significantly overrun the original estimate. The contractual arrangement called for Dover Cliffs to cover the construction contractor's direct cost with a possible bonus payment tied to schedule, cost, and quality targets. The contractual arrangement resulted from a lack of time to prepare traditional construction packages of final drawings and specifications. The compressed schedule required a significant amount of concurrent engineering in which construction drawings and specifications were finalized only 2 or 3 weeks ahead of the construction schedule. While this schedule did not impact line start-up or operation, it contributed significantly to project cost overrun. Also, because of a lack of proper labor tracking procedures, the total extent of this overrun was not known until late in the project.

PROJECT TRAINING

The workforce to staff the new coating line consisted primarily of experienced operating and maintenance personnel, along with some less-experienced workers. Working from a training needs evaluation conducted early in the project, the project team decided to use a mix of classroom training and hands-on vendor training. The classroom training was funded by the state government and provided through a local community college. However, as the training proceeded, the project team realized that the community college had failed to plan or prepare *specific* training on how to operate the equipment. This situation forced the project team to use Dover Cliffs' engineering and vendor personnel as hands-on trainers at the same time they were trying to start up the facility. Specific training needs were not developed until later in the project. These oversights were to have considerable impact on the project start-up.

PROJECT PREOPERATIONAL TESTING/COMMISSIONING AND INITIAL OPERATIONS

Approximately 4 months into construction, the project team began planning for preoperational testing, commissioning, and start-up. A separate commissioning manager was brought on board and a full-time preoperational testing and commissioning team established. A detailed testing and commissioning schedule was prepared that covered each piece of line and auxiliary equipment in the facility. The commissioning team coordinated the completion of all construction testing activities and supervised preoperational testing through coating-line cold runs.

Vendors were used extensively during commissioning. The construction contractor provided labor resources. Some equipment problems were encountered, requiring field correction or redesign. Process control testing proved successful, although testing results documentation was not optimal because of a limited workforce.

As soon as preoperational testing was complete, the project team turned the facility over to operations for hot runs (commissioning). During initial operations, the facility experienced both equipment failures and what appeared to be a general lack of competency among the operations staff. The equipment failures were handled by adjustment and redesign as required after consultation with vendors. Operator competency problems appeared to be rooted in inadequate and hurriedly prepared equipment-specific training. The equipment malfunctions and poor operator performance resulted in lost production. Three months after start-up, production was still considerably inconsistent.

PROJECT CLOSEOUT

At the time of closeout, final project tallies indicated the following:

- The project actually completed 2 months ahead of schedule, finishing in 12 months instead of the original 14 months. Missing from this "completion evaluation," however, is the fact that operators were having considerable difficulty in operating the line.

- Additionally, and of far more concern, project cost was exceeded by several millions of dollars, primarily because of poor construction cost control and errant estimating of engineering and commissioning costs. Engineering and commissioning costs were originally estimated by using numbers from an existing coating line. However, modifications to the Dover Cliffs line resulted in increased engineering and commissioning efforts.

The projected ROI and payback as stated in the appropriation were not attained. Although the project team considered this project a qualified success because the project met or exceeded its schedule and technological goals, the unexpected multimillion dollar overrun was a major blow to the corporate bottom line.

PROJECT CRITIQUE

PROJECT JUSTIFICATION AND APPROPRIATION

Executive management justified this project by reacting to a compelling commercial need to consolidate and exploit Hartford's share of the construction steel market and to take aggressive steps to outpace competitive challenges. The appropriation process, which consisted of a competition among the plant sites, resulted in the plants' skewing, or overstating, of benefits and advantages. For example, Dover Cliffs claimed that it could build the plant for several million dollars less than the cost of a greenfield site, yet the project overran its budget by approximately that same amount. Also, Dover Cliffs claimed that its well-educated, trained workforce would enhance and accelerate start-up. As it turned out, poor operator training and performance hampered, rather than enhanced, start-up and initial operations.

The fact that this plant was to be a duplicate facility drove project scope, cost, schedule, and risk definition. Consequently, very little risk assessment or preplanning was completed and the costs of engineering, construction, and commissioning were underestimated because the scope was based on an existing line.

If the scope had been thoroughly defined and risks assessed relative to the specific requirements of the venture and this project, rather than results from the existing line, costs could have been more accurately predicted. (A higher cost estimate, however, would probably have convinced executive management to proceed with the greenfield installation instead of the Dover Cliffs site.)

Preshipment testing succeeded, for the most part, in assuring that equipment arrived on site in proper condition. (A major discrepancy occurred, however, when the project team authorized some equipment to be shipped without motors installed and aligned. This decision contributed to an already-bloated construction cost overrun.)

While project construction and equipment installations were completed within the overall schedule, the attending multimillion dollar cost escalation overshadows any success that was achieved during execution. The overrun can be traced back to poor project definition and woefully inadequate cost control measures by both the contractor and the project team.

Project training was a negative. Enticed by the state government's offer to provide massive amounts of training through a local community college, the project team lulled itself into a false sense of security that operations and maintenance personnel would be fully prepared to assume control of the facility for commissioning and initial operations. This was not the case; lack of proper training was a significant factor in extending the ramp-up to full production learning curve.

The most glaring omissions associated with preoperational testing and commissioning activities were that commissioning services were not incorporated into vendor purchase orders and that planning was not started until 4 months into construction. Waiting to negotiate vendor assistance until the time of commissioning caused the original commissioning budget to be exceeded. Waiting until 4 months into construction to begin preoperational testing and commissioning planning forced the project team to complete a tremendous amount of work in a short period of time.

Unfortunately, the project team's concerted effort during preoperational testing and commissioning was undermined by inconsistent performance of the line during initial operations, inconsistencies caused primarily by a lack of thorough workforce training.

CONCLUSION

Project teams must be always aware that the money spent on projects comes from venture profits (net income); therefore, any money spent during the project must be made up as venture profits, not gross sales. The construction industry will have to do a lot of one-stop shopping at Dover Cliffs and its new coating line to make up for the bottom-line profit this project left behind.

BASIC QUESTIONS

Perhaps if both management and the project team had asked themselves a few basic questions, this project might have taken a much more desirable turn, right from the start. Before starting your next project, you might wish also to ask yourself some of these same questions:

1. Has a reality check taken place; i.e., is this project really needed? What are the benefits? How will a successful execution of this project affect your venture's bottom line? If this project goes substantially over budget and schedule, how will it impact the bottom line?

2. Is there an operational way to obtain equivalent results? Is there any other way except to spend capital funds?

3. Were alternative suppliers considered? Were alternative systems compared and analyzed?

4. Was a life-cycle cost analysis performed? Is the system chosen the most economically feasible over the long range?

5. Has the scope been completely defined? Do all potential bidders have the same information?

6. Have the objectives of the project and the benefits expected been communicated to all bidders with total clarity?

7. If a design has already been selected, is it a proved design; has it worked out successfully elsewhere? How many locations? Has it been completely researched by your engineers? Have your engineers investigated other installations, questioned other users?

8. Has input been obtained from all concerned parties? Operations? Maintenance? Have these parties "bought in" on the need for the project? On the design that has been selected or is being considered?

9. Has a risk analysis been performed? *Has scope been developed sufficiently to identify all risk elements?* What are the risks of doing the project now? What are the risks of not doing the project now? Which holds greater risk to the venture's bottom line?

10. If risks have been identified, have they also been prioritized? Which risk item has the highest impact potential? Which item has the greatest probability of occurrence? Have the costs of reducing highest ranked-risks been estimated?

DEFINING VENTURE AND CORPORATE RISK

TO DO, OR NOT TO DO—THAT IS THE QUESTION!

As stated earlier, one of the first assessments that must be made concerns the question of viability. Is this project really viable? Isn't the answer to this question really just an assessment of the risks associated with doing or not doing the project? In order to assess viability, project planners must identify the risks in two areas: the risks to the venture and the risks to the project itself.

Assessing risks to the venture may be a bit hazier in nature than the assessment of risks to the project. In the assessment of project risks we deal with more finite questions and more familiar answers. The assessment of risks to the venture, on the other hand, will usually deal with such questions as "Is the market right?" "Have we read the trends accurately?" "If the project fails, how will it affect the bottom line?" And how about the big question, "Can we survive a failure?"

The risks involved may be so heavy as to preclude the continuation of project development. It is far better to face these questions and make a rational decision at the outset than to pour perhaps many millions of bottom-line dollars into the project and then make the same decision anyway.

A CASE IN POINT

Not too long ago a large, integrated steel producer began planning a project that some in key management positions felt would enhance the company's position in the "big beam" and other structural products markets. The project was popular, since it would be built in the steel producer's headquarters city and would enhance its standing and reputation among the hometown citizenry. Additionally, the project held a certain nostalgia for some, since the company would be returning to its roots; it had cut its teeth on structural steel.

The project would be large, approaching a quarter-billion dollars, and would include a beam caster, furnace, vacuum degasser facility, and other ancillary systems. It had been considered for several years and, although the corporate balance sheet was not as healthy as it had been previously, the decision was made to proceed with the project.

Some other key managers, however, were uneasy. Although previous feasibility studies had shown the big beam market was penetrable, the evidence was not overwhelming. These misgivings, however, failed to dampen the spirits of others and the project roared into existence. A project team was put together, preproject planning was accomplished, budgets and schedules were developed, and contracts were awarded to several contractors.

The project proceeded in this manner for several months. Meanwhile, the uneasy feeling about the efficacy of the project began to spread, the main worry being the company's ability to compete effectively in the large structural market. Another study was undertaken and the results were disturbing, to say the least. The numbers just didn't add up. In the new world economy, and taking into consideration costs, margins required for profitability, and the competition, the data predicted a disaster in the making.

Finally, the steel company bit the bullet, so to speak, and halted the project. It didn't come by the decision easily though. Egos, and some careers, were on the line. After all, approximately $12 million had been spent to date, with nothing to show for it. As bad as this was, however, it was nothing compared to the risk that was well on the way to becoming reality.

Had this project gone forward, it could easily have ended in disaster, leaving the corporate bottom line with a quarter-billion-dollar white elephant. This result, coupled with the high cost of the project in the first place, could have led to corporate financial danger.

The preceding case took place either because corporate strategic planning was inadequate or because individual project planning was out of sync with the plan, or both.

Now, there are two ways to view this event, one good, one not so good. Let's consider the not so good first.

One can only assume that some very high-level thinking went into the decision to spend over a quarter billion of the corporation's bottom-line dollars on this entry into a highly competitive market. Could it have been that the decision makers were given market scenarios or project outcomes that were based on emotion rather than hard-eyed fact? Wishful thinking, perhaps? In any case, subsequent assessments indicated that the decision to proceed needed to be superseded by a new decision, that decision being to stop. Had that been the *original* decision, several millions of bottom-line dollars that were expended on initiation of the project could have been routed to a project that held more viability.

But this story also has a good side. It is far better to bite the bullet and cancel a project that has all the indications of being a disaster than to forge stubbornly ahead and risk the venture's very survivability. Too many times we have seen these projects assume a life of their own and push right on to their inevitably bad ending, costing jobs, reputations, and investors' money along the way. It usually takes courage on the part of a decision maker to make a decision such as was made in this case. We commend that decision maker.

Assessing risks to the venture, then, will include assessing both the risk in going ahead, that is, of doing the project, as well as assessing the risk of not doing it.

If the proposed project need has been based on environmental concerns, then do/not do decisions must give consideration to the potential adverse effects on workers, people in the surrounding community, company reputation, and the collateral costs of potential governmental sanctions, possibly huge fines and even facility shutdown. The risk to the venture is, as always, that the proposed change will cause the facility to cross the line into nonprofitability, or possibly result in margins so slim as to make long-term operation nonviable.

If the need for the proposed project is driven by a desire to take advantage of market opportunities or to sustain current business, the risks to the venture of not doing the project are serious. They can include loss of market share, or perhaps of being put at a technological disadvantage vis-à-vis your competitors, which could have the same result, i.e., loss of customers, loss of market share. It is imperative, however, that market opportunity be viewed with hard-eyed intensity and that the project not be given the green light on the basis of emotion or wishful thinking. An error in judgment here can take the venture or the company right out of the game.

For example, one of the more common risks to the venture is that the intended benefits of the project will not be achieved, thus weakening the venture's financial or commercial position. To carry that thought one step further, the cost of the project, if heavy in comparison to the overall financial health of the venture or company, combined with failure to achieve intended benefits, could threaten the venture's very survival.

This second risk, the risk of venture demise, is particularly applicable to small or midsize companies that do not have the resources to absorb a catastrophic project failure. However, a series of high-dollar project failures can have the same disastrous effect on large companies; large ventures just struggle longer to stay afloat before finally disappearing beneath the surface.

How, then, do corporate decision makers determine a go/no-go project decision? Usually by careful consideration of basic questions such as these:

1. Is the market assessment valid? From a cost-of-money standpoint, is the timing right?

2. How will the venture's bottom line be impacted over the next year if we don't do this project now? The next 2 years? The next 5 years?

3. How will the venture's bottom line be impacted over those same years if we do this project now within budget and schedule and achieve intended benefits? Is the ROI sufficient to justify the risk?

4. How will the venture's bottom line be impacted over those same years if we do this project now but don't achieve budget, schedule, and intended benefits?

5. Is there an operational method of attaining the desired benefits (as opposed to capital funds expenditure)?

6. On the basis of projected bottom-line impacts (both positive and negative) over the next several years, which option has the greatest chance to improve the venture's bottom line; which has the least chance for harming the venture's bottom line?

Let's take these questions, one at a time, and see if we can't arrive at some reasonable method of looking for answers.

IS THE MARKET ASSESSMENT VALID? IS THE TIMING RIGHT?

First, let's look at the validity of the market assessment. It would seem that the first question regarding the validity of the assessment should be "Who did the assessment?" If the assessment was performed by an entity with a vested interest in the outcome, then that assessment must be considered suspect. We're not saying here that something nefarious might be involved, only that human nature being what it is, most assessments, surveys, feasibility studies, or any undertaking of a similar nature that is performed by an agency, group, consultant, or individual with a bias will almost always result in a biased report. It's just the way we are.

If we rely on our own marketing and sales groups to assess the market potentials of a particular product, a particular market segment, or market area we may run into some of the same biased outcomes. Again, it's only human nature.

The only way to gather information of this nature and avoid the problem of skewed reports is to use a nonbiased third party having no interest in the outcome. We've already related one example of a company using the front-running prime contractor candidate to perform a study concerning the feasibility of the project in question. (It never ceases to amaze me when an otherwise erudite client company makes a move of this type!)

The market must be viewed not only in its present context, but also in the context of where it *might* be next year, the year after that, in 5 years, and yes, even in 10 or 15 years. Of course, any prediction of future events is uncertain, to say the least, but much can be learned from the past. Experienced people looking at trends can interpret data nuances that may be missed by less experienced observers. Politics, financial events, other market pressures and demographics will influence these trends. The seers who can read these trends, and from them make the most accurate deductions, obviously stand a better chance of coming up with the right answer as to just where corporate financing should be aimed for the best long-range results.

There are diverse views on the subject. Emerson Corporation recently experienced its "165th quarter of uninterrupted net-income growth," as chronicled by Carl Quintanilla, a staff reporter for *The Wall Street Journal.*

According to Emerson's Chairman and CEO Charles F. Knight, writing in the 1992 *Harvard Business Review* in an article entitled "Consistent Profits, Consistently," "The 'long term' consists of a series of 'short terms.'" His highly successful company, and record-setting run are testaments to his fixed-goal, low-risk strategy of carefully planning the future, quarter by quarter.

However, we recently watched Wall Street, although professing a fondness for consistency, rewarding "irrational exuberance" with booming stock prices. But, as it turned out, the "promise" of good returns was not sustainable on its own. Sooner or later that promise had to deliver, and too many new start-ups were unable to post a positive return. Today's market (since the dot.com bubble burst) has again become more conservative, favoring longer-range planning and aggressive (but more tactical) acquisitions, as long-range trends are targeted. This strategy, however, sometimes tends to interrupt quarterly profits as strategic moves require resulting charges to be recorded.

All decisions that are based on market trends hold risk. The real trick for executive planners is in gauging just *how much* risk is entailed. "Nothing ventured, nothing gained," goes the old saw. To capture a share of the market, and then to retain that advantage over the coming years, may dictate that some risk be taken. However, it is our considered opinion that one should never "bet the farm" on any risk situation. All the above is predicated, of course, on the company under discussion having a dedicated strategic planning group and practicing the selection of projects based on a strategic plan.

BETTING THE FARM

All the above being said, however, we shall watch with great interest the outcome of a recent decision by a huge corporation to, in effect, bet the farm on a course that may be fraught with risk. (The outcome may prove us wrong about betting the farm, at least in an isolated instance.) The company to which we refer is Airbus Industrie, the European giant and rival of America's Boeing Corporation in the manufacture of large jet aircraft.

An earlier *Wall Street Journal* article by another staff reporter, Jeff Cole, laid out in detail the pros and cons of the risks being taken by Airbus in its decision to design and build a huge new passenger airplane that could seat nearly 1000 people (in an all-coach-class setting).

The most interesting item of the piece, however, was in the disparate thought processes of the rival companies' strategic planning teams. While Boeing's executive planners considered the venture too expensive and too risky, Airbus' executives studied the same data and concluded that the greater risk to their company was in *not* proceeding.

The planned new Airbus, identified at the time as the A-3XX, will be the largest jetliner built to date, with spiral staircases, elevators, 10-abreast seating in a double-deck arrangement, an 8800-mile range, *and a development cost estimated at more than $12 billion.*

We have recently seen megabuck mergers and buyouts that stagger the imagination in their immensity. Risks of that nature, however, are usually not as great as they may seem; the net worth of the company being acquired, taken over, or merged with is usually easily ascertained and will increase the net value of the resulting entity.

But this—this is *real* risk! The outlay in development expense is tremendous. Even a senior Airbus executive said that while they will do their best to limit the risks, "this is one of those 'bet-your-company' decisions."

Boeing's response? Much more conservative. A bigger, longer version of its workhorse 747 called, simply, the 747X-Stretch. The new version, with an 8625-mile range, will be about 30 feet longer and will seat 500 to 520 passengers in a three-class arrangement. The big difference will be project cost. Compared to the Airbus $12 billion plus budget, Boeing expects to accomplish its goals in the $2 to $3 billion range.

THE STRATEGIES

As stated, both companies started from the same data. The data told them that "jumbo jet" use over the Atlantic had flattened over the past decade, even as midsize jet usage had increased many times over. The reason is because smaller jets are easier to fill and can be used more strategically in "point-to-point" service, bypassing the large "hub" airports.

According to the *WSJ* article, the same trend appeared, at that time, to have just begun over the Pacific, i.e., pinpoint destination service, as Southeast Asia and other Asian markets open new airports and the usual hub cities are bypassed.

Both companies had studied the data that led to these findings, but their take on the strategy to follow in order to capitalize on the emerging picture was totally different. Because of these differences, those involved—the corporate executives, the various airlines, the investors—all were watching in fascination as the scenario began to unfold. Boeing will be first into the market with its upgraded and expanded 747. But, they wondered, will it get the jump on Airbus and "define" the market? Some think it can. Lufthansa's Dietmar Kirchner was quoted by *The Wall Street Journal* article as stating that by the time Airbus has what he calls its "testosterone jet" ready, Boeing can "spoil their party by having a party next door."

Some worried that perhaps Boeing was being too conservative; was relying too much on retooling older models. Airbus has grown rapidly by introducing new designs. One such worrier, Stephen Hazy, president of International Lease Finance Corporation of Los Angeles, a big customer of both Airbus and Boeing, was quoted in the same article as stating that without new products, "Boeing is going to be falling behind Airbus. There's just no question about that."

Although Boeing appears to have no plans to develop one of the giant airliners (its chairman, Phil Condit, says it's "not worth it"), the company has revealed that there is always "low-level" research under way on all possibilities.

And as stated by Jeff Cole of *The Wall Street Journal*, "Ultimately, the question comes down to which is the bigger risk: moving too quickly, or not quickly enough. Both manufacturers insist they have done their homework. And Airbus says its gamble is simply good business. The A-3XX, says Mr. Forgeard, Airbus's managing director, should not be seen as an extraordinary risk, 'but as very well thought through by a conservative, no-nonsense team of people.'"

Is the timing right? To answer this question, executive planners must look at other issues in addition to market forces. For example, one of the most important questions to answer in any industrial decision of this magnitude is "How strong is the corporate balance sheet?" If the last several quarters have been weak, and market analysis shows that the window of opportunity will last for a while longer, perhaps the project should be put off for another few quarters. We never know when unfolding events will drastically change the game plan. For example, the horrendous events of September 11, 2001, have shaken the airline industry to its very core. Are these aircraft giants' balance sheets strong enough to survive a serious disruption to the strategic plan? We shall be watching the Airbus versus Boeing strategies very closely over the next few months and years to see what decisions they take now and just how those decisions play out.

WHAT IS THE IMPACT IF WE DON'T DO IT NOW? IF WE DO IT NOW? IF WE HAVE OVERRUNS?

These questions require not only an analysis of corporate finances, but also, in some cases, an analysis of corporate strategy. If the proposed project is of strategic importance and is tabled until the next budget cycle, the delay might begin an entire string of events that does real harm to the venture or corporate bottom line. This is why strategic planning must be very seriously pursued. Any "elective" capital improvement project should be weighed against the strategic plan and "what if" scenarios and models studied. One of the biggest problems we see across many industries is the tendency to take on large projects without this discipline being observed. This tendency results in poor returns resulting from unneeded capacity, deprivation of funding for other, more strategically needed projects, and, if the ill effects are serious enough, venture demise.

THE REAL OPTION VALUATION

One of the latest methods being used by corporate strategic planners to assess risk is real option valuation (ROV). This method could quickly become the new standard for assessing risky ventures and billion-dollar-plus bets such as the bet-the-farm case we have just discussed.

ROV uses complicated models to weigh all possible scenarios, probable and possible outcomes, and the value of all possible contingencies over the lifetime of a venture. It can be used to justify paying astronomically high development costs (such as we have just seen) or as a warning sign to "walk away."

It is true that some skeptics dismiss ROV as a complex and time-consuming gimmick that diverts attention from and undermines common sense and "dynamic leadership." However, anything that can truly *quantify* the variables, or even bracket the *probabilities,* is always better than those gut decisions that usually end in disaster. (Strange that the only gut decisions we ever hear about are those rarities that turn out well!)

ROV has many variations, but in its basic format it attempts to build a dynamic road map of potential paths, risks, and outcomes. The valuation techniques of ROV also tend to break with traditional valuation methods. For example, under the discounted cash flow method weighing expected revenues against costs, two products with the same probability of success, identical revenue potential, and similar development costs would be equally valued.

However, by using ROV techniques, i.e., laying out all the various steps in development, including the associated risks, products and projects that would tend to fail later rather than sooner would be valued less, as a result of the steeper costs involved.

ROV is a relatively new methodology, and, although it can help companies map out potential future risks, it is complicated and not yet totally proved as a risk analysis tool. Still, any analysis method is better than decisions based on gut, corporate politics, or egocentricism.

Other Factors

Another type project that must also be weighed from a strategic standpoint is the mandated project, i.e., the project that must be executed to satisfy an environmental or safety mandate. These projects can cost in the millions of dollars and have significant effect on operating costs. Sometimes there is no choice; it's either do it or face shutdown of a facility by the authorities. In some cases, however, there may well be a choice. The alternative to not doing the project may be a fine, albeit a hefty fine. In these cases, many things must be considered. For example, is it only delaying the inevitable; that is, will we pay the fine and end up being required to correct the situation at a later date anyway? And what effect will avoiding the project have on community relations, or on our workers? And if we accede and build a mandated facility, will the cost of operation drive up our product cost to the point that we become noncompetitive in the marketplace? Again, the strategic plan may provide the answers to even these questions. The point is, all projects, capital improvement as well as mandated, affect the bottom line and go/no-go decisions should always be gauged against the strategic plan.

IS THERE A SUFFICIENT RETURN?

In Chap. 2 we presented our first principle of commonsense, *Project Bottom-Line Success!* management: If project need cannot be justified on the basis of a realistically sufficient contribution to the venture bottom line, then the project should not go forward.

Project decision makers should assume, in this case, that the project will be executed flawlessly, that it will be completed within the stated budget and schedule. Now, leaving that risk out of the equation, the big question is, "Will this project make a realistically sufficient contribution to the venture or corporate bottom line?"

Looked at from a purely business standpoint, many projects would fail this test. These projects not only are usually totally out of sync with any long-range corporate interests, but the company could probably get a better return investing in mutual funds! Why do these projects go forward? *Usually because they are emotionally or ego driven, or because the company does not have an effective corporate strategic plan in place.* When we put the risk back into the equation (it may *not* be executed within the stated budget and schedule) it makes it doubly important that a good ROI be the basis of any decision to commit capital funding.

WHAT IS THE IMPACT IF SCHEDULE AND BUDGET ARE OVERRUN?

With some projects, schedule is really not an issue, other than its effect on the budget. In other cases, however, schedule is everything. Not making schedule can mean anything from missing a window of opportunity to losing a major customer. The decision to go, or not to go, with a project should be based on the worst-case scenario impact on the bottom line. Is there a risk alleviation factor available? If not, can the venture, or the corporation, survive the worst-case scenario? The answer here *must* be yes, or the project must be disapproved. No board in its right mind would ever bet the farm.

In most instances, one project will not make or break a corporation. However, a series or a string of overrun budgets and schedules, combined with insufficient ROIs, can, and often do cause irreparable harm to a venture or corporate entity.

IS THERE SOME OTHER WAY?

Many times, facility operators are "too quick on the trigger" when it comes to spending corporate dollars in the attempt to solve a problem. As stated earlier, it is highly important that project origination begin with a reality check, before capital improvement funds are committed. Let's restate that reality check:

> Everyone in the loop must take care that the need for a project is real, that it is not undertaken simply because it *can* be done or as an emotional answer to a perceived need or problem. Sometimes an operational change or further training will suffice. Decision makers should thoroughly evaluate and critically analyze the evidence supporting project need by actually conducting a reality check to verify that the need for a project does, in fact, exist.

Reality checks can take the form of feasibility studies, surveys, modeling, or fact-finding meetings. The point is this:

Not only are capital projects expensive (they consume bottom-line dollars), they also hold risk. If another way is available to solve the problem, then it is usually better to avoid the spending of capital funds. (There are other projects out there where the funding really *is* needed.)

FINDING ALTERNATIVES: AN EXAMPLE

We were asked by a manufacturer, not too long ago, to investigate alternatives to installing a modification to both equipment and software on a major production line in an attempt to improve productivity and quality. The effort appeared headed toward a capital improvement project, since a "feasibility study" by a large equipment supplier had shown that production line output could be increased by at least 15, and perhaps even 20, percent if the project were to be undertaken. Since the production line was constantly in operation, and demand for its product was high, it was a very tempting proposition to attempt an upgrade during regular maintenance outages. After all, the reasoning went, an immediate market existed for everything this line could produce.

The only hitch was the risk. If the several maintenance outages it would take to install the upgrade were to be delayed, the losses would be substantial. A further risk was potential loss of customers if any resultant outage overrun were to become substantial.

Management felt secure in the belief that the line could produce more than it was currently producing, since on many occasions one of the shifts had, in fact, been able to obtain production levels of almost 20 percent above the other two shifts. (Much of the difference centered on quality, since substandard quality meant rework and rework meant lower productivity.) Never, however, had the other shifts been able to duplicate this feat and management appeared ready to upgrade both equipment and control systems in an attempt to make them more "automatic." A capital improvement "idiot-proofing," according to some. The upgrade to equipment and control systems would probably work. But still, there was that risk factor.

An in-depth survey was begun, primarily to see why one shift was able to outproduce the other two shifts on so many occasions and to see if the performance could be maintained on a consistent basis.

Interviews with operators from each shift, observations of actual operations, reviews of procedures, and meetings with both labor and management revealed that there was no one thing that could be cited as the reason for the productivity differences between shifts. Rather, the study revealed that there were many differences, some almost minute, that when taken collectively added up to significant differences in the way the production line was being operated. For example:

- Although procedures existed for most parts of the operation, unit personnel tended to employ their own methods of task completion based on experience.

- Most of the practices employed were learned through on-the-job experience and the buddy system rather than through formal training. Each individual responded to operating requirements and any encountered problems in his or her own way, instead of using a standard, proved procedure or practice.

- A lack of communication between the front-end (operating) and back-end (packaging) groups many times caused production line backups.

- Training for replacements consisted of a break-in period, rather than a formalized training program.

- Problems with product identification were frequently caused by glare on control room windows that reduced visibility.

- Many problems occurred during shift changes since some operators had the habit of adjusting settings according to personal preferences rather than to the current processing schedule.

It was decided to shelve the upgrade, for the time being. Management was beginning to sniff a solution to its problem without either the risk of outage overrun or the high cost of the upgrade.

A series of meetings was held with all operators, maintenance personnel and shift foremen to standardize certain operational and maintenance practices, patterning them after the most successful, in all cases.

A training program was carefully designed to correct the deficiencies so noted in a training needs assessment, again using the most successful individual's skills and knowledge as the target.

A training contractor was hired to implement the detailed training specification that had resulted from the training needs assessment. Some personnel transfers and shift trades were effected in order to spread the benefits of best practices among the three shifts.

Soon, results were being felt. Production on the off-shifts began to rise. Even the previous bests were bettered by the first shift. In less than 2 months, overall production was increased by over 18 percent! (Over the next several months, production topped out at 22 percent, with sustained average only a little lower.)

Needless to say, management was elated. Not only had the desired benefits been obtained at a fraction of the expected cost, they had also come without the very high risk that would have accompanied a capital improvement project.

WHICH OPTION TO CHOOSE?

If all the proper steps have been taken, the decision won't be all that difficult. The decision being, of course, which option to go with—to do, or not to do, the project in question. The option to select is the one that best answers this question: *On the basis of projected bottom-line impacts (both positive and negative) over the next several years, which option has the greatest chance to improve the venture's bottom line; which has the least chance for harming the venture's bottom line?*

As can readily be seen, the choice in the foregoing example was easy to make; i.e., don't do the project that had been originally contemplated. The risk would have been great, the capital expenditure high, and there was another way to get the desired benefits.

Not all decisions, of course, are this easy. But if the proper *methodology* is in place, the decisions can become almost automatic.

We were told recently of a large paper company that had customarily spent over $1 billion per year on capital improvement projects. In an attempt to cut this figure to around $600 million per year, this company adopted many of the same methods we have discussed thus far, i.e., strategic planning, benchmarking, feasibility studies, preproject planning in detail, etc.—in short, methods never before used in that company. The new methods of critically appraising the need for a project, the fit with the strategic plan, and potential contribution to the corporate bottom line were firmly backed (and enforced) by a now fired-up management corps.

The corporate engineers and facility operators are now finding it difficult to *even come up to* the $600 million figure estimated for annual capital improvement projects! Needless to say, this company's margins have improved; its stock is up.

Regardless of which rung of management an individual holds, his or her input into the big picture is vital. Upper management must have options. Options derive from information; information comes from all sources. I am constantly amazed that lower-echelon engineers fail to recognize the impact that they have on the decision-making process. Their collective suggestions and desires are the driving force behind many a project.

PREPROJECT PLANNING

THE ORGANIZED APPROACH

The term, *pre*project planning is foreign to many project teams and project planners who, having hit upon a change, or an idea that they feel will yield some tangible benefit in the short term, quickly appropriate the funding felt to be necessary and begin organizing for a project. An ad hoc, or unorganized, type of project planning, usually devoid of any real risk analysis and ignoring any semblance of long-term strategic thinking, will usually fit within the confines of a "budgetary number" already established by executive management.

Preproject planning, on the other hand, is the planning that takes place *before* the project funding is appropriated, and which is both dependent on, and feeds corporate strategic planning efforts. The Construction Industry Institute's (CII) definition of this process is succinct and to the point:

> The process of developing sufficient strategic information to enable owners to address risk and decide whether or not to commit corporate resources.

The assiduous application of this process is *essential* to maximizing the probability of successful project outcomes. Anything else is just guesswork.

The nuts and bolts of this process begins with putting together a preproject planning team and gathering sufficient information leading to a pro-forma authorization to proceed with preproject planning. As you may recall, we discussed the pro-forma authorization step in Chap. 2, but briefly; we stated:

> The preparation of a full-blown project authorization document will take time, in some cases many hours of work and considerable expense, before enough information is in place to cause investors to agree to the bulk release of the funds necessary to actually start work on the project. Additionally, some of the information that will be required in order to obtain this funding must come from equipment suppliers or major service contractors who are hesitant to spend funds estimating a project that might be doubtful. *Pro-forma authorization,* then, is a quick-look approach taken by upper management to see if, in their scheme of thinking, the project holds enough merit to proceed with the expenditure of preauthorization funding.

The steps leading up to, and then succeeding, this critical juncture, or first major decision point, are laid out in Fig. 24 in their usual order. We say *usual order* because, all projects

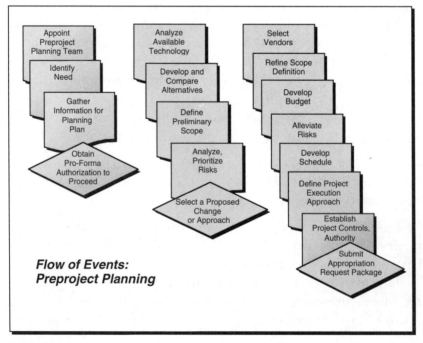

**Flow of Events:
Preproject Planning**

FIGURE 24

being unique, the order, even the content, may vary. In this chapter we will then address each of these points in order, bearing in mind that these are all steps that should *precede* the bulk appropriation of funding. The product of this series of steps is, in fact, the appropriation request (AR), or as referred to by some companies, the project authorization document (PAD).

APPOINTMENT OF A PREPROJECT PLANNING TEAM LEADER

A member of executive management (usually the Vice President and General Manager of Engineering) will select a qualified individual to spearhead the preproject planning effort. The individual selected should be one who not only has a good understanding of corporate goals and strategic plans, but also is unencumbered by any preconceived bias either for, or against, the proposed project. Other desirable traits that should be considered in the selection of this individual would be: a penchant for structured thinking, i.e., a "logical mind," as opposed to a free-thinking, inventive genius (make *use* of these types—don't let them *run* things!) and the ability to select other team members and then get the most out of them. Above all, the team leader must have the ability both to communicate well and, when required, to make decisions.

The composition of the team itself may be dynamic. The team may, and probably will, be composed of different individuals from time to time as the requirement for input changes. Above all, the team must be made up of individuals with the required skills, knowledge, and authority to provide true and factual input to the process (that process being preproject planning). Team composition will usually consist of persons with expertise in project management, technology, engineering, operations, and business systems.

It should be pointed out that some from the preproject planning team will, in all likelihood, become the nucleus of the ongoing project team—that is, if, indeed, the project is ultimately approved. Much more will be said about the organization and makeup of the ongoing project team in the next chapter.

IDENTIFICATION OF THE NEED; ECONOMIC FEASIBILITY

Identification of need has already been discussed at length in previous chapters. The only point we wish to make here is to reiterate that the venture or corporate strategic plan should be the focal point in determination of need. In many instances, short-term gain and long-range strategies do go hand-in-hand. When this is the case, fine. When the two are not complementary, however, or if strategic planning is not a corporate priority, the stage may be being set for execution of a project that will not live up to expectations—a project that may even weaken the venture or corporate position.

In many instances there will be a need to perform a feasibility study. The problem with most feasibility studies is that they are very often used as a tool to *reinforce,* or back up, a position already taken. In almost all cases they are performed by an entity with a vested interest in the outcome.

> How many times have we seen the feasibility study being performed by a large engineering company, the same company that is almost a shoo-in to become the prime contractor or primary equipment supplier? Does anyone really expect that the study will indicate anything other than that the project will be tremendously successful and will be completed at a very attractive price? We're not advocating that feasibility studies should *not* be done, only that they be viewed for what they are, i.e., a gathering of information and estimates that, in some instances, may provide a rather "parallax" view of the project.

Regardless of the outcome of the feasibility study, corporate planners should make use of methods such as risk analysis and, where equipment selection is concerned, life cycle cost analysis to determine the economic feasibility of the project. To analyze economic feasibility means to predict the project's financial performance and its results over its life cycle. The question to be answered is this: will potential profits resulting from successful project execution outstrip potential costs? If so, how long will it take? What are the risks? Additionally, economic feasibility should be stated in terms of discounted cash flow–return on investment (DCF-ROI).

DCF-ROI is a calculation of the rate of return on the investment in the project that takes into account the time value of money. It calculates project return on investment in a way directly equivalent and comparable to such financial measures as bond yields, return on shareholders' equity, mutual fund performance, etc. Thus, using DCF-ROI as one of the critical measures of feasibility facilitates a meaningful comparison to real-world financial returns, and helps in assessing whether the level of predicted DCF-ROI really and truly offsets the risk involved.

THE PLANNING PLAN

Gather Information for Planning Plan

One of the first orders of business for the preproject planning team will be to formulate *its own plan*, documenting the resources, budget, and schedule it feels will be required to (1) deliver a preliminary project estimate for possible *pro-forma* approval and (2) deliver a completed appropriation request, including definitive budget, schedule, scope, and project need justification.

The planning document should include at least the following key components:

- An outline of project requirements, keyed to the corporate strategic plan
- An outline of possible solutions (may be added to)
- An outline of required resources or input
- An outline of permitting requirements
- An outline of pro-forma and appropriation document requirements

- Definitive tasks and reporting requirements of team members
- A detailed schedule of preproject planning tasks
- A detailed budget for preproject planning

Other components will undoubtedly come to light later as the planning cycle gains momentum. Also, this list will vary from project to project, as different projects have different planning priorities. (For example, an environmental project may require defined tasks related to public awareness and public relations programs.

Planning is both time-consuming and tiresome. It is not a glamorous part of project management and it will take a dedicated leader with a desire for detail to keep the team on track and resistant to the cutting of corners as they sort through all the detail. Also, executive management must make it clear to middle managers that the commitment of team members is an absolute necessity. They must be given the time to carry out their team responsibilities. The preproject planning plan, however, is an absolute necessity if the project is to get off to a good start. The penalty for attempting to initiate a project without adequate control of the preplanning process is delay and additional cost later due to missed items of concern, items that may later hit the project team like a ton of bricks.

Another point to consider is the ease with which changes can be accomplished in the planning and conceptual engineering stage of the project. Changes can be made with a pencil and eraser, or with a keystroke on a computer. *Make that same change later, during the late construction or preoperational testing phase, and it will take workers, tools, cutting torches and, more than likely, additional funding.* (See Fig. 25.)

GATHER INFORMATION; OBTAIN PRO-FORMA AUTHORIZATION TO PROCEED

Gathering information is vital not only to the interest of comparing protagonists' project desires against the realities of corporate

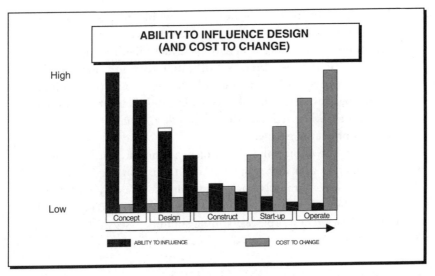

FIGURE 25

strategic planning, but also to the equally important requirement that a knowledge base of facility need, risk, options, and preliminary cost estimates is built. These items need to be known if we are to put forward a preliminary justification that holds enough water to cause executive management to approve, *pro forma,* the funding that will be required to complete the following steps of the preproject planning element.

Preliminary cost estimates of the available technologies will be a target of the gathering of information. This will involve at least a preliminary analysis of available technology including preliminary life cycle cost analysis of major equipment, availability of the various potential systems, obsolescence factors, preliminary costs of installation, and, of course, the cost of the hardware and software itself.

From this information gathering by the preproject planning team, preliminary budget and schedule estimates along with a reconciliation statement of strategic planning and project benefits should ensue. The estimate at this point should be within a ±20 percent range and should be used only as a reference number or order of magnitude. In no case should it be seized upon by anyone in a senior management position and passed on up the ladder as the final project cost.

If the order of magnitude number is within reason to senior management, if the project is considered a real fit with corporate strategic planning, if benefits are identified and are verifiable, and if the risk factors (although still only marginally identified) are within acceptable levels—then the project should be viewed as "highly probable" and additional funding should be authorized. Additional funding, that is, to proceed with preproject planning.

If, on the other hand, the project cannot be justified under the principle that any project (other than mandated safety or environmental projects) must return a reasonably sufficient contribution to the venture bottom line, then the project should not go forward and project planning should cease.

ANALYZING AVAILABLE TECHNOLOGY

Analyze
Available
Technology

The process of analyzing available technology is critical in assessing the comparative value of the various technologies in relation to venture and/or corporate needs and constraints. This process not only identifies and addresses the knowledge and technology gaps that may exist and must be overcome, but also assists in pointing out the risks involved in such frequently overlooked factors such as potential early obsolescence and insufficient knowledgeable resources, both in house and outsourced.

What do we mean by this? In many instances over the past few years, especially since the phenomenal growth of, and switchover to, computerized control systems, the advent of new and better materials, the requirement for closer and closer tolerances, etc., we have seen companies spend large sums on capital improvement projects only to find that the new installation was obsolete almost as soon as it started up. They have come up behind the wave, so to speak, and must then play a catch-up game.

By the same token, the technology may be so new that few in the field can understand it, or know how to service it. These are not "showstoppers" necessarily—that is, they are not insurmountable problems—but they do represent risk, and probably additional cost.

As the technology analysis proceeds, the process should be completely documented and contain at least the following:

1. *A statement of objectives.*   The statement of objectives must lay out the parameters of the analysis (which will sometimes trigger a requirement for a secrecy agreement, if the depth of analysis requested will intrude into a potential supplier's proprietary design).

2. *A list of potentially viable sources.*   These potentially viable sources must fit, generally, within the parameters of the statement of objectives.

3. *Previous applications.*   A detailed examination of previous use, including variations of the application. Previous applications would include also pilot plant testing and any scale-up problems encountered.

4. *Regulatory and environmental issues.*   The process must include a complete review of safety and environmental issues in order to ensure that a system, process, or equipment is "permittable."

5. *Financial comparison factors.*   This will include not only the initial cost of equipment, hardware or software, but also operating and maintenance considerations, including compatibility with the existing workforce.

6. *Legal and/or licensing requirements.*   The legal ramifications of acquiring any one of the alternative technologies, especially any licensing limitations or incompatibilities with long-range corporate strategies.

Again, projects vary from industry to industry and this analysis listing may change. However, these foregoing items, at least, will usually require the close attention of the preproject planning team.

THE FINAL REPORT

A final report, including the team's recommendation, should be compiled and should be in sufficient detail that senior managers will have a good understanding not only of the results, but also of the issues that were considered. Of special interest will be those issues that address operating constraints and company objectives of quality and productivity factors. In the event of new technology the report should also address both risk and obsolescence issues.

Let's look now at a case we came across not too long ago where many of the tenets and principles we have been discussing were either overlooked or ignored. In this case, we can see the pattern developing early in the project. I would bet that you can predict the ending by at least the halfway point in the reading of this case. The predictable ending brings up a curious point: if we can so easily see the route this project will take here, why couldn't the people involved see and correct the course there? The answer is many-faceted. They were too close to it to see the trends. They were experiencing it in a much slower time frame and the clues and signs were not so readily apparent. They were emotionally involved. And we have the luxury of 20/20 hindsight. A famous philosopher once stated, however, "Those who forget the past are doomed to repeat it." I think the same can be said for those who don't study and learn from past mistakes.

C A S E   S T U D Y   **4**

Granular Coal Handling System—Unchained Melody

HISTORICAL SYNOPSIS—PROJECT BACKGROUND

A long-time employee and manager at the Technical Center of Monolith Steel, Inc., a major American steel-producing company, conceived a project that could significantly lower production costs at a blast furnace operation. He drew heavily on prior mining industry knowledge and combined that with information about processed-coal use as a fuel and carbon source. He had observed this use at the site of a foreign steel producer. He found appropriate participants for a project of this sort in two Monolith Steel holdings: Whitfield Works, which contained a blast furnace operation and Collier USA, a coal-mining facility several miles away.

Collier's coal-drying process generated a granular by-product, and until now this material had simply been recombined with the coal before sale. Whitfield, located in a southern-tier state, bought natural gas from a local supplier to fuel the furnace, but normally experienced allocation cutbacks in winter. The cutbacks were caused by the natural gas utility's giving priority to residential and commercial users' heating needs. Technical Center studies indicated that the granular by-product from the mine could be used as both a fuel substitute and as source of carbon in place of coke for the furnace operation.

PROJECT APPROPRIATION

There were good commercial considerations in a potential project for both Monolith Steel operations. Collier saw an opportunity to increase both customer base and profit by marketing its by-product for this new application. The value of the granular coal when it was simply readded to the mine output was about $35 per ton. However, its value to a blast furnace operation was closer to $55 per ton. Whitfield saw an opportunity to replace a fuel that was subject to varied supply. As an added benefit, the use of the by-product lowered the cost of carbon input from $115 per ton of coke to about $60 per ton of granular coal injectant. Whitfield committed to the project in mid-1993. And, back on Collier's side, whenever the output of granular coal exceeded Whitfield's needs, there was an excellent probability that it could be sold to another blast furnace operation in the area operated by Bay Coastal Steel.

Whitfield had an effective working relationship with North American Technical Services (NATS) and a contract was let to have this company conceptualize the Whitfield project and conduct preauthorization engineering so that an appropriation request could be prepared. Although there was more than one bidder, Collier saw symmetry in having NATS do the same for the Granular Coal Handling System (GCHS) and engaged them for similar tasks. From a process standpoint, in dryer operation, new ground was being broken. But Whitfield and Collier were enthusiastic about the project, especially in light of NATS' confidence, which it projected during initial meetings.

THE BUDGET

Based primarily on the Technical Center study for process feasibility and on proposals by two engineering and construction companies (of whom NATS was one), an appropriation request was submitted in the summer of 1994 to proceed with the project, with a capital budget of

$5,500,000, a 14-month schedule, and a 48 percent DCF-ROI. The appropriation request entailed no risks and no risk-alleviation steps, while the budget carried only minimal built-in contingencies, and there was no formal analysis performed to guarantee budget accuracy.

Although there was a concurrent blast furnace injection project occurring at Whitfield, this study deals only with Collier's GCHS project from this point forward and shall serve as a basis for project execution analysis by all concerned parties at that facility before, during, and after start-up.

PROJECT ORGANIZATION/MANAGEMENT

Collier began the project by assigning a team of two project managers, one for construction and one to oversee design engineering. Both reported to the general manager of staff services. A dotted-line responsibility existed between the two project managers and the director of coal preparation. Additionally, the plant electrical engineer, answering to the director of coal preparation, was to direct electrical construction. There were dotted-line interfaces between the electrical engineer and the two project managers. After initial contract awards and selection of technology, the general manager's and the coal preparation plant director's involvement was minimal. The two project managers had responsibility for project execution (see Fig. 26).

PROJECT PLANNING/DESIGN

NATS and the equipment suppliers were relied upon heavily to foresee any problems associated with the system. No formal risk analysis was undertaken.

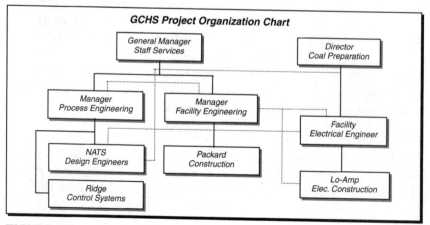

FIGURE 26

Because of the volatile nature of granular coal, and because Collier prided itself on its safety record, considerable attention had been given to the type of system to be used to move the product from the thermal dryers to the retention bin. Because the mine was located several miles from the blast furnace, special railroad cars would make that transfer and the same high-level safety precautions would be required. Considerable track work would be required, it was known, but there was no clear scope of this work and no definitive study had been done.

During preauthorization engineering, NATS had evaluated two methods of conveyance from the thermal drier to retention bin: a pneumatic conveying system and a chain conveyor. A technical investigation had revealed that neither method had been tried before on a granular coal system of the type being proposed. However, the construction project manager, the design-engineering manager, NATS and the corporate Tech Center favored the pneumatic system over the chain conveyor because such a system had been planned to introduce product into the blast furnace. The feeling was that if it worked at the blast furnace site, it should work at the Collier site. However, the general manager and the director of coal preparation felt otherwise, indicating concerns from both safety and cost standpoints. One concern was that a lack of process stability in the dryer would have made difficult the control of oxygen, methane, and dust levels in the pneumatic method; the other concern was that engineering out these factors would result in a much higher cost for this type system. Therefore, the general manager felt that a chain-type conveyor would represent a much lower overall cost.

Both project managers felt that cost was being used to justify the chain conveyor and that a bias against pneumatic systems was clouding management's judgment. In fact, both felt that, absent the negative opinions regarding control and potential hazards, a pneumatic system would actually prove to have a lower life cycle cost. Although no actual risk or life cycle cost analysis was performed regarding the use of chain over pneumatic, chain conveyor systems were common in the mining industry. That given, combined with the personnel safety element, made the choice of a chain conveyor seem the more prudent, viable, and cost-effective to management.

To reinforce the tentative decision to use a chain conveyor, several visits were made to installations that were using this method for fly ash and lignite movement. However, none of the locations visited used a vertical-rise chain conveyor like the one proposed for the GCHS.

Although the ensuing contract with the equipment manufacturer included no preshipment tests, plans included a full on-site system pretesting to prove adequate performance with granular coal. However, this test was never performed. As schedule pressures increased, this lack of critical testing was rationalized as follows: Since too little was known about the output of the dryers relative to filling the 400-ton retention bin, it was not possible to make a realistic process simulation. Nor was there information available on the life cycle of the product while in the bin. These facts and assumptions were to haunt the project team later.

PROJECT PROCUREMENT/VENDOR SELECTION

In the early part of the project, the Collier team was trusting NATS to run with the GCHS concept, keeping their (Collier's) best interests in mind. However, this confidence may have been misplaced. When the chain conveyor system was chosen, the NATS design appeared to favor a particular vendor. Collier's usual practice was to obtain at least three bids; however, in the case of long-delivery items such as the nitrogen gas system, the special railcars, and the chain conveyor, the number of vendors bidding would be increased to five. Although initial Purchasing Department involvement had been minimal, it was now called into the project to place orders.

The vendor whose design seemed to be reflected in the NATS specification was included in the bidders' list. But it was subsequently revealed that the favored vendor's proposal could not deliver the system within the now-accelerated time schedule. A contract awarded to this vendor would mean a 6- to 9-month start-up delay. As a result, ChainCon was the successful bidder. ChainCon stated that it would adhere to the specifications as contained in the bid proposal. But it did not comment on design or operation.

Collier chose Packard Construction and Lo-Amp Electrical Construction as contractors for a construction effort that included:

- A new silo for holding the clean coal product
- A new electrical motor control center
- The GCHS

Packard was included on the list of bidders because of previous good work and amenable relations with the facility's bargaining group.

Neither specifications nor purchase documents spelled out clear lines of authority or dispute-resolving methods.

CONSTRUCTION/INSTALLATION/TESTING

The project had an estimated 14-month completion time. Construction, overall, went well with completion 3 months ahead of schedule. (In actuality, this was a full month ahead of Whitfield's ability to receive the product, even though Whitfield also was completing ahead of schedule.) Schedule pressure, already high, began to increase. Whitfield was anxious to receive the granular coal to save the coke costs, and its own project schedule had been shortened by early completions. As construction completed within the foreshortened schedule, problems soon began to appear, especially in the areas of off-site and on-site testing.

Equipment inspection personnel could not always hold to their visit schedule because, in the zeal to complete early, priority was given to site construction. Personnel assigned to perform these inspections were, at times, distracted by vendor entertainment. Because of absence of preplanning, conveyors could be shop-tested for horizontal operation, but not vertical operation. Testing of railroad cars' differential pressure at the fabricator's shop was successful; however, because the Whitfield offloading site wasn't ready, offloading tests were not done.

Rifts between the Collier design-engineering project manager and NATS began surfacing very early in the project. NATS didn't have the same trusting relationship with Collier that they enjoyed with Whitfield, and soon differences began erupting over the cost of services. The design-engineering project manager soon became aware that the design for the chain conveyor had been written to favor a particular manufacturer. When the resulting competitive bidding and the need to hold to the schedule caused the contract to go to ChainCon, it was a bitter blow to NATS.

Communications deteriorated even more because the design-engineering project manager had a fear of flying and missed many of the NATS-suggested meetings to handle problems. Reliance on telephone and fax did little to fill the deepening chasm. NATS' attitude toward the project worsened further when the programmable logic controller (PLC) portion of the work that NATS had assumed would be included in their contract was awarded instead to Ridge Electric, the company that had done this type of work on the other two phases of the Collier project. NATS provided Ridge with a PLC functional design specification for the GCHS, but the loss of this portion of the contract was a bitter pill to swallow. No major problems occurred with any of the PLC programs.

Early on in the project, a pattern of change-notice requests became normal procedure and centered around a basic disagreement with NATS on the scope of work. These aggravations resulted in the Collier design engineering project manager's taking a rigid position, insisting that NATS uphold its contractual responsibilities, regardless of confusion over scope. However, these communications were invariably done by phone or fax rather than in person.

START-UP

The conveyor system operation was undertaken without the benefit of preoperational testing. It was soon discovered that the chain conveyor vertical lifts were experiencing a carry-back problem; i.e., the granular coal was not being offloaded completely at the top of the vertical lifts. Some product was being carried over into the return leg of the conveyor run and tended to clog the system at the bottom of the vertical sections. This clogging would eventually bind the conveyor and cause chain failure. Dissent soon erupted over the placement of blame and responsibility for corrections. Collier maintained that the conveyor was at fault, and ChainCon pointed to NATS, claiming that a filter screen clogged and that chutes were designed too small. Each failure required that the closed system be opened, the product removed, the end of the chain retrieved, repaired, and reattached, and system integrity reestablished.

It must be remembered that other equipment, systems, and facilities were under the start-up gun at the same time, requiring just as close attention. The main thrust of start-up problems, however, remained with the chain conveyor system.

Additionally, two events occurred at approximately the same time that most certainly did not help the situation. The process engineering manager retired and the facility engineer took vacation. The absence of two key team members at a critical time in start-up could not help but contribute negatively to an already problem-plagued situation.

PROJECT OUTCOME

Although irritating and maintenance-intensive, the conveyor clogging situation created no interruption of the product delivery to the retention bin, due to the redundancy of the systems. However, throughput was not as designed and, although not included as a benefit on the appropriation request, the hoped-for sale of excess product to Bay Coastal was not possible, lest flow to Whitfield be interrupted. NATS' contract was extended to troubleshoot the equipment and to stay on until all problems had been resolved. Problems with the chain conveyor and the presence of NATS on site to deal with those systems have resulted in a significant cost overrun for the project. Additionally, as budgeted money was directed toward problem fixes, basic project inclusions, such as training, were either canceled or diminished in scope. Track repair work, another major budget item, experienced an overrun of its estimate in excess of 100 percent.

ROI dropped from 48 percent to 33 percent. Payback time was lengthened from 3 years to 4 years. The project experienced an overrun of 44 percent on the budget because of the need for additional funding ($2.4 million added to the original $5.5 million approved) for redesign, troubleshooting, and general problem solving). Although Whitfield is satisfied as long as it gets the product to which it has now become accustomed, interruption of service could occur if one or both chain conveyors were to be out of service for an extended period of time. Although some problems have been solved, operation of the two conveyors is spotty, to say the least. Expected redundancy of these systems was not attained, since lower-than-expected throughput requires that both conveyors run continuously, or as continuously as possible, in order to maintain an optimum average throughput. The expected and hoped-for sale of excess material to Bay Coastal has not taken place.

Perhaps if more preproject planning had taken place, especially when it came to the analyzing of available technology, many of the problems (and much of the overrun) on this project would have been avoided. It would be helpful to keep this project in mind as we discuss the comparison of alternatives.

DEVELOP AND COMPARE ALTERNATIVES

Develop and Compare Alternatives

Another major function of preproject planning involves the comparison of alternatives. For the most part, we are referring here to the various mechanical and electrical devices that will serve to provide the answers to the goals of the project team—i.e., the process or production equipment. Equally important, certainly, is the comparison of the cost and quality of materials, and many of the same comparative methods should be invoked.

Once the "preferred technology" decisions have been settled, the preproject planning team will usually have another decision to make, that being the particular brand of equipment they will purchase. There are usually several suppliers or manufacturers of equipment that will, in the end, perform the same function. The reason one supplier is chosen over another is usually a mixture of several things, chief among them being cost, quality, availability, and preference.

There is a knee-jerk reaction on the part of some project planners to head immediately for the supplier with the lowest cost. However, as we shall see, the lowest *price* is not always the lowest *cost*.

One of the most effective tools that project teams have in the comparison of alternatives is *life cycle cost analysis*. As with project costs, the project team's ability to influence life cycle costs is greatest during the project's conceptual and design stages (see Fig. 27).

As can be seen, the ability to influence costs, including life cycle costs, decreases significantly as the project moves into construction and installation, start-up, and production. Conversely, the cost of change rises dramatically through those same periods.

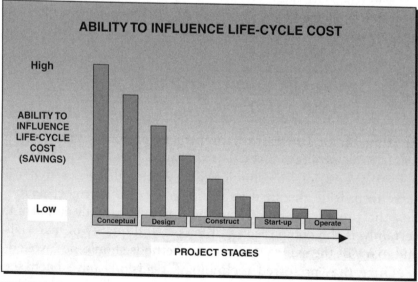

ABILITY TO INFLUENCE LIFE-CYCLE COST

FIGURE 27

The influence of the project team's decisions and selections will be felt in the facility long after the team has moved on to other projects, long after the issues of project budget and schedule have been forgotten. Well-thought-out selection of equipment and components; considered decisions as to process design, equipment, and controls placement; ease of maintenance—all are vital to the long-term health and *bottom-line success* of the facility or venture.

A life cycle cost analysis is an analysis that will determine not only the expected life term of the comparative systems or equipment, but also the *efficiency of operation* over the life term. There are many versions of life cycle cost analysis systems on the market; in fact, many equipment manufacturers will send one to you free, if you ask.

Most project managers and planners are aware that the lowest priced item is not always the most economical over the long run, and, conversely, the highest priced item is not always the most expensive when looked at long range. However, it may take more than a perfunctory look to arrive at the true costs, thereby enabling a project team to make a completely informed equipment selection. The following are factors that should be viewed carefully when comparing alternative selections.

INITIAL ACQUISITION COSTS

Initial acquisition costs to be identified and compared include the expenses required to purchase and receive equipment. These costs will include such items as sales taxes, preshipment equipment testing, spares, and traffic and shipping. Vendor and supplier pricing lists and quotations will be the source of this information. Remember, also, that these initial quotes may not be the final quotes. Comparative analyses many times are the first steps in negotiating price.

INITIAL INSTALLATION COSTS

It is about here that the true cost of equipment and materials begins to surface. Installation costs will include such things as the cost of design and design review (including first and second engineering submittals, which we will be discussing in a later chapter); process hazard analysis; environmental permitting; installation labor and training of personnel; and start-up costs (including the costs associated with vendor or supplier service engineers and consultants). The *amount* of these costs can vary significantly from brand to brand. And, some brands are just downright more difficult to install than others! Some designers of equipment, even equipment that, in the end, turns out the same product or does the same function as others, just seem to be better designers.

To illustrate this point in a very basic way: At my home I maintain about $2^1/2$ acres of lawn and meadow. In addition to a hand mower I use two lawn and garden tractors, one a 15-year-old Wheelhorse, the other a much newer, slightly more powerful piece of equipment produced by another manufacturer. Any time I go to change accessories, i.e., from snow removal equipment to mower deck, the differences between the two pieces of equipment become painfully obvious— changeout of accessories on the Wheelhorse is a piece of cake; on the other tractor it is a difficult and time-consuming task. And yet they both do essentially the same thing. Needless to say, whenever possible I "saddle-up" the Wheelhorse! It's simply a difference in design.

One should consider these issues when comparing alternatives. Which is the easier installation? Usually, easier equates to faster, lower cost, and less risk. How to spot the easier installation? Usually fewer electrical terminations, fewer design drawings required, fewer factored feet of conduit, simpler design, fewer bells and whistles, more factory testing, fewer field-installed components, etc., etc.—the list could go on and on.

OPERATING COSTS

Sometimes there is just no reason to debate the obvious; one particular alternative may be the clear, and sensible, economic choice. The object may be, for example, the exact duplication of an existing system, or production line. There will be no "learning curve," spares already exist, duplicating tie-ins had been designed into the existing system or line, etc.

However, in the case of installations that are not foreordained, there can be a huge difference in operating costs from equipment to equipment. The production line supplied by one equipment supplier, for example, may require five operators for optimum operation while a similar line, furnished by a different supplier, will require only three. The long-range difference here is tremendous. And it may well be that the lowest (initial) cost line just doesn't have the control system setup that reduces the need for the extra operators. *That's why it's priced so low!* Operating costs are a vital link in establishing the comparative cost of equipment and systems.

Maintenance Costs

The differences in maintenance costs among the potential selections can also be significant. If the lower-initial-cost equipment requires 12 maintenance outages per year and the higher-cost equipment requires only quarterly maintenance cycles, which equipment is most economical over the life of the equipment? And what about the price of spare parts? This, too, can be significant. These factors should be carefully considered when comparing alternatives.

Costs of Lost Production

For the project itself, outage costs can be significant. Whenever the schedule allows, project planning teams should certainly attempt to execute what we shall refer to as a "transparent start-up," an installation and start-up that does not affect production. These type projects and project start-ups are normally associated with equipment and system upgrades rather than with installation of complete new facilities and/or systems. These projects usually involve precisely planned and executed installation and start-up during regularly scheduled equipment/system maintenance outages.

When the work must be done on special outage, the cost of lost production must be considered in the overall project expense estimate. And finally, the cost of the *learning curve*; that is, the cost of familiarizing the operating group with the proper operation and maintenance of the new equipment and systems must be considered. This cost can be significant and is the downfall of many a budget.

Because operating and maintenance costs are ongoing, these expenses will be significant. Certain costs, such as spare parts usage and repair call charges, are incurred each time a process or system component fails. Additional costs, such as start-up, environmental reporting, fines, and incident investigation, are costs that are incurred with each failure event. The assessment of these costs will, in all likelihood, require a life cycle cost analysis.

Quality Issues

> The bitter taste of poor quality lingers long after the sweet fragrance of low price has faded.

This quote by an unknown philosopher was framed and hanging on the office wall of a major corporate buyer whom I once visited. It was so succinct and to the point that I have never forgotten it, and to this day, I use it in my seminars. Quality issues are probably the most difficult issues to assess in comparing alternatives.

For the most part, the old adage "the higher the quality, the higher the price" is probably true. However, there is always a line between adequate quality and inadequate quality. Get stuck on the short end of that stick and the project may never yield the benefits it was designed to provide.

On the other hand, the spending of capital for unneeded levels of quality can, and many times does, cause the project to be overpriced, depriving the venture of funding needed for other projects. Quality needs should be studied very carefully in analyzing alternatives.

Decommissioning Costs

Potential decommissioning costs include shutdown, demolition, and decontamination expenses. Back in the good old days, project teams would probably have given little time or consideration to these costs in their equipment selection process. However, with the environmentally sensitive eyes of so many groups and agencies now watching, these issues must be of real concern to today's planners. Some equipment, some systems, will contaminate the surrounding area more than other equipment or systems that essentially perform the same function. It is sometimes upon removal that the problem must be confronted at its fullest extent. *Sometimes, even the dirt must be decontaminated!*

We cannot overstate the importance of analyzing the alternatives to the greatest extent possible, especially in the scope of the solution and the equipment selection itself. It is at this point that project teams will make a *lasting impact,* either positively or negatively, on the facility. For one thing, and as stated earlier, changes can be easily effected at this point in the project with a pencil and eraser, or with a simple keystroke. In the later stages, it may take expensive labor, tools, even cutting torches and other added expense to effect those same changes!

Define Preliminary Scope DEFINING THE PRELIMINARY SCOPE

We discussed the *absolute* importance of scope development in Chap. 3, primarily as it related to project risk. However, let's state again the second principle of *Project Bottom-Line Success!*

> **Detailed scope definition is the cornerstone of achieving Project Bottom-Line Success!**

Now, consider the mechanics of, first, defining a preliminary scope and, later, the *refinement* of the scope package to the point where it is a detailed project specification that will serve as the basis for the appropriation of project funding.

After thoroughly analyzing available technologies, comparing alternative solutions within the preferred technology, and assiduously conducting life cycle cost analyses on those same alternatives (to ascertain exactly which holds the most promise for the good of the venture), the planning team is undoubtedly ready and anxious to outline a preliminary project scope.

Project scope packages are sometimes put together by the owner's project planning team, but more often than not this task will be accomplished in conjunction with one or more of the potential preferred major suppliers. In the event that the final decision (or in some cases, even a heavy preference) regarding the primary supplier has not yet been firmed up, the suppliers' input at first may be little more than a standard proposal.

Assuming that the development of the project scope package will, in fact, be a joint effort with a major supplier, let's put forward a definition of this function. First, however, let us introduce the term *first engineering submittal*. Some engineering groups and project teams are familiar with this term, some are not (although they probably perform the same function under some different designation).

FIRST ENGINEERING SUBMITTAL

A first engineering submittal is a detailed document, usually prepared by the primary supplier or the process control supplier, that includes

1. A detailed functional description of the system
2. The system's process control operation
3. Configuration of systems and equipment including hardware, software, user interface and preliminary design specifications

The first engineering submittal (FES) will respond to the project team's technology selection criteria. In most instances the submittal will be from the preselected supplier and is usually a paid-for work. (In a relatively few instances the first submittal will be in the form of competitive proposals from two or more equipment, control system, or primary supplier organizations.)

The FES will provide a functional description of the system, including technical capabilities and physical attributes such as dimensional requirements. Also included will be product yield and quality projections (if applicable) and a detailed description of the process control system operation.

The FES should provide a complete description and configuration of all systems involved, including all proposed hardware, software, user interface, and preliminary design specifications.

Obviously, if there is a *first* engineering submittal, there must be a *second* engineering submittal. We will refer again to these issues, including value engineering, the second engineering submittal, and stakeholders' input a bit later, when we discuss scope refinement.

ANALYZE, PRIORITIZE PROJECT RISKS

In Chap. 3, as you recall, we also discussed the process of analyzing and alleviating project risk factors. Theoretically, if we were to throw enough money into studying, analyzing, and alleviating risk, projects could be made risk-free. However, as we have already seen, that's not a practical approach. But we must alleviate all that we can. Recall, for a moment, the third principle of *Project Bottom-Line Success!*:

> **The probability of project success increases proportionally to the degree of project risk reduction.**

The reason that we put a discussion of project risk alleviation in such close proximity to a discussion of project scope development is that they are so closely intertwined. In fact, it might do well to recall our *PBLS* maxim: *The greater the detail of scope development, the greater the opportunity to identify project risks.*

In almost every case study where the project outcome is not as expected, i.e., is over budget, over schedule, returns less than it should, etc., we find that one of two things has happened: (1) the risks were not known, because of insufficient scope development, or (2) the risk was there, staring everyone in the face, but was ignored (usually owing to inexperience or an emotional approach by the project leader).

Let's look first at methods of identifying project risks. First and foremost, of course, is the detail of the scope definition package. If we were to perform a formal risk analysis at or near the beginning of the development of the scope definition package, using one of the well-known Monte Carlo probability methods, we would undoubtedly find that we had a very risky project. Perform the same analysis a few weeks later in the planning process and we would find a dramatic drop in the risk factor. Why? Because we have better knowledge of the scope and have factored in some alleviating steps, perhaps vendor shop testing, more inspections, quality checks, training, etc.

So, the first requirement is that the project team have the experience not only to recognize the importance of detailed planning and scope development, but also the "structured project attitude" that will cause them to take the necessary steps to alleviate risk wherever possible.

We have already discussed many of the "risk elements," but, for the sake of clarity (and repetition!) let's put them in the form of a list:

- *Corporate strategies.*   Is the project in consonance with long-range planning?

- *Market considerations.*   Have sufficient nonbiased studies been completed?

- *Technology.*   How well have the technological aspects been analyzed? Will there soon be a problem with obsolescence?

- *Environmental issues.*   Will permits be forthcoming? How would delay in obtaining them impact any "window of opportunity?"

- *Public concerns.*   Will there be a "back-lash?" What would be the effects?

- *Quality.*   What are the quality issues in design, procurement, installation, and construction?

- *Overruns.*   What would be the effects of overruns of schedule and/or budget?

- *Labor.*   What are labor issues, including incentives?

- *Construction labor.* Is the construction labor pool adequate?
- *Site conditions.* Any unknown conditions?
- *Logistics.* How will you get equipment and materials to site on schedule?
- *Contractors/subcontractors.* What is their performance, reliability, fiscal condition?
- *Weather.* What would be effects of delays caused by bad weather?

Certainly, this is not an all-inclusive list of potential risks that a project team must be aware of. But it's a starting point. It's a fact that no two projects are alike and the only thing a project team can do is play a "what if?" game. (It might be a good idea to play this game almost to the point of absurdity because, believe it, some really absurd things happen!) At any rate, the list will be prioritized.

Prioritizing the Risk List

As already stated, alleviating all risk is impractical; ignoring all risk is foolhardy. Using the results of the risk analysis, the project team should rank items according to the magnitude of their potential impact, then rank them again according to the degree of probability of occurrence.

Some risk items may be high-impact items, but may also be impossible to alleviate short of canceling out the project. This answer should be seriously considered and, by all means, the existence of a high-impact risk should be made known to supervisory management. If the decision is still to proceed, then the situation should be carefully examined for any congruent areas where alleviation efforts might lessen the overall impact of the risk.

And although we've already stated the following before, it bears repeating. After looking at risk alleviation strategies that could be implemented, estimate the cost of reducing the risks to acceptable levels, beginning with the risk items rated highest potential impact, highest occurrence probability, and alleviate all risk possible.

SELECT A PROPOSED CHANGE OR APPROACH; MAKE FINAL (PRIMARY) VENDOR SELECTIONS

It is at this point, usually, that enough facts are present, enough scope is determined, enough risks have been uncovered, to make final decisions regarding process and equipment preferences and to make final vendor selections.

VENDOR QUALIFICATION

Vendor qualification begins during the preproject planning stage and continues until the project team has determined which vendors will be selected to receive requests for proposal. During qualification, the project team should determine, among other things, just what type vendor organization, or organizations, best suits the scope requirements of the project. We sincerely hope that a commitment to the principles and tenets of *Project Bottom-Line Success!* would be the first requirement placed on a proposed vendor or supplier. (By the way, we will usually use the term *vendor* to refer also to suppliers of equipment, materials, or services, except for those more easily identifiable as *consultants, contractors,* or *major suppliers.*)

COMPATIBILITY

We would list, as another prime prerequisite of vendor qualification, the compatibility of business and operating philosophies and goals. This particular prerequisite may seem picayune, or too nitpicking to some; however, if you will consider for a moment, I think you will find it a valid point of concern.

You are, for example, a mature and established company with a standard method of engineering, procurement, project execution, operating methods, and plant maintenance. Unless you are embarking on a major change in your operating philosophies (a paradigm shift, as it were), you should probably not engage as your primary supplier a company that is using "new age," cutting-edge methodology in management or in its approach to the equipment, materials, or services it would be supplying to you. These differences will be just another potential source of project problems and will present another unneeded area of risk.

The teaming up of such dissimilar philosophies and goals can also lead to adversarial relationships and difficulty or delay in problem resolution. Capital improvement projects are difficult enough to bring to successful completion anyway, without adding the weight of having to confront problems in an adversarial manner.

Another attribute of the prospective vendor must certainly be good fiscal status. The last thing you want as a project team is to have one of your vendors go "belly up" on you at a critical phase of your project (or at any phase of the project, for that matter). The usual result of that event is delay and extra cost to your project while you either (1) bail the failing vendor out or (2) look for a replacement vendor. Bringing a new vendor up to speed will, in all probability, mean further delay.

We must look also at the proposed vendor's technological expertise. Is it *proved* expertise? Talk to past clients or users. Were they satisfied with this vendor? You may sometimes be surprised with the answers you get. Marketing brochures and sales presentations can say anything; the proof is in past performance.

Another factor somewhat akin to this is the availability of, and the commitment by the vendor to, supply the "right" personnel to the project. Many times we see the client company select a vendor because of its corporate size and reputation. Only after a less-than-successful (possibly disastrous) project start-up is it sometimes learned that the personnel the large and famous vendor was able to bring to that particular project were mediocre at best and, at worst, incompetent. Additionally, this "Cadillac" supplier may have been more expensive. It is sometimes found that better expertise could have been provided more economically from a smaller, less-renowned vendor.

Look also at the proposed vendor's historical performance. For example, look at its ability to work within budget, schedule and scope, its ability to adapt to change when required.

Look closely at the vendor's ability to handle its subcontractors, its ability to deal with other providers of equipment, materials, and service. How does the proposed vendor handle environmental issues and labor problems? Quality assurance and quality standards? Is the vendor certified to an ISO (International Standards Organization) level? If not, is it working to become certified?

Utmost care should be taken in the selection of contractors and suppliers of equipment. If your candidate company is coming off a string of poor project performances (don't hesitate to check with previous customers) you may just be the next point on its going-out-of-business curve.

By the same token, if your candidate company is coming off a string of successes, you will more than likely be featured in its next advertising campaign. Lucky you!

PROJECT PARTNERING

When contemplating the benefits and risks inherent in ventures and projects, planners should consider the "partnering" approach to project management. The Construction Industry Institute (CII) defines partnering as "a long-term commitment between two or more organizations for the purpose of achieving specific business objectives by maximizing the effectiveness of each participant's resources."

Partnering is founded on three principles: mutual trust, dedication to common goals, and an understanding of each partner's individual expectations and values. If prospective partners attain this common ground, then mutual benefits such as improved efficiency, increased opportunity for innovation, and the continuous improvement of quality products and services can be achieved.

The cornerstone of partnering is sharing, which may require significant cultural changes among the partners. Ingrained traits such as secrecy and corporate centrality must be replaced with open communication and teamwork. While partnering is not suitable in all situations, it can provide an excellent way of sharing both risks and rewards among compatible organizations. Additionally, the very factors that are required to make partnering a success are the same factors that will make a failed partnering arrangement more bitter when it does come apart. Partnering is somewhat like a marriage; it is based on mutual trust, and there is a feeling of betrayal when it doesn't work to each partner's satisfaction.

As already stated, partnering is not the best arrangement for all situations. It usually results in more protection for the contractor than for the client company. "Why do it then?" you may ask. Because in certain situations you may want the added flexibility that a partnering arrangement can bring. For example, you may find it necessary to begin a project without knowing the full scope of the job; i.e., the full extent of the work cannot be ascertained until a first portion of the work is accomplished. It may be found that many more hours of, say, electrical work is required than was previously thought. The partnering arrangement may allow what would have been "extra work" at full or premium rates to proceed on a rate scale that is graduated downward. In this case then, the contractor is protected against loss such as could occur in a lump-sum-type contract, while the client company benefits from getting the extra work accomplished at a somewhat lower rate than that to which it would have been obligated under a firm-price arrangement.

Other benefits? More flexibility in work accomplishment methods by the contractor. Potential long-term commitment by the client to utilize the contractor in similar projects in the future. More amicable problem solving. Better, more familiar, lines of communication. A feeling of partnership in a joint undertaking. In the proper setting, partnering is an excellent management method.

ISSUANCE OF INQUIRIES; SELECTION OF VENDORS

After a thorough evaluation of suppliers, the project team selects those few that are most compatible with the project requirements. Requests for proposals (RFPs) should be issued only to those vendors who would be selected if they submitted the best overall bid. When proposals have been received, project managers and adjunct personnel (operating/maintenance, etc.) analyze the proposals and, following the commercial analysis by Purchasing, award the contract to the supplier, or suppliers, they believe are best qualified to achieve the project's objectives. (More will be said about the procurement process later.)

> The importance of buy-in by operations at this point cannot be overstated; select equipment without this buy-in and stakeholders may well turn into roadblocks later on.

Once the suppliers have been selected, the project manager must integrate primary supplier personnel into the project team. To ensure economy of effort and to avoid redundancy of labor and territorial conflicts, the project manager should complete the following tasks before order placements:

- Devise a clear statement of each team member's (organization or person) specific responsibilities and tasks.
- Set out clear lines of communication and authority (both vertical and horizontal).
- Establish a specific mechanism for prompt dispute resolution.

> Regardless of the type of vendor arrangement finally selected (prime contractor, turnkey, etc.), the client company project manager retains overall responsibility for successful project completion.

Why do we state this so emphatically? Because too often we see project teams that have just placed a turnkey contract take the position that it is now the contractor's responsibility. They, in effect, wash their hands of it.

There certainly *is* responsibility on the part of the turnkey contractor. The contract may even call for some penalties to the contractor in the event that it fails to make schedule. But that's only money. Whose schedule is it, really? If it's *your* project, then it is your schedule! It's your facility, your company's investment, your customers at stake, your company's *venture*. The project manager and his or her team should never lose sight of this fact.

REFINE THE SCOPE!

Refine
Scope
Definition

Following the selection of at least the primary contractor, or vendors of equipment and services, the project scope must be refined. The first engineering submittal should have been received, studied thoroughly, and commented on by the project team. The review and comments by the project team should then form the basis for the preparation of the second engineering submittal (SES) by the primary contractor or vendors.

SECOND ENGINEERING SUBMITTAL

The second engineering submittal is a document submitted by the primary supplier following the client's review and comment on the first engineering submittal. The second engineering submittal document:

1. Contains revisions and refinements to the process control design, equipment, and configuration (including the final software design, final interface design specification, I/O list, database, and start-up strategy).
2. Details changes in plant production and maintenance equipment, systems, and components.
3. Provides a detailed specification of the scope of supply for the project.

> am·big·u·ous (am big' yoo ës) *adj* **1:** having two or more possible meanings **2:** not clear; indefinite; uncertain; vague—**syn**
> OBSCURE

The process of supplier selection also incorporates refinement of scope so that suppliers will have a detailed understanding of the product or service on which they will be bidding. In an article in the December 1991 issue of *Project Management Journal,* consultants Peter Beale and Mark Freeman present the results of a study they conducted to determine what variables most affect the success of a project. Clarity of objectives, defined as "the extent to which project details are specified and unambiguous," was identified 59 percent of the time by respondents as a reason for project difficulties. The authors go on to suggest that the best way to avoid ambiguity is to provide a detailed specification to prospective contractors. We wholeheartedly agree. The most common cause of both totally failed projects and those that are only partially successful is ambiguity of scope.

When a request for proposal lands on the bidder's desk, the bidder should see, in print, the full scope of work required by the client. It is the document on which the bidder, as well as the project manager, is going to stake its professional reputation and some amount of fiscal resources. Any ambiguities and unresolved issues will eventually impact the project somewhere down the line, and that which impacts the success of the project will impact the success of the venture. Therefore, all scope ambiguities must be resolved in the early stages of the project.

VALUE ENGINEERING AND SCOPE REFINEMENT

The rigorous pursuit of both detail and clarity in the development of these documents (which are, after all, the project specifications) is absolutely essential to successful project execution. The process used in pursuing this detail and clarity is usually referred to as *value engineering*. The *value* in value engineering means that early, detailed scope development will prevent cost escalation caused by scope creep later. Value engineering, properly conducted, will not only eliminate unnecessary bells and whistles from project specifications, but will also include life cycle costing methodology to help pinpoint *actual* low price. This process will have a positive influence on cost and schedule estimates for both the owner company and the suppliers.

Building on the scope definition already completed, the project team should continue to refine project scope through value engineering. Value engineering, as the name implies, is an analysis of the alternative solutions to project requirements such as the type of process, the type of control system, the types and brands of equipment and components to be used. Value engineering is an indication that the company is willing to spend money up front on sufficient conceptual engineering and planning to determine specific scope boundaries before final contractual terms are set. Don't forget, we're talking *preauthorization* here! At this stage, scope refinement is undertaken in consonance with selected or anticipated suppliers to pinpoint process, equipment, and design requirements. (Although to a project team the term *scope* is all-inclusive, for our purposes at this point let us consider *scope* to mean the project specification or specifications.) Just to bring this scope definition and refinement process to its core constituencies, consider the following methodology:

1. Conduct a thorough review of the scope definition, noting particular strengths and weaknesses of current design concepts.

2. On the basis of the established scope definition, require development of a first engineering submittal by anticipated primary and key secondary suppliers.

3. The project team should review and revise the first engineering submittal to refine details of design, life cycle costs, operability, and maintainability.

4. Working from the review, the anticipated primary and key secondary suppliers should develop a second engineering submittal.

5. Working together, the project team and the selected supplier and key secondary suppliers should review and finalize the second engineering submittal to a level of detail that will provide a clear and solid scope for both the client and the suppliers.

INPUT FROM STAKEHOLDERS

Another essential ingredient in the development of project scope—both preliminary scope development and later scope refinement—is the value of input from various entities that will become stakeholders in the project. Primary among these entities is Facility Operations, whose personnel will actually have to live with the results of the project over the next several years. Failure to obtain operators' input will, in almost all cases, result in design changes and additional cost later on.

> It has been my observation, over many years of watching project development and execution, that Operations will eventually get its way in the end anyway, so why do Engineering groups resist it so much? Seek out Operations' input early in the game and, within fiscal and professional reason, accommodate the desires of Operations wherever possible. It will save time and effort in later changes!

Develop Budget   BUDGET DEVELOPMENT

The budget is the heart and soul of a project. Reputations are built and lost, in project management circles, on the ability of a project manager and team to bring a project to a successful conclusion within the confines of a budget to which they have been committed. Therefore, it certainly stands to reason that a project manager, *and the project team,* should leave no stone unturned in efforts to achieve the looked-for end result.

Which stone, then, should first be turned? How about the one with the big red sign on it that says "realistic budget"? Many project budgets are overrun simply because there wasn't enough money allocated to start with, rather than for failure to manage well during the course of the later project phases. Why are unrealistically low budgets set so often? Many times for one of three reasons:

1. An insufficient identification of the true project scope. An inexperienced or inadequately informed project team can bring on this situation.

2. Upper management may refuse to authorize the level of preauthorization funding that will enable the project team to identify the true scope of the project, i.e., to the extent that project risks can be identified and alleviation strategies worked into the overall budget.

3. A refusal by either the project team or upper management to accept the true magnitude of the project, resulting in an arbitrary decision to hold project funding to an unrealistic level. (In the case of the project team, this behavior might also be an indicator of inexperience.)

In the instance of the insufficiently developed project scope package, the reason can, in fact, usually be traced to inexperience on the part of the project team or, more often, the team leader. It's unfortunate that experience must sometimes come through on-the-job training, by far the most expensive method. (It sometimes costs the company millions!)

In other cases, upper management may fail to authorize sufficient funding for any one of a number of reasons; too many projects for the overall budget, lack of understanding of true costs, a desire to raise the bar of performance just above reach in an effort to keep project costs as low as possible, etc.

When either the project team or someone in an upper management position refuses to accept the true magnitude of the project after it has been shown to be reasonably accurate in its appraisal and instead announces that it will be accomplished at some lower percentage number, it indicates that an "emotional" project is about to start. This type project will usually end up as a case study, or as a newspaper write-up concerning its deleterious effect on the corporate bottom line.

Let us assume, however, that none of the above conditions exist and look instead at some of the methods of arriving at a realistic budget.

PROJECT COSTS

Look, first, at the more common costs usually associated with a project. These costs will probably include:

The cost of engineering services
- Preauthorization engineering
- Feasibility studies and other consulting costs
- Postauthorization engineering

The cost of controls and instrumentation
 • Vendor shop inspections

The cost of equipment and materials
 • Associated shipping costs
 • Associated sales taxes
 • Vendor shop testing and inspections

Installation and construction
 • Site preparation
 • Labor costs
 • Third-party assistance costs

A contingency sum*

Actually, project planners and teams usually have a pretty good handle on these costs. Not only are they easy to list, they're also easy to see. Other costs associated with the project execution, however, are sometimes a bit more difficult to ascertain. These costs might include, for example, the time value of the funding, and the lost production costs during the outage or multiple outages that may be required for construction and installation of the new systems or equipment. Some might say also that "contingencies" represent a project cost (we include them in the budget). Actually, contingencies, when spent, simply become an increase in the cost of one or more of the identified costs.

The time value of money, however, is a cost that is seldom considered by a project team and is usually not identified as a line item in the budget. Consider, for a moment, this definition of the *time value of money*:

> Currency, as with any medium of exchange, has an inherent ability to appreciate in value over time when invested, and the diversion of capital to any other use interrupts this potential appreciation. Thus, the time value of money in a capital appropriation is a real and actual expense to the venture.

Perhaps the cost of money *should* be a line item in the budget. Another area that should be of much more concern to project managers and their teams than we usually see is the

---

*A contingency, although never expected to be spent, is usually carried as a line item on the project budget document. More will be said concerning contingencies in Chap. 8.

entire area of life cycle cost analysis. Although most project teams make at least a half-hearted stab at this issue, the overwhelming majority of the project teams with which I have broached the subject has never used a life cycle cost analysis program in its equipment selection process. And it's really a shame—they are missing a golden opportunity to wring the most value possible out of those very valuable bottom-line dollars. They are dollars they will be spending as they select the equipment and components that will undoubtedly be on the firing line of the venture's business over the next several years.

COLLATERAL COSTS

There are other costs associated with the project budget, certainly. The problem is, these costs are sometimes more difficult to pin down. Sometimes, they're even overlooked by the project team. For this reason, we call these costs "collateral costs." They are

The cost of training
- Vendor training
- Training needs assessment
- Training contractor costs
- Attendee time costs*

The cost of spare parts and materials

Production outage costs (and cost of extended outages)*

Project staffing (before and after start-up)
- Staffing for preoperational testing
- Consultants and service engineers
- Overtime and round-the-clock operation

Time value of money
- The cost of interest charged or discounted cash flow (DCF) calculation

Learning curves (start-up)
- The cost of commissioning (all costs from initial start-up to design capacity)

---

*Costs may be Operations charges.

Once planners have identified these initial costs, they have a basis for identifying life cycle costs for major equipment. (Although we have discussed life cycle cost analysis earlier, it is of such importance that we should probably refer to the subject again as we discuss budget development).

In an article in the June 1995 issue of *Chemical Processing,* William M. Goble and Brayton O. Paul identify total life cycle costs as the following:

- *Initial acquisition costs.* Initial acquisition costs include the expenses required to purchase and receive equipment. For capital equipment, these costs are readily available from a price list or a quotation.

- *Initial installation costs.* Installation cost estimates should include design, design review, process hazard analysis, installation labor, training, and start-up costs. In order to obtain realistic numbers, in-house labor and engineering costs must be included, as well as any cost-saving installation innovations.

- *Operating and maintenance costs.* Because operating and maintenance costs recur each year, these expenses can become significant. Certain costs, such as spare parts usage and repair call charges, are incurred each time a process or system component fails. Additional costs such as start-up, environmental reporting/fines, and incident investigation are costs that are incurred with each failure event.

- *Lost production costs.* Often, a process system or equipment failure can result in significant financial losses due to lost production, including unused capacity and out-of-spec product.

- *Decommissioning costs.* Decommissioning costs include shutdown, demolition, and decontamination expenses. Salvage or residual value is a negative cost.

The many details that go into establishing a realistic budget may be difficult to get your arms around, but it is absolutely essential that these details be brought out if the budget is to be a true and dependable document. Defining project installation and life cycle costs of selected project equipment, materials, and systems is the best starting point for both budget development and benefits calculations, including the ROI.

PROJECT COST ESTIMATING

Once all project costs have been identified, the project team may want to enclose these figures in an estimate framework that provides more comfort from an overrun-budget standpoint. One of the methods currently becoming popular in this area, a methodology also based in risk analysis techniques, is *range estimating*.

At the heart of range estimating is the philosophy that it is better to be approximately correct than exactly wrong. "Ranging" allows project teams to produce a target number (e.g., an estimate of construction cost) along with a subjective confidence factor that the target number can be achieved. A mathematical model is used to bracket the target with a series of outcomes that fall within acceptable limits above or below the target estimate.

Project managers and upper management should take care, however, that the need for a comfort factor doesn't lead to larger-than-necessary contingencies simply to avoid overruns. When contingencies are present, they tend to get used up.

Alleviate
Risks

ALLEVIATING RISK

The alleviation of risk must go hand in hand with the development of both the budget and the project schedule. Prioritizing risks and applying alleviation factors may affect both documents since the alleviation of risk is not free.

> This is the prime reason why so many projects get into trouble. There is a mindset that the risk item, although uncovered and known, will not come about anyway, and that budgeting to alleviate the risk is a waste of funding. This mindset is exactly the reason you can go bust at the gaming tables in Las Vegas or Atlantic City. Sooner or later, the dice roll will go against you. And, sooner or later, the risk you fail to alleviate will appear in

all its project delay and budget-overrun glory, sometimes costing more than all the alleviation efforts put together.

There are at least five general areas of risk alleviation that are open to the project team. These areas are:

- Reduction of risk consequences
- Reduction of risk uncertainty
- Avoidance of risk items
- Transfer of risks
- Sharing of risk

There are, of course, many methods of alleviating risk under each of the above headings. We have listed a few of these in Fig. 28, below. We couldn't possibly list all the options available, since there are so many different types of projects, each with its unique set of risk items. It's important that project teams play the what if game, naming *every* risk they can think of, regardless of its size. The important thing to

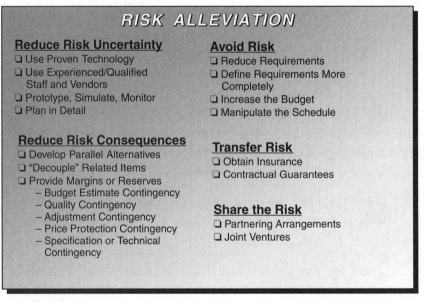

RISK ALLEVIATION

Reduce Risk Uncertainty
- ❑ Use Proven Technology
- ❑ Use Experienced/Qualified Staff and Vendors
- ❑ Prototype, Simulate, Monitor
- ❑ Plan in Detail

Reduce Risk Consequences
- ❑ Develop Parallel Alternatives
- ❑ "Decouple" Related Items
- ❑ Provide Margins or Reserves
  - – Budget Estimate Contingency
  - – Quality Contingency
  - – Adjustment Contingency
  - – Price Protection Contingency
  - – Specification or Technical Contingency

Avoid Risk
- ❑ Reduce Requirements
- ❑ Define Requirements More Completely
- ❑ Increase the Budget
- ❑ Manipulate the Schedule

Transfer Risk
- ❑ Obtain Insurance
- ❑ Contractual Guarantees

Share the Risk
- ❑ Partnering Arrangements
- ❑ Joint Ventures

FIGURE 28

consider is the size of the consequence, in the event the risk comes about in its worst-case scenario. At least the risk will have been considered!

 # DEFINING THE SCHEDULE

If, as stated earlier, the budget is the heart and soul of a project, then surely the schedule is the mind, the definer, of the entire effort. Some schedules are driven by project needs; some projects are driven by the schedule. Within the *Project Bottom-Line Success!* (*PBLS*) methodology, proper schedule definition relies on five basic requirements:

1. *Clearly defined objectives.* How can project planners determine how long it will take to achieve a project objective if they don't have a clear understanding of what that objective is?

2. *Detailed definition of project scope.* Accurate scheduling is impossible without detailed scope definition.

3. *Reasonable contingencies.* Contingencies must be appropriate to the project requirements. If a project comes in well under schedule, perhaps too much slack was built into the schedule. In these cases, projects usually take longer and, therefore, cost more to complete than they should have.

4. *Defined start-up date.* Vague, mushy start-up dates lead to longer and poorly executed start-ups. The start-up date and subsequent ramp-up to full production should be well defined and categorically stated.

5. *Attainability.* Ruthless honesty from owners and contractors is essential to identifying an attainable schedule. Self-deception is self-defeating.

The importance of the foregoing five items cannot be overstated. For the most part, they are self-explanatory. Common sense would decry most argument. However, some may miss the significance of the last item—attainability. Ignoring this basic schedule requirement has probably sent more projects down in flames than any other single cause.

Reader and author Peter Limber offers this parable regarding attainability and competition for business, culled from the newsletter of a London insurance group:

> Know ye, brethren, it came to pass that a great prophet once addressed a herd of donkeys, saying thus: "What would a donkey require for a three-day journey across the desert?"
>
> And they answered as one: "Verily, six bags of hay and three bags of dates."
>
> Then spake the prophet: "That seemeth a fair price, but I cannot give six bundles of hay and three bags of dates. Is there one among you who would go for less?"
>
> Behold! All stood forth!
>
> One would go for six bundles of hay and three bags of dates. A second would go for only four bundles of hay and two bags of dates. Yet another vowed he needed only three bundles of hay and one bag of dates.
>
> There was much bargaining.
>
> Now, one donkey, long of ear and lean of rib, stood forth from the rest. "I agree to go across the desert for only *one* bundle of hay."
>
> Whereupon spake the prophet: "Thou art a disgrace to the herd, and an ass. Thou surely canst not undertake the journey and profit thereby. Thou canst not even live for three days with only one bundle of hay for nourishment and shalt die of hunger, leaving me there in the desert to perish as well."
>
> "Verily, thou speaketh truth," replied the ass, hanging his ears in shame, "but I just wanted that order *so* badly."

Project teams must beware of and avoid the temptation to impose an unrealistic schedule on their bidders for, if they are not very careful, they may get what they asked for! Suppliers *want* your order. Savvy, reputable vendors will usually resist an unrealistic schedule when they see it—for a while. But as pressure to embrace the unrealistic schedule mounts, you may begin hearing words like, "Well, it's pretty tight, but I think we can make it." These are warning signal words. What they're really telling you is, "There's no *way* this schedule can be met!" We will examine this commonly occurring problem at some length later, when we will be discussing time management.

FAST-TRACK SCHEDULES

As a part of schedule development, the project team should also consider fast-track scheduling. Fast tracking is not simply doing everything faster, or spending more money to hire more people to get things done in a shorter period of time. *Fast tracking* is a method of saving time and shortening a project schedule by executing two or more identifiable project components concurrently rather than consecutively. To be successful, fast tracking requires meticulous planning and superior execution.

There are many places in the project schedule where fast-track techniques can be used. Two that come immediately to mind are in the areas of construction start and preoperational testing. As can be seen in Fig. 29, fast tracking can save time *and* budget. In this example, the fast-track method allows construction to begin prior to completion of all design drawings.

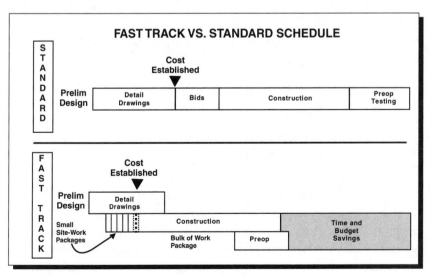

FIGURE 29

Obviously, the first drawings to be issued must be the site preparation drawings so that construction forces can get started.

We see also that preoperational testing begins when construction completion stands at about 75 to 80 percent. This formula will allow testing to complete at about the same time as construction, or shortly thereafter. On some projects, testing is not considered seriously until construction is "substantially complete." This is a waste of valuable time! When properly planned and scheduled, testing can begin much earlier, resulting in an earlier start-up.

Fast-track scheduling is an excellent project management method and should be used. However, to be successful it must be meticulously planned and executed.

DEFINING THE PROJECT APPROACH

Since all projects are unique, all projects will, to a certain extent, have a unique approach. But (and this is a rather important *but*) some planning items must remain more or less constant if the project is to be successfully executed.

PROJECT PLANNING

The fourth principle of *Project Bottom-Line Success!* emphasizes the importance of planning:

> The challenge of achieving *Project Bottom-Line Success!*
> lies, primarily, in planning.

Truer words were never spoken! In looking at case study after case study over the past several years, we have found that the fate of most projects is set in the early stages, the planning stages. The word *planning*, you see, can have any one of several qualifiers: There's good planning, poor planning, little planning, no planning, even ill-conceived planning. The planning we're speaking of here is, obviously, *good* planning.

Good planning means attention to detail. And it means writing it down. Planning should be clearly stated in logical, sequential segments so that omissions become obvious and correctable.

Project planning considerations should include:

- Value engineering and scope refinement
- Management planning
- Start-up and outage planning

MANAGEMENT PLANNING

Successful project execution seldom just happens. It usually occurs only as a result of careful and assiduous preplanning of a number of project factors and parameters. Project teams should consider and carefully plan their approach to quality management, time and cost management, and the impact that the project will have, not only on the immediate facility, but also on facilities upstream and/or downstream of the facility.

Planning for Quality Management. Quality issues should be defined in the bid specification as a part of the project's scope. This requires that the project team determine and communicate quality standards and the kind of program the contractor must have in place to ensure that these standards are achieved. When appropriate, ISO 9000 and other company standards should be included in quality requirements as a part of the specifications.

The project team should require that prospective vendors identify their quality organization and how they will maintain specified quality standards for engineering, purchasing, equipment fabrication, materials, receiving and storage, erection, testing, and site installation.

Additionally, the specification should contain provisions for quality hold points, third-party inspections, release for shipment, shop field testing, and nondestructive testing. Prospective vendors must demonstrate that they have the capability within their organization to police and enforce a quality program. If not, the project team should consider a third-party quality assurance contractor.

Remember that much of the equipment that will be supplied to the project will actually originate from subsuppliers to the primary or major equipment suppliers. For this reason the major suppliers' quality programs must be carefully scrutinized.

How do we do this? By carefully *reviewing* the supplier's quality document, by carefully *reading* the supplier's procedures, by carefully *surveying* the supplier's entire quality program, and by carefully *observing* the supplier's personnel list to see exactly who will be actually policing the quality of workmanship at each level. If you don't see the "policemen," you may not see the quality!

> *Note:* Just to help get your team started in this critically important review of the supplier's quality program, we have included in App. A a fairly thorough survey format that you might wish to use to gauge the merits of the proposed quality program. You will also find some other basic forms that you may wish to adapt as you formulate your entire project quality assurance effort.

Planning for Time Management.   A decision that results from tight or impossible schedule pressures can sometimes be disastrous. In many cases, an overrun schedule will be exacerbated by the decisions that are made under the duress of the overrun.

The project team must specify realistic schedule constraints for the bidders, and bidders must respond in kind. Too many times clients and bidders, each for their own reasons, reach erroneous conclusions about how long it will take, or should take, to complete a project or a critical portion of a project. To avoid schedule overruns and their attending costs and problems, project managers should ensure that a schedule contingency is built into the proposed *reasonable* schedule before the contract is awarded. However, the end start-up date should then be fixed and not changed after order placement.

Project teams must avoid the temptation to force an unrealistic schedule on a prospective supplier. If you do, be prepared—you may get just what you're asking for. The supplier wants the order and, after trying diplomatically to warn you that your requirement is unrealistic, may acquiesce with a statement like, "Well, it's going to be pretty tight, but I think we can make it." If you hear words like this, the warning flags are flying. What that supplier is really saying is, "There's *no way* it can be done in that time frame!" (This supplier is probably reasoning that if you are making mistakes of this magnitude at this early stage in the project, you will be so deep in problems by the time he is required to produce that you won't notice that the supplier was late!)

In the December 1990 issue of *Project Management Journal*, consultant David E. Hamburger underscores the need for project managers to create schedule contingencies during the bid specification and contract award process. "The theory of probabilistic PERT [Program Evaluation and Review Technique] suggests that a project schedule that perfectly fits its specified time constraint, i.e., concurrent expected and required project completion dates, has less than a 50 percent chance of success. Additionally, the degree by which this probability falls below 50 percent is a function of the degree of project uncertainty."

What this quotation is telling us is that even a realistic schedule requires some contingency. It must be understood, however, that contingencies are stopgaps, i.e., *emergency* funding. As such, contingencies are intended to be saved, if at all possible. Contingencies sometimes tend to be too tempting to ignore as the project draws nearer to completion and, as we shall see in a later chapter, they may be put to use by overzealous project team members.

Planning for Cost Management.   Project engineers are usually required to establish the cost of a project as part of an appropriations request. More important, perhaps, is that executive management approves the appropriation based on a documented projection that profits earned by the venture will exceed costs. In some cases, the project manager is in the position of being committed to bringing in the project at an established cost that is based on a bidder's budget estimate. This practice can lead to overruns or, worse yet, to curtailing critical project elements (thus increasing risk) in an attempt to avoid an overrun.

The best way to deal with "cost commitment before firm bid" is to design, specify, inquire, and receive formal (firm) proposals *before* requesting the appropriation. This can occur only when sufficient preauthorization engineering is accomplished in order to provide a sound basis for establishing total project cost.

Even when following this approach, project managers still must control costs over the life of the project. Effective cost management requires diligent and unrelenting pursuit of several factors by the project team. The first is cost forecasting, which is a projection of the costs of identified project elements, coupled with the contingencies that have been built in to protect against unknown factors. When costs are properly monitored and controlled, escalation and job growth can be contained within the confines of the contingencies. As contingencies are drawn down, *reforecasting* will be necessary if the project team is to have a realistic chance of avoiding overrun.

Cost reporting, consisting of detailed statements of funds that have been expended as of a designated date, must be both timely and accurate or they are of little use in controlling project costs. In fact, inaccuracy could be a real danger to the project.

The most important component, by far, of effective cost management is cost containment. Cost containment reviews should be held throughout the project to evaluate costs and make adjustments as required. The cost containment review becomes, then, the meat of the reforecast.

In addition, the project team should require that contractors develop a critical path schedule for work completion. The critical path should include milestone payments tied to the schedule. These schedules can then be reviewed during cost containment sessions, and problem areas affecting cost can be addressed and resolved.

Planning for Facility Impact.   The building of a new facility or the installation of new systems, upgrades, or expansions will almost invariably have an impact on facilities and other systems upstream and downstream. It is possible that the effects of the project will be felt far afield from the locality of the project itself: in sales offices, with raw materials suppliers, on product shipping capability, and in the area of labor relations.

Planners must consider the commercial consequences associated with the project. Commercial effects should be evaluated in view of the potential impact on product market share, product quality, and bottom-line efficiency.

Planners must determine what impact the project will have on the upstream and downstream operations within and without the facility and design the project to minimize or eliminate those impacts. If product flow will be interrupted, for example, planners must determine how long the interruption will last and how this will affect the facility and its customers. Special arrangements may be required to safeguard product supply to customers.

Project planners must weigh the project's short- and long-term impact on the surrounding community and environment. This impact is a sensitive issue that must be addressed realistically in order to help ensure that the project will go forward without damaging, and possibly derailing, either public relations or political understandings.

Planning for Employee and Labor Relations Impact. One of the most important items to consider is the impact the project will have on corporate employees and labor relations. Remember that resistance to change is a human trait, and that this trait must be considered in project planning. When word of your planned project begins to get around on the plant floor, the first question that most facility workers will ask will be, "How will *I* be affected? Will I be laid off? Will I get less pay? Less incentive opportunity? Will I have to work with a different group? Will I have to work harder for the same money?"

These are all real concerns to the workforce, and should be addressed with candor. If there is to be a reduction in force because of a change in the system or process, this reduction must be brought forward and dealt with. Let displaced workers know just what steps the company is taking to help them find other employment. Let retained employees know just how the change will affect them and the steps that the company is taking to ease the transition: new training, perhaps, or possibly new incentives.

To avoid problems, project planners should consider involving the appropriate labor groups' personnel in the appropriation process to determine how, or if, the project will affect employees and labor. Dissatisfied employees can wreak havoc with the best-laid start-up plan.

Incentive issues should be discussed and sticking points resolved within an atmosphere of teamwork and cooperation. Making labor and employee relations personnel a part of the planning team will ensure that the legitimate concerns of these groups are represented and addressed prior to finalization and approval of the appropriation. Their participation in planning will enhance the probability that all parties will work together as a team toward the achievement of *Project Bottom-Line Success!*

Start-up and Outage Planning. *Start-up planning belongs at the beginning, not the end, of any project.* Unfortunately, many project teams wait until the project actually enters, or is about to enter, the start-up phase before they begin planning this critical activity. That's too late! Start-up strategies are usually dependent upon construction and equipment installation strategies and schedules. The key to a structured, orderly, and ultimately timely preoperational testing and start-up phase is early planning—right from the start.

Therefore, the project team must include start-up and outage planning as an integral part of the project organization process. In effect, the project team *designs* the start-up by identifying objectives, by carefully integrating the construction and preoperational testing schedules, by identifying early the key start-up personnel, and by planning the entire preoperational testing and start-up phase in detail.

Identifying Basic Start-up Objectives

In some project scenarios, there is no need to identify start-up objectives—they're already identified for you. If the sole purpose of the project is to satisfy a customer requirement for a different size or a modified product, for example, and orders are already in the book, it's a no-brainer. Get up and running in the shortest possible time, begin producing that particular product, adjust for quality, and begin filling those orders!

In other project scenarios, however, the objectives may not be quite so simple. The project may involve a speed increase for a production line that produces several product sizes and grades. The start-up objectives may be more complicated because of product mix, customer orders, and complexity of products.

In any case start-up objectives must be identified and a plan initiated early so that construction and installation schedules, fabrication and off-site testing schedules and upstream and downstream facilities can be manipulated to the greatest advantage possible. We shall discuss manipulation methods of these schedules a bit later.

Identifying Key Start-up Personnel

Just as important as identification of start-up objectives is the early identification of key start-up personnel—*beginning with the start-up manager.* The individual who will be responsible for start-up activities should be identified at the time that the project team is first organized.

This person should not only have input throughout the execution of the project, but should also be planning the start-up in detail, looking for potential bottlenecks, working out the alternatives, writing or overseeing start-up procedure writing, and establishing the testing standards, both off site and on site. This project team member will have much to do, if the project is to conclude with a seamless start-up. Again, unfortunately, many project managers put off the start-up manager's appointment until too far into project execution, thus denying this position the opportunity to have the impact on the project that it should have.

Other key start-up personnel, or persons who will have impact on the start-up phase, are consultants, testing personnel, shop-test inspectors, and in some instances, pre-start-up audit teams. And, oh yes, don't forget environmental—someone will be needed to verify the required environmental permit checks!

Identifying Outage Dates

Many projects are upgrades or refurbishment and must be completed during maintenance outages. Some projects cannot be completed without taking a special outage. Regardless of which way it goes, it is absolutely imperative that the outage be planned in detail. An hour-by-hour plan must be developed along with a critical path of events. Outage planning must be carefully coordinated with operating and maintenance forces. Outage overruns can be very, very expensive in loss of revenue;

they can be even more expensive if they lead to the loss of a customer who can't wait any longer.

INITIATION OF TRAINING NEEDS ASSESSMENT

Operations and maintenance training is a critical requirement for the *bottom-line success* of a project. Training plans must be initiated early so that sufficient funding for the training program is a part of the appropriation request document. Permanent operating and maintenance personnel must be fully trained and ready to participate in preoperational testing, commissioning, and start-up.

Planning begins with a training needs assessment, which should identify:

- Number and types of personnel to be trained
- Current skill level of personnel to be trained
- Specific types of plant systems and equipment that personnel will have to be trained to operate and maintain
- Specific skills and knowledge areas that personnel will have to learn in order to operate and maintain the plant systems and equipment

The result of the training needs assessment (TNA) should be the development of a list of specific training objectives to ensure that personnel receive the exact training they require. The training objective list should be in sufficient detail to become the basis for subsequent training program development. (Training, and the development of a training needs assessment, will be addressed in Chap. 11.)

ESTABLISHING PROJECT CONTROLS

It is imperative that strict controls and clear lines of authority be established as part and parcel of the project plan. If this control and authority is not established, almost everyone involved will sooner or later be attempting to stamp the project with a personal imprimatur. Although creativity and individualism are great things, this is not the place where these attributes should be given free and unbridled rein. When this does happen, it invariably leads to a chaotic project with a delayed start-up.

PROJECT CONTROLS

Project controls should be placed on all facets of the project. The following is a partial list of project elements that should be tightly controlled:

- Document transmittals and revision hierarchy method
- Design changes and change approval method
- Receiving inspection and storage of materials and equipment
- Drawing changes and redlines
- Project monitoring and cost containment reviews
- Vendor and contractor quality of work
- Procurement and traffic requirements
- Environmental issues, including permitting requirements and checks
- Safety of personnel

Although there are many more, these items can just about be considered a "must" list of things to be controlled. (The above list is not in any particular order of importance.)

LINES OF COMMUNICATION AND AUTHORITY

Although lines of communication and authority must be firm and clearly understood by all who are involved with the project, the atmosphere must still be harmonious. Lines of communication must run in both directions; communicators must be able to provide input to the project effort without being summarily cut off. This may seem unimportant to some, but a project that is managed in an arbitrary or dictatorial manner will soon see its lines of communication break down. Soon, the input won't be forthcoming and the project will certainly be problem plagued.

Although we will be discussing some of these same issues in the next chapter, some key issues in maintaining good lines of communication are as follows:

Make sure they're informed.   A project team leader or project manager must make certain that all those with a stake in the outcome have the information needed to accomplish their part in the effort. Whether the effort is in the preproject planning stage, or later, when the project has been approved and is in actual work, everyone should know:
  • The project goals; the project benefits (even the long-range strategies).
  • The project schedule and the effects of schedule overrun or delay.
  • The project budget, including the budgeted areas in which they will be working.
  • The project organization and lines of authority. Lines of authority must include both signatory requirements as well as informational reporting.
  • Record-keeping and document transmittal requirements.
  • Individual responsibilities.
  • The "critical path" flow of events.
  • Project risk factors (and the project leader's philosophy of dealing with them).

Invite, solicit input.   The most successful project teams are those that actively request, even *search* for input. All input may not be used, or even useful, but just having it broadens the base of options. (It also heads off that famous statement we hear so often when the level of "alligators" is rising: "Well, if you had asked me I could have told you!"

As you may recall from the mission statement at the very beginning of this book, the fundamental precepts of the *Project Bottom-Line Success!* methodology are: clearly defined objectives, recognition of risks, teamwork, and preproject planning.

We have attempted (successfully, we hope) to address these fundamentals throughout this absolutely vital project period, the preproject planning phase. If this phase has been addressed properly, the final segment, appropriation approval, should come quickly and easily, because the request itself is backed with reasoned fact, not fantasy.

PROJECT FUNDING APPROVAL

Submit Appropriation Request Package

Project planners should consolidate the results of their work into a concise document for submittal to executive management. The format and contents of the document will vary from company to company but must serve to (1) clearly identify the need for the project; (2) state the precise scope, schedule, cost, and risks of the project; and (3) justify the investment in the project.

Based on the information and recommendations assembled by the project planning team, executive management will evaluate the justification for committing capital resources (funding) by:

- Evaluating the ROI
- Evaluating the availability of funding
- Evaluating business strategies and risks (as outlined in the appropriation documents)

It is critical to *Project Bottom-Line Success!* methodology that the submitted project appropriation document (PAD or AR) be composed of the absolute best work of which the project manager and his project team are capable, that it be completely candid, and that it address the risks as well as the benefits of the project's execution.

Executive management is depending on its professionals, the project team, to provide the evaluations, the factual information and the justifications that will lead them to the making of wise and profitable decisions.

> Once an appropriation is approved, executive management assumes, and rightly so, that the benefits described by the project team in the appropriation documents will be fully attained within the stated budget and schedule.

ORGANIZING THE TEAM

PROJECT TEAM ORGANIZATION

The ultimate success of a project depends, in most cases, on the makeup and abilities of the project team. Given the same set of originating circumstances and information, one project team might have an eminently successful outcome, while another team might find the same project problem-ridden. This brings us to a very important point—*problems occur, for the most part, as the direct result of people's actions or inaction, not because "things happen."*

How often have we heard, "But the start-up was delayed by glitches in the..., etc.," or "but the entire project was plagued by gremlins, leading to significant start-up delays." Now, I have been involved in many projects over the past several years and I must admit I have yet to see my first gremlin. (I'm almost ready to believe there is no such thing!)

Since problems are caused by people, it is vitally important that the project team not only be led and made up of the people best suited for that particular project, but also that clear lines of communication and responsibility be established early in the project's formative stages.

The project team organization, when in the hands of an expert project manager, is like a fine instrument. It can be both firm and flexible, large or small, fast-tracked for speed or detail-oriented for critical applications. Whatever its intended approach, the project team organization will usually include both the intracompany team and the representatives of the major supplier or suppliers. Let's look, for a moment, at a typical project organization chart (Fig. 30).

Most people say, when viewing this chart, "It's too big—we don't run our projects with a team of that size," or "We've downsized; we run much thinner than that." And except for very large capital projects, they're probably quite right.

However, regardless of the size of the project, the *functions* are still going to be there. You, as a project manager or project engineer, may be wearing several hats, but you or someone else will, in all likelihood, be accomplishing most of these functions.

Let's look, then, at just how team selection takes place and why some project teams seem to fare better than others.

INTRACOMPANY TEAM SELECTION

A project's ultimate success depends on the organizations and people that participate in the project. General managers should try to assemble a winning combination of company personnel for the project team based on well-thought-out and considered reasoning. Major factors that must be considered are the type of project and the technical expertise required.

THE PROJECT MANAGER

The first position to be considered, obviously, is the position of project manager or, as referred to in some organizations, the project engineer. (Actually, many larger projects will maintain both positions, with the project manager holding ultimate, overall authority and operating primarily as an administrator, while the project engineer, reporting to the project manager, oversees the technical aspects of the project.)

In considering the factors of project type and technical expertise required, the general manager should strive to select a project manager who has had experience in the past with this particular type project, this particular type application. If the general manager fails to do this, he or she is immediately

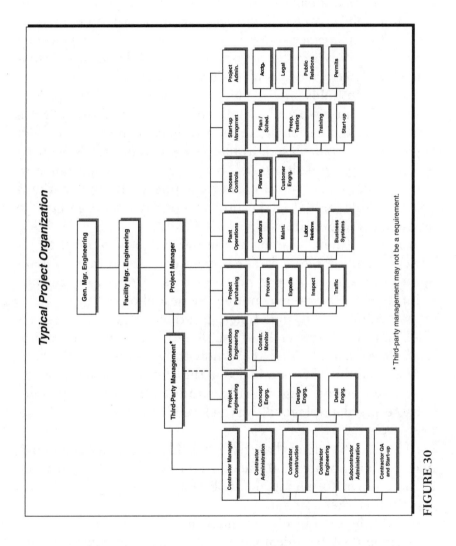

Typical Project Organization

* Third-party management may not be a requirement.

FIGURE 30

149

introducing a risk into a project that hasn't even started. Usually this risk is explained away with the reasoning, "This was the only person we could spare," or "This was the only one of our engineers available at that particular time." Now, I ask you, are these valid reasons to entrust perhaps a multimillion-dollar project to an inexperienced leader? Why not *hire* the needed expertise, if only for the project duration! Taking on risk that can so easily be avoided is like asking for trouble.

The same holds true for technical expertise. If the project is primarily an electrical installation, why would you select a civil or mechanical engineer as a project manager or project engineer? The old reason, availability, shouldn't really be used in this age of consultants. If the project is of importance to your company's or venture's bottom line (if it isn't, perhaps you shouldn't be doing the project anyway), then *go get* the expertise, whatever it takes.

In many (most) instances, the individual who led the pre-project planning effort will be appointed to carry on and manage the execution of the project. This brings up a curious point; that individual may not be the best choice!

We wonder why, sometimes, top-rated engineers (perhaps the best in the company) have such a difficult time with a project. After all, we reason, they know the process "like the back of their hand." They worked out the thorny problems of the first and second engineering submittals, yet the project became problem-plagued, was delayed, and came in seriously over budget.

This doesn't mean that these individuals are not good engineers; it only means that they were out of their element when it came down to management. Perhaps a simple graphic will explain this phenomenon.

As can be seen in Fig. 31, many projects require a considerable amount of technical expertise, thought-provoking discussions, experience, and creativity in the early or conceptual stages of a project. However, the further the project progresses, the less the need for this level of process expertise, the more the need for *management* expertise. The highly intense makeup of many conceptual engineering types doesn't always equate to the

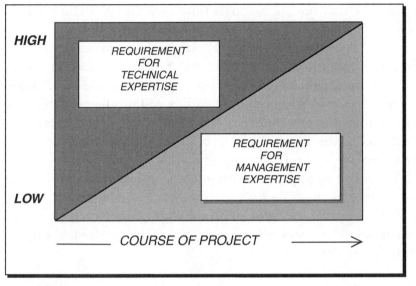

FIGURE 31

skills necessary to handle the everyday nitty-gritty of *managing* the project.

For this reason, it is sometimes in the best interests of the project that a change in management take place. This is especially true on the very large projects that are sometimes located in remote regions of the world and are of several years' duration. The very nature of these projects usually requires people with very different levels of expertise to be at the helm at various times.

For example, early requirements might be in the "expertise area" of a highly qualified civil engineer as remote areas are opened, roads and work camps are built, and the site is prepared for the influx of workers and materiel.

Next might be the requirement for a process-knowledgeable manager as process decisions are being made, and process equipment and suppliers are being selected. For the execution of the project itself (which may be heavily construction oriented) a third change in project managers might be a wise decision.

Many executive or supervisory managers will say they "hate to change horses in midstream." Personally, if I were on a horse that was having a tough time swimming, I think that I would quickly switch to the best swimmer I could find!

In all fairness, however, the supervisory manager should know the limitations and capabilities of his or her potential leaders, and management changes on a project should be planned and scheduled in advance so all parties will be aware not only of impending changes but also the reasoning behind them. (In most cases, the personnel affected will usually welcome the arrangement—nobody likes being a square peg in a round hole.)

Executive or supervisory managers should look carefully at the project *management* versus project *technical* requirements as they assign the responsibilities of project manager to any individual. That decision can mean success or failure for the ensuing project.

LEADERSHIP ISSUES

At least as important, and perhaps even more so, are the qualities of leadership that come with the selected project manager. These qualities can also spell success or failure, as much so as managing the project's nuts and bolts or as ensuring its technical correctness.

Most of us, by now, have all heard of the three basic types of management, i.e., autocratic or dictatorial, democratic, and laissez-faire, with all their relative positives and negatives. In this writer's opinion, the best leaders tend to draw from each of these management styles as they work their way through a project.

Perhaps if we looked at a descriptive list of each of these styles it would become evident that a savvy (and effective) leader *must* draw on all three.

Autocratic
- Makes all decisions
- Demands total commitment
- Calls few meetings, moves fast
- Is usually given the toughest projects
- Issues "public" reprimands
- Checks every detail personally
- Sets tight schedules
- Is inflexible; accepts no excuses

- Puts very little in writing
- Uses few procedures
- Dictates, uses fear as a tool
- Is a "loner," has few friends
- Refuses to listen to other viewpoints
- Doesn't accept blame, always passes it to others

Democratic
- Holds frequent meetings
- Seeks out, asks for input
- Discusses most issues, seeks consensus
- Sets realistic schedules
- Issues any reprimand in private
- Delegates responsibilities and authority
- Is flexible, listens to reason
- Works to procedures, written plan
- Leads, instills confidence
- Accepts responsibility, maintains an attitude of "the buck stops here"
- Has many friends, is respected by peers
- Is well-organized; is on top of day-to-day details

Laissez-faire
- Holds frequent, though irregular, meetings
- Lays out general goals, but with few specifics
- Makes few decisions personally, follows suggestions that proceed toward general goals
- Sets vague schedules, works best within a bracketed "range"
- Is a "people person," affable and pleasant
- Seldom issues reprimands
- Is most successful when schedule and budget are not top priorities
- Appeals to team loyalties to obtain results
- Exercises authority sparingly
- Accepts responsibility, but accepts it on behalf of the team

ESTABLISHING THE TEAM

The project manager should, in organizing a team, establish the organization chart that is to be used. Project team members shouldn't have to guess about their assignments. Tasks should be listed, in writing, to avoid any chance of confusion as to who is responsible for what. The project manager should establish clear lines of communication to ensure that he or she is knowledgeable at all times about the project's status.

WORKING GROUPS VERSUS PROJECT TEAMS

In all honesty, we have thus far been using the term *project team* pretty loosely. In reality, the project team is usually a small number of project engineering personnel operating within a larger *working group*. The core project team will usually be composed of a project engineer plus the discipline engineers (electrical, mechanical, process, instrumentation, etc.) whose responsibility it will be to watch over the project aspect that falls within their area of expertise. The engineering personnel may (should be) highly motivated and challenged by the technical aspects of the project. They will usually be assigned full time to the project and will look at it as a step in their engineering careers.

However, project managers and project teams cannot operate in a vacuum; they must have access to, and a firm commitment from, the expertise they require to help plan and execute the project if they are to achieve a smooth, bumpless start-up. Also, the project team needs the participation of project "stakeholders" to provide guidance and recommendations from the earliest stages of the project. It is particularly critical to solicit input from permanent operating and maintenance forces to help ensure a design that provides maximum operability, reliability, and maintainability and to avoid field design changes later in the project. These stakeholders, along with the core project team, make up the working group so essential to a project's successful outcome.

Much more will be said regarding the subject of stakeholder input and its criticality when we discuss the design element in Chap. 7.

MAJOR SUPPLIER SELECTION

Once assembled, the project team must evaluate and select the most important part of the final team, the major suppliers. Some company project managers and teams continue to look at the project organization as "us" and "them"—"them" being the contractors and suppliers of equipment and/or systems. Actually, the most successful projects occur when the major suppliers and contractors are integrated into the team. To accomplish this integration successfully, supplier selection begins with careful prequalification.

SUPPLIER/VENDOR QUALIFICATION

As stated earlier, the qualification process for major suppliers and vendors begins during the appropriation stage and continues until the project team has determined which vendors will be selected to receive requests for proposal. During this process, the project team should determine which vendor organization, or organizations, best satisfies the scope requirements of the project. (Again, we are using the term *vendor* to refer also to suppliers of equipment, materials, or services, except for those more easily identifiable as *consultants, contractors,* or *major suppliers.*)

Also as previously stated, another prime prerequisite of vendor qualification should certainly be the compatibility of business and operating philosophies and goals. This prerequisite may be far down on your priority list ("Compatibility? Come on, it's *price* that counts!"); however, if the compatibility issues are ignored your project may be in for some rough times.

Compatibility will yield more flexibility in standardizing the project's engineering, procurement, project execution, and start-up requirements. Noncompatibility, on the other hand, may mean inconsistencies in approach, resistance to change and/or standardization, constant irritation between team members, and slower solutions to differences in management philosophy. These differences usually yield more potential sources of project team problems and present one more unneeded area of risk.

The teaming up of dissimilar philosophies and goals can, and more often than not does, lead to adversarial relationships and difficulty or delay in the resolution of complex project problems. Although we've said it before, we'll say it again: Capital improvement projects are difficult enough to bring to successful completion without adding the weight of having to confront problems in an adversarial manner.

FISCAL STATUS AND TECHNOLOGICAL EXPERTISE

The importance of selecting vendors with both good fiscal status and technological expertise cannot be overstated. Deficiencies in either of these areas will usually result in delay and extra cost to the project while the project team looks for a replacement vendor. Bringing a new vendor up to speed will, in all probability, mean further delay.

> Not long ago we observed a project team encounter this same situation when it invited proposals for the purpose of selecting a contractor to flush and clean hydraulic piping systems in a new finishing mill. Proposals were received from several firms, with mostly similar bids for the well-defined scope of work. All, except for one. One bidder, with which the client company had had no previous experience, submitted a bid that was far lower than those of the other bidders. After interviewing this low bidder the project team awarded it the contract, on the basis of the contractor's stated long experience in the field and its low, low price.
>
> The results were terrible. The old, used equipment the contractor brought to site was, for the most part, more contaminated (dirtier) than the piping systems it was contracted to clean! Technical expertise of the operator was also obviously lacking. The end result of this "cave-in" to low price was the replacement of the contractor and a loss of two weeks of valuable schedule time.

Checking the record of potential vendors and suppliers is imperative before bringing them onto the project team. Sales presentations will *always* provide you with the positives; a former customer may provide you with the negatives. Look carefully at the proposed vendor or supplier's ability to work within budget, schedule, and scope, and its ability to adapt to change when required.

The project manager must also make sure that the vendor does, indeed, supply the high-quality personnel to the project that was undoubtedly promised in the presentation. When it comes to the larger suppliers we find, in many cases, that after a vendor has been selected based on its corporate size and reputation, the personnel the large and famous vendor actually brings to the project are mediocre or, possibly, even incompetent. By performing due diligence checks, the project team may find that it can buy better expertise for less money from a smaller, less-renowned vendor.

The selected vendor's ability both to handle its own subcontractors (including environmental issues and labor problems) and to interact well with other providers of equipment, materials, and services are of vital importance to the ultimate success of the project.

These are all issues that must be addressed by the project manager as he or she works to bring together an effective project team.

THIRD-PARTY MANAGEMENT

Referring again to the typical project organization chart (Fig. 30), we see a management line entitled "Third-Party Management." Most small projects won't have this line, but some larger projects will. The reasons for, and the methods of handling, third-party management teams are varied.

On large, multimillion-dollar projects the sheer amount of detail generated requires a massive effort by many people, including intracompany departments, consultants, outside companies, supporting contractors and vendors, and, yes, government agencies (sometimes local, sometimes state, sometimes federal, sometimes all three).

Because of downsizing, because of lack of large-project management expertise, or perhaps simply because most of its personnel are engaged in production, the client company may be unable to personally direct the entire project effort. In these instances, the client may elect to hire a "surrogate," or third-party contractor, to actually direct the day-to-day details. The third party may be a contractor with only that role, or a "turnkey" contractor that will provide the entire project structure including engineering, procurement, construction, installation, and start-up services.

In the first case, that is, in which third-party management is the only role played by the contractor, a full project team of third-party discipline engineers (civil, mechanical, electrical, structural, instrumentation, etc.) is usually provided along with the third party's project manager. Working closely with, and given the authority of (speaking for), the client, the third-party team will direct the project, interfacing with the cognizant client departments, other contractors, and subcontractors. It is usual, in this arrangement, that the client project team "mirrors" the third-party team for purposes of oversight. In this manner, the client team can go on with pure management details (budget and schedule monitoring, cost control, procurement and traffic issues, etc.) rather than be totally consumed with daily field installation and construction details. However, the client team must take great care not to get *too* far away from the nitty-gritty that is going on in the field. The monitoring and overseeing of the third-party management team must not be allowed to lag; this is, after all, the *client's* project, the *client's* schedule, and the *client's* bottom-line dollars that are at stake, not the third-party manager's.

In the second case, that of a turnkey contractor, the benefits can be great—the client keeps on operating its profitable facility while someone else engineers, procures, builds, tests, starts up, and then hands it another facility to run, hopefully also profitably. The only drawback is that this arrangement is usually more expensive than the management-only arrangement and can become even more so if the facility falls behind schedule or overruns the budget in a serious manner. These scenarios are usually brought about when the completed facility fails to come up to the client company's expectations of quality workmanship or production capability. One measure to avoid these situations is to issue a turnkey contract with a good deal of oversight responsibility residing with the client company. Unfortunately, that arrangement also can lead to adversarial encounters as the turnkey contractor usually feels a sense of proprietorship until the finished facility is turned over.

SCOPE REFINEMENT

Although the refinement of project scope was discussed at length in Chap. 5, it should also be mentioned here as it is such an integral part of the supplier selection process and, therefore, has a bearing on the makeup and organization of the project team. All potential vendors and suppliers must have an in-depth and detailed understanding of the product or service on which they will be bidding. This understanding must be unambiguous, that is, there must be no gray areas in which clarity is lacking. If clarity is lacking it will usually be revealed by bidders' questions that, to the project team, may be construed as a lack of basic knowledge. That is usually the furthest from the truth. What this situation should tell the project team is to go back and review the scope definition in detail—something is lacking. The most common cause, both of totally failed projects and those that are only partially successful, is scope ambiguity.

PROJECT PARTNERING

Partnering, defined as "a closer-than-usual commitment between two entities or organizations for the purpose of achieving specific and mutually advantageous business objectives," may become an important factor as the project team is formed. Project partnering, when entered into for the right reasons, can give the project team much more flexibility in its approach to handling difficult project problems. We say, "when entered into for the right reasons" because a partnering arrangement is not always the best way to go. For example, if the scope is cut and dried, and there are no ambiguities, get a firm price on the work and get it done—no need for a partnering arrangement!

If, however, the team has found it necessary to enter into a partnering agreement with one or more of the contractors or suppliers, remember that partnering is founded on three principles: mutual trust, dedication to common goals, and an understanding of each partner's individual expectations and values. Care should be taken by the project team that the trust remains intact. When the partnership's original good feeling is maintained, the mutual benefits such as improved efficiency, increased opportunity for innovation, and the continuous improvement of quality products and services can be achieved.

On the other hand, when the partnering contractor feels that it has been taken advantage of, big problems usually develop: adversarial meetings, nonresponsiveness, lack of flexibility, etc.

The cornerstone of partnering is sharing, and it may require significant cultural changes among the partners. While partnering is not suitable in all situations, it can provide an excellent way of sharing both risks and rewards among compatible organizations.

SELECTION OF VENDORS

After a thorough evaluation of suppliers, the project team selects those few that are most compatible with the project requirements.

Once the suppliers have been selected, the project manager must integrate them into the project team. To ensure that any territorial conflicts or miscommunications are avoided, the project manager should complete the following tasks:

- Set the project team's basic operating agenda.
- Devise a clear statement of each team member's (organization's or person's) specific responsibilities and tasks.
- Set out clear lines of communication and authority (both vertical and horizontal).
- Establish a specific mechanism for prompt dispute resolution.

In the next chapter, Project Execution—Design and Procurement, we shall explore in much greater detail the duties and responsibilities of the various team members, including the "stakeholders," whose contribution to the project team is so important.

CHAPTER
SEVEN

PROJECT EXECUTION— DESIGN AND PROCUREMENT

IN GENERAL

The execution of the project usually begins immediately following the approval of the appropriation request document. (We say usually because in some instances a project may be temporarily shelved following preproject planning and approval of funding.) All work that occurs prior to this event is *preproject planning,* regardless of how extensive that work may have been.

Project design and quality procurement of equipment and materials are critical elements in the transition from project planning to execution. Future operational characteristics and the chance for a smooth start-up will be greatly influenced by the actions of the project team in the development and implementation of these elements. Stringent application of *Project Bottom-Line Success!* precepts, particularly in relation to seeking out, evaluating, then including the input from stakeholders, subject matter experts, and qualified vendors and suppliers, will certainly have a positive impact. The impact will be apparent not only in the short term, but also in the continuing contribution of the project to the venture bottom line for years to come.

THE DESIGN ELEMENT

In this discussion of the design element, we shall assume that the actual engineering will be under contract to a key supplier of this type service. We will also assume that development of design criteria (specifications) and selection of process and major process-related equipment will be under the direct control of the client company's project manager and project team. Final approval of all design drawings and related documentation would also rest with the project team.

We will continually stress the absolute need for detail and clarity of objectives in the equipment and systems design of every project. However, we wish also to make this point: the detail to which we refer is *necessary* detail. Elaborate specifications with nothing left to the discretion of the design-engineering company will serve only to run up the cost of the project. And yes, we've seen and read much lately about "minimal engineering." Care must be taken that this isn't used as an excuse for poor or incomplete engineering. Some engineering houses have been known to use terminology such as this to "low-ball" their competition, knowing full well that the client will require and request more detail later on, after the contract has been awarded.

However, it would certainly be to the project team's advantage to carefully go over the specification they intend to "lay on" the designers and make a serious effort to purge it of all unnecessary or outmoded boilerplate. Much of this language and unnecessary requirement for documentation, redundancy, and detail may have accumulated over the years and, when carefully read, may not even make much sense. Don't overdesign. Whenever possible, specify equipment to the standards of the accepted engineering associations, i.e., ASME, AISE, ISA, AIEE, to name but a few. "Why reinvent the wheel?" to quote an old saw.

The project design element consists of many factors, but most can probably be captured in the following seven considerations:

1. Gathering input from a multidimensional project team
2. Evaluating and analyzing team input for selection of the best design

3. Procuring on a quality basis
4. Considering labor relations and incentives issues
5. Initiating training program development
6. Planning for off-site integrated testing and inspection
7. Revision and refinement of start-up planning and strategy based on design, schedule, and testing requirements

INPUT FROM A MULTIDIMENSIONAL TEAM

To help achieve a truly successful project—that is, a project that not only achieves its promised benefits but also contributes to the venture bottom line in the best possible manner—design planning should use an interdisciplinary approach. This approach will bring the experience and insight of multiple disciplines and positions into an atmosphere that encourages the free exchange of information, ideas, and requirements.

We should, perhaps, state right here that we encourage and espouse the gathering of input from all possible sources and the project team's discussing and comparing alternatives. But the project manager, bearing the ultimate responsibility, must make final decisions. It would be nice if the project team and project manager could always reach a consensus. With human nature being what it is, however, this is not always possible. Our observation has been that, whenever divisive issues are involved, and absent a project manager with a decisive leadership style, the strongest personality in the group will usually bring consensus to his/her viewpoint.

This interdisciplinary approach requires, at a minimum, that design activities include input from the following departments, groups, or areas of experience and expertise:

OPERATIONS AND MAINTENANCE

We have listed this group first for one obvious reason: we consider it an absolute necessity that the people who will be operating and maintaining the equipment and systems affected by the design effort have input very early. Ignore this and your project team will almost certainly be instituting design changes later, possibly leading to budget and schedule overruns.

SAFETY AND ENVIRONMENTAL

In today's increasingly environmentally aware world, these issues must certainly be taken into consideration as the design or design specification is being developed. Early input by experts in this field will also help the project team to avoid potentially huge environmental or safety-related pitfalls later. (In the next chapter we will take up the special requirements and problems associated with "the environmental project.")

CONSTRUCTION

In some projects, construction expertise may not be a requirement, i.e., small projects or perhaps projects involving only control systems changes or upgrades. In other projects, however, the input of a construction expert or experts may be of inestimable value in questions of constructability.

INDIVIDUAL ENGINEERING DISCIPLINES

Certainly the individual engineering disciplines (mechanical, electrical, civil, structural, chemical, etc.) will have input to the project. The trick is to bring the needed expertise to the table at the proper time, i.e., soon enough to provide the input needed to make the right design decisions. Waiting too long to bring the required discipline aboard can lead to hurried decisions caused by schedule pressure.

SYSTEMS/PROCESS CONTROL/COMMUNICATIONS

It is equally as important that input from this group be sought as early as possible in the development of the design or the design specifications, if the project team is to avoid major error in control system selection. Input here can include knowledgeable advice relative to hardware and software standards, level 1 and level 2 control parameters, the man/machine interface (MMI), data collection and data access, networks, business systems, and the interface design specifications. All too often, the project team will ignore this in-house expertise until after critical decisions have been made, relying instead on input from system vendors who, after all, have a more vested interest.

QUALITY ASSURANCE/CONTROL

As design specifications and inquiries to potential suppliers are being developed, there will be a need to include the desired quality levels, including inspection and test requirements, in all documentation. To ensure that these requirements are made perfectly clear to all bidders and suppliers, they should be put in that special quality language that borders on "legalese." Team input from someone with this quality-type background will go a long way in reducing misunderstanding by suppliers and fabricators later as they respond to the team's request for proposal.

As stated earlier (Chap. 5, "Preproject Planning"), all potential suppliers of equipment and/or services to the project should be very thoroughly investigated for quality capabilities. (See App. A for a suggested supplier survey questionnaire and some generic quality forms that you might wish to adapt to your project.)

PROCUREMENT/LOGISTICS

As in all other project activities, procurement of equipment, materials, and services must be planned in detail and executed with precision, not only to ensure that quality standards for procurement are attained, but also to ensure that late-arriving shipments do not impact the start-up date. For this reason, early input from purchasing and logistics experts is critical. Designers may sometimes feel that they have a good enough handle on exactly what is needed in equipment, materials, and services procurement when, in reality, they know very little about the track record or fiscal status of many of the suppliers. Somewhat like the Internal Revenue Service, Purchasing has a long memory based, in many companies, on extensive files that go back several years and perhaps extend through the experiences of other divisions within the corporation.

START-UP GROUP

Many of the decisions made during the design element will impact start-up. This is reason enough to establish start-up representation and input at the outset. However, other reasons are equally as important. Start-up planning should start at the beginning, not the end of the project. The requirements of a well-planned, orderly, preoperational testing and commissioning program will also impact design. Off-site testing and inspection requirements, for example, must be included in the specification packages.

HUMAN RESOURCES/LABOR RELATIONS

A disgruntled or uneasy workforce can wreak havoc with start-up, even though the design is perfect and the project has been executed flawlessly to that point. Incentive issues, new or changed work rules, layoffs or impending layoffs, all can have a chilling effect on start-up, leading to long, drawn-out learning curves and delay in achieving promised benefits. If these issues are pertinent, then input from both human resources and labor relations experts is an absolute necessity!

PROJECT TEAM INVOLVEMENT

In many instances, project team involvement will be brief, and may perhaps be only attendance at the initial planning meeting. (In a few cases, the team involvement may consist only of a phone call or a letter.) Regardless of the time of involvement, however, this input is highly important not only from the aspect of the information gained, but also because the status of the one providing the input has now been changed from bystander to stakeholder.

The fifth principle of *Project Bottom-Line Success!* recognizes the critical importance of having these personnel become, by virtue of their input, stakeholders in the success or failure of the project:

> **Input from all stakeholders is imperative, if the project is to be successful.**

Up-front involvement of each group that will impact implementation of the project and operation of the facility is a key factor in the achievement of *Project Bottom-Line Success!* Let's consider, for a moment, just how that up-front involvement may be sought out and used to the project team's advantage.

SELECTION CONSIDERATIONS

One of the project team's first tasks is to select the design that *best meets the project's objectives.* (Note that we did not say, "Select the low-cost design"—it may or may not best meet the project objectives.) The project team will certainly use the engineering submittal developed during project origination and definition as the primary resource document for this task. Let's list just a few of the considerations that might be included in arriving at the best design selection.

Process Performance Parameters.   These are the parameters that are required to meet production and quality goals. These parameters may ultimately have a huge impact on project cost and must be very critically reviewed by managers as to the value to be received from meeting them. (Example: Is it really necessary to get to *that* level of quality to be competitive?)

Process Technology Reliability, Availability, and Maintainability.   The "abilities" that should be right at the top of design selection criteria! These will be discussed in more detail as we discuss life cycle cost analysis.

Cost of Initial Procurement and Installation.   Certainly, initial procurement cost and installation should be one of the selection factors. However, lowest price may not always be the most economical selection. By the same token, the high-priced selection may turn out to be the most economical selection over time.

Life Cycle Costs for Operation, Maintenance, and Environmental Concerns.   This is really what it all comes down to; i.e., what will the selection ultimately cost. The only real way this can be determined is through life cycle cost analysis. (Several excellent programs are available on the software market.) Effective modeling of the costs and benefits over the entire equipment or system life cycle can improve the selection process tremendously. Computer-based spreadsheet tools are adaptable for the purpose of modeling the life cycle of any system, whether automated or not. Costs to consider include initial acquisition costs, installation and start-up costs, running and maintenance costs, loss-of-production costs during maintenance outages, costs of unscheduled downtime (based on historical data), associated environmental costs, and estimated decommissioning costs at the end of the life cycle. Only through such an analysis can project teams arrive at the true cost of selected equipment.

Personnel Requirements for Operation and Maintenance. These are extremely important considerations in establishing criteria. Higher or lower cost considerations may become irrelevant if a significant difference exists in the number of personnel required to operate and/or maintain.

Each of the above will benefit greatly from early input of operations and maintenance personnel. How many times have we repositioned equipment or redesigned it during (or even after) construction to correct some deficiency that was overlooked in the early design stage and then heard the words, "If you had asked me, I could have told you"?

These words, although grating, are usually only too true. It is absolutely *imperative* that operations and maintenance people thoroughly review the design and operational characteristics of any new facility, system, or system change.

It has been our observation, over the years, that Operations and Maintenance will ultimately have the system they want anyway, so why not get their early input and give them what they want (and *need*) sooner, rather than later.

We hear over and over, however, that Operations input is very difficult, if not impossible, to obtain. We hear that Operations people refuse to attend project meetings, claiming that they haven't the time, that they are too busy.

ENLISTING OPERATIONS SUPPORT—AN EXAMPLE

We were invited, not long ago, to consult with a project team that was experiencing a few problems in kicking off a project involving the upgrade of a major steel mill system, an upgrade that would, among other things, reduce the process-produced pollutants, long an irritant to workers.

One of the problems, it seemed, was the noninterest that Operations people exhibited: a failure to attend project meetings that the project manager had called, failure to return design drawings they had been asked to comment on, failure to provide input on outage requirements, etc., etc. The project manager had listed this pattern of noninvolvement as a risk to the successful execution of the project, a project that needed to be completed during the next maintenance outage. Miss this outage and the entire project would have to wait at least a year.

Under these circumstances, the project manager was at a loss to understand what he perceived as operation's lack of cooperation. One of the most important aspects of the project was to improve a very undesirable situation involving air pollution that affected Operations personnel. It was decided that an interview with the Operations area manager by a third party might be in order.

The interview with the Operations manager revealed the other side of the story. He stated that although Engineering might think that he had no interest in the project, he actually had great interest and wanted to see it successfully accomplished during the upcoming maintenance outage. "After all," he stated, "we were the originators of the request for this upgrade."

This manager had several very good reasons for his "failure" to respond; the most overriding one was that he simply hadn't had the time. "They call a meeting, usually on very short notice, and expect me to drop everything and attend," he said, "but I just can't do that. Their responsibility might be to execute projects; mine is to make steel. I have very important responsibilities here—I just can't attend a meeting whenever Engineering sees fit to call one!"

The operations manager went on to relate the reasons behind his seeming episodes of failure to respond, his not reviewing the design drawings, for example. "They send over a 17 drawing set of engineering drawings and ask me to review them," he stated. "Now, although I can read a drawing," he went on, "it's not something that I do every day—and I don't have the time to study every detail of a set of drawings to assure engineering that they haven't screwed up somewhere!"

Another problem this manager recounted was a problem we have all faced: the interminably long wait in an hours-long project meeting we have been asked to attend to offer our "input." From the manager's viewpoint, these meetings were an unnecessary infringement on his busy schedule.

As we discussed these issues, I began to see a possible solution, a solution that could perhaps be considered a "win-win." I asked which day of the week was the least busy for this Operations manager. "Thursday," he replied without hesitation.

It was soon established that if he knew there was to be a project meeting every Thursday and that his part (operations-related issues) would be taking place at approximately 10:00 A.M., he could easily be there.

It was also soon arranged that, if a project engineer would bring a set of drawings to the operations manager's area, he would "walk them down" with the engineering representative and offer input, from Operations' standpoint, on the spot.

In a later meeting, the project manager and the project engineer readily accepted these offers from the Operations manager. They struck a deal! As I last heard, the situation had worked to everyone's satisfaction. The "lack of cooperation" had been nothing but a scheduling problem all along. All it took to arrive at a solution was just a bit more of project management's effort.

Project teams must take every step possible to make it easy for concerned groups to offer input to the project effort. Only by sometimes making this extra effort will you be able to look at your project team as a truly multidisciplined, cross-functional team. And remember that when you ignore a potential stakeholder, he or she can just as easily become a roadblock!

These considerations preclude the definitive need for early involvement of *all* stakeholders. Also remember, the best design is not always the most expensive or the least expensive. The best design is one that provides the greatest cost efficiency over the life cycle of the facility while sustaining production quality and quantity targets. Input from all stakeholders will aid the project team immeasurably in arriving at the best design.

INCENTIVES AND LABOR RELATIONS

Project planners should be familiar with the requirements of any corporate or negotiated incentive programs or labor issues. Early negotiation and equitable resolution of incentive and labor concerns will help ensure that these issues will not delay or impede the project facility's start-up and initial operation. Project team members should consider the following:

- Possible incentives for achieving a shorter learning curve and smoother start-up
- Incentive programs for achieving production goals as scheduled, or sooner
- Incentive programs for achieving product quality goals as scheduled
- The ramifications of labor force reductions or job shifting
- The ramifications of new technology requiring new skills
- Meeting or achieving safety goals

The absolute *worst* time for these issues to come to the attention of the project team is during the commissioning element. A smart project team will tackle them up front where there is some maneuvering room.

INITIATION OF TRAINING PROGRAM DEVELOPMENT

Putting a multimillion-dollar facility into the hands of a poorly trained workforce is like giving the keys to your brand new Corvette to a teenager who's never driven anything but a go-cart.

Operations and maintenance training is a critical requirement for *Project Bottom-Line Success!* for any project. Training program development must be initiated early so that permanent operating and maintenance personnel are ready to participate in preoperational testing, commissioning, and start-up.

As stated earlier, a training needs assessment should result in the development of a list of specific training objectives to help ensure that personnel receive the exact training they require. The training objective list should then become the basis for subsequent training program development, regardless of whether handled in house, by vendors, or by a training contractor. (We shall be discussing project-related training in greater detail in a later chapter.)

PROCUREMENT ON A QUALITY BASIS

Procurement refers to the acquisition of the equipment, materials, and services required to construct and start up an industrial facility. Some business organizations tend to think of logistics in the form of purchasing and traffic as second-tier functions, not so important as engineering, operations, maintenance, or sales. We heartily disagree with this viewpoint and this approach to procurement functions. Purchasing is a highly important function in the execution of capital projects, and the intricacies of this process should be handled by people with experience in the areas of negotiation, traffic control, documentation, expediting, and both domestic and overseas purchasing.

In some organizations where the importance of the purchasing function is downplayed, these functions are left to the project team, usually to the detriment of the project. The project team is usually pressed for time by other vital project concerns (such as selection of the best design). Also, the full scope of the purchasing function is usually not within the project team engineers' knowledge and ken. Engineers should engineer; buyers should buy!

A strong Purchasing group can be a major factor in holding down the cost of a capital project simply by requiring justi-

fication for "sole sourcing" or for selection of the higher bidder from a group of "qualified bidders."

In a recent conversation with the Purchasing manager of a
major corporation, I asked his viewpoint on awarding through
sole source or to higher bidders. "I have no problem with
either one, as long as it's *justified*," he said, adding, "whatever
is best for the company. Unfortunately, our engineers usually
don't want to take the time to justify this type of selection;
then, when we shoot it down, they complain that Purchasing
is holding them up!"

Typically, owner project procurement activities fall into
four categories. These activities are:

1. Long-lead direct purchase
2. Services procurement, i.e., primary and secondary systems
   contractors
3. Ancillary equipment and construction services procurement
4. Start-up materials and services procurement

KEY CONSIDERATIONS FOR PROCUREMENT

Critical items that the project team should consider during
the procurement process will usually include the following:

- Supplier selection
- Placement of orders
- Expediting
- Traffic planning and control
- Material receipt
- Documentation/administration

Although there are variations from company to company,
many times even from facility to facility within the same company, most modern procurement departments operate in
essentially the same way. (See Fig. 32.)

The process begins when a requisition is received from
Engineering requesting the procurement of equipment, services,

PROCUREMENT MANAGEMENT ACTIVITIES

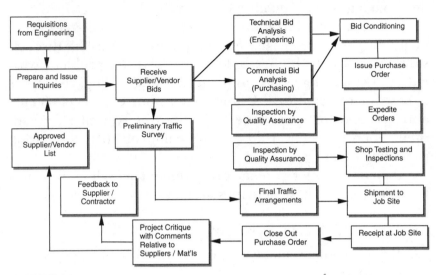

FIGURE 32

or materials in support of a project. Generally, the Purchasing department, working from an "approved vendor list," will prepare and issue inquiries to qualified suppliers of the equipment, services, or materials. (We will discuss the origin of the approved vendor list a bit later.)

BID CONDITIONING

After receipt of bids from qualified, interested bidders, Purchasing will usually forward a copy of the bidder documents to Engineering for a technical evaluation of the bidders' offers. Bidders' "numbers" may or may not be revealed to the evaluating engineer. Some companies with especially strong Purchasing departments black out the numbers to avoid any cost bias during the technical analysis.

The Purchasing department itself will perform the commercial analysis, making sure first that all "apples and oranges" are identified so that the commercial playing field is level and true cost comparisons can be made.

As stated earlier, true cost comparisons are sometimes impossible without a life cycle cost analysis. In this event, the total commercial analysis may or may not be done by Purchasing. Life cycle issues may need to be researched by Engineering, Operations, or both.

AWARD OF PURCHASE ORDER

Following the bid conditioning exercise, a purchase order is issued to the winning bidder. The purchase order should not necessarily be issued to the bidder with the lowest price, but *to the bidder who best meets the needs of the project*—and the project goal must be to contribute the best possible return to the venture or corporate bottom line.

True, we should never issue an inquiry or invitation to bid to any supplier that we would not honor with an order upon presentation of the low bid; however, the bid conditioning process may prove that the low bid is not in the best interests of the project's success. There may very well be factors relevant to the several bidders that "negate" the factor of low bid, for example, standardization with similar equipment already installed, availability of spares, and size and installation differences. All these issues have merit and must be considered. Where possible, of course, these factors should be revealed in the prequalification of the supplier; however, such issues may not be apparent at that particular time.

The purchase order should be looked over very carefully by *knowledgeable* Quality Assurance personnel, to ensure the inclusion of the proper quality clauses, quality standards, tolerances, inspection and testing criteria, fabrication "hold points," etc. Never forget, you receive only what the order calls for—no more, no less. If something is overlooked, or if the wording of the order is unclear, it will cost more later; perhaps even delay of the project.

Once the order has been issued, a series of events will take place, beginning with expediting of the order and ending with payment of the supplier and a critique of the purchase. However, several vital functions must take place between these two events.

EXPEDITING

Many large Procurement departments handle their own expediting function, and have people (called, naturally, expeditors) who are trained in this function. Their job is to visit supplier and subsupplier shops and ensure that the order schedule is being met, that the project is not going to be impacted by late deliveries. The role of the expeditor is *not* to inspect for quality, but for maintenance of schedule. The mandate of the expeditor is to get the item moving to the field as quickly as possible.

INSPECTIONS AND SHOP TESTING

Shop inspection and testing may be accomplished by several methods. In some cases, this function may be carried out solely by the project team, while in others a third-party professional quality assurance entity may be contracted. On most large projects it is usually a combination of the two. The role, or mandate, of the person or persons charged with the responsibility of vendor shop inspections and testing is to ensure that the equipment or materials do not leave the fabricator's shop until all requirements of the purchase order have been met.

On some projects, we see an attempt to *merge* the responsibilities of expediting and shop testing or inspection. The problem with this practice is that the two functions tend to be diametrically opposed. Unfortunately, whenever the dichotomy of schedule need versus quality need exists, the person performing the function will tend to favor the activity with which he or she has the most experience or to which he or she feels the most loyalty. Where possible, it is probably best to separate the two functions. (Although this should not preclude, for example, a shop inspector or testing person *reporting* the status of equipment or materials observed during the inspection or testing trip.)

SHIPMENT TO JOB SITE

Shipment to the site is accomplished via a carefully considered and detailed traffic plan. In too many instances, the initial traffic survey and planning for shipment to site isn't afforded the importance that it deserves. Most major corporate Purchasing departments maintain a traffic unit consisting of employees who are skilled in the movement of large shipments of materials and, in some cases, massive pieces of equipment.

It is important to get input from these units very early, since the cost and schedule requirements associated with the movement of purchased items can have an enormous effect on project risk factors and decisions relative to vendor selection.

If there is no traffic unit specializing in this aspect of the project, these factors must be handled by the project team. They can be daunting to someone untrained in the ins and outs of bulk material and specific equipment movement over long distances, especially imports from overseas. For example:

- By road, through various countries, en route to a seaport: What are the local regulations, weight limits, tariffs, permits, etc.? What are the risks of delay?
- By sea: Which ports of exit and entry will move the material or equipment with the least amount of delay? What documents are required? Tariffs? Permits?
- In the United States: various state regulations; permits, weight limits, oversize loads; physical impediments en route; potential delays.

Certainly this is not a complete list of all potential problems. The main concern here, the point we wish to emphasize, is *risk of delay* to the project. Every potential problem that is investigated and solved (or at least brought within an acceptable comfort zone) will improve the overall probability of a successful project outcome.

RECEIPT AT SITE

As equipment and material are received at site, they must be handled properly. After all, they represent a considerable investment in bottom-line dollars. Since this is generally a construction phase requirement, the receiving and storage procedures will be discussed in a later chapter. However, any discrepancies with the order, or damage observed, should be reported to Purchasing so that corrective procedures can be immediately implemented and expedited.

CLOSEOUT OF ORDER

Once it is evident that all purchase order terms have been satisfactorily completed and there are no outstanding items, the purchase order will be closed and final payment can be effected. The performance of the contractor or supplier should be well documented. Only in this way can project teams hope to avoid making the same mistake again and again.

One method used by many companies is the project critique, a formal look at all aspects of the project, including contractor and supplier performance. Not only will a close look at supplier performance and product quality aid in preventing costly repeats of project problems, it will also close the loop by providing information for an approved vendor list.

PRIMARY AND SECONDARY CONTRACTORS

Primary contractors are those contractors to whom owner companies assign major responsibilities, responsibilities that may include overall facility design, construction, and commissioning. These contractors will usually be purchasing considerable amounts of project equipment, components, and services themselves under the auspices of their project contract. In this area project teams must closely monitor not only the quality requirements the primary places on its subsuppliers but also must ensure that the primary's component selection is in line with component standardization efforts already underway by plant maintenance forces. (Another *excellent* reason to seek input from the maintenance faction early in the project!)

Secondary or nonprimary contractors are those to whom owner companies, or primary contractors, assign discrete, specialized, craft, equipment, or process-oriented responsibilities necessary to complete the facility design, construction, and commissioning.

PLANNING FOR PROCUREMENT

As in all other project activities, procurement must be planned in detail and executed with precision, not only to ensure that quality standards for procurement are attained, but also to ensure that the carefully planned start-up date will not be impacted by late or incomplete equipment deliveries. Here are some of the ways these goals can be accomplished:

Include purchasing and traffic personnel early as integral members of the project team. Use their expertise in procurement planning. Why? Because usually, the Purchasing department of any company keeps detailed files; *they have a long memory!* Purchasing departments maintain records of past projects and past services. Chances are, they will have some kind of record on almost any supplier the project team can come up with.

Traffic, usually a function of purchasing, is also crammed with valuable information. Information such as the best and quickest routing to ship purchased equipment and materials to site. Your schedule might just hinge on this information! Additionally, if the equipment or material is coming in from overseas, traffic personnel can direct entry into the United States through the port of entry with the least amount of delay.

To take full advantage of these valuable services, however, traffic personnel must be brought aboard early; otherwise, you will just be making paper shufflers out of them.

Include warranty evaluation and stipulations in procurement planning. If possible, specify favorable warranty conditions, for example, warranty to begin on equipment installation. Also, contrary to what most people think, warranties are not engraved in stone; they're negotiable items. However, they are negotiable only before and until the order is signed; *then* they become engraved in stone!

Qualify suppliers and provide inquiries only to those that have a proved track record. Qualifying should include an inspection of supplier facilities, procedures, and workforce, as well as contacts with previous clients of proposed suppliers. Qualification should also extend to identifying a supplier's ISO 9000 certification status and its ability to comply with company standards.

Stringent qualification of a potential vendor/partner. A partnering arrangement is a closer-than-usual method of cooperation and involves trust and mutual respect. Make absolutely sure of the potential partner's commitment to the project goals and of the project team's ability to accept a supplier company under this type arrangement. When a partnering arrangement does go sour, it tends to foster more bitterness than does a more ordinary contractual arrangement. Why? Because one or both parties end up feeling betrayed.

Plan for purchase of modularized, preassembled, or skid-mounted equipment. It's simple, with faster installation, less on-site assembly and testing, and less chance of mistakes.

Plan for the standardization and blanket ordering of equipment. Wherever and whenever possible, standardize the design and procurement of structural shapes, piping, valves, fittings, instruments, motors, electrical materials, and small driven equipment. Standardize entire systems, if possible. Not just the hardware, but the control system software, too. Just think of the bottom-line dollars that could be saved if systems were cookie-cutter produced!

Develop and enforce stringent quality standards and inspection and testing requirements. These standards and requirements should be a part of the requisition and clarified in face-to-face meetings before the purchase orders are issued. One of the main purposes is to help ensure that defects and nonconformities are identified and corrected before the equipment is released for shipment. If the vendor is ISO 9000 certified, quality enforcement should encompass verification of compliance with ISO 9000 standards and requirements. If the project team does not have sufficient human resources to do the procedural development and the actual inspection and testing of fabricated items and equipment, third-party assistance should be contracted. To ignore these inspections and tests simply by thinking, "We don't have the people to spare," is an invitation to a failed project.

Tie project plan milestones to payment schedules. This assists not only in forecasting expenditures but also in keeping suppliers on schedule.

Include commissioning services in the purchase order. The cost of these services is negotiable prior to issuance of an order; postorder, it will usually increase.

Make unannounced visits to vendor shops. Sometimes, this can be a good way to find out just where your vendor's priorities are; your project may not be the supplier's No. 1 priority after all!

Integrate planning and scheduling for acquisition of spare parts and material required for preoperational testing, start-up, and initial operations. The last thing in the world you want is for the project start-up to be delayed for want of a spare. That spare could be extremely expensive!

Establish realistic delivery schedules. Setting of delivery dates for equipment and materials is an extremely important function since the construction and/or installation schedule and ultimately the start-up date itself depend on timely deliveries.

The knowledgeable project team will, however, beware of forcing an unrealistic schedule on a supplier. Ignore this advice and you may just get the schedule you're looking for; however, the actual delivery date may be far different than the schedule!

Remember what we said in Chap. 5, "Preproject Planning"—suppliers *want* your order. Savvy, reputable vendors will usually resist an unrealistic schedule when they see it—for a while. But as pressure to embrace the unrealistic schedule mounts, and the supplier realizes that the client is making the schedule a condition of award, you may begin hearing words like, "Well, it's pretty tight, but I think we can make it." (Remember what we also said in Chap. 5: what they're really telling you is, "There's no *way* this schedule can be met!")

Now, why would a supplier do this? First, because you insisted on an unrealistic schedule and the supplier didn't want to give up on the order. Second, the supplier probably figures that if this project team isn't any brighter than this, they've probably erred in other areas, the project schedule will slip anyway; nobody will realize the supplier's tardiness!

Far-fetched? Not too much; we see this scenario play out in project after project. Let's look at a case in point. We call it "The Case of the Troublesome Roll Grinders." (Roll grinders are machines used in mill facilities to refurbish the rolls used in the rolling of steel into long thin sheets or coils. Rolls must be ground to extremely smooth and close tolerances.)

C A S E   S T U D Y   **5**

The Case of the Troublesome Roll Grinders

HISTORICAL SYNOPSIS—PROJECT BACKGROUND

An integrated steel company contracted a machine-tool company to refurbish and computerize three existing roll grinders. The contract was a part of the modernization of a hot strip mill (HSM). The roll grinders were critical to sustain the productivity and quality requirements of the modernized HSM.

Originally, the steel company considered contracting roll grinding to an outside facility. However, because of labor negotiations, the steel company reconsidered and decided that its needs would best be suited by in-house grinding.

The steel company then evaluated the purchasing of new roll grinders versus the alternative of refurbishing the existing three grinders. On the basis of price, and of *schedule and production requirements for the HSM start-up*, the company decided to refurbish the existing grinders. (The steel company estimated that the rebuilt grinders could be furnished within 12 months.)

Because the steel company needed the grinders to support HSM operations within 13 months, they asked bidders to commit to a 12-month work schedule. From the outset of the bid process, the steel company emphasized and bidders understood that the ability to deliver completed machines within the schedule was critical to the steel company's needs (thus implying such delivery as a condition of contract award).

During the bidding process, the eventual winner conducted an aggressive sales campaign designed to convince the steel company that it was fully capable of satisfying the performance specification and work schedule for the grinders. The sales campaign was replete with the vendor's representations that it was the premier and largest

American systems integrator for rebuilding and automating existing grinding equipment. These qualifications were exactly what the steel company was looking for when it put out the bid.

The successful vendor used its proposal, supplemented by correspondence, brochures, conversations, recommendations, and newsletters to persuade the steel company that it could meet the explicit requirements of the contract. In spite of some adverse reports from one of the vendor's former clients, the steel company awarded the contract in August to the vendor and the project got underway.

CONTRACTOR PERFORMANCE

According to the original schedule, the first grinder was to be shipped from the vendor shop to the steel company in June of the following year (10 months after contract award); the second grinder was to be shipped in July and the third in August. In fact, the first grinder was shipped in August (2 months late), the second in December (5 months late), and the third in December of the following year (16 months late!).

None of the machines, when shipped from the vendor, had passed the contractually required factory test. The steel company made the decision to ship the machines because of the vendor's sustained lack of progress and because the steel company, in desperation, had assembled a team of grinder experts to resolve control problems in the field.

The inability of the machines to pass their shop tests is indicative of the vendor's technical performance. Although the mechanical rehabilitation of the grinders proceeded as planned, the vendor seemed unable to master the electrical and software requirements for computer automating the machines. This resulted, at least in part, from a turnover of key vendor personnel. The vendor's software engineers who were familiar with the project left the company; the vendor hired replacements, who were unable to complete the job. Finally, 8 months into the project, the vendor contracted out the software work.

Vendor personnel problems continued to hamper the project. According to the steel company, the first grinder that was shipped to the field was accompanied by the vendor's only two capable electrical and control people. These vendor personnel were required to help start up the machine and assist in the field software automation effort. Although the steel company was glad to have the vendor engineers' assistance, their absence from the vendor shop left no qualified personnel there to work on the remaining machines.

As the grinders arrived at the roll-grinding shop, the vendor's field personnel and the team of grinding experts that the steel company had assembled set to work finalizing the automation of the machines. The team included several of the steel company's engineers, as well as experts hired from outside engineering and manufacturing firms.

As work progressed, the vendor continued to assure the steel company that resolution of problems was about "2 weeks" away. But weeks turned into months, and months into years. Three years after contract award, none of the three machines were operating according to the original design specifications. During this time period, HSM rolls were transported for servicing at great cost and effort to other grinding facilities within the plant area.

PURCHASER/CONTRACTOR RELATIONS

As is always the case when a contract goes awry, the relationship between the purchaser and vendor steadily deteriorated. The vendor alleged that its failure to fulfill schedule and performance criteria resulted from excessive interference by steel company engineers and from inherent deficiencies in the grinders supplied by the steel company for refurbishment.

The steel company disputed these allegations, arguing that they had provided assistance in the engineering effort only after it became obvious that the vendor could not perform the work. The steel company pointed out that the vendor had thoroughly inspected the grinders before the contract was awarded, without expressing any reservations about the existing grinders' ability to meet upgraded performance criteria.

Furthermore, the steel company asserted that, during the proposal process, the vendor was given the opportunity to take exception to the technical and schedule requirements of the contract but had declined to do so. Also, the steel company maintained that, at no time during the performance of the contract, did the vendor suggest that the schedule was unrealistic or that the steel company was responsible for schedule delays.

Eventually, relations between the purchaser and vendor degenerated into a work and payment stoppage, with the purchaser threatening legal action to obtain satisfaction and recover financial losses.

CONTRACT RESULTS

THE PURCHASER'S POINT OF VIEW

The steel company considered the vendor's performance of the contract to be a complete failure, in terms of both schedule and performance criteria. Simply stated, the vendor delivered a product late that didn't work. This failure resulted in lost profits. According to the purchaser, the vendor's inability to perform its contract has caused the steel company to fall well short of projected production levels.

THE VENDOR'S POINT OF VIEW

The vendor maintained that its performance of the contract was in good faith and that contract failure was caused by the purchaser's failure to cooperate, by undue interference, and by management deficiencies within the purchaser organization. Vendor losses include both financial losses (cost of performing the work far exceeded the agreed-upon contract price) and damage to professional reputation. News of the vendor's failure will inevitably spread throughout the industry, impacting the vendor's ability to secure contracts with other companies.

CONCLUSION

The project to upgrade the three roll grinders to support a modernized HSM failed to achieve even a modicum of success. Mistakes were made on both sides of the contract and throughout the spectrum of project phases. *The failure of the project impacted the performance of the venture, which was to achieve certain production and quality goals for the HSM.*

The project to upgrade the roll grinders was critical to the HSM modernization, yet it appears to have been planned and executed as an adjunct, rather than integral, part of the HSM project.

The steel company contends that it is not an expert on roll grinding technology or design, and it was therefore dependent on the vendor's engineering expertise to determine if the contract's performance criteria could be met. Yet, the steel company insisted that rebuilt grinders could be furnished within approximately 12 months and made this schedule a term of the contract. If the steel company was not an expert on roll-grinding technology and design, how did it arrive at the conclusion that the grinders could, in fact, be refurbished and automated within 12 months?

If the vendor took no exception to the terms of the contract, it must be assumed that (1) it believed it could fulfill the schedule and performance criteria and then grossly underestimated the job or (2) it knew going in that it couldn't fulfill the terms of the contract and decided, for reasons of its own, not to take exception in its proposal. If the first scenario is correct, how could a company with this vendor's experience have underestimated the job by such a wide margin? If the second scenario is correct, what logic and motivation would have made it decide not to take exception to the schedule and performance criteria laid down by the purchaser?

In our considered opinion, emotion overcame good judgment on both sides of this project. On the client side, the emotion of egotism was expressed as, "We *need* it by that date—therefore, it *will* be done by that date!" On the vendor side, greed—expressed as, "We *want* the order—regardless of what we must *say* to get it!"—appeared to be the driving emotion.

Close coordination, planning, and communication between the project team and Purchasing are essential in achieving *Project Bottom-Line Success!* Purchasing must be integrated into the initial project planning stages and kept active, involved, and informed throughout project implementation. Above all, however, cold, hard facts must rule the day; leave emotions at home!

Life cycle cost analysis by the project team will assist greatly in the bid-conditioning process. Low price may not always be the most economical way to go.

There's an old maxim that says:

The bitter taste of poor quality remains long after the sweet fragrance of low price has faded.

OFF-SITE INTEGRATED TESTS AND INSPECTIONS

Another task, absolutely vital to the success of the project is the task of identifying and setting up the program of off-site testing and inspection of systems and equipment that are being fabricated in various vendor facilities all around the country and perhaps the world.

For the purpose of this discussion, the term *off-site testing and inspection* encompasses all actions taken to ensure that equipment and materials meet design specifications before shipment from the manufacturer's location to the construction site. This includes individual component testing, as well as integrated testing. *Project Bottom-Line Success!* holds as its sixth principle that

Testing in the factory reduces problems in the field.

In almost all cases, it is easier, cheaper, and quicker to correct problems with equipment and controls at the vendor's site rather than at the project site.

KEY CONSIDERATIONS FOR PRESHIPMENT TESTING

There are some critical tasks that the project team must consider if it is to accomplish an off-site testing and inspection program that will be effective in helping to ensure the functionality and reliability of equipment and materials. These tasks will usually include at least the following:

- Identification of equipment and material testing requirements, standards, and schedules, and the project team's inclusion of this information in specifications and purchase orders.
- Establishment of fabrication testing and inspection standards and procedures.
- Establishment of functional testing standards and procedures.
- Establishment of a procedure for notification that equipment or materials are ready for testing.
- Performance of preshipment inspection or testing at the vendor location, including documentation of equipment and material testing results. This inspection and testing may be performed by the project team or, in some cases, by a third party contracted for this service.
- Examination and evaluation of testing documentation by the project team (or material review board) and initiation of corrective action if test results do not meet standards.
- Release of equipment and materials for shipment by the project team (or third party) only if the vendor has achieved testing/inspection standards.

It may be useful to remember the famous statement by Dr. W. Edwards Deming, the father of modern quality assurance: "True quality is fitness for use." By this maxim he meant that a project or a production element should not be held hostage to a *meaningless* quality standard, but should be judged on its own merits as to "fitness for use." Hence, the rise of the material review board. If the material review board reviews an *anomaly*—an item that does not meet the exact letter of the original specification, test requirement, or material content—and finds that the desired end result will still be achieved without further action, it may elect to waive that particular requirement. This waiver, in effect, changes the specification and the previously offending item now complies and may be shipped without violating quality standards. Be cautioned, however, to avoid the use of this method simply as an excuse for poor quality.

A well-planned off-site testing and inspection program is vital to attaining *Project Bottom-Line Success!* If preshipment testing is not done, or if the testing is not well planned, coordinated, and verified, start-up teams are likely to spend many hours testing, repairing, or even redesigning equipment in the field. This situation will inevitably lead to delays in plant start-up, additional costs, and a negative impact of the project's bottom line.

To ensure that off-site testing is properly planned and completed, the project team should require preshipment testing as a term of award for contract or requisition order. The team should ensure that testing requirements include not only all elements of testing (mechanical, hydraulic, pneumatic, electrical, hardware, and software) but also all types of testing required, such as destructive or nondestructive tests, where necessary.

The project team should establish the acceptable standards with which a successful bidder's quality organization must comply prior to contract or purchase order award. This should include both quality procedures and, if applicable, verification of compliance with ISO 9000 standards.

The project team should develop complete, thoroughly written procedures for testing, including off-site integration testing. Perhaps we should precisely define the term *off-site integration testing* right here, since it is such an essential element in the successful execution of a capital project:

> Off-site integration testing encompasses the testing of a plant's process control system's software and hardware at the supplier's facility to ensure that each control system component operates

within the overall system as designed. Integration testing requires that the process control system be tested and functioning as a whole. There are two types of tests: the preshipment integration test (PSIT), which is performed off site prior to component shipment and installation, and the site integration test (SIT), conducted at the facility after installation.

Why do we espouse *off-site* integrated tests? Because the last thing the project team needs is for the control system supplier to install, on site, a system that is unproved and full of bugs. *Require that the control system vendor, or any other vendor, for that matter, correct the problems at its place, not yours.* Follow this rule religiously, and you will enjoy your start-ups much more!

In many cases, the project team will be pressured by contractors to waive this requirement. They will say that they can "save time" by installing and "working out any minor problems" on site, using the real equipment for "meaningful testing." Don't be swayed. Control systems can be tested in the vendor's facility, simulating process changes. Contrary to what suppliers sometimes say, there is *nothing* that cannot be simulated. Gemini, Apollo, Skylab, and Space Shuttle have taught us that!

Test each subsystem fully during integration testing, ensuring that test procedures include simulation of actual equipment or system operation.

Establish a sequential testing schedule by equipment, by system, and by test that is to be applied to each equipment and system, including integration testing. Identify hold points for equipment and material testing and inspection. Then be on site to witness and verify testing and documentation, maintaining a consistent test team to the greatest extent possible. (Also, if at all possible, arrange for hands-on preshipment testing of equipment and systems by operating and maintenance personnel. This testing will give operations and maintenance personnel the opportunity to receive training on the equipment, as well as to evaluate the equipment's operating and maintenance characteristics.)

Test. Correct defects. Retest. This is one of the most important axioms in the testing business! Many times, after a test reveals only a minor deficiency or bug, the supplier, eager to ship, will say, "Well, we'll correct that little item and ship, okay?" The answer should be an unequivocal, "*No*; not until you correct it and perform a retest!"

If this practice is not followed, you will surely be shipping problems to your project site. So many times, the correction of one problem will reveal another one, or maybe more, on a retest. This is especially true in the case of software systems.

> Do not release equipment, material, or systems for shipment until the vendor has fully achieved the fabrication or functional standards identified in the contract or purchase order.

Preshipment testing cannot be left to the good word or good will of the vendor. To achieve *Project Bottom Line Success!,* preshipment testing must be planned, specified, witnessed, and enforced to ensure that equipment and systems are structurally and functionally complete before they arrive at the job site.

START-UP PLAN REVISION AND REFINEMENT

If not already in place, a start-up team should be assembled at the outset of the design element. The start-up manager should be identified. This team's primary focus is to develop a detailed start-up plan, with input from all disciplines, so that first-time success in facility start-up can be achieved. This technique will help to reduce operations' learning curve time and will tend to minimize facility downtime.

A start-up that drags on for weeks, months, or even years longer than intended before arriving at design capacity is leaving considerable revenue behind, revenue that will never be recovered (see Fig. 33).

Start-up team planning during the design phase, or element, should include the *refinement of start-up objectives* that the project team established earlier. With the refinement of objectives should come the development of responsibilities for start-up activities, procedure development, investigation and

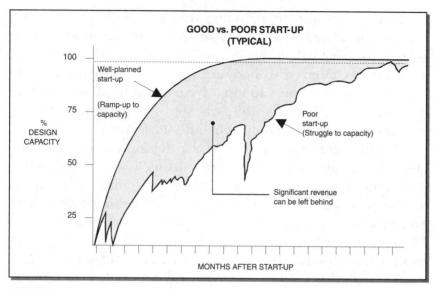

FIGURE 33

initiation of environmental permitting steps, and a key events or milestone schedule of every activity that must take place, leading up to and including the start-up itself.

Early planning for start-up during the design element will help to ensure that designers will be able to allow for such things as, perhaps, a bypass mode of operation so that systems and processes can be tested off line. Or, perhaps, the analysis and advance remediation of potential spillover or "plugging" points that could delay start-up or the achievement of design capacity.

If the project involves a production outage for installation of new equipment or control systems, it is absolutely essential that the outage activities be planned in detail. An hour-by-hour schedule of every outage task should be developed. These activities must be examined very carefully, with a view toward avoidance of an unrealistic or overly aggressive schedule. (One problem we observed on a recent major upgrade involved an unrealistic schedule of outage tasks—not the installation of the new equipment, but rather, the demolition and removal of the old. Regardless of where the problem originates, the end result will usually be delay.)

Other early start-up planning should include procurement planning to ensure that sufficient spares are on order to support start-up and that services will be on site when required. The services referred to here are not only vendor or supplier support, but also the support of consultants, if required, of process experts, and of third-party start-up specialists. *All* may be required to ensure an on-schedule start-up.

Planning for start-up during the design and construction elements should also include both detailed schedule development and development of the required equipment and systems testing procedures for the preoperational testing phase. This project phase, or element, should begin at the approximately 75 percent point in construction completion. (This project element will be discussed in much more detail in a later chapter.)

A successful start-up will depend on quality equipment performing as specified. A major effort of the project team will be the witnessing of tests and fabrications at vendor facilities. Early planning and scheduling plays a major role in this effort.

And, finally, planning and development of standard and emergency operating and maintenance procedures, the O&M manual, should take place early in the project. Operations and maintenance personnel won't have the time (or, in our experience, the inclination) to prepare this manual later.

There are many, many details that the project team must "get its arms around," especially in the early stages of a project. There is an old saying that the devil is in the details. But not in project management. In project management, *angels* are in the details. The more detail addressed, the higher the probability of a successful project. Go for it!

PROJECT EXECUTION— CONSTRUCTION AND INSTALLATION

The construction and installation element in any project symbolizes a time of transition for the project team. In attitude, if not in fact, construction marks the project's point of no return. What previously existed only on paper will now become real.

It is during construction and installation that the project team's planning begins to significantly impact project efficiency. However, if facility construction and equipment and systems installation is not properly planned, choreographed, implemented and *monitored*, the benefits gained by planning the previous elements in accordance with *Project Bottom Line Success!* principles can be lost.

RESPONSIBILITY

During construction and installation, project managers must always remain aware that they, not the primary or construction contractor, are ultimately responsible for successful execution of this element.

Why do we state the obvious? Because we have observed, on many occasions, a tendency to view the letting of the primary contract as also the relinquishing of responsibility for the outcome of this critical element in the overall project. So many times when critiquing a project that has enjoyed a less-than-successful outcome, we have heard a project team member or manager heaping blame on a contractor with the words, "It was *their* responsibility to...." Then the sentence will be finished with whatever the project shortcoming was. In those cases the project team has, in effect, washed its hands of responsibility, and is comfortably sitting back and relying on a contractor to, perhaps, decide the corporation's or venture's fate.

KEY CONSIDERATIONS

In almost all cases, the root causes of failed or less-than-successful projects can be traced back to the project team's poor planning (which may include poor contractor selection) or failure to monitor the primary or key contractor's construction and installation. Let's look, for the moment, at what we would describe as the key factors that a project team should either consider in its planning for this element or should closely monitor during its execution.

RESEARCH SIMILAR PROJECTS

Identify positive and negative aspects of similar projects. These projects may be past triumphs or failures within your own company or perhaps within your experience with former employers. Keep abreast of capital project management successes and failures in the engineering and trade journals, excellent sources of lessons in managing projects. (The many detailed articles concerning the Denver International Airport project should provide study material for years to come.) Perhaps the worst feeling that a project manager can have is the realization that he or she has repeated a past mistake—and has suffered the same outcome.

REPEATING PAST MISTAKES—AN EXAMPLE

Several years ago, I was lead start-up engineer at the construction of a uranium "yellow-cake" plant, located in a southwestern U.S. state. Because of the caustic and abrasive nature of the slurry materials involved in this in situ facility, most of the plant piping was of fiberglass. This included the valves. Many of the plant's valves were of the large, motor-operated variety, Teflon lined, and designed for installation in fiberglass piping systems. We called them saddle valves, since the valve body was equipped with what resembled a large saddle for cementing the piping in place with fiberglass resins.

As we began preoperational testing of plant systems, we began to experience valve-sealing failure; i.e., the valves would leak through and fail to isolate piping sections as required. Investigation revealed that the Teflon lining was wiping, or scoring, because of the abrasive nature of the slurry we were putting through the system. As valve after valve failed and our changeout rate accelerated, we began to feel the magnitude of the problem. We were en route to a changeout of almost the entire plant piping system, and this plant was almost nothing but piping. This situation was turning into a disaster!

It was about this time that I heard the words that I'll never forget. A field engineer, from our own company, said, "Hell—I could have told them that this would happen; we had the same valves at Spokane and they gave us the same problems there!" (He was speaking of a similar project that had been completed perhaps 2 years before.)

I could hardly believe what I had just heard: we had repeated a major design error in less than 2 years and Engineering had never bothered to make an issue of valve selection. Evidently, we had short memories. Even worse, our project team had totally failed to research a similar project *within our own company!*

The result? What should have been a profitable job turned out to be a $7.5 million loser. Also, to our board, this was the straw that broke the camel's back. They shut down the regional office that was responsible for this project—permanently.

DEVELOPMENT OF A DETAILED CONSTRUCTION PLAN

A detailed construction plan is *vital* to efficient execution of project construction and installation. Project team members should consider developing at least the following planning documents:

The Construction Organization and Division of responsibilities. We're speaking here not of the construction contractor's organization, but of the project team's organization, whether it be organized as its own general manager or as an interfacing team with the general contractor. The project manager must ensure that the major interfaces (mechanical, electrical, civil, process and control systems) are represented, from the client standpoint, by project team members. These project team members should be completely knowledgeable not only of the intricacies of the equipment and systems that will be installed but also of the project's *goals*, from both the operational and business points of view. It is imperative also that the project manager identify specific responsibilities of construction management and establish clear lines of communication.

Close monitoring should be the order of the day throughout the construction and installation period. When poor workmanship or mistakes in installation delay the start-up and subsequent gain of project benefits, it is not enough to say, "It was the contractor's responsibility to...."

The Construction Master Schedule. This schedule, usually produced by a primary contractor, will lay out construction in the most economical manner possible for the contractor. However, the most economical manner of construction and installation for the contractor may not always be the best route for the client's project team. It is imperative that the project team member or members having responsibility for preoperational testing and commissioning work closely with the construction contractor in the planning of the construction master schedule. The reasoning behind the importance of this liaison will become very clear in a later chapter when we discuss preoperational testing in detail. Suffice it to say at this point that in order for the testing sequences to begin in a timely way, i.e., at 75 to 80 percent construction completion, the preop start-up team *must* have input into the master construction schedule.

The master schedule must be realistic and should contain some contingency. (The amount of contingency held by the contractor will usually be dependent on the type of contract that was let: lump sum, contingency will be there; time and material, probably not.)

The Detail Schedule.   The project will certainly require and have a detail schedule. The important thing, however, is that this schedule be of sufficient detail that nothing is left to chance, that nothing can fall through the cracks. Key events, or milestones, must be carefully scheduled along with contingency time, or float. The detail schedule must be realistic and must depict construction completion dates and items *in the proper sequence* to support a logical preoperational testing program and start-up schedule.

> Construction sequence should be addressed in the bid specification to potential construction contractors. Although planning and scheduling for sequential construction may add to cost and schedule because of overlap or the presence of different crafts on site simultaneously, the cost will be returned in start-up schedule efficiency and rapid ramp-up to full production. This efficiency will result from conducting preoperational testing during the construction element, rather than after. This factor will be discussed in more detail later.

It is doubly important that the construction and installation schedule be in even finer detail if the project work is taking place during a production outage. To avoid delays from unexpected events with resultant late start-up and lost production, this part of the detail schedule, the construction-and-installation-during-outage schedule, should be reduced to an hour-by-hour scenario of required actions.

Plan for Establishment of Construction Forces on Site
Another key consideration for the project team is planning for the presence of construction forces on site. Proper location of the various contractor and subcontractor facilities is absolutely essential to the efficiency of the construction element. Not only must planning include adequate space for construction supervision and management but also for worker facilities (safety meetings, parking, toilets, tool trailers, phones, janitor service, etc., as well as sufficient water and power for these facilities).

Plan for Construction Power Requirements.   On many projects, construction power requirements can be considerable: power for welders, for lighting, for compressors and pumps, for tools and equipment. A detailed plan to satisfy the power requirements of the construction forces is imperative, if this phase is to proceed without needless delays.

Plan for Labor Relations.   An extremely important consideration of the project team in construction and installation phase planning of any project is smooth labor relations. There will likely be several bargaining units on site at the same time. Any contractual differences must be settled; all parties must understand jurisdictions and responsibilities. There will come a point in time, for example, when care and custody of equipment will pass from the building trades to facility operators and maintenance forces. When will this be? What is the key to turnover? What if the equipment must go back to the construction trades again for some reason, how will that transfer take place? Any of these questions, if not addressed and planned for, could trigger a period of labor unrest, perhaps even a walkout. And that could be disastrous to the project.

Plan for a Safe Job.   Accident-free jobs don't happen by accident—they're planned! Let's begin with what should be a given in anyone's thinking: projects are not worth human life. By the same token, it is a necessity that capital projects take place.

Since a construction site is a dangerous place, steps must be taken to ensure the safety of all personnel, whether they be contractor or facility employees: All test procedures should be reviewed by safety personnel for inclusion of site safety rules and clauses. A stringent tag-out/lockout procedure must be provided and then strictly enforced (immediate termination for violation). Frequent safety meetings should be held. Employees should wear proper protective clothing. Fire protection systems should be up and running. Emergency medical service should be available and used consistently, even for minor injuries. All accidents, even minor ones, should be documented and analyzed, to determine whether a pattern of accidents is evolving. And finally, strict site housekeeping rules should be made and enforced. (Show me a haphazard and dirty work site and I'll show you an unsafe work site; the two go hand in hand.)

Plan and Schedule for Site Preparation. In many instances, before new equipment can be installed, old equipment must be removed, mounting pedestals must be demolished, structural changes may need to be made. In fact, there may be considerable demolition work to be done. If the work is to be accomplished in an operating facility, as opposed to a greenfield site, it is absolutely imperative that this work be planned and scheduled in precise detail. This planning and scheduling will help to avoid production interruption (other than scheduled outages). Special attention should be given to the detailed scheduling of the demolition work; it has been our experience that these tasks are usually underestimated.

Look carefully at anticipated field conditions when planning the opening of field operations. If the project is located in Michigan, for example, site preparation will face more possibility of weather delay in January than it will in June. So often we have seen project teams carry straight through in their detailed planning with one of those schedules that was originally planned on a "0 to 14 months" basis but had been set without any consideration of seasonal weather impact.

Plan for Equipment Receipt, Inspection, and Storage. A critical aspect of any capital project, many times either overlooked or looked on as a low-priority concern, is the receipt, inspection, and storage of the equipment, components, and materials required for construction and installation. If material is not stored properly and receipt and inspection is done haphazardly, critical items can be lost (in some instances, stolen), damaged, or destroyed. These losses can be the result of either mishandling or improper storage.

Environmentally sensitive equipment, components, or materials must immediately go to an environmentally safe staging area, that is, a place with proper temperature, proper humidity, etc. Failure to adequately plan and handle this aspect of the construction and installation phase can seriously jeopardize the project schedule—you simply won't have the things you need when you need them.

Plan for Environmental Permitting Controls.   By the time your project team begins to plan for construction and installation, the environmental permits should have long since been requested and/or received. However, now you must consider the application and control of the permits. As permits are put into effect, checks and reporting will be required. The control of the project's environmental aspects cannot be left to the contractors, without the project manager's or an assigned project team member's diligent supervision.

As stated in Chap. 5, environmental violations can be extremely expensive and, in some instances, can mean the unexpected shutdown of the project until some requirement is satisfied. Environmental permitting control requires procedural-type planning and close surveillance.

CONTRACTOR SELECTION

Certainly, a key to successful project completion is the selection of the construction and installation contractor. There are many, many contractors out there to choose from. Choose the contractor that best fulfills project requirements. Notice we didn't say, "Select the lowest bidder." The lowest bidder may not be the best to fulfill your project's requirements.

When selecting a construction contractor, look carefully into the contractor's quality program and track record. Try to choose a contractor company that is coming off a string of successes. If your project team has done its homework (planning) properly, perhaps you'll be the latest on that string!

INVESTIGATION OF "CONSTRUCTABILITY"

Look closely at the constructability of your project requirements very early in project planning. Some facilities are easy to construct; others, very, very difficult. It may be the substrate, it may be the terrain. In some instances accessibility may be a major factor (can a crane of sufficient size get in there?). Can the local hall provide the needed crafts in sufficient numbers and with the competency necessary to make your schedule? How about rigging and utility requirements?

You may not have the expertise within your own organization to analyze constructability, and overlooked factors can lead to unexpected delay. If you don't have this expertise on board, *then go out and get it*—hire a consultant, if need be! It may just be the best purchase you'll make on your project. And, if you hire this consultant, don't hesitate to also have him look very closely at your schedule. A tentative schedule may have been set in the conceptual period of the project, and, without too much thought or study, is still in place almost by default. But is the schedule realistic? You may get a surprise when a real construction expert looks it over.

SUBCONTRACTOR COORDINATION

Another key factor for the project team to consider is the proper coordination of subcontractors. In some contractual situations the coordination of the subcontractors will fall under the jurisdiction of the client project team; in other arrangements this responsibility will be delegated to a primary contractor. In either case, it is in the project team's best interest to provide strong overview of subcontractor coordination.

> We observed a case recently where the client project manager and his team paid scant attention to the work of on-site subcontractors, since the subs were under the jurisdiction of a primary contractor who was responsible for subcontractor coordination. Unfortunately, although the primary was performing above expectations on its own work, it was weak in its ability to coordinate and monitor the subcontractors' work. Since the work was being performed during a production outage, the electrical sub's poor-quality work led to delays and, ultimately, to considerable production loss.
>
> It may have been the primary's responsibility to monitor the sub's work, but it was the *owner* project team's outage, schedule, and customers at stake. The project team should never assume that any facet of the project is someone else's responsibility and can therefore be ignored.

Field Changes

We could have put field changes at the top of our list since it is such an important topic, and is certainly one of the key considerations of the project team. What *is* a field change, anyway? As a matter of fact, field change is just another name for "scope creep," that other dreaded phrase! Field changes are the bane of capital projects, and in almost all cases result from one of two causes:

1. A failure to adequately define the scope at the outset, or early in the project. This failure leads, in many instances, to budget overruns.

2. Succumbing to the temptation to use up contingent funds or overestimated fat budgets. This practice may lead to a balanced budget and perhaps a pat on the back for coming in right on the money—but the venture or corporate bottom line is the loser. Figure 34 demonstrates this project phenomenon very clearly.

As stated earlier, changes in scope late in the project are generally more expensive. For this reason if for no other, doesn't

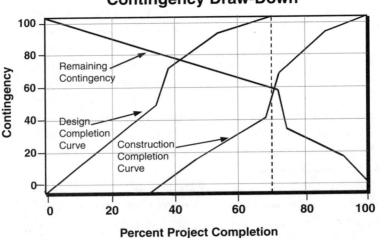

FIGURE 34 (*Source: CII Research 1994 Conference—"Managing Project Change"; 104 projects, $3 million to $2 billion.*)

it then make much more sense to get input from *all* concerned parties very early in the project? We are assuming here, of course, that everyone has the company's or the venture's bottom line at heart. Of course, if the budget is being controlled by an operations manager who has the attitude, "If we don't use it we'll lose it," the project will probably see some bells and whistles added that may not otherwise have made it past the first cut. This type manager will also usually ensure that all contingencies are totally consumed. Let's hope that the *Project Bottom-Line Success!* message comes through to them. Bottom-line improvement requires universal acceptance.

There is one other design change or form of scope creep that should probably be discussed because it does occur more often than we would like to admit. This type of change should be referred to as the "nice-guy change" and usually occurs on projects that are lacking in field cost control measures. It goes something like this:

> A construction crew is installing an electrical panel on an operating platform, or "pulpit," and is approximately 50 percent complete when one of the client's project team members, an operator, happens by. After studying the situation for a few moments, the operator remarks, "Man, it sure would have been better if that panel had been located over there," pointing to a spot down the catwalk about 15 feet from the spot where the construction crew was installing it. "You want it down there?" asks the lead man, "No real problem—it'll go there just as easy as it'll go here." "You can do that?" asks the operator. "Sure, no problem," replies the installer.
>
> The operator walks away thinking, "What a nice guy that was." Meanwhile, a construction foreman begins to prepare his extra work document. The scope has just crept.

Start Outage Only When Ready

In many cases a portion of the construction work will be accomplished during a plant production outage. The work may be done in conjunction with a regularly scheduled maintenance outage or series of outages, or, on the other hand, the outage may be called specifically to accomplish the project's construction phase. In either case, as the outage date draws closer, the project team should refine the detailed outage plan and then start the outage only when ready.

Starting a production outage when it is obvious to the casual observer that you are not ready for the outage is an invitation to a disaster. How many times have we heard those famous last words, "No more excuses! We're taking it down, ready or not!"? From there it goes on to become a future case study in how not to do projects. The bottom line suffers, usually to salve some misguided manager's ego. It is usually far better to find some other way around the problem than to go into an outage before the preliminary work is complete. (How about rescheduling it, even if it does hurt the ego a bit?)

FIELD COST CONTROL

If the project scope has been properly defined and the budget has been realistically estimated, good project cost control procedures will not only help keep project costs in line but might also allow saving of the contingency. The procedures will, of course, require aggressive implementation and follow-up.

One of the primary tools of field cost control is the *extra work authorization*. This document should be backed by a field procedure that prohibits any out-of-scope work that has not been both priced out by the contractor and approved by the client project manager. The procedure should be an inclusion in all inquiries, specifications, and purchase documents. It must be made clear to all contractors and suppliers that any unauthorized work, i.e., work that is performed outside the confines of this procedure, will be at the performing party's expense.

Another primary tool of field cost control is the *cost containment meeting and report*. Cost containment meetings should be held weekly with major contractors and subcontractors. Construction completion and equipment installation progress should be reported by contractor representatives, line item by line item. As items of schedule and budget begin to deviate from the detail construction plan, corrective measures can be instituted to bring budget and schedule back to plan.

This method of cost control should be reinforced with close project team monitoring of construction and installation activities.

FIELD MATERIAL CONTROL

Close control of materials certainly must be a key consideration for the project team during, and even before, the construction phase. (But we could probably say that the construction phase actually starts much earlier than the day it goes to the field.) Regardless, construction material control, including, of course, process equipment, begins the moment the material arrives on site, and its handling and storage are essential factors in a smooth construction phase.

INSPECTION OF WORK

An absolute key consideration in any successful project is the monitoring, or inspection, of the work in progress. Unfortunately, too many project teams consider this responsibility to be "not my job." The reason usually given for this thinking is, "That's what we hired the contractor for; it's *his* responsibility." Of course it's the contractor's responsibility to do the work—but the ultimate responsibility for project execution rests with the client project manager and his or her team. And this responsibility includes both quality of installation and keeping to the schedule. We're not proposing here that client engineers hang over the contractor's shoulder and watch every move that is made; however, a project team that will sooner or later be accepting or rejecting systems for testing and start-up will be far ahead of the game if they are generally aware of the work in progress.

Close monitoring will, in many instances, spot problems or potential problem areas early enough to be corrected before the schedule or budget is compromised. The multifunctional project team should develop procedures for monitoring and inspecting the following items, when applicable, both for progress and quality:

• Layout and construction of building foundations

- Erection of structural steel
- Installation of piping components
- Erection of roofing and siding
- Installation of electrical components
- Installation of mechanical components
- Installation of instrumentation and process control equipment
- Construction testing of installed equipment

PROGRESS MEASUREMENT

When monitoring construction progress, it would be to the project team's benefit to know something of the methods used by construction contractors to determine the status of construction completion. The contractor will use terms such as "factored feet" of piping and wiring, "yards" of concrete placed or of "overburden" removed, numbers of "cables" pulled or "terminations" made, and so on and so on. Although the project team isn't expected to be composed of construction experts, the team members should have a basic knowledge of construction terms and methods if they are to intelligently monitor the project construction phase and discuss problem areas in the daily or weekly project review meetings. There are many reference books available on this subject. Clear benchmarks should be established and the project team should obtain updates on a daily basis. Only in this manner can a close watch be maintained over the all-important project schedule.

> We cannot overstate the importance of keeping to the schedule. Study carefully Fig. 35. The result of a review by the CII of over 100 projects indicates that if a project is *on schedule* at the 75 percent construction completion point, it *still* has only an approximate 80 percent probability of completing on schedule! Often, this situation is the result of the project's having consumed float, or schedule contingency, too soon. The result of using all the float time in the construction schedule too soon is that there is no room for error during preoperational testing, i.e., there is *no time left* in the pot. In fact, if construction uses more than its allotted time, the testing and start-up element will be compressed, unless the start-up date is pushed further out.

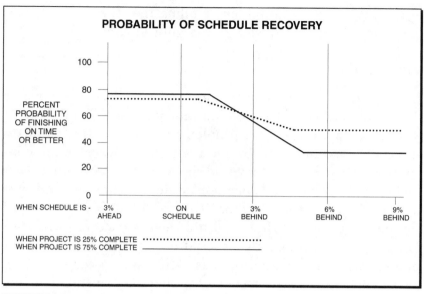

FIGURE 35

DRAWING REVIEWS

Institute continuous drawing reviews. Many of the construction element delays the project team will be facing will be attributable to incorrect or incomplete drawings. This statement is especially true when it comes to the interface between vendor and contractor drawings, or between vendor drawings and as-built or existing configuration. Ongoing drawing review, even if assigned to a beginning or junior engineer, can save much delay time when caught before becoming a real field problem. By the way, some project managers view interconnect drawings as superfluous, or an unneeded luxury. It has been my observation that the cost of these drawings will be returned several times over through elimination of error and resultant delays.

The project team must also ensure that all drawing changes are captured, redlined into field drawings, and forwarded to engineering for inclusion in the final revision. No change should be permitted without the resultant field sketch or drawing change notice submittal. There is nothing worse than to get into preoperational testing or commissioning and, when proceeding to work a problem, finding that the drawing does not match the installed wiring. It might just ruin your day!

VENDOR EVALUATION

Evaluate the vendors, contractors, and suppliers of service as the project unfolds. How well do they interface? Do they want to work with you to solve problems, or do they just want to argue with you about them and get into a fingerpointing contest? Can they do what they said they could do when they were selling you on their skills or their products? How well did they stick to the plan, the schedule? How well did their product or equipment start up? How well did their service rep perform? These are all questions that should not only be answered, but should also be circulated to areas within your company where the lessons will not be lost; i.e., perhaps to a vendor history database coded under headings that would bring them up when similar projects are considered at some later date.

Let us look now at a capital project that took place not too long ago, one that followed very few of the tenets of good project management that we have just gone over. As you read through this case study, you will probably be saying to yourself, "Come on now, nobody would approach a multimillion dollar project like that!" But the people in this case study did, and others do. If you read between the lines in industrial publications and newspaper articles about start-up problems and glitches, and how these things are causing poor financial returns in the last quarter, you will know that a project team has "executed" its way to a very poor outcome; an outcome that has had a disastrous effect on the company's bottom line.

CASE   STUDY   6

Modernization of the Continuous Annealing Line

HISTORICAL SYNOPSIS—CONTRACT AWARD

In early 1988, a plant in a large, integrated steel company identified the need to increase the throughput rate of the continuous annealing line to meet projected market demands for tin mill products, used primarily by the can-making industry.

An engineering company was contracted to perform an extensive study to outline the objectives and scope of work required to increase line productivity and efficiency. The study identified improvements to increase the maximum line speed from 1650 to 2000 ft/min, with a corresponding increase in the throughput rate from 309 to 410 tons per turn.

The installation of the proposed improvements would require a 6-week outage to coincide with the planned annual maintenance outage of the electrolytic tinning line in January. There is a traditional commercial lull in the can-making business at this time of year. Full production would be reached 12 weeks after start-up. The outage would drive the project.

These changes would cost $17,500,000 and yield a before-tax annual savings of $1,887,000 and an after-tax annual savings of $1,510,000. These savings would recover the investment in 13.9 years with a project DCF-ROI of 13 percent.

Plant engineering prepared an appropriation request that was submitted to and approved by upper management in April. Attached to the request for funding was an internal memo from the manager of tin mill products detailing market trends and growth, the quality benefits of proceeding with the project, business that would be lost if the project were not undertaken, and current and projected product flow and loading.

ORGANIZATIONAL/PROJECT MANAGEMENT

Plant management assigned one of the engineers who worked on the appropriation request preparation as project manager. Plant engineering was understaffed and a process design expert was not available to supervise the project. However, a second plant engineer was provided to assist the project manager. A lead electrician was borrowed from the maintenance department and assigned to the project. No other request was made for operations and maintenance department involvement.

The can-making industry experiences a slowdown the first 2 to 3 months of each year. An electrolytic tinning-line outage is planned to coincide with this slowdown every January. The project would be delayed a full year if the January slowdown were missed. Although plant engineering and the project team were undermanned, plant management decided to take advantage of this window of opportunity and placed the project on the fast track.

The project manager prepared five RFPs, one for a construction management contractor, one for a construction contractor, one for a mechanical equipment vendor, one for a furnace vendor, and one for a software, electrical, and controls vendor. An RFP was not prepared for a design engineering vendor because of the fast-track nature of the project. Two to three vendors responded to each proposal. The bids were evaluated, the five contracts were awarded, and the project manager established the organization chart in Fig. 36. The plant engineer was to oversee the mechanical aspects of the project and the lead electrician was to oversee the electrical aspects of the project.

PROJECT DESIGN

The project manager met with each of the vendors and reviewed the project objectives and scope of work outlined in the appropriation request. Each of the contractors/vendors was directed to proceed with the design phase for its individual scope of work. Each vendor was also directed to procure equipment and services to support its area of responsibility.

No engineering or installation engineering submittals were prepared. The vendors prepared their designs from the original engineering drawings and only a cursory field verification of these drawings or the existing equipment condition was performed.

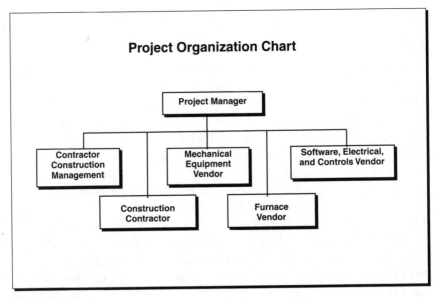

FIGURE 36

PROCUREMENT

Purchasing assigned two individuals to the project team who prepared, issued, received, and evaluated bid specifications. The orders were placed, most often verbally. No integrated off-site or on-site testing was specified.

The procurement process proceeded without a purchasing plan or QA/QC requirements. For example, new gears were ordered from three or four different vendors. When the gears were received, they were shipped, with the gear boxes, to nine different vendors for assembly.

PRESHIPMENT TESTING

No preshipment or integrated testing was planned or performed because of the fast-track schedule required to meet the outage window.

CONSTRUCTION/INSTALLATION

As stated previously, each of the vendors proceeded with its contract independently. This situation was intensified by the loss of the second plant engineer for 3 months, through fire in another facility. This left only the project manager, with no turnkey contractor, to handle a $17,500,000 project. The project manager was never able to establish or maintain effective communications channels with the project vendors.

Because of a lack of management availability, no one expedited the vendors and there was no tracking of the vendor's manufacturing and fabrication progress. Many of the vendors were not informed that this was a fast-track project, and, subsequently, much of the equipment was not delivered until the project was well into the outage.

The construction management contractor proved to be ineffective. It also became apparent that the steel company had selected a construction contractor who had never installed a process line. The contractor failed to prepare an outage plan or schedule.

The engineer who had been removed from the project because of the fire returned to the project and visited the software, electrical, and controls vendor. He found all facets of this vendor's work behind schedule. It was obvious that there was not enough time for adequate engineering and procurement. He met with the project manager and recommended canceling the outage.

As the outage approached, the construction management and electrical vendors also told the company that the project could not be completed during the allotted outage time. With no realistic critical-path outage schedule, however, the company decided to proceed with the outage, although it was apparent to most stakeholders that there was now little chance of successfully completing the project within the outage schedule.

Several design edicts created additional obstacles. The electrical control scheme, designed in an attempt to salvage usable components, retained most of the existing relay panels and connected them to the new programmable logic controller (PLC). The lack of accurate engineering drawings transformed this project segment into a wiring fiasco.

Regenerative/recuperative burners, specified for the line but never used in this type of application, created additional problems. Much on-the-spot engineering was required to make the burners operate effectively.

Needless to say, the outage was extended an additional 4 weeks. The control vendor eliminated the input/output (I/O) verification process to get the job done in the time allotted for the outage.

These and other administrative and technical problems forced an on-the-fly redesign of the line and a rewrite of the system software, causing even more delay.

TRAINING

No training of any kind was planned or specified and no start-up plan was developed. (Operator training would have been very difficult, under the circumstances, since no one at the time knew how the process was supposed to operate.)

PREOPERATIONAL TESTING/COMMISSIONING

No formal preoperational testing or commissioning plan was developed. Eight to twelve months of trial-and-error tinkering and redesigning was required after the outage to bring the facility to nominal production.

INITIAL OPERATIONS

The initial production results were marginally adequate and maintenance costs were very high. Projected production wasn't reached until well over a year later, and then only on an intermittent basis.

CONCLUSION

The project to modernize the continuous-annealing line was an unmitigated failure. Plant needs were never realized and project objectives were not met. The facility has since never run to specification, and the speed and productivity requirements of the appropriation request were never met.

Most of the factors contributing to the project's failure were a direct result of a project team's muddled fast-track approach to project management. This team didn't really understand the term *fast-track*. (As you recall, we said earlier, *fast-tracking* is a method of saving time and shortening the project schedule by executing two or more identifiable project components concurrently rather than consecutively. To be successful, fast-tracking requires meticulous planning and superior execution.) This manager's misguided approach required an understaffed project team to proceed without process expertise, without proved technology, with inadequate engineering design specifications, and without detailed planning or adequate scheduling. This isn't fast-track; it's *fail*-track!

This true case offers some very valuable lessons. One such lesson is the affirmation of the belief held by many project management experts regarding the ultimate attainment of design capacity and quality. G. Brian Jones, general manager, systems and process control, United States Steel, states, "I believe that in *all* instances where capital projects are ill-conceived, poorly executed and suffer long, drawn-out start-ups, they *never, ever* come up to full capacity or expectations of quality."

Another lesson to be learned is the foolhardiness of crashing ahead into a production outage when not only other knowledgeable people but also good common sense tells you to wait, that you can't possibly make it. Ignoring such warnings would appear to be pure emotionalism, perhaps even ego at work here. Emotional and ego-driven projects usually never live up to expectation.

ON-SITE (PREOPERATIONAL) TESTING

IN GENERAL

Anyone with any knowledge at all of industrial construction or industrial plant operation will know that a new or upgraded facility, regardless of the degree of design sophistication, does not start up with the push of a button on some predetermined or magical start-up date.

A start-up, whether successful or trouble plagued, occurs only after much careful planning and arduous work, and then usually over a segmented schedule period as supporting systems are brought on line.

A start-up can, however, be attained more successfully (read sooner and at a lower cost) if certain preoperational steps are taken. The actual commissioning, or start-up, period, is not the time to be tracing circuits, troubleshooting faulty equipment, or correcting malfunctions. However, if an effective preoperational testing program has not been implemented, these types of problems will in all likelihood occur, and will confuse and delay the planned start-up. This leads us then, to the eighth principle of *Project Bottom-Line Success!*:

> **Preoperational testing is a preemptive strike against start-up problems.**

When construction is approximately 75 to 80 percent complete, or sooner if practical, preoperational testing of equipment and some supporting systems should begin. The preoperational testing and commissioning elements will proceed smoothly if detailed planning has preceded them, and will greatly increase the probability that a successful project start-up will be achieved.

Some will say, "Let's just get this thing built; *then* we'll take care of testing it." But just consider for a moment what they are saying. On a major installation, this testing period may go on over a 4-, 5-, or 6-month period.

In today's highly competitive economic climate, plant owners or investors can't afford the luxury of such long testing and start-up curves. If the preoperational testing element is properly and thoroughly planned and scheduled, testing can complete at approximately the same time as plant mechanical completion. We can *save* that 4, 5, or 6 months of schedule! (See Fig. 37.)

The previous statement assumes, as stated in an earlier chapter, that the preoperational testing and start-up manager was identified when the project team was organized. Preoperational testing usually will not begin at the 75 to 80 percent construction completion point, however, unless the

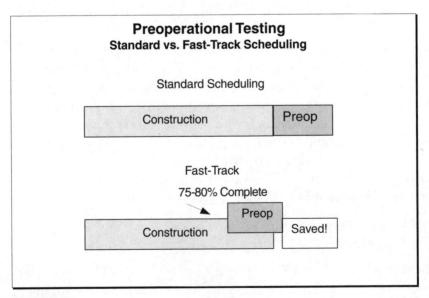

FIGURE 37

designated preoperational testing manager has had *early* input into the construction schedule.

Why is it so important that this position be filled early and that this input occur so early? Because the construction master schedule is being formulated at that time, and without this input, construction planners and schedulers will *not* schedule the construction effort in a manner that lends itself readily to logical, sequential testing.

Construction managers normally prefer to construct by area, i.e., concentrating their forces in area A (see Fig. 38) and, after this area is essentially complete, moving the scaffolding, welding machines, tools, and workers over to area B to begin work there. This process will continue through area C, and so on, until the facility is, in construction parlance, "essentially complete," at which time they will then offer the entire facility over to the project team for testing and start-up.

There is a simple explanation for a construction manager's preference to construct in this manner—this method is more economical. Given the choice, construction managers will structure both their bid and the schedule on this construction pattern.

A well-structured preoperational testing program cannot proceed under this arrangement, however. It is only logical that a testing program must have *systems,* and these systems generally will extend through all areas (see Fig. 39).

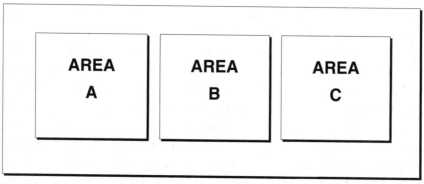

FIGURE 38

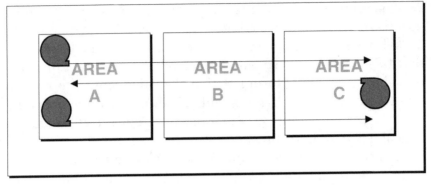

AREA A   AREA B   AREA C

FIGURE 39

If construction forces are approached late in the construction phase with a request for system completion so that preoperational testing can proceed, you'll most likely hear words from construction managers such as, "Sure, but that will be extra. We didn't *bid* it that way!" And they will certainly be within their rights.

However, if the project team has made it clear in the inquiry documents that preoperational testing will occur simultaneously with the last quarter of construction and that *system* turnovers will be required, construction estimators will include this requirement in their bid offering. This fast-track method may result in a slightly higher construction cost, but the yield in earlier profits from a much shorter start-up period will more than make up for the cost-of-construction increase, sometimes many times over!

To make this project element work smoothly, the designated preoperational testing manager must work closely with construction schedulers to form the master construction schedule. The testing manager must make it clear to them the order in which specific systems and individual pieces of equipment must be completed and handed over to testing forces, including the dates required, in order to attain an accelerated start-up schedule. "Scoped-out" drawings, showing the equipment, systems, and supporting control loops, must be turned over to construction forces, along with the dates on which construction must have the equipment and systems ready for turnover to the preoperational testing group.

Using these system descriptions, preoperational testing forces must sit down with the construction contractor's schedulers and ensure that the master construction schedule is formulated to accommodate the required system and equipment start-up dates. A further product of this meeting should be a finalized key events schedule, showing the construction and testing completion dates for all plant systems and major plant equipment.

The preoperational testing and start-up group should follow up this meeting of the minds, so to speak, with development of what we shall refer to as a *detailed sequence schedule*.

The detailed sequence schedule is a computerized listing of all plant equipment. It provides the following information: each piece of equipment by name and number, equipment description, a description of the test to be performed (for example, installation inspection, electrical preoperational test, mechanical preoperational test, run-in, line blowdown, line flush, energization), a "weighted unit" to allow for tracking, and, most important of all, the date on which each test will be performed. (See Fig. 40.)

TEST SEQUENCE SCHEDULE
VACUUM DEGASSER PROJECT
Project No. 147 – Turnover No. 29 – Refractory Repair System

Equipment Number	Equipment Description	Sequence Number	Wtd. Unit	Test Description	Sched. Date	Actual Date
10-52001-103-1	Excess Air Blower	029-055-01	1.0	Instal. Inspec.	08/04/98	/ /
		029-055-02	2.0	Elec. Preop.	08/11/98	/ /
		029-055-03	1.5	Mech. Preop.	08/18/98	/ /
		029-055-04	3.0	Run-in	08/25/98	/ /
10-52001-103-2	Excess Air Blower	029-056-01	1.0	Instal. Inspec.	08/04/98	/ /
		029-056-02	2.0	Elec. Preop.	08/11/98	/ /
		029-056-03	1.5	Mech. Preop.	08/18/98	/ /
		029-056-04	3.0	Run-in	08/25/98	/ /
10-52001-104-1	Recirc. Fan	029-057-01	1.0	Instal. Inspec.	08/04/98	/ /
		029-057-02	2.0	Elec. Preop.	08/11/98	/ /
		029-057-03	1.5	Mech. Preop.	08/18/98	/ /
		029-057-04	3.0	Run-in	08/25/98	/ /

FIGURE 40

It is extremely important that, upon completion, the detailed sequence schedule is forwarded to and then discussed with the construction forces. This discussion is done to obtain agreement that the schedule represents attainable, realistic goals for construction completion and testing.

Concurrently with the development of the detailed sequence schedule, the testing and inspection procedures should be developed, along with the test result forms that will be required in order to capture the testing data as it occurs. The procedures should be "cookbook," leaving as little to chance as possible.

> Some will say that they don't need procedures, that procedures only "slow us down," and that, "I've started up a lot of these plants; with my experience I don't *need* to read a piece of paper!" These are probably the people who have "screwed up" a lot of start-ups! We make enough mistakes when we have detailed procedures; it is foolhardy to attempt to start up or operate complex, modern machinery without them.

TESTING AND START-UP MANUAL (TABLE OF CONTENTS)

The developed procedures and testing schedule should be incorporated into a manual that we will refer to as the *Preoperational Testing and Start-up Manual*. Our suggested table of contents would include:

- *Division of Responsibility.* At testing and start-up time, many interests will be represented on site: construction forces, the preoperational testing and start-up group, vendor representatives, subcontractors, operators, maintenance personnel, project team personnel, engineers, and consultants, just to name a few. It is imperative that clear lines of responsibility and authority be established as they apply to testing and start-up, or the entire effort will become unfocused, resulting in a chaotic, delayed start-up.

- *Sequence Test Schedule.* The previously described detailed sequence schedule should be incorporated into this manual, and excerpts from this section distributed to the cognizant construction superintendents or foremen.

- *Key Events Schedule.* This agreed-upon schedule should not only be incorporated into the manual, but also should be distributed widely throughout the site work areas for posting on bulletin boards.

- *Test Completion Curves Forecast.* The weighted units, as identified on the detailed sequence schedule, should be plotted to a forecast testing curve and posted in the manual. These curves can then be compared to the plot resulting from entering actual weighted unit totals weekly as testing is performed. (Weighted-unit credit is claimed as testing items are completed.) In this manner, a close watch can be held on testing completion status and increasing priority can be put on areas or systems that indicate, by divergence of curves, that they are falling behind.

- *Test Result Forms.* Carefully designed forms to capture all test data should be displayed in the manual. Forms that the project test and start-up manager wish construction or vendors to use should be reproduced and forwarded to them with firm instruction that these are the official forms and the only such documentation that will be accepted. This instruction will help to avoid a hodge-podge of different forms when it comes time to prepare turnover packages for operating and maintenance forces.

- *Test Procedures.* All test procedures should be reviewed and signed off by the cognizant and responsible parties. The final approving signature should be that of the owner project manager. All procedures should be displayed in the manual with reproduced and *numbered* copies distributed to the cognizant and responsible parties. In the event a procedure is changed after it is issued, a revised copy should be sent to all concerned parties with instruction to destroy previous versions.

DEVELOPMENT OF PREOPERATIONAL TESTING PROCEDURES

To help ensure that all critical testing tasks are accomplished and documented, the project team should consider development of procedures for the following:

- Verifying that construction punch list items are complete
- Notifying testing forces that equipment/systems are ready for testing
- Conducting and documenting safety and installation inspection
- Conducting and documenting electrical preoperational tests
- Conducting and documenting mechanical preoperational tests
- Conducting and documenting equipment run-ins
- Conducting and documenting instrumentation testing
- Conducting and documenting on-site integrated testing of process controls
- Completing and documenting final completion list items
- Conducting and documenting final safety inspection
- Conducting and documenting equipment performance demonstrations
- Compiling and turning over test documentation and turnover packages
- Turning over the facility for commissioning

When we point out these "procedural necessities" in one of our *PBLS* project management workshops, we usually hear a lot of ohs and ahs, along with statements such as, "But we don't have the time or the people to do this" or "It's too expensive—we would overrun our budget; we can't afford to do it!"

My answer is always the same—you can't afford *not* to do it. Remember what we said earlier—we make enough mistakes when we *have* detailed procedures; to attempt to start up new, complex equipment and/or systems without them is just asking for trouble.

Now, to help you in getting a good head start on *your* next project, we have included many of these needed procedures in the back of this book, under App. B. Although these procedures are generic in word and format, they should provide you with a good basis for developing your own more specific procedures. (In some cases, you may be able to adapt ours, almost verbatim). Additionally, many of the forms you might use with these procedures are also provided in App. A.

TESTING DEFINITIONS

This would probably be a good time not only to review the definitions of both construction and preoperational testing, but also to point out the absolute necessity of completing these project-testing elements prior to the commissioning phase (which is the actual introduction of feedstock).

Construction testing. Construction testing is the testing performed by the construction contractor prior to turnover to the preoperational testing group. This is normal construction testing and usually includes wiring ring-out, motor bump, and a mechanical completion punch list. Other construction testing requirements may include pressure tests, line flushes and blowdowns, and rotating-equipment alignment. These tests, however, will probably be under the direction of, or at the least witnessed by, the preoperational testing group.

Preoperational testing. Preoperational testing, on the other hand, is more advanced testing that demonstrates both the functionality and reliability of equipment and systems. This testing, which *must* be well-documented, should be performed by procedure and will include such items as:
- Detailed installation inspections
- Freedom-of-rotation checks
- Lubrication checks

- Coupling alignment verification
- Line blow-down and flushes
- Wiring verification
- Uncoupled motor run
- Equipment run-in
- Instrument calibration and loop checks
- Control system simulations
- Bearings and gears; temperature and vibration checks
- Component sizing (fuses, overloads)

As preoperational testing commences, the project team would be well-advised to examine the project safety considerations, that is, the safety procedures, the safety program, the safety *attitudes* prevailing. Why? Because things are about to change! Equipment that has been inert or unmoving since installation, perhaps for months, can suddenly start up, either intentionally or inadvertently, and can pose a danger to personnel in the immediate area. Previously dead electrical circuits can suddenly become energized. Safety of personnel should be the number one priority of any project team. No project schedule is worth human life.

> We were just into the preoperational testing and start-up of a large nickel mine and smelting operation in Indonesia. In the course of initial testing and start-up of the huge forced-draft fan in the furnace area, the usual steps had been taken. The area had been "walked down" and roped off, and people in the immediate area had been warned that this large rotating equipment was about to be turned on for the first time. We hit the start button, and the large fan wound up like a jet engine. Imagine our surprise when three Indonesian workers came flying out of the open end of the huge ductwork! (Imagine *their* surprise!) These workers had been catching a nap several feet back in and around a bend of the duct and hadn't heard the warnings. Moral: We should have checked it out more thoroughly. This time, we were lucky; the workers were only shaken up. Too often, these situations end in more tragic circumstances.

The goal of a good preoperational testing program is to reveal any equipment faults or weaknesses *before* commissioning. If a malfunction is to occur, it is far better to have it occur during this period than later when the malfunction would delay the start-up. Also, an equipment or component malfunction during start-up could be mistaken for a process or design flaw and create confusion.

Equipment suppliers should be on hand to assist in the testing and commissioning of the equipment and systems they have provided. The project team should review the terms of all purchase orders to ensure that suppliers are providing the amount and length of service promised. Some major suppliers may be called upon later, during commissioning, to prove the capability of their equipment or systems in performance demonstration runs.

If needed, the project team should not hesitate to call in engineering specialists or consultants. Sometimes, when unusual problems arise, a knowledgeable consultant can get you from here to there in a much shorter time than can your project team. It might be the best money spent on the project!

Let's discuss for a moment the mechanics, so to speak, of how best to handle the actual testing and commissioning phase, i.e., team makeup, interfaces, scheduling, tracking, reporting, etc.

Please refer, if you will, to one of our definitions, the definition of preoperational testing:

> *Preoperational testing:* That testing performed by the designated preoperational testing and start-up group upon notification by the construction manager that a system, subsystem, or equipment is mechanically complete, and which will demonstrate that the system, subsystem, or equipment is reliable and ready to safely perform its function in the process. Preoperational testing includes installation inspections, electrical and mechanical functional checks, and run-in without product.

The "designated preoperational testing group" will vary from project to project. On the smaller projects, the preop and start-up functions are usually handled by the client project team and plant forces, aided as necessary by the equipment supplier or suppliers. Larger projects, however, will usually require the services of a professional consulting company specializing in the testing and start-up function.

These companies will not only perform the testing and start-up function, they can also *plan* this phase in detail. However, the contracting out of preoperational testing and start-up functions does not, in any way, reduce the responsibility of the project team to manage this phase of the project; it simply makes the job a little easier.

There are many ways to organize and work a contracted preop and start-up group into the team. One good way is to "shadow" the contractor with a project team member monitoring each contractor position (see Fig. 41). By the way, don't be too concerned about "duplication of effort." You can be sure of one thing—if it's like most projects, there's plenty of work for everyone.

As testing completes, equipment should be thoroughly run in. Run-in period length will vary, depending on several factors. One, obviously, is the manufacturer's recommendation. In all cases, equipment run-in time should not be less than

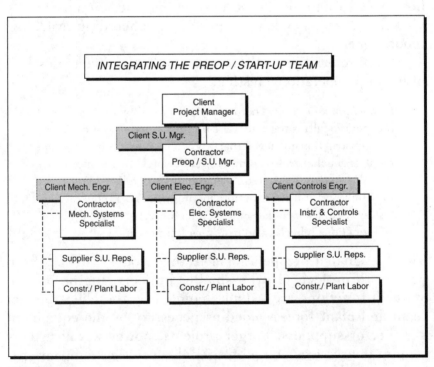

FIGURE 41

that recommended by the supplier. Another and more important consideration when determining run-in length is test reading stabilization.

During run-in, if meaningful testing is being accomplished, a number of readings will be taken—bearing temperatures, vibration readings, motor loads, etc. The run-in should continue until all readings have stabilized, that is, until the equipment has reached a steady state of operation.

> A project manager once told me, when discussing the need to take a series of bearing temperatures on a newly installed production line, "I don't need to waste time taking all these readings; I can tell when a bearing is too hot just by putting my hand on it." "Of course you can," I replied, "so can I—but I can't tell if it's getting hotter, or when it's going to *stop* getting hotter!"

Upon completion of satisfactory testing, the equipment and/or system should be demonstrated and turned over to the operating forces. The equipment should be started up from a cold condition and, according to procedure, put through its paces. Manual, automatic, and emergency shutdowns should be demonstrated by introducing over- or undertemperatures, pressures, flows, speeds, etc. to the sensing element that would initiate the control signal. All related instrumentation, including alarms and shutdown flags on electrical relaying instruments, gauges, dials, and recorders should be included in the demonstration. When operation is properly tested, *and demonstrated,* the preoperational testing team should have no problem in gaining acceptance from the commissioning team and turning the system over to them.

All testing must be thoroughly documented. The importance of complete documentation cannot be overstated. The readings taken serve not only as indication of testing parameters satisfied, but also as valuable baseline documentation for the plant operating and maintenance forces. The documented results of the testing phase are snapshots of the equipment when it was new. Future trends will be based on this documentation, these baseline readings. Additionally, start-up problems are much easier to solve when there is solid data to analyze!

A case in point came to our attention recently, a case that demonstrates how lack of a carefully planned and well-executed preoperational testing program can lead to problems later on, during the start-up period. We call it the Achilles' Cone Case.

Cooling the Achilles' Cone

In ancient Greek mythology, legend has it that the Styx river flows through the nether world of Hades. Were you to be immersed in this river and somehow able to rejoin the mortal world, you would be invincible to any mere mortal weapons. Further, according to legend, the only mortal to have accomplished this was Achilles, the greatest of all Greek warriors who, at birth, was immersed in this river by his mother and was thereafter totally immune to his enemies' arrows and spears—all except for his heel, where his mother had held him tightly as he was immersed. Thus, Achilles' heel was vulnerable, and he was later slain in battle when a Trojan's poisoned arrow struck him in that single vulnerable spot.

HISTORICAL SYNOPSIS—BACKGROUND

The success of other projects is no guarantee your own project will follow suit. What appeared to be a no-brainer to the Engineering group of a southeastern integrated steel manufacturer ultimately turned into a no-gainer that cost over 4 days of lost production time and created the potential of severe injury to personnel.

Improvements in refractory materials and practices have enhanced basic oxygen process (BOP) vessels to the point where significantly more heats can be produced before a reline is necessary. However, the BOP vessel of the southeastern steel manufacturer had an "Achilles' heel": the vessel's cone section. Wear and tear on the cone was severe enough that replacement was required during every reline operation. The engineering group considered various solutions to the problem and decided that a more economical approach would be an upgrade to a water-cooled cone.

To verify the proposed solution, a team of operating, mainte-nance, and engineering personnel visited several BOP shops where water-cooled cones were in service. The team was favorably impressed. User experience indicated that water-cooled cones had the potential to last through at least five campaigns before requiring replacement. (At the time of the visits, none of the cones had been in service for more than five campaigns.) Thus far, none of the observed water-cooled cones had required replacement. Plant personnel at the visited sites reported no problems with their cones. After reviewing several designs, the project team agreed on the following:

- Piping for the cone would be connected in series with the water-cooled trunnion ring.

- The successful bidder would design, build, and deliver a complete cone.

- Plant personnel would install the cone. With the exception of piping, the new cone could be installed in the same manner as the old cone.

- A contractor would install the water connections.

PROJECT EXECUTION

During the prebid meetings, engineering provided the necessary existing equipment drawings; however, those drawings did not clearly highlight the water supply arrangement. Also, the project team conveyed its requirements to the contractors but did not document those discussions.

After an acceptable bid was selected (the successful bidder was a Japanese firm that had designed and built water-cooled cones for 12 BOP shops), the appropriation was submitted. Among the other budgetary items, funds were requested for preoperational testing and a contingency; all requests were approved. The successful bidder's local engineering office was assigned the tasks of detail design and construction supervision.

During the review stage of the design, the steel company hired another engineering firm to check the piping route for any interference with the vessel supports and any effects on the trunnion ring strength. On the basis of the engineering firm's report, the routing was revised to minimize stress in the ring and to maintain clearances. In addition, the cone manufacturer made corrections to the drawings and proceeded with fabrication.

To ensure the quality of work, weld inspections, measurements, and static pressure tests were performed during assembly. The cone was completed several months ahead of the scheduled reline.

In preparation for installation, drilling and welding quality parameters were established for the piping work. The reline schedule was developed so piping would occur concurrently with the cone-changing activities and other repairs. A structural inspection of the trunnion was included in the scope of reline work.

Extensive cracks were found in the trunnion interior during inspection. The steel company's Engineering department was aware of the cracks, but they did not take into consideration how extensive the cracks actually were. Piping installation was delayed until repairs to the trunnion's interior were made. However, the connections were finished prior to completion of the crack repair work, so no time was lost for that project phase.

TESTING

Engineering knew about the cracks in the trunnion ring yet took no action to adjust the schedule. Repairing the cracks would take additional time that cut into the scheduled downtime. Engineering made the decision to not test intermediate piping stages to compensate for the shortened downtime.

In order to check the piping without affecting other work in progress, an air pressure test was set up. The drain ends of the piping were blanked, and the water shutoff valve was used to seal the supply side. The test revealed a forgotten gasket and several loose flange bolts that needed tightening. Pressure was maintained for several hours, then the piping was bled and the blanks were removed. Water was not turned on at this time since welding was still not finished on the cracks in the trunnion. It was decided to close the trunnion ring when repairs were completed, then flow-test the full-flow path through the cone and the trunnion ring together; however, this test did not take place. The decision to not fully test the cone as originally planned came back to haunt the project team later.

During the construction phase, the project team experienced a turnover of key operating and maintenance personnel. Additionally, no formal, written commissioning report was ever developed, a fact that would later impact the project.

START-UP AND INITIAL OPERATIONS

Upon completion of the reline, the system was put into operation. Within a short time, problems began to surface. Leaks developed at the piping flange connections. In each case, either the flange bolts were loose or the gasket failed. Engineering felt that the bolts must have been loosened either by vibration or from stretching because of radiant heat. High-temperature gaskets and stainless steel bolts were installed; the bolts were tightened by using higher torque. Steel temperature near the piping was measured at 700°F; the water channels on the cone were at about 300°F. These measurements convinced

Engineering that temperature was the problem, so changes to increase the flange fitting size were initiated.

After a few weeks of operation, several small leaks were discovered in the cone piping. The manufacturer of the cone could not explain why the leaks were developing and stated that no cone designed by it had experienced a similar problem, either now or in the past.

The vessel was again taken out of service for leak repairs. During this downtime, the flanges connecting the water piping to the cone were loosened, then water was turned on to observe flow at the flanges.

What happened next was completely unexpected. The water did not come from the inlet, but appeared at the outlet of the cone, coming from the trunnion ring. Looking closely at the existing drawings of the supply side trunnion block, engineers discovered a note indicating that the view shown was of the return side trunnion block. From the view, the water supply side block was upside down. This discovery indicated that the piping to the cone was connected to a closed cavity and that water was bypassing the cone completely and entering the cone only on *backflow* when the vessel was rotated. High pressure from steam generated in the partially filled cone, which was blocked at the supply end, caused the leaks.

Water piping was disconnected from the cone and the vessel was returned to service in an uncooled, dry state until a plan for correcting the pipe routing could be developed. A 4-day outage was scheduled to correct the piping and repair all leaks in the cone. Piping between the cone and the trunnion was revised to reduce the number of connections. This time, the water route was checked for flow entering *and* exiting the cone, and a pressure test was run to detect leaks. After these modifications were performed, there were no further problems with either leaks or lack of cooling to the cone.

CONCLUSION

Achilles, the greatest of all ancient Greek warriors, was dipped in the river Styx by his mother to make him invincible. However, the part of his body that was not dipped in the river, his heel, ultimately lead to his death during the Trojan War.

Poor planning and poor communication can topple any project, the one being discussed no exception. Poor planning and overlooked details resulted in 4 days plus 12 hours of lost production and brought serious personnel injury risk. (The problem was discovered not by design, but by luck.) Poor planning and oversight was the "Achilles' cone" of this project. Had a sound preoperational testing and start-up plan been developed and then strictly adhered to, this project would, in all probability, have had a much happier ending.

COMMISSIONING!

Commissioning, the initial operation of the systems in a production mode, encompasses introduction of feedstock and demonstration of plant design capability and product quality. During commissioning, as the project team, operations, suppliers of equipment, and technical support personnel begin to put the new systems through their paces, it is doubly important to follow procedural methodology and to document all the changing variables. (If a problem does occur, lack of this documentation can sometimes delay problem resolution.)

If the project has been well planned, well designed, and well executed, the start-up, or commissioning, phase should be uneventful, almost a nonevent. Some project management consultants pride themselves on how well they can help a client company work through the problems of start-up and get into production. Personally, I'd rather have a dull, boring start-up with absolutely no surprises! In either case, one thing that can help get a project team through the commissioning phase of a project sooner, rather than later, is planning.

One of the major purposes of extensive project planning throughout all project elements is to ensure that initial and continued operation of a new facility is conducted safely, efficiently, economically, and *as soon as possible*. When this is accomplished, the learning curve is short and the facility operates as designed. Result: the new facility or installation begins immediately to return the investment of resources that have gone into its creation.

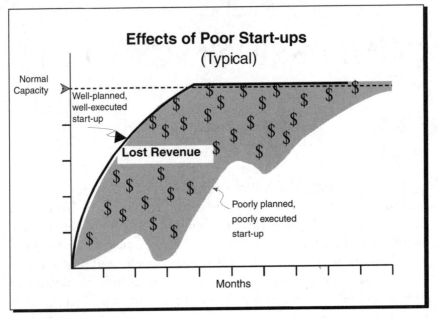

FIGURE 42

The absolute importance of an as-short-as-possible learning curve cannot be overstated. Every day, every week, every month that passes before the facility or production unit attains design capacity results in lost revenue, revenue that would have gone to the venture's bottom line (see Fig. 42). The sad part is, this is revenue that is lost forever; *it will never, ever be regained*. On large capital projects, these lost revenues can mount into the millions of dollars!

KEY CONSIDERATIONS FOR COMMISSIONING

Although a complete listing of all the important factors that the project team should take into consideration would take up several pages (since *all* items are important!), we shall list here the elements within the commissioning phase of any capital project that we would consider key, or absolutely essential, to a successful start-up.

DEVELOPMENT OF A COMMISSIONING PLAN

Probably the most important piece of the project management puzzle is the commissioning plan. Yet, time after time, the commissioning plan is a last-minute, ill-conceived, quickly put together chronology of events that the project team hopes will happen by a certain date, given that there are no problems.

Hannibal Smith, the fictional leader of the A Team, concluded each episode by lighting a cigar and saying, "I love it when a plan comes together!" Wouldn't it be nice to make the same declaration at the end of your next project? You can, you know; it just takes proper planning. Let's take a look at some of the salient features of a commissioning plan.

Start-up Objectives. Preliminary start-up objectives should have been identified early in the project—back in the conceptual stages. Why? Because the start-up duration and the strategies to be employed to obtain the best product mix at start-up will affect the cost of the project. As the project becomes better defined, as equipment selections are made, as primary suppliers and their systems are selected, the start-up plan must be refined. Remember, we stated earlier, "Start-up begins at the beginning, not the end, of a project."

Provide for Adequate Staffing. The project manager must recognize the need to provide adequate staffing for start-up early in the project planning. To wait until preoperational testing and start-up begins is to wait too long. If the need is for discipline engineers, they should be brought aboard early enough to help in the planning of the start-up. If the need is for third-party assistance, this should be a part of *preappropriation* planning, or the budget probably won't allow for it. Most experienced project managers know the importance of adequate staffing for start-up; it is usually the less experienced or first-time project managers who feel cocky enough to go at it with marginal team strength. Usually, they fail.

Develop the Start-up Procedures. The designated project start-up manager should develop procedures for every facet of the start-up. (Actually, start-up procedures should be developed in tandem with the preoperational testing procedures since, in many cases, they both address the same issues, i.e., the start-up and running of equipment and systems.) We say *every* facet of the project for a very good reason—we miss enough details when we *have* procedures; we will *certainly* miss details when we don't! Some of the procedures that might be required are:

- Detailed safety checkout procedures
- Valve lineup procedures
- Detailed operating procedures
- Procedures for heat-up or cooldown
- Procedures for capturing technical data
- Procedures for handling nonconformance items
- Procedures for sampling and for quality control
- Procedures for guaranteed performance testing
- Procedures for satisfying environmental-permitting requirements
- Procedures for turnover to operating forces

Ensure That As-Built Drawings Are on Hand.   One of the most exasperating events that can be experienced during a start-up period occurs when one is attempting to troubleshoot a process or equipment problem and the wiring or mechanical configuration is found not to correspond with the drawings. This is caused, in almost all cases, by failure early in the project to set in place detailed procedures regarding the design change documentation. Lack of this planning will inevitably lead to start-up delay.

Refinement of Start-up Objectives.   Start-up objectives should have been identified very early in project planning. As the project firmed up, i.e., as selection of equipment, systems, and components became firm orders, the start-up objectives may have required refinement. For example, the planned product mix may have changed; the method of start-up, of bypass operation, of start-up sequence may have changed or been slightly modified. As the final start-up plan is developed, nothing should be left hanging.

Review the Commissioning Plan with All Parties.   On large projects, there will be numerous entities represented on site, especially as the project nears start-up. Besides the project team, there will be operations personnel, vendor service engineers, third-party consultants and testing engineers, and possibly environmental or other official agencies. Start-up is no time to be keeping secrets (unless of course there are proprietary process secrets); the wise project start-up manager will call all parties into meeting prior to actual start-up and review the plan with them. Lack of knowledge can be dangerous.

Establish Firm Lines of Communication and Authority. Let there be no misunderstanding in regard to exactly who is calling the shots regarding start-up. This issue sometimes becomes confused when major suppliers are involved; they tend to forget just who is the buyer and who is the seller! The project start-up manager must make clear the requirement for detailed documentation of all start-up operations, i.e., readings, test numbers, changes made as process optimization proceeds, loading, process parameters, etc. The project start-up manager must also make it clear that all communications regarding the start-up phase must flow through his or her office. Instructions or authorizations to proceed with the various segments of the start-up plan must be firm and unequivocal. Firm leadership is imperative; ambiguity is dangerous and will lead to confusion and a chaotic start-up.

START-UP OF ANCILLARY AND SUPPORT SYSTEMS

Most, if not all, of the supporting systems will be required to be up and running prior to energizing, or bringing up, the production equipment. We're speaking here of electrical systems, instrument air, cooling water, fire protection, process gases, environmental protection systems, and any others not classified as production equipment. Since, in most cases, it is impossible to run the primary production system or systems without these supporting systems, it is obvious that these systems hold as much importance as the primary systems to the start-up. Unfortunately, many project teams fail to recognize this factor and give short shrift to the proper testing, run-in, and start-up of the support systems. The result is usually a poorly executed facility start-up with many delays for supporting equipment and systems corrections.

Field and Control Room Checks.   All instrumentation should have been bench-checked prior to ancillary systems start-up. A field-to-control-room loop check should have been performed to verify proper operation of the entire instrument loop. Instrument and loop-check data should be recorded, including the settings of all controllers, relief valves, limit switches, etc., for later turnover to permanent operating and maintenance forces. This is valuable baseline data, providing a snapshot of these systems when they are new. (After some future tweaking, someone just may want to get back to the starting point!)

Begin the Turning over of Systems and Documentation to Permanent Operating Forces.   Once the support or ancillary systems are up and running and all instrumentation indicates that the operation is nominal and reliable, turnover to permanent operating forces should begin. The start-up, stabilization, fine tuning, and performance testing of primary equipment may take some time; there is no point in the project team's continuing to use its resources in the operation of the proved ancillary or support systems. Start up, demonstrate, and turn over these systems, along with the completed turnover package. The *turnover package* is a complete compilation of the data, procedures, settings, and vendor literature pertaining to the system. The turnover package is further discussed in the section titled "Turnover of Documentation" later in this chapter.

COMMISSIONING: THE INTRODUCTION OF FEEDSTOCK

As stated earlier, the project's commissioning or start-up phase is not the time to be solving equipment problems; these should have been taken care of earlier, in the preoperational testing phase. If the preparatory steps have been properly carried out, the start-up itself should be almost an anticlimax. However, there are many important steps to be taken in the commissioning phase, if this anticlimax is to actually be achieved. In the first place, permanent operating personnel should be playing a key role in the start-up—in some instances, running it. Outside staffing for the start-up will certainly be provided by vendors, consultants, and the bulk of the engineering project team. But when it comes to making product, operators rule! However, this is the time when good planning and discipline will make a real difference. The plant operators are eager to get the plant running as soon as possible, while the engineers', vendors', and consultants' motivation is more toward process confirmation rather than the achievement of an instant production record. On top of this, plant management usually tends to underestimate the need for timely application of key personnel during the start-up period. Start-up is not an easy task. It requires teamwork and individuals who are enthusiastic and flexible. The hours are unusually long and tiresome. However, the satisfaction of a good start-up makes up for a lot of tiresome hours spent bringing it off.

Gradual Ramp-up of Systems. In commissioning new equipment and systems, it is usually best to "crawl before you walk; walk before you run." This is especially true if you have the option of a production mix. Start with the simplest product and gradually ramp up to the more complex products. This isn't, by the way, a decision that should be played by ear. The product mix should have been determined much earlier, during start-up plan refinement. Keeping to the scheduled ramp-up and the predetermined product mix may be more difficult than it sounds here. Management may take a keen interest at this time and begin insisting that ramp-up proceed at a more rapid pace. They smell *profit* and, perhaps, a betterment of the projected ROI. However, the project manager must resist the pressure to change the start-up plan. Changes such as those that are based on emotion are usually not well thought out, and can lead to delay and a stumbling or erratic start-up curve. By the way, if the project team does give in to these pressures and the result is a problem-ridden and delayed start-up, who do you think will get the blame—Management?

Fine Tuning and Documentation.   As the system or systems are brought up, engineers and operators will undoubtedly adjust and fine-tune the process in their attempt to bring the system to design capacity as quickly as possible. Fine tuning of the process is certainly usual in any start-up. However, the adjustments, *any adjustments,* must be accompanied by complete documentation of the change. If this is not done (and in too many instances it is not), problem solving can be significantly delayed. By "significant" we're talking extra weeks, months, or even *years* of production that can't be brought to design capacity. By failure to document all testing and process adjustments, one can make it next to impossible to track a design problem or deficiency. Resultant revenue losses can be disastrous.

The Guaranteed Performance Test.   During the start-up period, equipment vendors and major suppliers will usually be required to demonstrate the design capability of the equipment or systems they have provided. These tests or performance runs are intended to prove contractual obligations, and the project team and plant operators must monitor and evaluate them very carefully. Any nonconformance must be corrected and the performance run recycled to the beginning. Detailed procedures should be in place for the performance demonstrations.

System Acceptance.   Likewise, a detailed procedure outlining Operations' method of acceptance must also be in place. When contractual obligations are fulfilled, Operations must accept. To drag out acceptance of an obviously operational unit or system is not only contractually illegal, but also unethical. These situations are usually a result of animosities that have been built during project execution and reflect the project team's lack of sound planning and management. ("Why the project team?" you ask. Because if contractor deficiencies were the problem, the project team should have moved to nip the problem in the bud!)

Consultants. There may be several consultants and contractor experts on site during the commissioning phase. The project team's job is to get these specialists on site at exactly the right time to support their area of project expertise and then to get them off site as soon as possible. The project team should meet with the consultant or specialist upon his or her arrival at site, not only to inform the specialist of the project team's expectations but also to summarize the status of the project, site rules, safety procedures, lines of communication, and anything else that might help in accomplishing the task at hand. The specialist's activities should be closely monitored and, before departure from site, an exit interview should be conducted by cognizant project team members. The interview is intended to make sure that no small piece of information is overlooked, information that might lead to a more successful start-up.

Prompt Resolution of Problems. If the project has been initiated, planned, and executed properly, let's hope the problems will be nonexistent or minuscule! However, if a problem is encountered, the project team must take steps to analyze and solve it completely. Never, ever, should a project team demobilize and leave a problem unsolved. The solution of process problems, however, can sometimes be elusive. That is why it is so vitally important that every start-up action and reaction be fully documented. Without this intelligence, problem resolution may impact the start-up date and, eventually, the promised project benefits.

Quality Tests, Sampling, and Environmental Checks. The product mix that is produced during the commissioning and ramp-up phase is valuable and is intended, in almost all cases, to be a marketable product. Quality procedures must be in place, with constant monitoring of quality. This monitoring may involve "cuts" or samples taken from the line or process. To accomplish this, sampling procedures, equipment, and knowledgeable technicians must be available and ready during the first and subsequent runs.

Environmental checks may be required as a condition of permitting. Failure to supply these mandated checks may cause a shutdown of the facility or a delay in permission to start up. In today's world, environmental issues are an absolute priority item on almost every project.

TURNOVER OF DOCUMENTATION

The data collected during construction testing, preoperational testing, and commissioning must be neatly packaged and turned over to the operating and maintenance forces. The best format for data collation and turnover is the "turnover package," wherein all documents that have been kept on file throughout these phases is collated by system or major equipment item and plainly labeled. The turnover package should contain a table of contents and all the original data sheets, forms, and instrument settings. This valuable information will serve as baseline data for the permanent operating and maintenance forces. The importance of getting this information into the right hands cannot be overstated. Additionally, all warranty information must be entered into the warranty tracking system so that warranty work can be charged to the proper entity.

GAUGING THE SUCCESS OF THE START-UP

The start-up may be a roaring success, but the project as a whole may be a failure. On the other hand, the preceding elements of the project may have been executed flawlessly, but the planned 8-week start-up dragged on for 18 months, practically bankrupting the venture. The point here is that the project must be viewed in its entirety. We can't take one part of the effort and say, "Well, at least that part was a success." It just doesn't work that way. The phases, or elements of a project are interdependent, and failure in any area will usually lead to the same outcome; delays, budget overruns, and long drawn-out start-ups. Let's close out this chapter with a case in point.

CASE STUDY 8

PLTCM and CA Line—"Where Did We Go So Wrong?"

HISTORICAL SYNOPSIS—CONTRACT AWARD

In 1985 a large, American integrated steel company entered into a joint venture with a major Asian steel company to revitalize an outdated and unprofitable finishing plant on the U.S. West Coast. The joint venture was incorporated under the name AmRok Steel. The two joint venture partners were to split the project costs 50/50, and the AmRok Project Team was comprised of management personnel from both partner companies. The American partner, however, supplied a majority of the project personnel and generally held the upper hand in the decision-making process.

The existing facility was composed of cold-rolled sheet and tin mills, with tinning, galvanizing, and pickling facilities. The overall project goal was to replace the existing facility with a new continuous annealing (CA) line. Both the CA line and the pickle line tandem cold mill (PLTCM) were designed to handle both sheet and tin products, although sheet would be the primary product. Also included in the project was an automated coil handling facility that would transfer product between the PLTCM, the CA line, and other existing facilities.

AmRok management personnel selected Obilisk, Inc., an international engineering/design/manufacturing firm, as the primary contractor. Obilisk, in turn, selected the major subcontractors, with input and approval from the AmRok project team. The PLTCM was planned and constructed first, with the CA line to start up shortly after the PLTCM and coil-handling facility. Plant start-up was to coincide with an orderly shutdown of the old facilities. Although the project team had prepared no detailed start-up plan, the line operation checkout was performed in a systematic way (bypass mode, followed by cold and hot trials). Unfortunately, these trials were conducted on the fly and without documentation. In addition, no integrated testing had been performed on the control system prior to installation, and operator training had been less than optimum.

Obilisk selected a nonunion contractor to perform construction for both the PLTCM and the CA line and chose a well-known electrical firm to design and install the electrics and controls on the PLTCM. Originally, Obilisk had intended to award the CA line's electrics and controls contract to the same company. Although AmRok agreed with this plan, high-level managers from the American partner's headquarters overruled AmRok and Obilisk, deciding that the CA line electrics should be designed and installed by Zebest Electrics, Inc.

Zebest was widely acknowledged throughout the industry as the undisputed premier designer and supplier of electrics and controls for process lines of this nature. The decision to award the CA line contract to Zebest was based on the American partner's belief that a company of Zebest's experience and track record was required in order to ensure that the CA line's electrics and controls could adequately handle both sheet and tin products.

According to the CA line's appropriation and specification, the line was to operate at a maximum speed of 750 ft/min with a throughput of 655 tons/turn for sheet product and a maximum speed of 1975 ft/min with a throughput of 454 tons/turn for tin.

HISTORICAL SYNOPSIS—CONTRACT PERFORMANCE

Project design, procurement, and construction proceeded primarily as scheduled. Zebest Electrics, Inc. designed and installed the CA line's drive systems, electrics, and controls with only construction supervision and oversight from AmRok, Obilisk, and the American parent company. After all, AmRok had paid a steep price to acquire Zebest's expertise and services; AmRok had employed the best in the business and felt secure that the Zebest name would guarantee that the electrical drive and control systems would meet contract specifications.

The PLTCM was started up in mid-1988, along with the coil-handling facility. The CA line went into production in early 1989 and slowly began ramping up in an effort to achieve the production rates identified in the appropriation.

Prior to actual start-up of the CA line, many weeks were spent running the line in a bypass mode. Bypassing the furnace allowed engineers to check out and tune up the basic strip-transport system and debug line sequencing, without expending the time and money incurred by threading the furnace.

After the CA line's furnace was threaded, additional weeks were spent running the line with no heat on the furnace, "cold trials," and tuning up the furnace tension regulators. Following this, hot trials were conducted to fine-tune the furnace tension-control system. By systematically conducting these various trial runs, first in bypass mode, then in cold and hot trials, start-up engineers made every effort to ensure that the furnace drive systems and controls were operating properly.

The initial CA operation in 1989 was poor because of a variety of entry-end sequencing problems. The PLTCM and automatic coil-handling system were experiencing difficulties of their own, and consequently impacted the CA line operation. In addition, the line was plagued by strip breaks in the furnace. CA line production increased very slowly and peaked in 1992 at 430 tons/turn sheet and 350 tons/turn tin, well below the appropriation level. The subpar production levels meant that the DCF-ROI targets were also being missed—*big time.*

For a period of over 3 years, 1989–1992, CA line operation was supported by two full-time Zebest field service personnel under a maintenance contract. Technical support from the Zebest field service engineers was limited primarily to assisting AmRok with line malfunctions. The focus of the technical support was maintenance of the line to retain the status quo rather than to provide analysis and proactive effort to bring the line production up to appropriation levels.

The role of the Zebest field service engineers became a point of contention. For the price they were paying, some AmRok managers, as well as managers from the American parent company, expected the Zebest personnel to assume responsibility for bringing the CA line up to targeted production levels, not to just provide reactive maintenance support whenever a malfunction occurred. However, the fact was that the Zebest personnel were there under a maintenance contract, and AmRok had not specifically defined what duties the Zebest personnel were to perform, other than basic maintenance support. Also, the AmRok team did not inform Zebest management that they were dissatisfied with the scope of support being provided. Therefore, no effort was made by Zebest management to alter the situation.

By mid-1992, CA line management personnel, as well as the Zebest field service engineers, concluded that line operation had reached optimum performance levels, even though production was still far below appropriation levels.

With CA line production levels below appropriation, engineering managers at the American parent company, along with a group of engineers from AmRok, were unwilling to accept that optimum performance levels had been achieved. Consequently, they undertook efforts to determine why a successful start-up had eluded them and what could be done to remedy the situation.

FINDINGS

In mid-1992, a chart recording surfaced showing a CA line furnace tension oscillation having a period of 60 seconds. Suspicions immediately turned to the furnace tension regulating systems. When questioned about the 60-second oscillation period, the Zebest field engineers indicated that they considered this insignificant.

Initial investigations revealed that there were tension transients that were totally unacceptable, and that the tension regulating system had been detuned. (The gear motors supplied by Zebest to drive the furnace rolls had significant backlash. This fact, coupled with the inertia of the rolls, resulted in unstable speed-regulating system operation. The speed-regulating system was subsequently *detuned* to prevent tension oscillation.) In addition, no documentation (chart recordings) showing the original tune-up or the subsequent detuning could be located. Complicating the situation further, the field prints had not been marked up.

On the strength of these findings, AmRok hired a third-party consulting firm to evaluate the CA line's entire regulating scheme. The outside firm's investigation revealed that drive-system problems existed in all sections of the CA line. After an in-depth analysis, the firm concluded that the drive systems and controls designed and supplied by Zebest were totally inadequate for the job, including both hardware and software. The bottom-line cause of the low production rate was that the drive systems could not react quickly enough to properly regulate line speed and tension change requirements. Consequently, operators were *running the line slow* to avoid strip breaks and downtime. In addition, random line stops were occurring frequently, because of incorrect protective interlocking.

CONCLUSION

The project to replace the outdated facilities with a PLTCM and CA line was far more costly than anticipated, primarily because of the inability of the CA line to attain its sheet and tin products' productivity goals. The failure of the project to produce as planned subsequently endangered the joint venture's ultimate goal: namely, to reach profitability for both partners according to the appropriation's

DCF-ROI projection, while achieving low-cost, high-quality producer status for their customers.

The immediate cause of the CA line project failure can be said to have resulted from the inadequacy of the Zebest-supplied drive systems and controls. However, the root of the problem was in the project's management. Not only did this project team abrogate its responsibilities of superintendence—of close examination of the design philosophy being used by their big-name supplier, Zebest, and of monitoring and questioning the activities of the contractor's field team—but they also came up quite short in the basic requirements of project management.

"Where did we go so wrong?" How about training? How about start-up planning? How about documentation? How about giving up, and saying, "That's as good as it gets?"

After revisiting the problem of slow running for 3½ years (and through many millions of lost-revenue dollars), the control system was redesigned and the line was brought to capacity (even to exceed design capacity). The sad part is, *it could have been there the first time.*

PROJECT-RELATED TRAINING

In a world brimming with ever more sophisticated technology, it is sometimes easy to put too much faith in machines and diminish the role of humans in the work process. It seems, however, that the simpler we try to make the job, the more complex it becomes. For this reason, there is no substitute for good training. One of the most critical aspects of achieving *Project Bottom-Line Success!* is ensuring that permanent operating and maintenance forces are ready to assume control of the plant. This can be achieved only through training, and its criticality is expressed in the seventh PBLS principle:

> **The ultimate success of any project or venture is dependent not only on how well you design or build, but also on how well you train those who will operate and maintain.**

We have seen, in case after case, the detrimental effects of lack of training. These effects can sometimes be seen in long, problem-ridden start-ups and, in some cases, in accidents resulting in personal injury and damaged equipment. The results will usually show up in a measurable part of the project, the learning curve. A *learning curve* can be defined as:

> The percentage of reduction in average costs as output and/or production increases. More generally, a learning curve refers to the time and cost of familiarizing personnel with the requirements of performing specific tasks and functions.

This definition may sound like a very simple statement, and indeed it is. However, its very simplicity can be taken as a

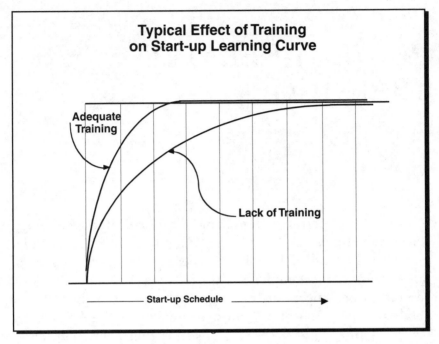

**Typical Effect of Training
on Start-up Learning Curve**

Adequate
Training

Lack of Training

Start-up Schedule

FIGURE 43

statement of its importance in bringing a project through to a successful completion—*successful completion* being a positive contribution to the venture bottom line. All else being equal, the graph in Fig. 43 depicts the difference in the learning curve we usually see in projects where training is a factor.

KEY CONSIDERATIONS IN THE DEVELOPMENT OF EFFECTIVE TRAINING

The pure truth of the matter is that many project teams fail to recognize the criticality of a well-trained workforce or the connection between a well-trained workforce and the success of their projects. The gap we see between the two curves in Fig. 43 can represent revenues in the millions of dollars. These are revenues that will never be recaptured—they're gone forever.

Why do we say that project teams often fail here? Because they often start thinking of the training element too late, give it short shrift in planning, set aside too little funding, or make it the first thing to be cut when budget concerns arise. The result of any of these can be a poor start-up, leading into a poorly operated and maintained system, a system that may for years contribute far less to the bottom line than it should.

Additionally, project teams sometimes fail to realize that, in almost all cases, they have full commitment from executive management to *all training necessary*. Executives want to be assured that the facility, when commissioned, will have the well-trained operators, maintenance personnel, and management who can operate and maintain at full capacity in as short a time as possible. Why should anyone imagine anything different? The problem is that when executive management puts on the pressure to "Get those numbers down," training sometimes suffers.

Let's look, then, from the training standpoint, at some of the key considerations and tasks that a project manager and his team will be taking up in their pursuit of a successful project.

THE TRAINING-NEEDS ASSESSMENT

Before the project team can make any informed training-requirement decisions, it must know the current status of workforce knowledge, skills, and ability. In a *brownfield* project— an upgrade or refurbishment project or the insertion of a new system or product line in a mature facility—learning the workforce's knowledge, skills, and ability is best accomplished with a training-needs assessment (TNA). The TNA should not be confused with a task analysis, which is an in-depth analysis of operations and maintenance tasks. Task analyses are usually used in determination of workforce classification and the task responsibilities of those classifications. Testing, based on these types of analyses, are used many times in greenfield, or new-facility, settings.

The training-needs assessment should take place early in the project, in the preauthorization period, so that sufficient funds are budgeted for training. Properly done, the assessment will serve as the specification for training and can be used in negotiations with both vendors and training contractors.

An effective training-needs assessment will identify, by classification or title, all personnel who will require any type of training to satisfy project requirements. The assessment will have three other primary goals:

- To identify the knowledge and abilities required to properly operate and maintain the equipment and systems to be installed
- To identify, through examination of relevant documentation and individual interviews, the current knowledge and experience level of the personnel to be trained
- To provide detailed training objectives, including training-class outlines, for each of the noted assigned groups

The "knowledge and ability required" identification will come from several sources: design specifications, vendor manuals and procedures, similar equipment procedures, and previous plant work orders, to name just a few. This identification will require some research, whether in a new installation or in an existing facility (see Fig. 44).

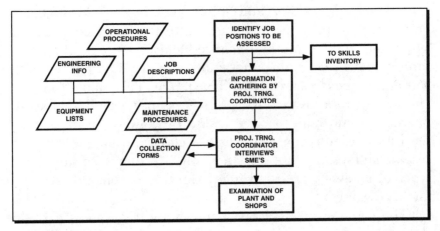

FIGURE 44

Identification of the current knowledge of the personnel to be trained is a bit trickier, however. Again, some research will be required, using both individual interviews and existing documentation. Depending on the training requirement complexity, interviews may be few and random or more inclusive in nature; in some cases, up to the full classification involved. When these interviews, coupled with documentation reviews, i.e., research involving past job requirements, educational level, current and past training courses attended, bid process criteria, operations and maintenance procedures, and entry test criteria, are not enough, testing may be required. Tests may be aptitude tests or tests of specific knowledge and skills, for example, certification testing (see Fig. 45).

The results of these skills inventories should be compared against equipment and system requirements to determine the amount of training that will actually be required for the project. The very simple graphic in Fig. 46 may help to explain.

The result of the assessment should be a detailed list of training objectives and class outlines. It should also contain a

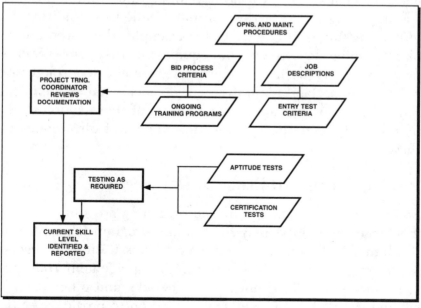

FIGURE 45

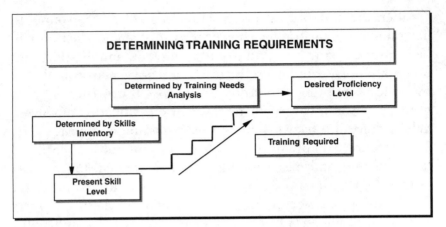

FIGURE 46

detailed schedule of class presentations, visits to similar facilities, vendor training requirements, and any safety or human resources–type training or indoctrination segments felt necessary to overall project success. In short, the result of a training-needs assessment should be the project training specification.

Another key consideration of the project team will be the decision of just *who* will be developing and conducting the training program. Entities normally called on for this all-important function could be, for example, the corporate or plant training department, the equipment or systems vendors or suppliers, or perhaps a third-party training contractor or public-training facility (junior college, vocational or technical school, etc.), or perhaps a combination of these sources. Let us take a look at the specific functions and differences of these entities.

IN-HOUSE TRAINING PROGRAM DEVELOPMENT

Some companies maintain in-house training-program development capability, especially for training programs that fit into the human-relations or employee-relations training category. These might include safety training, management training, self-improvement programs, craft upgrade, and other technical courses. Although sometimes called on to provide specific training for smaller capital projects, most in-house training departments today tend to leave the large-project, specific-equipment training programs to the project team. The project team then usually relies on the vendors' training capability, a third-party training contractor, or a combination of both. An in-house training representative, however, can well be a member of the project team, lending training expertise and guidance to the project-training requirement.

VENDOR TRAINING

Vendor training is an essential ingredient of the project training requirement. The vendor representative knows (or should know) more about the vendor's equipment or system than anyone else. Additionally, vendors have an obligation, usually within their purchase order or contract, to provide a certain amount of training. However, project teams must be aware of several factors:

1. Vendors normally provide training only on their own furnished equipment. Any training on ancillary or supportive equipment or systems must come from "others." One very good reason for this is the liability involved. If a vendor were to present misinformation on equipment or systems other than its own and that equipment or system failed, the vendor would in all likelihood find itself in a liability situation.

2. Vendors are not in the training business; they are in the business of selling equipment. Training, being an added expense to their package, will usually be held to only that amount expressly requested or written into the order.

3. Vendor training is usually presented at an engineering level; that is, vendors seldom attempt to write or present material that is geared to any predetermined grade level.

4. Vendor presentations, especially by foreign suppliers, may be difficult to understand because of language barriers (accents, idiomatic differences, dialects). This situation is especially true in the United States, where the ear is not attuned to "foreign" accents. (Remember those classes you had that were taught by a Japanese, a German, an Italian, or a Frenchman who, although very knowledgeable, had a tough time getting through to American trainees? Not so in Europe or Southeast Asia where most people are accustomed to many different languages and accents! Here, however, the training must usually be "Americanized.")

It is highly advisable that, as the purchase order is prepared, the project team not only specify in detail the training requirements it expects from the vendor, but also investigate fully the vendor's capability to successfully develop and present the training expected. Too many times, the training program that is presented by the vendor falls far short of the project team's expectations. The reason is usually that the project team's training requirement, as stated in the order, was too vague or otherwise ill defined.

TRAINING CONTRACTORS

In some cases, and especially on the larger capital projects, the project team may find it necessary to employ a third-party training company. Companies specializing in these services can provide, for example:

- *Task analysis.* A detailed description of actual job requirements.
- *Training-needs assessment.* A comparison of existing skills within the workforce with the actual job requirements.
- *Training specification development.*
- *Training coordination.* Off-site and on-site training, vendor coordination, and training-schedule development.
- *Overview training* and other training not normally considered by equipment vendors.
- *Ongoing training capability.* Training companies can capture and encapsulate the training program on video or multimedia so that future employees can have the benefit of much of the same program.

PUBLIC TRAINING FACILITIES

For some projects, the use of public training facilities may be advantageous. By *public training facilities*, we are referring to colleges and universities, technical, and vocational-technical (vo-tech) schools. Several factors may influence the project team to lean heavily toward this training method.

One factor might be the need for simple remedial training of certain classifications of the workforce. In these cases, a few evening or off-shift classes of vo-tech style training might be all that's needed to get personnel ready for the serious training, i.e., the specific equipment training, that is coming later.

On the other hand, one of the prerequisites for obtaining many thousands of dollars of state training funds often is using a state-funded school in the development and implementation of your training program. Although this is an enticing path (and one followed by too many project managers), these programs seldom live up to expectations, and the project team usually finds itself in start-up with a poorly trained workforce. As long as the project team recognizes this shortcoming in public-facility programs and moves to augment the program with in-depth training by vendors and specialty training contractors, no harm done. However, project teams sometimes view the "free" state-supported training programs as a windfall and fail to add sufficient training funds to their project budgets.

Regardless of the development or delivery method chosen by the project team, the important thing to remember is that training is the best investment in success that money can buy. You can have the best facility with the most modern equipment and controls money can buy, but only a well-trained workforce can use that equipment to its greatest potential.

The quality of training will reflect the quality of the planning and preparation that the project team has put into the training program development and delivery.

Evaluate and select training providers, i.e., in-house training capability, vendors, and/or training companies during the project design, procurement, and pretesting element. Why then? Because it is during the design element time frame that training program *development* must begin in order to ensure that a quality training program is in place and ready to train the workforce at exactly the proper time in the schedule.

DEVELOPMENT OF THE TRAINING PROGRAM

The project team must take care that sufficient time is allowed for the training program development. On very large capital projects it is not uncommon for development of training to take 8, 10, or perhaps even 12 months. Regardless of which entity develops the training, training material review will usually be a task requirement of knowledgeable members of the project team. Remember, as project team members, you will be very busy!

Training material review, however, is essential to development of an effective training program. If the material is not reviewed, the training program you get may be far different from the training program you had thought would be delivered. As an example, figures and drawings may be lacking in sufficient detail. Vendors may be instructing from generic references, such as manuals or manufacturer's bulletins, which require that trainees remember the differences in generic diagrams and the specific equipment that has been installed. The reading levels of instruction materials may vary greatly from vendor to vendor. As stated previously, some information will be coming at the trainees from an engineering level, some from the equivalent of a junior high school level. To avoid a hodge-podge of training materials, review of material will be required. Allow sufficient time for this—a good training program depends on it.

TRAINING OBJECTIVES

We have mentioned, several times, the term *training objectives*. Perhaps it is time to define this training term a bit more fully. *Training objectives* are statements that identify specifically what the trainees will learn relative to the facility's technology, systems, and equipment. Training objectives can generally be classified in three categories:

1. *Overview objectives.*   Covering process and equipment basics:
   - Identifies function of equipment, process, or system
   - Identifies location and boundaries of equipment, process, or system
   - Identifies basic operation of equipment, process, or system
   - Identifies major components of equipment, process or system
   - Identifies related safety items and concerns

2. *Operations objectives.*   Covering process and equipment operations and control specifics:
   - Identifies equipment operating procedures under normal conditions
   - Identifies equipment operating procedures under emergency conditions
   - Identifies location, function, and operation of equipment, process, or system controls
   - Identifies detailed operating characteristics of equipment, process, or system
   - Identifies checks for proper operation of equipment

3. *Maintenance objectives.*   Covering mechanical, electrical, and instrumentation control systems maintenance details:
   - Identifies location and operation of maintenance panels and cabinets
   - Identifies required lockouts while performing maintenance functions
   - Identifies types and location of equipment sensing devices
   - Identifies equipment troubleshooting procedures
   - Identifies equipment predictive and preventive maintenance procedures
   - Identifies inspection and adjustment items
   - Identifies specific repair and replacement procedures
   - Identifies major overhaul items and procedures

This listing is by no means a complete listing of the types of objectives that should be identified in any good training program, but it will serve, at the very least, as a starter list.

ORGANIZE AND SCHEDULE THE TRAINING PROGRAM

In anticipation of implementation, the training program must also be very carefully organized and scheduled. Scheduling, in the training world, has a significance that is sometimes overlooked. This significant facet can be boiled down to a single word—retention. When we learn something in a training class, as opposed to learning it through experience, we tend to begin losing the instilled knowledge very quickly if it is not soon put to use. This is a natural tendency—when information is not used soon after learning, or frequently thereafter, the brain considers the information to be of relative unimportance and begins sloughing it off, a bit at a time. Use it, it becomes knowledge; use it frequently, it becomes habit.

It is imperative that the project schedule be watched closely and that the training program implementation be in consonance with it. Trainees must get their training at *exactly* the right time if they are to get full benefit from the training and are to be able to immediately apply it during start-up. The cost of training is high. Vendors' charges for training, when broken out from equipment costs, are significant. Then there are materials costs and the cost of a training contractor, perhaps, along with one of the most significant costs, the cost of trainees' *time*. It would be a shame to fail to get full benefit from all the training dollars being expended simply because the scheduling effort was lax.

IMPLEMENT AND COORDINATE THE TRAINING PROGRAM

Project training, especially on large projects, can be a daunting undertaking and must be carefully coordinated. When upwards of 200 people must be trained in the operation and maintenance of technologically complex equipment and systems, the program must run like clockwork. Training text materials, training aids, instructors, and the proper trainee classification must come together at exactly the right time, in the right classroom or field training location.

Coordination will certainly become an issue when outside training is a part of the mix. For example, portions of the training may be conducted at other locations, where similar equipment or systems are already in use. These locations may be in another area, another state, or even overseas. On the other hand, portions of the training may be *remedial*, i.e., training in the basics in order to bring all trainees quickly to at least a minimum prerequisite level so that they all may go on then with the intended training.

Another area of training that will require considerable attention and coordination is the area of state-supported training. Since this training is at least partially funded with public funds, the state entity that authorizes the grant will undoubtedly require some modicum of control, probably planning in advance, establishment of segment costs, then draw-down against the overall state-supported program.

In all these instances, the wise project manager will bring a training contractor aboard early in the project to plan and coordinate. Wait too long, and the workforce will not get the depth of training required for a successful conclusion to the project.

EVALUATE AND ADJUST AS REQUIRED

Your training program may come off like clockwork; then, your project goes into start-up and suddenly, things start going wrong. Operators don't respond properly, maintenance personnel don't seem to be able to make repairs or adjustments properly, people just don't seem to know how to run or maintain the new or upgraded systems.

What you are probably experiencing is the result of inadequate training, an inadequacy that you weren't really expecting because you had taken great pains to provide the best in training for the workforce.

The problem may be, however, that you failed to include a provision for *evaluation of the results* and adjustments to the training program based on that evaluation. Evaluations can usually be obtained through frequent testing, both on paper and with hands-on simulators. Let's look at a case in point:

C A S E   S T U D Y   **9**

Operator Training: Are They Ready?

BACKGROUND

Forty-two operators and eight supervisors were assigned to blast furnace operations. The operators have an average of 22 years with the company and 16 years' experience operating the furnace. The supervisors have an average of 12 years with the company and 8 years' experience with the furnace. Six of the operators and five of the supervisors have limited computer experience. No one has experience in the operation of a computerized process control system.

A primary training contractor was hired to design an operator training program incorporating 1 week of systems overview classes and 2 weeks of operations classes, based on the requirements of the training specification as developed by a project team member. A formal training-needs assessment was not performed.

PROBLEM

During presentation of the first operations class, the instructor quickly began to notice blank stares and confused looks from the trainees whenever the subject turned to operations involving the distributed control system (DCS). This was a computerized system employing state-of-the-art computer control of the entire blast furnace operation, which had previously (for years) been an almost totally manual operation.

Only one of the four or five trainees with some limited computer experience answered the follow-up questions that had been directed to the class. Further questioning revealed that the majority of the trainees not only did not understand how a computer functioned but also were even doubtful that a computer could properly operate the furnace. Being thoroughly familiar with the volatile nature of a blast furnace and the dangers inherent therein, they were very apprehensive about operating the furnace with a computer.

After the initial operations and maintenance classes, evaluation tests were given. A review of the test results clearly showed that at least 80 percent of the trainees had failed to understand the presented material. (The average test score for these students was 27 percent.)

The instructor immediately contacted the project manager and revealed the classroom experience. The instructor felt that any continuation of the program would be futile until the trainees were familiar with, and comfortable with, computerized control.

The project manager agreed and, after revisiting the entire area of project training, authorized an in-depth training-needs assessment, this time looking not only at the new system requirements but also at the background knowledge and experience of the operations and maintenance workforce.

The assessment revealed an almost total lack of computer background for most of the intended trainees. In addition, most of them seriously doubted that a computer could control such massive and volatile equipment.

If you were the project manager in this situation, what would *you* do? The answer as to what was actually done is revealed at the end of this chapter.

PROVIDE FOR ONGOING TRAINING

Project teams should face this fact—the workforce being trained under the auspices of this, their current project, will not be the same workforce operating the same equipment a year from now. Turnover will inevitably alter the workforce. Workers will bid out, workers will bid in, workers will retire, move, quit, get fired, get promoted. The project team may say, "But that's an operations problem; our responsibility is only to train *this* workforce."

The principles of *Project Bottom-Line Success!* take us to the next level, however; the project's long-term contribution to the health, the success, of the venture. Here is one of those areas where just a small amount of extra effort from the project team can result in an extended benefit to the bottom line.

And, in keeping with our principles, the responsibility *does* rest with the project team to provide an ongoing training capability, if possible.

In years past, it was difficult to provide for much ongoing training capability. To provide new employees with the same training that the workforce received when the equipment and systems were originally installed was virtually impossible or, at the least, economically unfeasible.

Now, however, things have changed. Most training programs, whether developed by vendors or training contractors, is developed on computers. This means that the text material, the drawings, the figures, the tables, etc., are simply a *database,* and can be manipulated. One of these manipulations can be the fairly simple task of converting this material to a one-on-one computer-based training program, a program that can be used over and over again as new employees come into the workforce. It behooves the project team to take this extra step in providing for the future health of the venture by providing a method of continuing training as the workforce changes.

All too often, training tends to be given a lesser priority among the critical objectives and tasks for bringing a facility on line. It is easy to get caught up in the technology and frenetic activity of making sure that the plant systems and equipment operate as designed.

> Project teams should keep in mind that people can't be programmed, tweaked, or adjusted like a piece of equipment; they have to be trained.

SOLUTION TO BLAST FURNACE TRAINING PROBLEM

An in-depth remedial training program was developed to, first, familiarize all attendees with computer knowledge and operation basics (for those who needed to learn the basics) and, second, train all operators in the basic theory and operation of computerized control systems in general. Maintenance personnel were given overviews of these classes, along with instruction on system-troubleshooting techniques.

In order to build confidence within the operator workforce, trips were arranged to a similar facility where the operators could observe, first-hand, operation of a blast furnace utilizing a distributed control system.

Following these remedial steps, the previously scheduled and developed training was successfully resumed and completed. Because of delays in the project construction effort, there was enough float time in the schedule to allow these steps to be taken. In many instances, this will not be the case. That is why it is so vitally important that a comprehensive training-needs assessment be completed early in the project.

THE SMALLER PROJECTS

To this point, it may appear that we have addressed only the billion-dollar (or at least the multi*million*-dollar) projects. In actual fact, almost all of what has been put forward thus far is as applicable to the smallest project as to the largest. We'll even go one step further—most of what has been put forward is *more* important to the smaller project!

Why would we say this? Because everything is not always relative. The smaller project usually has much less room for error. The loss through accident, error, or omission of, say, a 30-horsepower motor will probably not throw a $90 million project into a failed category; the same loss, however, in a $1,200,000 production line upgrade may completely skew the return on investment that justified the upgrade (especially if the loss occurs during a production line outage, resulting in extended production downtime).

The same principles still apply, regardless of industry, area of endeavor, or size of project. In fact, let's review for just a moment the steps we've put forward that support the rock-solid principles of *Project <u>Bottom-Line</u> Success!* Regardless of size of project, *before authorization of project funding,* the focus must be on:

- Justification of project need
- Detailed scope definition
- In-depth project preplanning
- Aggressive risk assessment and alleviation

JUSTIFICATION

We have seen in previous chapters the importance, even criticality, of justification of project need. In major project scenarios this factor can mean success or failure of the venture
itself. Large chunks of capital funding can be wasted if a
major project is, indeed, unjustifiably pursued. In a smaller
project being carried out within the confines of a large entity,
the risk to the venture may not be as high; however, a series of
unneeded or ill-advised smaller projects can, over time, seriously threaten the health of even a large venture.

Actually, there's another side effect to the execution of
unjustified or unneeded projects. The side effect is that this
practice sets the tone, many times, for the way projects move
forward within that entity. It seems to "slop over" into the
overall method of project approval. In other words, it's just as
important to take the same disciplined steps with *all* projects,
large or small.

Justification criteria may be, in fact usually is, different for
the smaller project. The very large project is usually tied to market factors; smaller projects are usually tied more to operating
factors. Where the megamillion-dollar project goal is to expand
the venture's presence in the marketplace either through a larger
presence or to capture bigger shares with higher quality or new
products, the smaller projects are the ones that keep the venture operating. Repair and refurbishment projects; productivity-
increasing projects; upgrades to improve operating conditions,
safety, and environment-related projects; all are within the
descriptive area of the smaller project.

Too many times these projects escape the scrutiny given to
the large project. The budget for the operationally related
small project may reside within the operating units, rather
than falling within the purview of Engineering and the annual
capital improvement budget. When this is the case, projects
may move forward without the all-important question being
asked and answered, that question being, "Is there another
way?" That is, could operational procedures be changed;
would further training suffice? Just as with the large project, if

it doesn't need to be done, don't do it. These small projects are also being funded with bottom-line dollars, regardless of whose budget is being used.

SCOPE DEFINITION

As with project justification, detailed scope definition is absolutely essential to the smaller project. Why so essential? *There's less room for error.* Poor scope definition is by far the biggest contributor to cost overrun on the smaller projects. To project teams, we say this: forget the fact that it's a small project—go into it as if your company's survival, and your jobs, were at stake. Look closely at factors such as:

- *Project design criteria.* Are the design criteria, i.e., drawing requirements, review and approval requirements, quality standards for materials and fabrication (including shop inspections and testing), well enough defined to preclude the receipt on site of substandard materials and equipment or, in some cases, ill-fitting equipment?
- *Site characteristics existing/required.* Have existing versus required site characteristics been examined sufficiently to be able to accurately estimate the amount of work required to complete site preparation and subsequent installation? In many cases the removal of equipment being replaced leads to far more work than was originally estimated and the construction costs skyrocket because of "extra work."
- *Lead discipline scope of work.* Have the discipline leads (civil, mechanical, electrical, etc.) defined completely the scope of work that will be required within their areas of expertise? Or will they come back later with a big surprise, e.g., piping or ductwork interferences, twice as many electrical terminations as estimated? These are surprises that will often double the cost of a smaller project.
- *Stakeholder input.* Have all stakeholders been heard from? If not, and previously unheard-from operations or maintenance

personnel come forward later in the project with requests for justifiable design changes, both budget and schedule will be in danger. It is far better to *actively solicit* stakeholder input right from the beginning, when it can be included in the original scope.

IN-DEPTH PREPROJECT PLANNING

The small project must be as assiduously planned as the large project. Also as with the large project, most of the planning should be accomplished early on, prior to actual commitment of funds. Why? If the preplanning includes definitive project justification and scope definition, it may be evident that the project does not hold sufficient benefits to justify the expenditure required. In other words, the ROI may not be sufficient to proceed. In any event, the more preplanning, the more detail uncovered, the better chance there is to establish a definitive cost estimate. And it is far better to know the facts beforehand than to learn of a serious miscalculation later on.

Let's take a look now at one of these smaller projects and see just what can happen when the project team, or the executives in command positions, fail to observe some of these basic project management principles.

CASE   STUDY   **10**

On the Links: Birdie or Bogey?

BACKGROUND

The Jefferson City Municipal Golf Course had been in operation for 14 years and was well established. In the town of approximately 80,000 population, the municipal course was the best in town. Although there were other golf courses in the area, most preferred to play the municipal course because of its design and condition, which was always immaculate.

There was only one problem; the course had no clubhouse. All that existed was a small structure that doubled as the pro shop and the cashier's desk. Under pressure for some time to improve the facility, and with firm backing from the mayor, himself a golfer, the council decided to authorize the building of a real clubhouse. With unanimous consent, and on the basis of some preliminary data supplied by the city engineer, the council authorized the project to proceed with a budget of $400,000.

PROJECT EXECUTION

Without too much thought, the overall management of the fast-moving project was ceded to the city engineer, partly because he had furnished preliminary data but mostly because he just assumed control.

As the project proceeded, problems began to develop. The council, for example, had long discussed among themselves, and expected, a nice eating establishment. In fact, they had anticipated that it would even be a bit elegant, a place to entertain. However, none had ever made it a requirement before funding.

As it turned out, the city engineer went for the cheapest option, a hamburger-and-beer snack bar. The decision was made, design was initiated by an architect, and some installation proceeded with almost no communication between the council and the city engineer. The kitchen design itself wound up with a small, under-the-counter dishwasher and without a walk-in cooler—a very frugal installation, to say the least.

The council, when it became fully aware, would have none of it. Although the design was 99 percent complete, the council demanded a shift to a more formal dining atmosphere. Bowing to pressure, the architect modified his design, routing the changes through the city engineer. The new design would require more kitchen and dining space. This was to be expected. However, several options were also presented to the engineer, including an option to substantially increase the size of the building. These options, though, were never communicated to the council. The dining area, originally budgeted to cost $20,000, shot to $80,000. The change in building design and size increased that portion of the budget by an additional $100,000.

The city clerk/finance director, when later trying to reconstruct what had happened, pointed out that in addition to the original design change fiasco, other midproject inputs from different council members and from the city engineer himself contributed to further overruns.

For example, a golf cart maintenance building, a fireplace, and more expensive furniture than anticipated were added during the project. The above-counter dishwasher was delivered 2 months late, causing delays in opening the dining facility. The delay, coupled with the change in machine selection, cost an additional $5000.

The original delay in settling on the building design caused construction to slip into the first of the cold winter months and the concrete pad had to be poured in cold weather, causing an increase in price of $10,400 for this line item.

More input kept coming. The Park and Recreation Commission wanted more lockers, while the newly hired golf pro wanted to maximize the restaurant and pro shop to make more profit. He contended that the trend is not to go for locker facilities, but for profit-making opportunity. The design was again changed, as the bigger kitchen and lounge area won out. "We were just doing as we were asked," said the architect. The mayor, now very concerned about the escalating costs, agreed. "The city engineer should have brought all this information to the attention of Council," he explained to an inquiring reporter.

Other contractors were frustrated and dismayed with the way the project was going. They complained to the mayor that "no one is in charge" of the project.

One of the loudest complainers was, justifiably, the contractor who was to run the restaurant and bar. "All it is, is politics," she said. "A total lack of communication." This contractor had a $1500 per month lease that was over 4 months late in implementation, since the facility wasn't yet ready. Not only did the contractor lose profits from not being in position to open, but also the city was losing $1500 per month while the facility wasn't open.

The project finally came to a close. "Jefferson City should give itself a pat on the back," said the architect. "It's a top-notch, A-1 facility, even though it did cost a little more than expected."

There will be "nothing but bigger and better things now" for the golf course and clubhouse, maintained the golf pro.

"We have a building that is going to serve our community well," stated the Mayor.

AFTERMATH

The "project team" may have put the best face possible on this project, but the cost to the taxpayers is not quite so sunny. The original estimate was $400,000. The final cost was $672,753. The overrun was $272,753, or 59.5 percent.

Cost overruns included:

- Original building design change: $100,000
- Dining area and kitchen upgrade: $55,000 to $65,000
- Added fireplace: $13,590

- Furniture upgrade: $26,000
- Cart maintenance building addition: $50,000
- Pouring building pad in cold weather: $10,400
- Losses in lease revenue and profits due to schedule slippage: $8000

Were the changes necessary and justified? Was the project even necessary to begin with? Perhaps. Perhaps not. The point is, this project did not go as planned. The project team had no real leadership, lines of communication were nonexistent, and the scope of the project was almost totally undefined before appropriation of funding, resulting in a "budget estimate" that failed woefully to deliver the results that the Council expected. In the end, taxpayers paid dearly for a surprising lack of applied project management.

RISK ASSESSMENT AND ALLEVIATION

If risk assessment and alleviation efforts are important to the success of a major project (and they are), they are *doubly* important to a small project. Again, there is usually very little room for error.

In the foregoing case study the major risks to the project were an ill-defined scope, poor project organization and control, and poor lines of communication. At least one or more of these conditions is usually present in almost every smaller project that either fails totally to deliver or returns less than it should.

In industrial projects, the risks may be centered on other factors, such as:

- Pinpoint scope refinement and equipment life cycle cost analysis
- Early attention to training and start-up issues
- Meaningful involvement of all stakeholders
- Procurement on a quality basis
- Preshipment testing of equipment
- Equipment and systems preoperational testing

In the industrial world, however, the smaller project often doesn't get the attention it deserves simply because it *is* a smaller project. Warning signs are sometimes overlooked in the concern over the larger projects that may be in progress at the same time.

The project team selected for the smaller project will sometimes consist of one person, a person who is expected to fill the role of project manager, project engineer, buyer, inspector, and any other job that might be associated. In addition, this individual may also be filling a role on a larger project at the same time. Is it any wonder that risk items fall through the crack sometimes; that scope development is not always in the detail it should be before project execution is attempted?

Regardless of the situation, the smaller project risks must be addressed. Risk alleviation efforts should include, for example, the use of proved technology whenever possible. They should also include planning in detail, providing for reasonable contingencies both in funding and scheduling, and the development of parallel alternatives (workarounds).

In some cases, "improvement upgrades" may actually be research and development (R&D) projects in disguise. R&D projects often fail, especially when carried out in circumstances that are less than optimum in preproject analysis, as they usually are when they are masquerading as improvement upgrades. Let's look for a moment at a relatively small (at least in the beginning) industrial project that fits this description.

C A S E   S T U D Y   1 1

The Autoweld System—Upgrade or Masquerade?

HISTORICAL SYNOPSIS—PROJECT BACKGROUND

To reduce weld breaks from a historical level of 35 per month to 10 per month on one of its cold mills, a large integrated steel company hired a small supplier company to design, build, and install an autoweld inspection system. The system was to use a magnetic transducer arrangement to detect bad welds for removal prior to downstream product processing.

A unit prototype by the same supplier had already been in place and operating on another line. The prototype, however, was unreliable, required too much operator intervention, and its sensitivity to some product flaws was not good.

Shift managers and engineering were sure, however, that they could get this system up and running properly by improving on the prototype design. The steel company proposed, therefore, that the supplier design and build a first-of-its-kind autoweld inspection system (AWIS). The new AWIS would use a magnetic transducer with a permanent magnet and would be automated by using a computer-based control system. This control system would allow the magnetic transducer to be placed on the strip through an up-and-down motion, instead of being pulled across the strip as was the prototype.

The automated AWIS would, it was felt, reduce operator error in decision making and would reduce inspection time, improve reliability, and increase sensitivity to product flaws. Additional design features for the new system included automatic tuning adjustments and inspection data capture and interpretation with minimal operator intervention. Since the system would operate automatically, elimination of the requirement for a full-time operator would be an added cost reduction benefit.

The appropriation did not clearly state that the project was developmental. As a result, the risk assessment, reduction, and management strategies normally employed in a developmental project were never considered. Further, no specification was ever completed for the new AWIS. Instead, the client company (steel company) accepted, as specification, the supplier's vague project description, submitted as a part of the proposal.

PROJECT EXECUTION

The project to build the new AWIS system had engineering, design, and procurement difficulties from the very beginning. Working from the vague description it had developed instead of a detailed specification, the supplier soon ran into significant design and engineering problems. The software engineering effort, in particular, resulted in unanticipated changes in input/output (I/O), hardware, and other electronic circuitry. Also, the supplier did not take seriously the line maintenance personnel's expressed concern over the design because the steel company's upper-level management had already approved the original design.

Attempting to get the project back on track, management consulted with an outside firm to review the design and engineering of the AWIS and to recommend changes. Needless to say, the project began to seriously overrun its budget. Finally, the steel company's upper-level management acknowledged that the supplier did not have the experience, personnel, or resources to handle this project. At this point, the steel company assumed responsibility for all adjunct project activities, including control building design, fabrication, and installation. This arrangement left the supplier with only AWIS equipment design and fabrication to complete.

However, 9 months after contract award, the AWIS manufacturer filed for Chapter 11 bankruptcy. As a result of this announcement, several of the contractor's key project members left the company. Only part of these vacancies were filled, and the newly assigned personnel were unfamiliar with the project.

The steel company brought the system on line, but it operated for only a short time before failing and damaging the unit. With most of the appropriation spent and a machine that didn't operate, the steel company considered the following courses of action:

- Scrap the project altogether
- Contract another manufacturer to complete the project
- Finish the project using in-house resources

The steel company was unable to locate a qualified contractor and decided to finish the project using in-house resources. However, inadequate drawings and documentation, a lack of personnel knowledgeable in magnetic transducer electronics, and unforeseen design changes delayed completion of the rebuild for several months.

By this time, the original prototype system had been improved to the point where weld breaks averaged 10 per month, the project target. Therefore, the company decided not to install the rebuilt unit. They attempted to find a cost-effective method of automating the prototype, at least, but they determined that the minimum additional cost to automate the existing system's displays and data storage capabilities would be cost-prohibitive. Since automation would still be a developmental undertaking with no guarantees, they closed the project.

CONCLUSION

At project closing, almost 1 million bottom-line dollars had been spent. Because the appropriation was closed without the system in operation, the capital expenditure was transferred to direct plant costs.

Perhaps a reality check would have pointed out that, at least for the primary goal of reducing weld failures to 10 per month, this project should not have gone forward. An operational change and minor adjustments would have solved that problem and the approximately

$1 million could, perhaps, have been put into a project that would have yielded a more tangible benefit.

This project appears to have been a research and development project masquerading as an improvement upgrade. The big problem with these projects is that they are so difficult to head off. Someone has a "great idea," it gains supporters and momentum, and it usually really does sound good. Executive management is particularly susceptible to this type project because it appears that great benefits can be gained for a relatively small investment. The result is that normally analytically oriented engineers bite, and a project proceeds without the feasibility studies and other safeguards that accompany the normal capital improvement project.

DESIGN AND PROCUREMENT

The careful consideration of both design and procurement factors is doubly important to the success of the smaller project, not only in the public sector, as we saw in the first case study, but also in the industrial setting, as we have seen here.

In the industrial setting the project, many times, will involve the replacement or upgrade of a particular piece of equipment or the installation of a new device to improve quality or production rate. The selection process can be vitally important and must be carefully thought through. Items to be considered, for example, might be:

- *Quality level.*   Should be sufficient but not overkill. (The selection of equipment or material that far exceeds the specified requirement is a needless waste of resources.)
- *Obsolescence factors.*   Although it is good practice to go with proved technology, obsolescence must be considered. This is especially true with electronic and/or computerized systems. The state of the art changes rapidly.
- *Ease of operation.*   Operational characteristics must be carefully considered; the equipment or material selected may be in use for the next several years.
- *Maintainability.*   The same holds true for maintenance characteristics. Some equipment requires considerably

more maintenance than other equipment that serves the same purpose. Life cycle cost analysis should be a high priority in the smaller project.

- *Initial cost.*   Cost is always a factor, and should be carefully considered. After all factors are taken into consideration and *true costs* have been ascertained, real comparisons can be made. Selection of the higher-cost product should always be first "dollarized," then justified.

CONSTRUCTION/INSTALLATION

As with all projects, large or small, it is during the construction/installation phase that the effectiveness of early planning and attention to detail will become apparent. If equipment, components, and materials arrive on schedule, if they *fit,* if testing reveals a problem-free installation, then the project manager (and team, if there is one) can claim credit for having taken the actions that significantly impacted project efficiency. However, if construction/installation was not properly planned, choreographed, and implemented, the problems can be frustrating, even on a small project.

Above all, in production line situations, the installation should be carefully orchestrated, perhaps "shadowed," to avoid disruption to production in the event that the installed equipment or change doesn't perform as planned. (*Shadowing* means leaving existing equipment in an operational mode so that it can be returned to service immediately, if required.) *These things require planning, and attention to detail.*

KEY CONSIDERATIONS FOR CONSTRUCTION/INSTALLATION ON THE SMALL PROJECT

Key items to consider during construction planning and implementation on the smaller projects are really not much different than we have discussed, in depth, when we considered the larger projects. These considerations might include, for example:

- Environmental permitting and controls
- Employee/labor relations
- Field planning and scheduling
- Contractor selection
- Construction or installation planning
- Field changes and cost control
- Start-up planning

DEVELOPMENT OF A CONSTRUCTION PLAN

A detailed construction plan is vital to efficient execution of project construction and/or installation, regardless of project size. Project team members should consider developing the following planning documents:

- A detailed project schedule
- A plan and schedule for site preparation, if applicable (tearing down existing structures/equipment, modifying foundations, etc.)
- A plan for establishment of necessary construction/project management forces on site
- A plan for equipment receipt, inspection, and storage
- A detailed outage plan, if installation is in a production line or in an operating area where normal work will be interrupted
- A plan for personnel training if operational changes result from the upgrade
- A plan for start-up and performance testing.

IN SUMMARY

Smaller projects should be taken much more seriously than they usually are. Why? *Because there are so many of them!* Many engineers (and others who are associated continually with the management of projects in one role or another) will never be assigned to a megamillion-dollar project. During the course of their careers, however, they may see literally *hundreds* of smaller projects. Taken collectively, the smaller projects, i.e., the upgrades, refurbishments, replacements, layups, decommissionings, etc., are the lifeblood of the venture. Usually, as was stated in the opening chapter of this book, it is the manner in which *these* projects are approached that will determine the health and longevity of the venture.

THE ENVIRONMENTAL PROJECT

IT'S A "DIFFERENT" PROJECT

Now that we have discussed, in some detail, the origination, definition, and organization of most (say 95 percent) of all projects, we should point out that there is one exceptional project type that sometimes defies many of the general rules of good project management. It might be said, in fact, that this type project sometimes defies the rules of logic. The type project to which we refer is, of course, the environmental project.

Although there are many differences at which we could point, perhaps the one that stands out the starkest is *bottom-line* contribution. Except in rare instances, the environmental project is not only non-revenue-producing, it is usually not even revenue neutral; in other words, the environmental project many times results in the construction of an ongoing corporate expense! We're speaking here, of course, of the construction or installation of water treatment facilities, emission controls systems, tailings holding ponds, monitored storage facilities, etc. These facilities, equipment, and systems are usually mandated by government decree or negotiation, or are built as a settlement of safety issues with labor force bargaining units.

Since these projects are, in actuality, corporate expenses rather than revenue generators, it is even more important for project teams to handle them as quickly and economically as possible in the ever-important battle of limiting negative impact on the corporate bottom line.

The rare instances referred to above, wherein the environmental project is, in fact, intended to result in a profit-making venture, i.e., hazardous waste incinerators, waste-to-electricity cogeneration facilities, landfills, etc., it can be even more daunting to a project team, for reasons described below.

THE FORCES AT WORK

The forces arrayed against the corporate entity in this battle can be formidable when the project in question is one of an environmental nature. Not only are the guardians of the environment (the governmental agencies) *seemingly* intent on delaying the project until everyone concerned is old and gray, but also the environmental activists and "fringers" may also make their presence loudly known. These individuals or groups sometimes resort to stirring the kettle of public fear in an effort to achieve their own ends. Although not generally addressed in project management courses and treatises, the handling of these forces is a reality that project teams must deal with. The projects involved may consist not only of environmental projects of a remedial nature but, in many instances, may also be those projects feared by some to be causative in air, water, or earth pollution or contamination. Public opinion is a powerful weapon that weighs in heavily when the responsible agencies arrive at a go/no-go decision point. A savvy project team will not abandon the field of public relations and awareness to the activists, but will instead go to a "full-court press" to get the real facts into the public's awareness.

If all concerned parties were to always use rational thinking to arrive at logical answers and logically applicable outcomes, these projects would not be so difficult or consume so much time; however, human nature being what it is, such is sometimes not the case. Therefore, let's take a look at an environmental project to see just where the differences might lie between the management of this type project and our normal industrial project.

First, consider the makeup of the typical industrial project. Most large projects are, certainly, concerned with environmental issues. However, although approvals and permitting are important issues, they are not usually the overriding factors. Using the project management bar as the base of reference, we can see most of the project elements depicted in Fig. 47, in their approximate relative times of appearance and duration. (Some we have already discussed; others will be discussed in later chapters.)

When the environmental project results in the construction of a new facility (or an upgrade or expansion of an existing facility), then the project will usually conclude in much the same manner as depicted in Fig. 47. It's what happens *before* this that makes many environmental projects not only difficult to handle, but also sometimes inordinately expensive. Why so expensive? Because these projects are under public scrutiny and are at the mercy of both government bureaucrats and activists of every stripe and nature. The personal and public

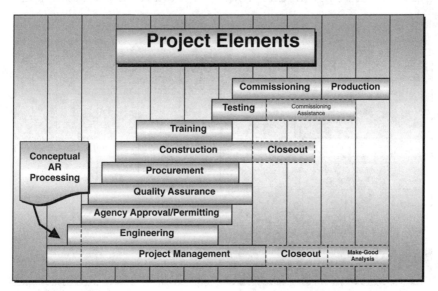

FIGURE 47

agendas of many of these groups may cause them to seek to delay the environmental or environmentally sensitive project at every juncture possible. It stands to reason that delay, on any major project, is expensive.

In this chapter, then, we will seek to identify the chain of events that usually must take place *prior* to bringing the environmentally sensitive project to a point, as shown in Fig. 47, where an appropriation request (AR) can be processed. Believe it or not, there are certain courses of action that can be taken to "speed up" the activities. (We put *speed up* in quotes, because the word *speed,* in this instance, is a relative term!)

Let us begin by constructing the first part of a chart (Fig. 48) that will depict the events that usually take place in an environmental project prior to arrival at the *beginning* point of the chart in Fig. 47. Later, we will attempt to tie the two types together as, in reality, this is generally what happens.

THE ORIGIN OF THE PROJECT

As discussed earlier, most projects originate from a desire of the investors to generate profit and, hopefully, after consider-

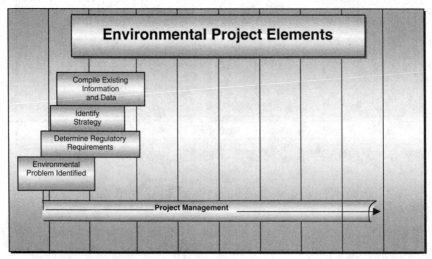

FIGURE 48

able due diligence has taken place in the form of feasibility and market studies. The environmental project, on the other hand, may sometimes be traced to emotion-laden environmental activists' complaints, citizens' meetings, or governmental citations for violations (or perceived violations) of environmental statutes or regulations. Any or all of these actions will eventually lead to the EPI, the environmental problem identified.

We will not attempt, in this writing, to study the huge machinery of the U.S. Environmental Protection Agency, other than at the points where its reviews and decrees come in direct contact with the project team's efforts to complete the project in a timely manner. Suffice it to say that after the identification of an environmental problem, a series of research investigations by concerned governmental units (usually utilizing the resources of the allegedly offending corporate entity) will lead to a Corrective Action Order by the Environmental Protection Agency. This is where we will begin.

DETERMINE THE REGULATORY REQUIREMENTS

The Corrective Action Order, though citing Resource Conservation and Recovery Act (RCRA) articles and regulations allegedly violated, may be somewhat general in nature and must be closely studied by the project team to determine *exactly* where the corporate entity is in violation. In short, the project team must determine for themselves the regulatory requirements and the degree of violation, if any. Only by closely studying the legal requirements can the project team take the next step, that being to identify the strategy to be taken in responding to the agency's order.

IDENTIFY THE STRATEGY

After carefully studying both the Corrective Action Order and the applicable regulatory requirements, the corporate *investigative unit* must decide on the strategy that best suits the corporate, or venture, bottom line. (Note that we referred, in this instance, to an investigative unit rather than to a project team.

At this early stage, an appeal to a legal authority may be the winning strategy—an ongoing project may not be necessary.)

Chances are, however, that the creation of a project team will be necessary, and the necessary strategization effort will be *to determine the minimum amount of reaction necessary to satisfy the order.* The identification of strategy should include a listing of all viable options, budget and schedule estimates, and detailed risk analyses of the salient factors involved.

The project team must recognize that the winning strategy will include not only precise, structured planning at all stages of the project, but also a certain amount of *negotiation,* and carefully considered public relations exercises. The importance, both of the negotiations with agency officials and of well-planned public relations exercises, cannot be overstated. The manner in which each of these strategies is handled can, many times, be tracked either negatively or positively to a significant corporate bottom-line effect.

In the event that an appeal is not a viable approach and project work must be undertaken to satisfy the order, both the Agency and the corporate entity will usually be required to name project coordinators within a short period of time.

INTERIM WORK

It is possible that the Corrective Action Order will be written in such a way that will include also a requirement for interim work to be accomplished in order to stabilize a situation that is in violation of agency guidelines or Resource Conservation and Recovery Act (RCRA) regulations. Work of this nature will require the formulation of a more immediate action plan. This work plan, and succeeding work plans for ensuing divisions of the work required to finally satisfy the order, will require a considerable amount of planning. Work plans may require, for example, a management plan, a quality assurance plan, a data management plan, a technology selection and construction plan, a health and safety plan, a public involvement plan, detailed task lists and, finally, schedules and reports.

COMPILE INFORMATION AND DATA

Supporting the determination of regulatory requirements, the identification of strategy and any interim work requirements, will be a need for a compilation of any pertinent information and data. If the order is concerned with earth or groundwater contamination, for example, samples will be taken periodically and usually at several different locations, in order to get an overall picture of the area or areas of concern. On the other hand, if the order is concerned with air contamination, then continuous sampling may be taking place. Sampling may be related either to gaseous or particulate content, or both. Regardless of the means, methods, or procedures used, it is imperative to the project interest that complete data be taken and results analyzed.

Compilation of information and data should not, however, be limited to *technical* information and data. Of equal importance is information concerning viability of approach, long-range effects of approach options, viewpoints of the citizenry, and the concerns of the various environmental groups. The level of Agency push is, many times, a function of the level of reaction to public concern. The level of public concern is, likewise, many times a function of the level and content of public relations awareness programs and press releases effected by the project team. It is far easier to negotiate with a government official when the public is on your side!

Armed with good, solid sampling information, a thorough knowledge of the environmental agency's regulations and guidelines, and with a well-conceived strategic plan that includes close attention to public concerns, it is time to meet with government officials. The purpose of this initial meeting is to present the corporate plan in an attempt to obtain a consent order so that remedial action may begin. Let's take the chart a few steps further (Fig. 49).

MEET WITH AGENCY; OBTAIN CONSENT ORDER

First and foremost, it important that the project has a knowledgeable *corporate sponsor* who has intimate knowledge of

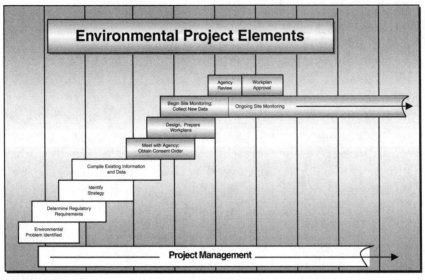

FIGURE 49

corporate strategic planning. This person should guide the project team as it prepares itself for this vitally important meeting with the governing agency. A lot depends on the outcome, as we shall see.

The secret to a successful meeting with *any* governmental agency is to be *ready*, as anyone who has ever been audited by the tax collector knows. And what do we mean by successful? We mean a meeting that results in the *best possible outcome* for the venture, or corporation. Success may be earlier completion, lower cost, fewer items to correct, relief from some responsibility, shared responsibility, etc., or perhaps a combination of all. However, it may be difficult for any of these to occur if the project team is ill prepared for the primary Agency meeting.

Consider, for example, the schedule. Although the project team may have a perfect plan, and has responded fully to every allegation and requirement, the government agency will almost always require 30, 60, or 90 days for review. This is to be expected and should be a factor of the project team's planning. However, when the project team is not sufficiently prepared, has insufficient data, or has failed to address items of concern in a satisfactory manner, they may find themselves playing the lawyer's or bureaucrat's game. This is a game of *back and forth,* each turn of which will also include another 30, 60, or 90 day period for review!

The lawyers and bureaucrats will welcome these opportunities to ply their trade. This is, after all, their bread and butter—it's the way they make their living! For the most part, however, unnecessary project delay means nothing but *added expense* to the venture, or corporate entity. (We recognize that, in some instances, the corporate entity may desire to resist remediation for as long as possible, or to avoid it entirely if it can, for various reasons. However, these are isolated instances and we usually find that even bitter medicine is better taken early—usually it is less expensive.)

The planning of strategy, the comparative analyses of the various approaches, the assiduous study of the regulatory requirements, all come into play in this first meeting with the Agency and the attempt to gain a consent decree, order, or agreement. In the words of an old adage, time is money, and the better prepared the project team is, the sooner the work will commence. Governmental agencies are detail oriented; therefore, the secret to success here is to be just as detail oriented—be prepared! And, the project team must remember— *the main criterion of success is obtaining the best possible outcome for the corporate entity.*

DESIGN, PREPARE WORK PLANS

At about this point in time on many projects, the project team will be looking forward to Agency review and approval of the project work plan. Again, this process can be relatively quick and painless or, on the other hand, long and drawn out. (The latter usually equates to "costs more.") It all depends on how well the project team designs and prepares the work plan.

As in the preliminary or interim work plan, this plan will, in all probability, also require a management plan, a quality assurance plan, a data management plan, a technology selection and construction plan, a health and safety plan, a public involvement plan, detailed task lists, and finally, more schedules and reports.

It is far better, at this stage, to err on the side of too much, rather than too little detail. (Too little detail will begin the back and forth of disapproval, rewrite, submit again, wait, perhaps another disapproval, etc., etc.) Delays will usually result in more expense to the venture or corporate entity.

Corrective measures studies (CMSs) must be finely detailed, in order not only that any disapproval might be avoided, but also to make easier the development and approval of the corrective measures implementation (CMI) plan that will be required.

Corrective measures studies will be based on the information that has been collected and compiled to date. This information will have come from sampling, i.e., taking samples of air or surface water, tailings, subsurface strata, radiation, heat, noise, emissions, etc., or whatever may have triggered the corrective action order in the first place. *The point is, the better the information, the better the studies; the better the studies, the better the implementation plan; and the better each of these, the fewer the Agency comments and delays.*

This, then, is one of those areas we mentioned earlier where good project team practices and attention to detail can speed up the project and greatly benefit the venture or corporate bottom line. Comments by the Agency can trigger penalties and/or fines when not acted on within stipulated time periods. These penalties can be severe, ranging from many thousands of dollars per day in fines to facility shutdown. Good project management that results in detailed studies and plans can help circumvent this.

This might also be a good place to discuss, just for a moment, the *personal* aspects involved. Many project teams look at this entire process as adversarial, and take citations, disapprovals, and comments as personal affronts to themselves individually, or to their companies. Unfortunately, the Agency does indeed hold the high ground and, when irritated, can usually be counted on to pull the knot a bit tighter. The wisest of project teams recognize this and gauge their conduct and comments judiciously. The cost of self-satisfaction can sometimes carry a very high price tag for the venture or corporate entity. The same advice holds true when considering the public, the activist organizations, and the fringers. But these will be discussed in more detail later.

SITE MONITORING; COLLECTING NEW DATA

During this period of time, a new protocol will probably be put into place, that protocol being the collection of new data at prescribed intervals. This is site monitoring, and if preliminary studies were soundly based, the new data will corroborate and reinforce the reports and plans already submitted to the Agency. However, if the original studies and planning were based on sparse, weak data, then the project will be delayed while new studies and plans are produced. As we have already stated, delay can equate to higher cost and potential danger to the corporate bottom line.

When the magnitude of the project is large, and the danger of reversal, system failure, or recontamination is present, the corrective action order may require that the site monitoring protocol be made permanent with periodic reporting to the Agency. This requirement, coupled with the cost of operating any resulting air, water, or other emissions control systems, forms the basis of what we described earlier as the non-revenue-producing project. It should be obvious why it is so important to the bottom line of the corporation that these projects be handled properly. The cost of this type project must be held to the lowest number possible.

AGENCY REVIEWS AND APPROVALS

During the course of the environmental project, there will be several occasions of Agency review and approval (or disapproval). These are "choke" points, and how they are handled, i.e., *prepared for,* can be a major factor in the ultimate cost of the project. We call them *choke points* because of the inordinate amount of time that can be consumed during the back-and-forth cycle of disapproval, return of comments, reaction to comments, and resubmittal for another review. Put 60 days on each transmission, multiply the entire process by two or three, and it becomes obvious that a simple approval of a work plan might take several months. And months can sometimes stretch into years!

> We spoke recently with some corporate personnel from the environmental affairs division of a large company. They revealed that they had fallen into this same back-and-forth trap. Their largest current project, which had originally been anticipated (approximately) as a 5-year effort, not including the ongoing monitoring that would be required, now appeared to be at least an 8-year project, at best. Eleven million dollars had already been spent, with really very little to show for it. The real problem seemed to be lack of an overall "finite" approach, resulting in writing and rewriting of work plans, answering Agency comments, seeking/waiting for extensions, and sometimes waiting months for an actionable response. Funds were expended almost carte blanche, since no detailed scope had been developed and no appropriation request had been submitted or approved. The project was proceeding almost at random, reacting, for the most part, to the Agency and outside pressures rather than defining the issues internally and then pushing for desired results. These are the projects that are so costly to the corporate bottom line.

The choke point can also be expensive in other ways. Usually, failure to respond to Agency comments calling for revision to any work plans, reports, or submittals will trigger the imposition of penalties that may range to thousands of dollars per day. Additionally, if responses are deemed inadequate, or failure to respond in a timely manner drags out the proposed or directed remediation efforts, legal liabilities for the venture or corporate entity may skyrocket. This is especially true in situations where there is a threat to public health or the environment.

PUBLIC RELATIONS AND PUBLIC AWARENESS PROGRAMS

Public awareness and the public's perception of the identified environmental problem, along with the proposed solutions and work plans, are potent factors in almost any environmental project. We have emphasized this point, because too many project teams view the public awareness effort as almost an afterthought, attaching far too little priority to it. With serious thought and some creativity on the part of a savvy project team, the public can sometimes be turned into a real ally; ignore it, and an environmentally uneducated but aroused public can cause a project to turn into a nightmare (or very bad press) for the venture.

The public is sometimes easily swayed by activist rhetoric that may exaggerate, or simply misstate, the true situation. Facts matter very little to an activist group with an agenda. We see this around us every day—the political scandals, the abortion clinic violence, the global warming controversy—the list could go on and on. A good project team will not abandon the playing field to activist rhetoric, but will take the steps necessary to not only inform the public of the true facts, but also to package the message in such a way as to *convince and sway* the public. As stated earlier, government agencies and the officials who run them are supersensitive to public opinion. If this were not the case, we would see much less of the activist organizations and the radical fringe groups who would return the planet to a pristine (and nonindustrial) condition if they could! *Of course* the environment is vitally important; *certainly* tough environmental laws and regulations must protect us all—but common sense and a reasonable reaction to the *facts* must prevail. The better project teams recognize the importance of this aspect of the project and take great pains to both educate and sway the public.

Obviously, the first thing that must be done is to get the facts of the matter identified. This should already have been accomplished in the earlier stages, i.e., back when the studies were underway to determine *exactly* the extent of all regulatory requirements so that strategic planning could take place. The compilation of all existing information and data should form the core of the public education and awareness program that now needs to be carefully planned and executed.

To be successful, the program must be carefully packaged. It might be wise to engage a professional public relations firm to handle this part of the project if the expertise is not readily available within the confines of the project team, or elsewhere aboard. Any public meetings called by opposing forces should be attended and reported on by someone from the project team. Errant or slanted information should not be allowed to stand unchallenged. The goal should always be to have the public see the project as a solution, and not as a problem or future concern.

Let's again add to our chart, to see just where this might fit in (Fig. 50). As can be seen, we have placed the public relations and awareness programs squarely beneath the agency review and approval functions. Why? Because we wish to better our position with the agencies through public support, if possible! We can accomplish this, however, only if our position is tenable and we have packaged it adroitly.

We will extend this public relations program further a little later on, if and when a facility construction phase is added to the environmental project. The reasons for extending the program will become obvious. But first, let us look at the other three steps we have just added to the chart (Fig. 50). Two of

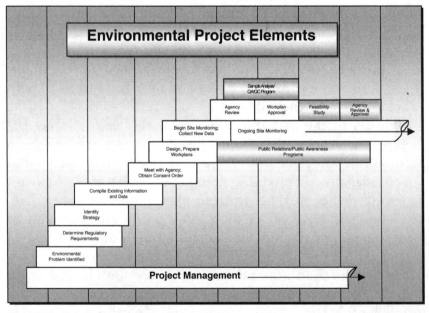

FIGURE 50

these can have an impact *on* the public relations/public awareness program; the third can be impacted *by* it.

SAMPLE ANALYSIS AND QA/QC

Top-notch sample, sample analysis, quality assurance (QA),
and quality control (QC) programs are essential to the reinforcement of the site monitoring program. This is worthy of
special note, since all of these are tools that provide the ammu-
nition for both the public relations program and the agency
review and approval milestones.

The planning for the sampling program itself should take
public concerns into consideration and should demonstrate
both completeness and the corporate desire to put any public
concern to rest. As an example, consider projects where air
pollutants are one of the articles of the order. Sampling in the
neighboring communities, and further in the downwind cone,
should be widespread and highly visible to the inhabitants.
The news media should be encouraged to take note of the
widespread sampling. Sample results should be made known
to the public. Even when sample results are deleterious, the
project team should publish the results, in order that projected
fix benefits can be also released at the same time. Make no
mistake, the results *will* be made public; they will, however,
sound far worse if activist groups put the information before
the public.

Sample analysis, in cases where public concern is an issue,
should be accomplished by a respected independent agency
(rather than a corporate or plant lab) to avoid any hint of
impropriety. Likewise, the attendant quality assurance program would best be served by an independent third party.
Quality procedures should be written in detail, and the project
team should ensure that the quality program includes all regulatory parameters. Much of the quality program will be concerned with the methodology of sample gathering, that is,
ensuring that each core sample, each air quality sample, each
water or effluent sample is collected and handled in strict
accordance with procedure. These programs must be carefully
planned and rigidly followed if the data obtained is to be of

value in obtaining workplan approvals and, later, permits to proceed.

It will be to the project team's advantage to err on the side of too many samples, rather than too few. If the team is eagerly awaiting an approval of a work plan and the word comes from the agency that more sample results must be considered before the work plan can be approved, another month (at least) has been added to the schedule. Remember our earlier statement—extended schedules usually equate to more cost.

THE FEASIBILITY STUDY

Following initial work plan approval, site monitoring, extensive sample gathering, and analysis, but prior to finalization of the project work plan and submittal for final agency review and approval, a detailed feasibility study is usually performed. Why? For the most part, to ensure that the whole thing makes good sense; that after the expenditure of perhaps millions of bottom-line dollars, the problem really will be cured. Also, to assure general managers that future operation of the overall plant facility can still be profitable. The feasibility study must, however, be brutally honest; it must not gild the lily, regardless of what it reveals. Feasibility studies should be reality checks.

PUTTING IT ALL TOGETHER

The foregoing has been a discussion of the steps usually followed by good project teams as they bring an identified environmental problem to solution. If the final solution and approved plan calls for site construction, that part of the project will now revert to more traditional project management and execution, perhaps even an additional site project team. Let's look now at how this might all fit together.

As can be seen by the chart in Fig. 51, the facility project team must work hand in glove with the environmental project team, usually starting with the feasibility study. The facility team will go on with the development of the formal facility appropriation request (AR), design engineering, pro-

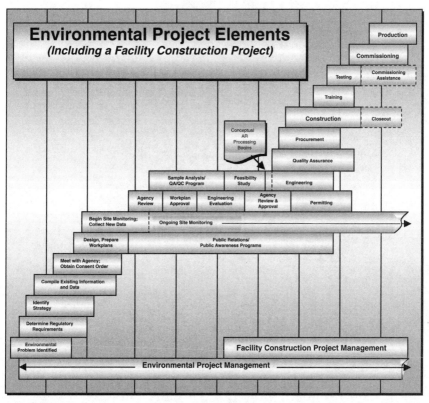

FIGURE 51

curement, etc., while the environmental team's responsibilities may continue on indefinitely with on-site monitoring, sample gathering and analysis, and periodic reports to the EPA. This is part of the overall environmental program management for the facility.

Please note, however, the one particular point where the two teams should work together very closely in order to attain a common goal—that goal being the obtaining of all necessary permits to complete the project. The point to which we refer is the public relations and awareness programs initiated by the environmental team. As can be seen, we have extended that bar further, so that it now encompasses the permitting process. Permits will sometimes be easier to obtain if there is no public outcry in process!

THE RE-ENGINEERING PROJECT

A TIME OF CHANGE

For the most part, business processes have changed very little for hundreds of years. For centuries, merchants have made investments, hired labor and craftspersons to toil at producing goods, have taken market risks, kept production cost records, bartered and sold, watched profit margins, and paid taxes. Nothing changed much—that is, *until now!* Suddenly we are being told such things as, "Throw out everything you've ever been told about how to conduct business" and "The company that fails to change will fail," and so on, and so on.

Well, only part of that is true—and that part is only partly true.

The tenets of business, the underlying principles, the driving forces, have changed very little, even to today. What *has* changed, and is still evolving rapidly, is the way that successful businesses *react* to those driving forces. We now have the means and the tools to analyze, evaluate, stop and start business functions; and compete at levels and to degrees that we would never have considered before. And there is one powerful, underlying reason this is happening: we now have the capability to evaluate almost infinite amounts of information, thus giving us the ability to *maximize profits* as never before! We have been given this capability through the advent of the computer.

It is true that the company that fails to change in today's business climate will, in many cases, be at a disadvantage; some may even fail. However, the business of drastically changing business methods and processes, or as it is commonly called, *business process re-engineering,* can also be disastrous if not handled properly.

The term *re-engineering* was coined by Michael Hammer and James Champy in their bestseller *Re-Engineering the Corporation* in 1993. The term, and the process of re-engineering became the buzz and the mantra of the first half of the '90s decade. Companies began revamping business and manufacturing processes to gain competitive advantage in an increasingly global marketplace. Every facet of corporate operation, from business systems to manufacturing processes and practices, became fair game for change. Companies re-engineered to eliminate redundant processes and to cut down the number of steps involved in manufacturing, marketing, selling, and shipping. With closer control on manufacturing, inventories could be reduced, freeing more capital for investment in profitable enterprises.

But as more and more companies jumped aboard, some bad things began happening. Many of the efforts aimed at re-engineering ended in failure. In many cases, expected benefits failed to occur; in some, production levels (and profits) went down rather than up. What had happened? In most cases, the re-engineering process wasn't being looked upon *as a project,* which, most assuredly, it is! Normal project planning, scheduling, risk analysis, and scope development weren't taking place. Operating people were, more often than not, being left out of the picture until time to introduce them to a completely foreign method of doing their jobs. By then they were ready to resist—sometimes in subtle ways, sometimes not so subtle.

Employees, from middle managers to janitors and laborers, could soon see, in many instances, that the contemplated changes that would result from re-engineering would drastically affect their jobs and livelihoods. Many would simply be unneeded, and many would be unqualified to perform newer, more technical functions. The *human element* was being ignored.

> We noted just recently that two large waste-hauling companies have opted out of a new, state-of-the-art software system after having gone several millions of dollars down the re-engineering project development path. The shocking part of the story, however, is the amount of money poured into these projects before pulling the plug. One company had spent $45 million of an estimated $250 million, while the other company had spent a whopping $130 million!
>
> It is commendable when a company's executive management sees the error of an earlier decision and moves boldly to correct it. However, these are tremendous sums of money to be throwing out the window. The statement that "We'll take a charge for it," attributed to one of the CEOs, seems to be oversimplifying the situation a bit. Surely, for the benefit of the shareholders, the original decision to purchase these business-management software systems should have been investigated more thoroughly.

TREAT IT AS A *PROJECT!*

The re-engineering project should not be viewed as anything other than what it is—a project, albeit sometimes a special project. If the re-engineering project is concerned simply with a business system, a process, or an isolated facility, then it most certainly should follow all the rules of normal projects. If, however, the re-engineering effort encompasses the entire corporation, if it goes to the very heart of the manner in which the corporation conducts its business, then it becomes not just *a* project but *the* project. Failure may mean the demise of the venture.

In too many instances, these multimillion dollar projects are treated as "works in progress." Their boundaries being somewhat nebulous anyway, they overrun both schedule and budget. Preproject planning is as important to this type project as it is to other major projects. Need we be reminded that we are, after all, spending the company's hard-earned *bottom-line* dollars on these projects, just as with any other?

IDENTIFY THE GOALS

The only way to *begin* to avoid those nebulous boundaries to which we just referred is to know exactly where you're going, especially when considering projects of this nature. That means starting with a very hard-eyed look by executive management, first at what *needs* to be done and second *how* it's *going* to be done. For example, the chairman and CEO of the waste management company just mentioned was quoted as stating, "They expect you to change your business to go with the way the software works." He was speaking here of a huge consulting company that provides a complex software system purporting to monitor and manage virtually all of a company's business systems. The only problem is that he was speaking *after* having spent $45 million.

And therein lies the problem with many re-engineering projects. None of the packaged software systems *work,* at least from the packaged state. They must be heavily modified, almost re-created. The cost, at least in the very large applications, is virtually open ended. A major portion of the cost arrives with the teams of consultants brought aboard to implement the software, i.e., "change consultants," who help companies standardize both operations and the monitoring methods required to adapt to the package software.

The re-engineering of any company, from the smaller factory to the corporate behemoth, is a serious, make that *radical,* step to take. Re-engineering should come from the top down. By that we mean the re-engineered vision must come from executive leaders, leaders who are firm in their strategic view of the corporate goals. Companies whose leaders have only a nodding acquaintance with software systems and the intricacies of re-engineering usually become sold by both the scare tactics (if you don't totally change your business systems you will lose out in the global market) and the grand promises (by totally changing your business systems you will save x millions and increase profits by x^2 millions) of very sophisticated consulting companies. After having been mesmerized by high-powered sales techniques many client companies then assign an executive sponsor who in turn assigns a manager to "re-engineer our company." Unfortunately, what they sometimes get, after spending tremendous sums of bottom-line dollars, is a cumbersome parody of a once proud company that now just doesn't seem to work.

Another point to consider when going with a heavily customized packaged system is that customized systems are almost impossible to upgrade. Extensively customized programs may mean that consultants will be aboard continuously, in order to keep the systems up to the latest versions.

Of course all re-engineering projects don't end this way. And of course re-engineering is a sorely needed change for many companies. But the resultant product of the re-engineering effort must be a result of corporate vision, not a change in corporate direction as a result of an attempt to comply with packaged software systems.

Let's assume, for a moment, that executive management has very carefully considered the alternatives and has assigned a corporate sponsor to spearhead a re-engineering project. The first course of action should be to see that corporate strategies and goals are addressed by a preproject planning group. One of their first tasks will probably be the formulation of a *mission statement*.

THE MISSION STATEMENT

Let us state right here that mission statements, organization charts, matrixes, schedules, and any other tool that we might discuss are nothing but pieces of paper, or keystrokes on a computer. It's what lies *behind* them that is important. Behind them must stand commitment, perseverance, and a clear view of the goal, or goals. Without these things the tools remain nothing but "pieces of paper and keystrokes on a computer."

The development of a mission statement by the preproject planning team will help to set the boundaries of the project by identifying the goals. This will in turn later allow the scope, the schedule, and the budget to be more firmly set.

The mission statement itself is a written description of the guiding principles by which the ultimate goal of the project (also defined in the statement) will be accomplished. Many of us have been through these mission development sessions. Usually facilitated by a consulting professional, these meetings are exciting, fast-moving, and challenging brainstorming sessions. (It is highly important, however, that the facilitator have an understanding of the difference between a project and a work in progress. If he or she doesn't, the exercise may take the wrong tack, right at the outset). The individuals making up the preplanning group are encouraged to let their minds and imaginations range far and wide in an effort to surround the problems to be addressed in a re-engineering project. In this manner, the worth of various goals can be discussed; the efficacy of remedial actions can be examined. Executive management, represented by an executive sponsor, should attend and lend vigorous encouragement to this effort.

When properly developed, the mission statement will finally boil down into a concise and clearly stated project goal (or goals), buttressed by firm management principles and guidelines that will be effective in keeping the project on a straight and narrow course, a course that will lead to a successful conclusion.

What, then, are the necessary components of a mission statement?

- Identification of the primary goals
- Encapsulation of management philosophy
- Delineation of major management guideline elements

Some of the focus items that might be raised during the mission statement development session:

- Corporate short- and long-term strategies
- Desired project benefits

- Production and quality goals
- Teamwork
- Communication
- Commitment
- Definition of success
- Risks
- Venture profitability
- The human element; manager and worker "buy-in"
- Executive management commitment

These are certainly not all of the items that will be focused on by the mission statement development group, but they all should certainly be included in the discussion. As an example of a mission statement, we herewith again reiterate our own carefully considered mission statement, the same statement with which we began this book:

> *Our Mission:* To teach project teams to execute capital projects more successfully by focusing not only on achievement of the promised benefits, but also on corporate and venture *bottom-line* improvement. This stated mission recognizes that the ultimate goal can be accomplished only by convincing project-associated personnel of the critical importance of maintaining a constant awareness of the potential long-term effects of project decisions, of teamwork, and of the importance of the stakeholder approach. The fundamental precepts of this methodology are:
>
> - Clearly defined objectives
> - Recognition of risks
> - Teamwork
> - Preproject planning
> - Detailed definition of scope

Let's look, for a moment, at a case in point, a case where some of these fundamentals were lacking. As you consider this case, bear in mind that we are viewing it in hindsight, and these fundamentals are sometimes almost indiscernible, especially when you're "up close and personal" with the project.

The case we have chosen is a relatively small re-engineering effort, taking place at the same time that a larger business process change is occurring. We have chosen the smaller case for our discussion, primarily owing to the complexities involved in the larger projects. (An entire book could be written on many of them.) However, as can readily be seen, the same principles apply regardless of project size.

CASE   STUDY   12

Reapplying Material to Maximize Profits—or Emotionally Yours

HISTORICAL SYNOPSIS—PROJECT BACKGROUND

A manufacturing company with multiple operating sites decided that, while it was re-engineering business processes in its primary manufacturing and finished product areas, it would, at one of its sites, make a concerted attempt to maximize profits on rejected material. Although any particular rejection is directed against the intended purpose of the primary product, it does not rule out reapplying the rejected material to another, less demanding purpose so long as the material meets those particular specifications. This reapplication practice had long been in effect; however, there was much room for improvement.

The information captured for in-process material was on a site- and process-specific set of databases and managed by a site-specific set of software. The concept called for identifying the constraints and interactions between these sets of data and common corporate ordering and inventory systems. A user-written query and report was employed to extract data from a variety of sources, resulting in a printed report that could be used as a decision-making tool. For the most part, this process was being handled, on a consultant basis, by very knowledgeable outside resources.

It was estimated that as much as $800,000 per year of "lost profits" was being recovered via this method. Material that would otherwise be sold to lower-margin markets was being reapplied to a prime order and sold for about a $150 per billable unit premium over these downgraded prices. One aspect of this tool, however, was that all needed data was not immediately available, and many phone calls to a variety of sources were required before the decision could be made.

Any defects existing in this material were not a hindrance to the reapplied order specification. (Actually, in some instances it was merely excess material on a given order and had no defects). In either case, there was no product liability in reapplying the material, but the determination of this fact depended on the knowledge and experience of the consultants. To ensure appropriate reapplication, the process required not only this determination by the consultants, but also a further sign-off by the Quality Assurance department that the application was acceptable.

PROJECT DESIGN/PREPROJECT PLANNING

Preproject planning took place in March 1994. The result of this preproject planning effort was a concept that described three phases. The first phase would deliver a consolidated relational database, or snapshot, extracted from the myriad data sources and a printed report that would draw on all necessary data to describe rejected material. A significant improvement of the breadth of data for a given material would improve the process of phone calls. It was recognized that there would be some data quality problems, but it was anticipated that these would be corrected through the process. A user manager was designated with both the responsibility for buy-in of the project, and the power to effect administrative changes when necessary.

The second phase would extract orders that were candidates for having material reapplied to them. These would be orders that had an open balance of material still to be supplied. The data for each set of material from the first phase would be logically matched to these candidate orders in a specific value sequence. External, user-maintained tables of parameters would be used to allow fine tuning of the matching criteria. The scope would be modest and geared to achieving the objective of organizing the data; there would be no attempt at Star Wars perfection of automatically applying material. A human would remain in the loop to select the best fit, or fits, for each case.

Databases for both of the above phases would be designed as interfaces, in order to leverage future efforts at other sites. Though data and manufacturing processes at other sites would differ, the underlying architecture would enable the use of this system as a pattern, or template. This, it was felt, would minimize rework in phase 1, eliminate it entirely in phase 3, and keep the changes required for phase 2 to a small effort.

The third phase would be a work flow system that would allow online applications and routing of these recommendations to the Quality

Assurance department for review. On approval, the application would be forwarded to the staff responsible for managing these reapplications.

PROJECT ORGANIZATION/MANAGEMENT

During early project stages, a user was placed in charge to ensure not only that all requirements were met, but also for purposes of coordinating the appropriate user resources. Eventually an experienced project manager (who also filled the role of system analyst) picked up the project and drove a very difficult data integrity problem to conclusion.

The project was sponsored by the manufacturing's site executive management. User personnel resources were identified, briefed, and committed to the project. Funding came from the corporate Information Systems (IS) function. Delivery of service came from an outside contractor's technical staff, both at corporate headquarters and the site facilities.

PROJECT EXECUTION

A technical project team was formed, consisting of a technical lead person at the site, a management resource at the corporate headquarters, and a pool of expertise at the site who were familiar with the site-specific systems and data. Users were part and parcel of the team, so they could take part in acceptance and refining of requirements.

Phase 1

The initial request was formally made of the IS contractor (an outsourced function) in late March of 1994. The work statement describing the cost, schedule, and approach to each phase was delivered in August of 1994. The first phase software system development was essentially complete and accepted in January of 1995. During this time the IS contractor replaced the project manager from the headquarters site with a manager who resided at the site.

> In July of 1994 a stabilization effort was begun to finalize and completely install, at all sites, the order entry system for all products. It was considered, however, that the most difficult site would be the one where the reapplication project was being developed.

The technical resources at the manufacturing site facilities were unfamiliar with the intricacies of the order entry system and data, and the HQ order entry team was unfamiliar with the intricacies of the site-specific data regarding work in progress.

During the course of Phase 1, many issues for resolution were identified, related to data that was wrong, not present, or the "wrong data" for the purposes of the project. This was not unexpected; in fact it had been anticipated, and an additional value this project was expected to bring was related to this very issue (i.e., a cleanup of mission-critical data).

Though Phase 1 took longer than originally expected, it ultimately delivered, and all issues were worked in a cross-functional way with full awareness of all parties involved. The remaining process-related problems were resolved by the users during February and March of 1995. Final reviews of these last issues revealed a desire by some end users to expand the scope. This desire was made known by the IS contractor's project manager, but was quickly resolved by end-user management— project scope was to be held to the original definition.

Phase 2

Phase 2, the actual extraction of orders that were candidate for having material reapplied to them, was directed to be started during the final cleanup of a few remaining issues in April, 1995. This phase was originally scheduled to complete in November, 1994; however, the unexpected delays encountered in Phase 1 had extended the Phase 2 kickoff by approximately 5 months.

Additionally, finding a technical lead person to apply to this phase took some time, even to the point of causing the contractor to take time to make a concerted effort to build a skills inventory of potential candidates. Although this action consumed some extra schedule time, it was deemed by project managers to be a needed process in order to secure the right resource to execute the work. (The personnel resources at the site facilities were unskilled in the use of the relational database employed.)

Eventually a good resource was found and the second phase delivered in early July, approximately 8 months later than originally scheduled.

Phase 3

Phase 3, the work flow system to allow on-line "applications" and the routing of these recommendations to the Quality Assurance department for review and approval, was begun in July 1995 and finished in the following month. The August completion was, again, approximately 8 months behind the original scheduled date of December 1994.

CONCLUSION

Early planning stages of the project assumed that if a data element could be identified, it existed and had integrity. This was a bad assumption, and this early overestimate and overassessment of the data quality resulted in a loss of profits to the outsourcer's (contractor's) fixed bid in the first phase. Appropriate tools to query and assess the data did not exist, and lack of fundamental knowledge of the system further complicated the planning. In short, possibly because it was difficult to assess the data, this step (assessment of data) was, by and large, ignored.

Not only did the site team have inadequate knowledge of the common order entry system and data, but the order entry system itself was undergoing a stabilization and reduction-to-practice activity. The convergence of both activities at the same time (order entry system and reapplication process changes) created more distraction to both efforts than had been anticipated.

The site resources were of insufficient breadth in that they were the only ones having knowledge of division-specific systems and, since these systems required day-to-day support, the overall effort on this project was diluted.

The site staff attempted to take on a portion of the project for which their skills were lacking. Eventually an appropriate technician who knew both the technology and the manufacturing business was relocated to the site facility to support this effort (with much better results).

A very urgent need and attitude of "hurry up and make it work" was coming from the end-user management. The complexity of the project's early stage was not clearly understood by this faction, nor was there any sympathy toward it. The occurrence, at the same time, of both a significant business problem and an opportunity that warranted an urgent, no-holds-barred effort further complicated the project by causing its priority value to recede on user management radar.

> User management, being under the gun to produce, usually will take a short-term approach to all activities. Although this in itself is not bad, it does at times lead to "emotionalism" and unrealistic demands on project teams and contractors alike.

There were also a number of contractor management changes during the course of the project, some of which involved the project manager position itself. Obviously, the best method would have been to involve the ultimate project manager from the inception of the project. Good project planning and personnel selection at the very beginning is absolutely essential to a successful outcome.

Right at the outset the contractor's work statement incurred a delay in approval by the client company. Although the delay was not hugely significant in this case, it was only one of many, and it does support the observation that the outsourced contractor should work closely with the client company's staff in preparing work statements, rather than wait until all the i's are dotted and t's are crossed. Requiring both a first and second engineering submittal would probably have negated this problem.

The actual benefits derived, although significant in terms of dollars saved by reapplying material, were disappointing in that only 50 percent or less, of anticipated savings were obtained as a result of the reengineering effort. Although the tool is valuable in the reapplication of secondary to prime orders, the human element is still very much in existence within the system. Could it be that the effort itself was misdirected? Could it be that too much effort was expended here in treating a symptom rather than in curing the disease? In this age of microchips and advanced computerized control systems, does there really have to be "nonprime"?

LESSONS LEARNED

All too often, emotion sets the course of a project. When this occurs, the results are usually less than planned and, in some instances, can be disastrous. In this case, emotion ruled the day, and a project was begun without the necessary consideration of very important and relevant precursors. In haste, considerations of risk and the abilities, knowledge, and expertise of those who would be involved were put aside. The project took longer, cost more, and returned much less than anticipated.

Planning in detail is essential to any project, not just projects of the re-engineering type. Although "planning" was done in the early stages of this project it apparently was not in sufficient detail nor was it complete. At almost every turn, it was found that the plan was lacking. The project team appeared at all stages to be reactive rather than proactive.

This project, though of questionable value, was not disastrous to the company. This was due largely, however, to its relatively small magnitude in the greater scheme of things. Imagine the outcome if this small re-engineering project were 100, or perhaps even 1000 times bigger.

PROJECT ORGANIZATION

Since there are so many varied types of re-engineering projects being called into existence in the marketplace each day, there are likewise many varied ways these projects are being approached, not only from an organizational standpoint but also from the standpoints of planning and execution. There is no cookbook method of organizing for them either, but there are certainly some tried and true methods that have led to successful outcomes for some.

THE STEERING COMMITTEE

Most re-engineering projects go deeply into corporate culture, including long-held and deeply ingrained beliefs about how to run the company's business systems. By business systems, we mean such systems as:

- Marketing
- Selling
- Order fulfillment
- Inventory
- Purchasing
- Manufacturing
- Production
- Accounting

Of course, there are other subjects that might be considered in a total restructuring of corporate business systems, but the foregoing are now relatively common as grist for the re-engineer's mill. Probably the most important aspect of this list is the extent to which these systems permeate all areas and levels of company activities.

Re-engineering, once adopted, must be ongoing as a company or corporate philosophy. It is not an incremental process. [That would be more akin to Total Quality Management (TQM).] To successfully re-engineer an organization, a company must usually *demolish* existing organization structures. In many cases, functions formerly performed within the organization will be outsourced. This is the very factor that causes the failure of so many re-engineering projects. Why? The organization *resists, fears* change. "Expect from your re-engineering effort that you will come out with fewer people," according to Walter Kiechel, editor of *Fortune* magazine, "but this is the paradox: if the principal aim is headcount reduction, then you're doing it wrong. You have to focus instead on the process of work, and how that can be improved."

Engineering projects usually bring together teams from different corporate functions. For this reason, if for no other, re-engineering projects should be coordinated by a steering committee composed of senior managers from each area affected. The steering committee should report to executive management (see Fig. 52).

THE STEERING COMMITTEE ROLE

A Reflection of Long-Range Corporate Strategy.   The re-engineering process must be firmly backed by executive

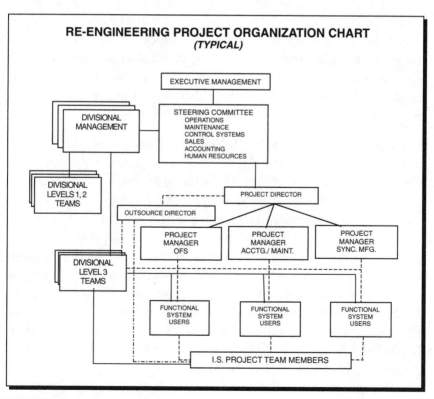

FIGURE 52

management. Corporate strategic planning and goals must be transmitted to the Steering Committee via the executive management overseer. Only in this manner can the ensuing, and inevitable, resistance to change be overcome.

Consistent Leadership and Direction.   In most re-engineering projects, multiple teams will be at work. The work must be coordinated, since few corporate functions stand alone. The organization chart in Fig. 52 depicts a possible Steering Committee position in an overall re-engineering project. Note that it is made up of representatives (senior managers) from all affected areas and that the direction of management is from the top, down.

We often see and hear of large re-engineering projects where the direction comes primarily from the outsourced contractor. In these cases, the corporate picture is being dictated by the contractor in an effort to make the business systems correlate with its, the contractor's, software systems. In some instances this may work, especially if the client company has a relatively unsophisticated system in place to start with (or if the project is greenfield). However, in most cases, the contractor's software must be rewritten in order to satisfy the various corporate factions. It is in this rewriting process that consistent leadership and direction is absolutely essential.

Ensure Adequacy and Availability of Resources.   Using the clout derived from the active oversight and direction from executive management, and the solid-line ties to both divisional management and identified project factions (teams), the Steering Committee must ensure not only the adequacy of resources, but also the *availability* of those resources.

The schedule, the budget, even the success of the re-engineering effort can be thwarted by powerful middle managers who, for whatever reason (usually alleged higher priorities) fail to make needed resources available to the re-engineering effort. And there is another associated problem that is seldom discussed: the *quality* of the resources that are made available. Do we really think that a manager will readily give up his or her *best* people, possibly for months (or even years) without being "significantly urged" by superiors? This leads to our next critical steering committee role—selling the concept.

Selling the Concept; Obtaining Buy-in.   The only way to get those powerful middle managers to willingly put their best personnel forward is to make believers of them. Even this is not enough; the resources committed to the project must also be believers. Let's go another step in that direction; the users of the re-engineered systems must be believers. Want another? The customers must be believers.

In short, to make a re-engineering project work, it must make sense, it must be shown to result in benefits to all concerned, *and it must be sold!* Buy-in by the affected populace at large is an integral and essential part of re-engineering success. It should be one of the roles, say responsibilities, of the Steering Committee to ensure that proactive steps are taken at all levels to educate this populace. Unfortunately, many re-engineering efforts are sadly lacking in this critical area.

Monitor Project Scope and Cost.   One of the problems associated with re-engineering projects is the tendency for overrun, both in time of execution and cost. This can, of course, be caused by failure of the Steering Committee to address any of the foregoing individual items, but in reality it's usually a combination of all of them. Poorly defined goals, insufficient preproject planning and a failure to obtain buy-in from the affected populace will almost always lead to overruns, in many cases substantial overruns. The scope must not be allowed to expand beyond the borders of the original *well-defined* plan. This can readily occur, in the absence of close monitoring by the Steering Committee.

THE PROJECT DIRECTOR

The project director must be knowledgeable and completely familiar with the intricacies of a majority of the current business systems. He or she should have held positions of major profit and loss responsibility at the corporation's divisional levels, should be completely in accord with executive management's view of the need and desirability to effect major changes in the corporation, and should be experienced in major project management.

As stated at the beginning of this chapter, a major re-engineering project—that is, one wherein the very basics of how a corporation conducts its business, services its customers, fills orders, keeps its books, and controls its costs and inventories—is the most important project there is; it is *the* project. For this reason, executive management must carefully consider the qualifications of the person who is to fill the position of project director. It must be filled by the best person for the position, not just the best *available* person. If the best individual is unavailable, then that person must be made available. There is no higher priority.

The project director should have great leeway in selection of the principal players on the re-engineering team. He or she will be looking for individuals who have the ability (and the sense of teamwork) to unselfishly subordinate their own part to the general effort of the group with whom they are working, whenever necessary.

Assuming that the re-engineering project will be utilizing an outsourced contractor's software system, the project director will require close coordination with the contractor's project manager. It is essential that the corporate requirements be made known, in detail, to the contractor's team. This should be accomplished through extensive and detailed preproject planning sessions by the individual project teams working with end users.

Likewise, it is essential that the software contractor then produce a detailed first submittal to the project director for review and study by the individual project teams. Second (and perhaps third) submittals should be required in order that the scope of the project can be defined and refined. When the Steering Committee is satisfied that the project is clearly understood and sufficient planning has taken place, then, and only then, should the project go forward.

THE PROJECT TEAM

The re-engineering project team will be composed of users, accountants, buyers, sellers, statisticians, information systems engineers, consultants, and possibly many others, dependent on the type and magnitude of the project. Since the very nature of the re-engineering project is usually intended to effect change primarily in business and information systems, the majority of the project team members will probably derive from these (the IS) classifications. This gets right to the heart of one of the main problems encountered in this type project: the lack of experience in disciplined project management by the project team.

For the most part, these are very talented people with an in-depth knowledge not only of how the systems currently work, but what needs to be done to vastly improve them. The problem is, these same people are used to viewing this type of activity as work in progress. To a certain extent they are *always* engaged in this type of work and tend to view the re-engineering effort as just a gigantic "slug" of the same thing. And, when viewed in this context, a huge project can drift aimlessly. This is why we stated so emphatically that one of the qualifying criteria for a project director should be experience in major project management. In all likelihood, the project director will find that one of the major tasks associated with the position will be the indoctrination of much of the team into the intricacies of this discipline.

PLANNING

As with any project, planning in detail is the key to success. It may sound ridiculous to some, but for major projects the planning process itself must be planned! Think of it for a moment; if the planning process isn't well thought through, a critical planning element may be left out.

With this in mind, we offer here a few questions that the preproject planning team should ask itself:

- Has a dedicated, dynamic preproject planning team been assembled?
- Does the preproject planning team have the required skills, knowledge, and authority it requires?
- Does the preproject planning team consist of personnel with expertise in the following areas:

Project management?
Technology?
Business?

- Has it been determined whether there is a valid business advantage to be gained?
- Has it been determined if the risks of not doing the project outweigh the risks of doing the project?
- Has it been determined if the technology is available and proved?
- Have the technology obsolescence factors been determined?
- Has it been determined if there is an operational method of achieving the desired result?
- Has a preproject planning plan been formulated with documentation of the methods and resources to be used in the planning process?

When these questions have been satisfactorily answered and the planning plan itself has been formulated, it must then be implemented and tracked. As the various resources report in, the preproject planning manager should evaluate the results of the tasks that have been set in motion. A generic evaluation list for preproject planning might consist of all, or some, of the following:

- Development of a statement of business need
- Mission statement development planning
- A definition of responsibilities for all preproject planning team members
- The development of a set of major milestones for preproject planning
- A defined schedule for preproject planning
- Preproject planning resources
- A defined budget for preproject planning
- Information availability and needs
- The locations of preproject planning work

- Defined planning deliverables
- Status reporting requirements
- Defined tasks for analyzing risks
- Development of a preliminary overall project outline
- Defined tasks for analyzing capability of in-house resources
- An available technology review
- An outline of known alternatives
- Preproject planning priorities
- A defined plan to obtain buy-in at all levels
- The quality of deliverables
- The development of an organization chart including defined responsibilities
- Outsourcer contracting

As stated, the foregoing is only a generic and partial listing of the many and varied task items that a preproject planning group might find on its plate. Bear in mind, also, that this is only preproject planning. The planning deliverables should provide not only a much clearer view of project need but also a much more informed picture of budget, schedule, benefits, and risks.

The bright light of a well-organized preproject planning phase will provide executive management with a better basis for ultimate decisions (decisions that will affect the bottom line of the company for years to come) by helping to illuminate the claims and counterclaims of the software providers. The preproject planning effort will set the stage for project approval, organization, execution, and disciplined monitoring.

EXECUTION

Although we won't attempt here to provide a complete primer on the subject of re-engineering projects (there are too many variations and there are already entire books out on the genre) a listing of some probable task items might be of value to the "re-engineer." Again, bear in mind that this listing is generic and cannot be considered all-encompassing. Many of these items will be subordinate detail tasks emanating from the broader definitions set by the preproject planning group. This listing of potential re-engineering project task questions is in no particular order of priority.

- Have the following been considered in a financial analysis:
  Sales forecasts
  Price/volume for each product (short and long term)
  Cost elements (labor, cost of goods, capital, etc.)
- Have regulatory items been assessed?
- Have all relevant technologies been analyzed?
- Have the economic benefits been defined, including:
  Sales volumes and pricing forecast for each product/by-product
    affected
  Obsolescence issues
- Has project investment and timing been defined, including:
  Capital cost
  Capital project timing with yearly expected cash flows
  Cost of financing the project with timing of cost
  Date of rollout
- Have inventory quantities and values been evaluated?
- Have the working capital requirements been evaluated, including:
  R&D expense
  Training and indoctrination
  Incentives
  Outsourcer fees and expenses
- Has general plant investment, including utility capital and investment in raw material manufacturing facilities been considered?
- Have changes in the tax structure, including any applicable subsidies, been evaluated?
- Have changes in the various labor types, usage, and costs been evaluated?
- Have changes in operating rates and percent on-stream and percent on-specification production been evaluated?

- How will any cost savings not previously identified be handled?
- Have other criteria been evaluated, including:
Future access to market
Future access to raw materials
Long-term access to labor skills needed
Fit with company long-range strategy
Political considerations
Company image/quality of life/safety
Environmental considerations
- Have the facilities ability to meet new requirements of quality, volume, or type of products been evaluated?
- Has the availability of selected technology been thoroughly examined in terms of price and timing? (Could it be better developed in-house?)
- Which legacy systems will be retained?
- What is the capability of the system to fall back to a legacy position in event of unforeseen difficulty?
- Have the business risks been identified and evaluated, including:
First costs (capital costs)—what is the worst case?
Operation and maintenance costs
Start-up and commissioning costs
Market considerations, such as product marketability, market size, market share, and life span
Uncertainty in process and technology capabilities
Steps necessary to alleviate resistance to change
Customer concerns
Public concerns
- Have the qualifications of potential contractor and designer resources been thoroughly examined?
- Have the qualifications of company resources been thoroughly examined?
- Has the availability of qualified contractor and designer resources been investigated?
- Has the availability of qualified company resources been ascertained?

- Have the installation risks been identified and evaluated, including:
  Resource availability and productivity
  Subcontractor, equipment, and supplier performance
  Strikes, work stoppages, and other adverse labor activity
  Unforeseen project conditions
  Unforeseen economic factors (inflation, shortages, etc.)
  System incompatibilities

- Has management and administrative risk been identified and evaluated, including:
  Cost and schedule estimates
  Human errors
  Timely decisions
  Necessity for and availability of experts or specialists
  Level of design documentation required

- Have project schedules been defined and developed, including:
  Rollout schedules that support the overall project need dates
  Development and installation schedules coordinated with the rollout schedules
  Procurement schedule for materials and equipment, including the need dates for outsource contractors and subvendor information required for completion of detailed engineering

- Does the procurement schedule for contractors consider time factors associated with the prequalification and selection of those contractors?

- Have business planning changes that may result from the project's success been addressed, including:
  Capacity/volume/inventory studies
  Location and market evaluation
  Profit plan
  Long-term funding plans and strategies
  Raw materials studies
  Process flexibility and expandability
  Delivery studies
  Unit price objectives
  Risk strategies

Corporate resource assessments
Business alliance evaluation
Government regulations
Technology versus competition

- Have risks been assessed, including:
Environmental risks
Social risks
Political risks
Processing technology risks
Equipment capability risks
Operational risks
Design engineering risks
Project estimate risks
Business risks

- Does the project execution approach include:
Basis of estimate
Basis of schedule
Selection of critical technologies for the project
Work breakdown structure
Procurement approach
Contracting strategy
System development strategy
Strategic objectives
Installation and rollout strategy
Legacy systems strategy

WHAT IT FINALLY TAKES

Mission statements, steering committees, studies, schedules, and strategies are certainly needed items in a re-engineering project. Yet they are all just nice pieces of paper without one critical additive—executive management commitment. Commitment and follow-through by knowledgeable and proactive executives is absolutely required if the project is to end up in the success column which, by the way, is far smaller than the failure column in re-engineering type projects.

The risks are great since, in some instances, large corporations are radically changing their business systems; business systems which, for the most part, had brought them to greatness. However, the rewards can also be great. In fact, as we race headlong out of the industrial age and into the information age the companies, corporations, and conglomerates that don't change may be the last dinosaurs!

Let's take a look now at one more case study—one where the first pass was not quite what its architects were looking for:

C A S E   S T U D Y   **1 3**

Before the Concrete Sets

HISTORICAL SYNOPSIS—PROJECT BACKGROUND

In March of 1996, NewAge, Inc., a large industrial tool and die company headquartered in Michigan, embarked on two ambitious re-engineering projects. The first project involved automating procedures for equipment purchasing and maintenance at the company's multiple work sites. The second project, dubbed Order Fulfillment System, or OFS, was designed to both improve customer service and to more accurately and efficiently process sales orders.

It was felt that the corporate needs and goals were simple and clear enough to management that there was no real need to formally prepare for the project; therefore no steering committee or corporate sponsor was assigned. Instead, a project manager was drafted from the Information Systems group to organize re-engineering teams composed of both corporate and field personnel. These teams were tasked to develop strategies for implementing the projects. Primary functions of the re-engineering teams included:

- The establishment of measurable re-engineering goals for each project.
- The re-engineering of the business processes to achieve the stated goals.
- The gathering of data and the empirical research needed to provide a foundation for the re-engineering effort.
- The development of plans, policies, and procedures felt to be necessary for re-engineering project implementation.

- The identification of the resources required to develop and implement the re-engineering project.

- The communication of re-engineering plans and information throughout the corporate structure to attain buy-in at all levels.

- The establishment of schedules for project development, training, and implementation.

- The research of and recommendation for the software required for implementing re-engineered processes.

- The shepherding of the re-engineering project implementation efforts in the field.

The re-engineering of the company's procedures for equipment purchasing and maintenance was perceived as critical to sustaining market competitiveness. The nature of the work, designing and building high-quality machine tools (much of it for the automotive industry), required the steady and precise operation of large and expensive equipment. The purchasing, maintenance, and repair of this core equipment was the company's highest functional cost area.

The goal of the equipment re-engineering project was to achieve a 25 percent productivity improvement by reducing staffing requirements and improving equipment acquisition and maintenance planning and control. This percentage estimate of possible productivity improvement had been put forward by a major software producer who had prepared and made a detailed presentation to a NewAge executive management group. The presentation had been very convincing.

THE PROJECTS START

To achieve this improvement, the re-engineering team devised plans to:

- Redesign and automate equipment preventive maintenance and repair scheduling.

- Track highly critical spare parts to ensure that they were on hand when required.

- Centralize and automate equipment purchasing and accounts payable processes to ensure economies of scale in equipment acquisitions.

After 8 months of planning and development in association with the outside software consultant (the consulting company that had presented its systems a year earlier to executive management), the re-engineering team began to introduce the new processes at the company's field sites. Field implementation was conducted in stages, three sites at a time, with implementation scheduled to be completed for all 12 company factory sites by the end of 1997.

THE PROBLEMS BEGIN

However, halfway through implementation, and with the re-engineered processes in place at six sites, the company began experiencing difficulties. Increases in productivity rates of 25 percent were not being achieved at any of the sites. Three sites had seen modest (10 to 15 percent) improvements, one site had achieved no improvement at all, and productivity at two sites had slightly decreased. In addition, project schedules were starting to slip and it was beginning to look as though implementation would not be achieved at all 12 sites by the end of '97. Some customers were beginning to show concern about the company's ability to meet increased product delivery schedules.

The manager of the re-engineering projects set about to determine why productivity goals were not being met, and why implementation schedules were slipping. But more important, he set about to determine how to correct these deficiencies.

A survey of the project's status at each site revealed several surprises. One was that workers seemed somewhat confused and just didn't seem to be getting the hang of the new procedures. The project manager knew that to interrupt the process would mean that the goal of achieving full implementation at all 12 sites would be delayed for several months. However, full implementation didn't seem to mean much if the implemented re-engineered processes weren't accomplishing the expected productivity improvements.

Meanwhile, the second re-engineering project to enhance sales-order processing and customer service (OFS) had also run into trouble. The sales-order and customer service redesign had been driven largely by the team's study of best practices at other companies. The re-engineering team had revamped the process accordingly, then ordered software from the same software producer, in order to maintain consistency of systems.

The team had been assured by the software consultant that its particular software would "more than satisfy" the process's new requirements. However, during a test of the new software, some team members suddenly realized that they were unnecessarily complicating what had originally been a relatively simple process. Stopping the re-engineering process at this point would require rethinking basic assumptions about the sales-order and customer service redesign. This would mean returning to square one and beginning the whole process over again.

The re-engineering manager now faced significant problems with both re-engineering projects—problems that would require further investment of time and resources, and would certainly delay by several months the completion schedules for both projects.

RECOMMENDATIONS AND CONCLUSIONS

After careful consideration, the re-engineering manager requested executive management to accept implementation delays and to allocate both additional funding and the required resources to ensure that, once in place, the re-engineered processes would achieve their productivity goals.

Reluctantly, executive management concurred with the re-engineering manager's recommendation to interrupt and delay both projects. The basic philosophy behind this decision was that the re-engineered processes had to be correct before the process was "set in concrete" at the plant level. If not, process goals would not be achieved and more time and resources would have to be expended in correcting a process already in place.

For the equipment purchasing and automated maintenance project, the project manager adjusted systems training so that employees were working with actual company data, rather than practice data supplied with the prepackaged software. Additionally, site-specific equipment registers and inventory data were loaded into test machines for training sessions. The Human Relations department was brought into the picture to help explain to the workforce the benefits that the new systems would bring (cleaner and safer maintenance and operation). It was also affirmed that projected savings in labor costs would be the result of improved machine productivity and, where necessary, to attrition rather than to layoff. Several employees were trained to run systems classes, and the installation eventually got back on track. The total delay was just over 6 months, but these midcourse corrections ensured that the system was working properly and that personnel were both well-trained and "on board."

Adjusting the sales-order processing and customer service re-engineering process was a bit more complicated in that it required re-engineers to begin all over again in the mapping of existing processes in detail. They discovered that their original mistake had been to rely too heavily on the successful practices of other companies as a basis for their own software decisions. What was missing was an in-depth assessment of their current process and how it needed to be changed, before ordering software. (In actual fact, the originally selected software was ultimately deemed not to hold the best solution and another software producer was brought in to satisfy the need). The systems were, in final retrospect, re-engineered to satisfactory levels—but at much greater cost and a full year later than the anticipated completion date.

OBSERVATIONS

The problems encountered during this corporation's re-engineering effort are typical, according to surveys conducted by re-engineering consulting firms. When planning and implementing re-engineering efforts, companies should bear the following in mind:

- Re-engineering will always take longer than you expect.
- Re-engineering will always involve more resources than you have.
- Re-engineering will always present problems no one anticipated.

To account for these vagaries, re-engineers and executive management should:

- Avoid taking re-engineering projects lightly; executive oversight is imperative from the start.
- Base decisions on achievement of re-engineering goals rather than adhering to a schedule.
- Be flexible; be willing to re-evaluate assumptions and adjust plans accordingly.
- Obtain buy-in at all levels to the greatest extent possible. Non-buy-ins are *roadblocks!*

Making corrections while the concrete is still wet is always easier than busting it up after it sets.

PROJECT CLOSEOUT; MAKE-GOOD ANALYSIS

IN GENERAL

After successful performance testing and subsequent stabilization of plant operations by permanent operating and maintenance forces, the project team must formally close out the project. This should be followed by a make-good analysis to determine if the project has achieved the intended benefits.

First, let us examine project closeout. The primary objective of project closeout is, of course, to leave the plant forces in full and confident control of plant operations, with no unresolved problems or unaddressed requirements.

However, proper closeout is essential not only to the ongoing success of the project, but also to the success of future projects. As we look at the components of this project element, you will realize just why we say this. As with any other element, this one must also be well planned.

Project closeout usually consists of the following primary items:

Turnover of Documentation.   It is imperative that everything learned during the project, from conception through initial operations, be captured and become a plant asset. To achieve this, and to ensure an efficient and thorough project closeout, project teams should include the following items in their closeout planning and implementation:

- Ensure that all project documentation is properly organized and filed for ease of use by permanent operating forces.

- Organize and turn over results of preoperational testing and commissioning to operating and maintenance forces. This critical information will constitute baseline data for system and equipment operating characteristics and for proper maintenance planning. This should include a detailed explanation of problems encountered during the project and how they were corrected.

- Develop and implement a warranty information tracking system. Tie warranty tracking into established management information systems, and instruct permanent operating forces in its use. Review warranty conditions and specifications to determine when warranty commences and the work that must be accomplished to keep warranties in force, and to ensure that plant forces are not conducting activities that should be accomplished under the warranty by the supplier.

Smooth Demobilization.   Implement team demobilization with the least possible amount of interference and disruption to plant operation. Remember, your project team has been a fixture on site for some time, perhaps for many months. In the final phases of the project, team members may have been working directly with operations forces as they became familiar with the new systems.

Schedule a predemobilization critique with operators and shift supervisors. Find out how they feel about the new system or equipment. Are they comfortable with it? Do they feel they have had sufficient training? Do they know of any unresolved problems; anything still not working quite right?

It is essential that the project team leave no project-related problem behind them when they demobilize and depart site. If they do, they are leaving an unfinished project, and unfinished or poorly performing projects usually cheat the venture or corporate bottom line of its due.

Recall Case Study 8 in Chap. 10. That project remained unfinished for over 3 years, depriving the venture's bottom line of millions of dollars of sorely needed revenue. Investors soon tire of a chronically ill facility and, at some point, will move to divest, to stop the bleeding. It was rumored that just such a solution was considered for that facility, that venture. Fortunately, the problems were finally solved and the facility was brought to design production in time to forestall divestiture.

Closeout of Contracts. The project team should ensure that all subcontracts are closed out and contract obligations have been fulfilled or resolved. If work by contractors and subcontractors has been satisfactory, see to it that the documentation required to trigger payment of their invoices is timely. Contractors, suppliers, and subs have payrolls to meet also. (As the ultimate client, your project team may sometimes need to pressure a foot-dragging contractor to pay *its* subcontractors.) Ensure that purchasing closeout has been initiated and that all outstanding items have been addressed. Turn over appropriate closeout information to Accounting to facilitate a future make-good analysis.

Project Critique. One of the most important aspects of this project element is the project critique, conducted by the project manager at the conclusion of the project. Critique the project by conducting in-depth interviews with project personnel and permanent operating forces to provide a wide variety of perspectives on the implementation of the project plan, on both the problem areas and successes of the project. Included with project personnel should be key contractors and equipment suppliers. It has been their project also, and, if the critique is handled in a businesslike manner by the project manager (as opposed to using it as a forum of recrimination and blame-fixing), valuable insights into causes and effects can be gained. This information can then be used to determine how future projects can be improved by application of *Project Bottom-Line Success!* principles.

Information and insights gained from the project critique must be captured, and a means found to disseminate the gained information throughout the company's other facilities and departments. The project team should prepare a detailed closeout report so that learned information can be applied to future projects. Only through a *planned* program of information sharing can you avoid the terrible fate that has befallen so many industrial projects, that is, repeating the same mistakes time and again.

MAKE-GOOD ANALYSIS—CLOSING THE *PBLS* LOOP

The primary objective of a make-good analysis is to determine if the project met the goals as contained, *and promised,* in the appropriation document. Upper management may not always take the time to read all the words in the appropriation document but, I guarantee you, they know how to read results summaries! It is absolutely vital that project teams develop a plan to measure, track, and evaluate the outcome of a project. By closing the loop, project teams will be able to assess overall project performance to determine if they have made good on the goals and benefits identified in the appropriations document. This leads directly to the ninth principle of *Project Bottom-Line Success!*:

> **Any project that costs more, takes longer, and returns less than it should cannot be considered totally successful.**

The primary objectives of the project evaluation plan are to pinpoint areas where the project could have been improved, incorporate these lessons into the application of *Project Bottom-Line Success!* on future projects, and analyze project goal accomplishment. The project evaluation process will also assist permanent operating forces in their ongoing efforts to exceed and enhance the basic goals and benefits achieved by a successful start-up.

During the evaluation, it is critical that team members keep in mind that it is not only the project execution process that is being examined, but also the overall contribution of the project to the corporate or venture bottom line.

The question that team members must answer is: "Did the process result in achieving a seamless, short-learning-curve start-up, while at the same time producing the benefits called for in the appropriations document?" No process is perfect; therefore, no project will be perfect. However, evaluation of the process in comparison with project goals will inevitably result in improvements in the process. This, in turn, will decrease mistakes on future projects and increase the likelihood of success. It is not instantaneous perfection we must seek, but steady, continual improvement.

Lastly, without feedback from evaluating the outcome of a project, the entire project process could become skewed to the point where scarce capital resources will not be allocated properly or used effectively and the venture's long-term financial and competitive viability will falter and, perhaps, become questionable. In a nutshell, *Project Bottom-Line Success!* methodology cannot be a long-term success without a consistent, vigorous, and open pursuit of actual project outcomes. This is the feedback loop leading to a project management process that is under control and being constantly improved.

The project team, as part of closeout and make-good analysis, must develop a full plan to evaluate the outcome of the project. There is no one set cookbook approach that can be applied to every project. The approach will be determined by many project variables, including the following:

OVERALL MAGNITUDE OF THE PROJECT

The project outcome evaluation can be as simple as a one- or two-page description of the project and its benefits, submitted soon after project closeout. At the other end of the spectrum, a large project where objectives and benefits will develop over an extended period of time may require an ongoing effort with continuing responsibilities assigned to each team member. This would naturally lead to an effective make-good evaluation that will be periodically submitted to management.

PROJECT STATUS AT TIME OF CLOSEOUT

Has the project made good on the technical, production, quality, and financial goals set out in the appropriation? It may be that some of these questions will be answered only over an extended period of time, especially if new product markets must be developed and sales results analyzed.

SOURCE OF BENEFITS EXPECTED FROM PROJECT

The source of the benefits to be measured can be quite varied. For example, the source of benefits for one project might be reduced manning requirements, which would result in lower unit cost of production, while the source of benefits from another project might be the satisfaction of a government environmental mandate, resulting in the staving off of huge government fines. Yet another source of benefits might be an increase in production capability and the capture of a larger share of the market.

At a minimum, the plan to evaluate project outcome should encompass the following items:

- Clearly identify the objectives expected to be accomplished from the project.
- Document the benefits pledged to secure the resources necessary to carry out the project.
- Assign responsibility within the project team to assess the extent to which objectives have been reached and benefits realized.
- State clearly the plan to be followed to evaluate project outcome.

Typical areas of responsibility for team members in the project outcome evaluation and make-good analysis may include the following, depending on the scope and nature of the project:

Project Implementation Parameters.   These will undoubtedly encompass budget and schedule performance, the performance of the project team itself, the performance of suppliers and vendors, and the project's ability to stick to the original scope.

Achievement of Operating and Maintenance Goals. Operating and maintenance goals may be varied, but will usually include such items as production rates, yield, direct costs, workforce changes, and product quality issues. The objective of the analysis will be to report on the status of achievement of these goals.

Engineering and Design Goals.   Engineering will, in all probability, be responsible for gathering the data regarding the capital cost of the project—whether or not the process control system objectives were met—and the operability, maintainability, and reliability of the new installation.

Achievement of Commercial Goals.   The project team must reach into Facility Management and the Sales department for data on improvement in product mix, market retention, and new or expanded sales resulting from the project.

Achievement of Financial Goals.   Accounting will, in most instances, be asked for input to the analysis with information related to venture or corporate working capital changes, total project costs, and finally, the calculation of that all-important number, the return on investment. This number will usually be stated in terms of the discounted cash flow (DCF-ROI) method in order to obtain a comparison with real-world returns.

SUMMARY

All project team members should agree on the status of project objectives and benefits. In some cases, bringing in an independent outside assessment might be the approach that is required to effectively convey the accuracy and authority of the project outcome assessment.

Most important, it is the project team's responsibility to see that an appropriate project outcome assessment is carefully crafted and effectively accomplished. It is the project team's final statement and justification for having spent their company's resources. *The loop is closed.*

MEASURING PROJECT SUCCESS

TRADITIONAL CRITERIA FOR MEASURING PROJECT SUCCESS

Project success means different things to different people. From an architect's point of view, a project might be an overwhelming success; from the perspective of the constructor who had to bring the architect's vision to reality, the same project may be an abject failure. Corporations, however, do not have the luxury of evaluating projects by single-source criteria; they must evaluate project success from a global point of view.

According to studies conducted over the past several years, industry personnel most often rate project success by the following criteria and usually in this approximate order of perceived importance:

Technical performance. The extent to which requirements specified at the beginning of a project are achieved.

Efficiency of project execution. The degree to which targets of time and cost were met, and the efficiency of suppliers, vendors, and manufacturers.

Satisfactory benchmark achievement. A measure of client, parent, and user satisfaction, including the facility's ability to meet industrial competitive benchmarks.

Manufacturability. The ease with which the product resulting from the project can be manufactured.

Business performance.   The success of its commercial performance as measured by quality, quantity, and client service.

Project start-up.   The completeness of project termination and the absence of commissioning problems.

Team technical capabilities.   The degree of success achieved in identifying and solving technical problems during project implementation.

Note that, according to the order, respondents to these type surveys almost always judge the success of a project by whether or not the project meets its technical, time, and cost objectives. It would be natural to assume then, that a project is a success if:

- It performs as designed.
- It comes in on time.
- It comes in on budget.

These are all admirable and highly sought after project parameters, and rightly so. In the *Project Bottom-Line Success!* philosophy, however, coming in on time, on budget, and as designed does not necessarily indicate total success. Consider, if you will, our tenth (and last) principle:

If the venture is not a success, neither is the project.

PROJECT AND VENTURE SUCCESS

Using traditional criteria for evaluating project success is like using the time of a single runner to determine whether or not a relay has been successful. A project is part of an *overall venture*, and the success of the project must be measured by its bottom-line impact on the venture.

This may be a difficult notion for project engineers and managers to accept. After all, once they turn the plant over to the permanent operating forces the ongoing operation of the facility is beyond their control, right?

Nevertheless, the success of the project and the success of the venture are undeniably and inseparably linked, whether we choose to admit it or not. This is especially true if we remember that the venture is shaped, over its life span, by the stream of projects that goes into it.

This idea might make more sense if you think of project implementation as an exercise in child rearing, from conception to the time the child leaves home. Once children are out on their own, the parent has no direct authority over them. Yet the health aspects of the gestation period, the birthing conditions, the upbringing, education, and values that parents instill in their children will influence the child's entire life. Similarly, the plans, decisions, and actions of project engineers and managers impact the operation, productivity, and profitability of a venture throughout its life cycle, long after the project engineers and managers are gone.

Project teams may wish to go beyond the traditional criteria of project success and evaluate success from a viewpoint not usually considered at the project level. Let us apply our *Project <u>Bottom-Line</u> Success!* principles in the consideration of project success and see where it leads us.

JUDGING PROJECT SUCCESS BY *PBLS* PRINCIPLES

PBLS PRINCIPLE 1

If project need cannot be justified on the basis of a realistically and sufficiently positive contribution to the venture *bottom line*, legal mandates, or safety considerations, then the project should not go forward.

The genesis of successful capital projects should be a clear justification of project need. Even if a project comes in on time, in budget, and within scope, it cannot be considered successful *if it was not justified to begin with!* If this is the case, the corporation's money and the project team's time has been ill used and the company is stuck with operating and maintaining a facility it didn't need in the first place. In the conceptual stage, be as one with the investors. Is it a project on which you would spend your own money?

PBLS Principle 2

> Detailed scope definition is the cornerstone of achieving
> Project _Bottom-Line_ Success!

If justification of project need is the foundation of project success, then project scope is the structural framework within which success must be realized. Detailed scope definition is something that should occur before, not after, appropriation of funds. Lack of scope definition leaves project teams open to the dreaded scope creep, which means items that should have been identified during scope development were missed.

Adding work to the scope after vendor contracts have been issued results in increased costs that may have been avoided if the work items had been a part of the initial negotiations. In addition, the lower the level of scope definition, the greater the degree of risk. When evaluating project success, project teams should compare the original project scope with the finished product to see how well they stayed the course and to calculate the cost of expanding the scope envelope.

PBLS Principle 3

> The probability of project success increases proportionally
> to the degree of risk reduction.

Risk is inherent in business, and particularly so in heavy industries that must continually invest huge sums of capital to sustain technical competitiveness and market share. All projects hold risk and all risk can be alleviated. That all projects hold risk cannot be argued, but the benefit of risk alleviation must be weighed against its cost.

Obviously, no private company can afford to reduce risk to nil. However, entering into a project without aggressively identifying and alleviating risks is tantamount to taking a bag full of money to the crap table; you may get lucky and break the house, but don't bet the farm on it! Project teams should revisit their risk identification and alleviation efforts to evaluate the impact of risk and risk reduction on the outcome of the project.

PBLS PRINCIPLE 4

The challenge of achieving *Project Bottom-Line Success!* lies, primarily, in planning.

In the *Project Bottom-Line Success!* philosophy of project management, project planners should strive to identify, up front, the correct level of resources required to attain project goals. This is accomplished by detailed preauthorization planning. Detailed project planning through multifunctional team participation, pinpoint scope development, and risk assessment and alleviation is the only way to determine the appropriate level of resource investment and return. Anything else is a guess based on experience; i.e., what's been done in the past. But conditions are fluid; technology, competition, markets, and costs all change. As conditions change, so do risks. The purpose of detailed up-front planning is to anticipate and respond to project needs and risks before needs turn into problems and risks into reality.

PBLS PRINCIPLE 5

Input from all stakeholders is imperative, if the project is to be successful.

Thorough risk identification, pinpoint scope development, and detailed preplanning require the participation of all the various groups that will impact the project. Groups that are left out of the planning process are apt to be recalcitrant in the later stages of the project, insisting on changes that will be costly to the project's cost and schedule. More important, project engineers should acknowledge the fact that they cannot be experts in every field; project teams would be wise to avail themselves of the expertise available both within the company and from supplier organizations.

Involvement of these groups will provide a sense of ownership that can be gained in no other way. When exploring the causes of project difficulties, project teams should assess whether early and meaningful involvement of groups with specific expertise or vested project interest might not have avoided or mitigated those difficulties.

PBLS Principle 6

Testing in the factory reduces problems in the field.

It is the vendors' responsibility to ensure that its equipment is complete and in proper working order according to specification before it leaves the shop. *But it is the project team's responsibility to make sure that the vendor makes sure that equipment is ready.* The only way to accomplish this is to conduct stringent preshipment tests that are witnessed and verified by the purchaser or a third party. Long, problem-plagued start-ups can often be traced to equipment or systems that were not tested prior to installation, particularly process controls. Allowing vendors to ship equipment from their shop to your site is tacit, if unofficial, acceptance of their product. Any problem with the equipment suddenly becomes a field problem, rather than a shop problem. When tracing the source of problem start-ups, look to equipment and systems for which preshipment or off-site integrated testing was not required or was waived.

PBLS Principle 7

The ultimate success of any project or venture is dependent not only on how well you design or build, but also on how well you train those who will operate and maintain.

Permanent facility forces *will* get trained, even if they have to train themselves during start-up and initial operations. It is not a question of *if* training will occur, but rather *how and to what end.* The *bottom-line* purpose of training should be to achieve a short-learning-curve start-up so that production can deliver the financial, quality, and quantity benefits stated in the appropriation documents as quickly as possible. Minimum-learning-curve start-ups cannot be realized unless permanent operating and maintenance forces have been thoroughly trained before commissioning; thorough training cannot be realized unless planning and preparation begins before appropriation. When contemplating project success, project teams should examine their attitude and approach to training as measured against the ideal of a zero-learning-curve start-up. An extraordinarily long start-up, or ramp-up to design capacity, can deprive the venture *bottom-line* of hundreds of thousands, perhaps *millions*, of dollars in revenue.

PBLS PRINCIPLE 8

Preoperational testing is a preemptive strike against start-up problems.

When preoperational testing has been ignored, the commissioning phase will usually suffer. When the process trips out on overload, is it due to an underdesign of the electrical system, or is it due to a defective bearing? Or, perhaps, a poorly aligned belt? The sole purpose of a preoperational testing program is to work through and eliminate the equipment problems before commissioning begins. If something is going to fail, we want it to fail during the testing phase; not when we are checking and fine tuning the process.

Some engineers consider a start-up successful as long as the facility eventually gets going. But how much time, money, and *bottom-line* dollars have been spent during such an "eventual" start-up? Case study after case study shows that start-ups that don't start up so well usually lack, among other things, a well-planned and detailed preoperational testing program.

PBLS PRINCIPLE 9

Any project that costs more, takes longer, and returns less than it should cannot be considered totally successful.

This *PBLS* principle may be the hardest for project teams to swallow because it deals more with degrees of success than success itself. The goals set for a project (budget, schedule, scope, venture contribution) are valid only *if the target numbers or standards are appropriate for the particular project*. Is a project a success if a company meets its established criteria of a $30 million budget, a 22-month schedule, and a return on investment of 25 percent, if that same project should have more appropriately cost $25 million, taken 18 months to complete, achieved an ROI of 30 percent, and paid for itself in 3.3 rather than 4 years?

This principle begs the question, "When is success successful enough?" Perhaps the answer should be, "When it cannot, realistically, be done better!"

PBLS Principle 10

If the venture is not a success, neither is the project.

For the sake of argument, let's assume that a project team has executed the perfect project as judged by traditional criteria: on time, under budget, within scope, and meeting all the production criteria identified in the authorizing document. Surely no one can argue with the success of such a project. Make-good analysis after the fact reveals that, even though the project has met its production goals, the annual costs of operating and maintaining the facility are actually lowering instead of increasing *bottom-line venture profitability*. Project success should be judged not just in relation to the cost and efficiency of the project itself, but by the contribution of the project *over its lifetime* to the *bottom-line profitability of the venture*.

The *Project Bottom-Line Success!* philosophy offers a fresh perspective on project management that, before authorization of project funding, focuses on:

- Justification of project need
- Detailed scope definition
- Aggressive risk assessment and alleviation
- In-depth project preplanning

During project implementation, *PBLS* calls for:

- Pinpoint scope refinement and equipment life cycle cost analysis during design
- Early attention to training and start-up issues

- Meaningful involvement of all stakeholders
- Procurement on a quality basis
- Adherence to preshipment testing requirements
- Equipment and systems preoperational testing
- Closing the project loop so good things are repeated, bad things avoided, and project make-good analysis proves worthy of its name

Most important of all, *PBLS* holds that evaluation of project success should be based on a positive contribution to the venture's bottom line. Any other criteria for project success, when you stop and think about it, is disingenuous and self-defeating.

Project teams cannot fully implement the *PBLS* tenets listed above unless they believe in and adhere to the principles that underlie the *PBLS* method. A methodology is a system of rules; a philosophy is a set of principles that shapes one's attitude toward a given subject. It is a set of 10 principles, then, that elevates *PBLS* from a methodology to a philosophy. Some companies may already be following this philosophy without ever having put a name to it; others may require only a marginal shift in attitude or method to accomplish projects in this same manner. Undoubtedly, there are a significant number of companies that will require a radical and sometimes painful change of corporate mindset if they are to adopt a methodology such as *Project Bottom-Line Success!* However, we believe the rewards for doing so will be well worth the pain.

A *PBLS* GUARANTEE

If the venture to which the pyramids of Giza contributed was the perpetuation of the ancient Egyptian's cultural legacy, then the project to raise these magnificent structures continues to be an enduring success.

If the venture to which the Apollo Space Program contributed was the opening of cosmic frontiers bounded only by the edges of the universe, then Apollo was a project whose success has known no equal.

Although there is no guarantee, *ever*, that a capital project of a more domestic and earthly variety will turn out to be an unmitigated success, you and your company will increase the *probability* of attaining the intended project benefits by applying the concepts of *Project <u>Bottom-Line</u> Success!* This we do guarantee.

DEFINITIONS

Most of the terms highlighted in the following listing are used somewhere in this book and definitions are offered here in an effort to answer, or clarify, questions of a definitive nature. Although some readers may have different definitions for certain of these terms, it was upon the following interpretations that this book was based.

Appropriation process: The formal process used to conceptualize, justify, and approve major projects.

Capital requirements: The financial resources necessary to fund all the goods, services, and equipment required for conceiving, designing, engineering, constructing, and starting up an industrial facility, whether these items are assigned in-house or purchased from outside agencies.

Commissioning or start-up: Commissioning, or start-up, encompasses start-up of demonstrated equipment, introduction of feedstock, and demonstration of plant design capability and product quality. During the commissioning/start-up phase, equipment and/or process suppliers may be called on to demonstrate or prove design capability of equipment or process. On successful completion of the commissioning/start-up phase, the stabilized plant is normally turned over to the permanent operating forces.

Component: A constituent part of a system or subsystem.

Construction punch list: A list of all deficiencies noted during any of the preoperational testing sequences. This list allows precise control over the remaining work status by the construction forces and ensures that all possible construction items have been completed before equipment/system start-up.

Construction testing: Testing normally performed by a competent construction contractor to prove, prior to turnover to the designated preoperational testing and start-up group, that the equipment installed by the construction forces is installed in accordance with the installation drawings and specifications. This testing encompasses wiring ring-out, motor roll, and the contractor's version of a final completion, or punch, list.

Discounted cash flow technique: A calculation method to allow a firm to quantify the time value of money for a series of positive and/or negative cash flows that exceed the firm's cost of securing capital.

Electrical preoperational testing: A series of electrical acceptance checks to ensure that equipment is electrically complete and can be operated without danger to equipment or personnel. This series of checks may include, as applicable, insulation resistance checks, high potential tests, electrical installation checks, component sizing, control circuit checks, and motor runs (uncoupled).

Engineering quality assurance/quality control: That portion of a quality assurance program responsible for ensuring that quality requirements are met during design; this includes preparation of drawing specifications.

Environmental permits: Those environmentally oriented permits required by a lawful national, state, or local regulatory agency prior to commencement of field work or certain operations affecting the environment.

Equipment: One or more assemblies capable of performing a complete function.

Facilities turnover: A sequence of events that includes a functional, sequential demonstration of equipment/systems to prove system integrity prior to release of equipment to operations forces, turnover of all facilities and buildings, and turnover of data packages that document the specific tests and results for each equipment item and system.

Field changes: Changes in the originally approved design, fabrication, erection, installation, or operation of facilities, systems, or equipment.

Field quality control: That portion of a quality assurance program pertaining to field inspections and tests to ensure that design specifications are met during construction, erection, installation, and testing.

Final completion list: Developed both prior to and during equipment demonstration, the final completion list is the vehicle for interfacing among construction, preoperational testing, and start-up forces to assure completion of as many open items as possible prior to turnover.

First engineering submittal (FES): A detailed document, normally prepared by the primary supplier or his process control supplier, that includes a detailed functional description of the system, the system's process control operation, and configuration of systems and equipment. This functional description includes hardware, software, user displays, and the preliminary interface design specifications.

Hold points: During equipment fabrication, a hold point refers to a stage past which work may not progress until an inspection of the equipment is accomplished.

Installation inspection: A forerunner to subsequent testing, the installation inspection ensures that a system, subsystem, or equipment item is correctly installed and operably complete, reveals any incompleteness or nonconformity to design criteria, and ensures that the equipment is in a state that will allow meaningful testing to be accomplished.

Instrumentation testing: Completed prior to run-in of concerned equipment or systems, instrumentation testing includes inspection of instruments on receipt at site, installation inspection, instrument setup, calibration checks, operational verification, and loop checks.

Integration testing: Integration testing encompasses the testing of a plant's process control system software and hardware to ensure that each control system component operates within the overall system as designed. Integration testing requires that the process control system be tested and functioning as a whole. There are two types of tests: the pre-shipment integration test (PSIT), which is performed off-site prior to component shipment and installation, and the site integration test (SIT), conducted at the facility after installation.

ISO 9000: ISO 9000 is a standard developed by the International Organization for Standardization to establish consistent methods for ensuring the quality of products and services. Particular emphasis is given to documenting the actions taken that relate to product quality.

Key events schedule: A schedule depicting the proposed construction and testing completion dates for all plant systems and major plant equipment.

Learning curves: The percentage of reduction in average costs as output and/or production increases. More generally, a learning curve refers to the time and cost of familiarizing personnel with the requirements of performing specific tasks and functions.

Marketing: The process of planning and executing the conception, pricing, promotion, and distribution of ideas, goods, and services, to create exchanges that satisfy organizational objectives.

Materials control: That portion of a quality assurance program that pertains to ensuring that quality requirements are met for materials, including material identification and certifications.

Mechanical preoperational testing: A sequence of tests designed to ensure that all necessary steps have been taken to allow run-in of a unit under test with safety and without damage to equipment. This sequence of tests may include, as applicable: lubrication checks, coupling alignment checks, internal inspections, pressure tests and flushes, installation of temporary screens, installation of special test instruments, and systems inspections.

Nonconformance: A fabrication or installation that is contrary to specifications for equipment fabrication, performance, or installation.

Operating philosophy: Establishment of the way an industrial facility will be run throughout its existence.

Preoperational demonstration: Systems, subsystems, and operational portions thereof are demonstrated to the operations group upon satisfactory completion of preoperational testing. This demonstration includes start-up, running, shutdown, and demonstration of system safety interlocks, including high-pressure, high-temperature, or other emergency shutdowns.

Preoperational testing: That testing performed by the designated preoperational testing and start-up group on notification by the construction manager that a system, subsystem, or equipment is mechanically complete, and which will demonstrate that the system, subsystem, or equipment is reliable and ready to safely perform its function in the process. Preoperational testing includes installation inspections, electrical and mechanical functional checks, and run-in without product.

Process control system: Integrated devices functioning to provide automatic control of a continuous operation.

Procurement cycle: The process of procuring equipment, from purchase order initiation, through fabrication, to delivery.

Product mix: The specific types, varieties, and amounts of products a single industrial facility is designed, engineered, and constructed to produce.

Project definition rating index (PDRI): A simple and easy-to-use tool, developed by Construction Industry Institute (CII), for measuring the degree of scope development on industrial projects. The PDRI identifies and precisely defines each critical element in a scope definition package and allows project risk factors to be quickly identified and/or predicted.

Purchasing quality assurance/quality control: That portion of a quality assurance program pertaining to ensuring that design specifications are met during the procurement cycle.

Quality assurance clause: A clause incorporated into purchase orders specifically stating that equipment must be fabricated/manufactured to meet exact specifications.

Quality assurance program: Management policies and systems designed to ensure that all construction-related activities, including procurement, fabrication, transport, storage, erection, installation, and testing are conducted, completed, and documented in accordance with design specifications and contractual agreements and instructions.

Quality control: Specific techniques, criteria, and procedures used to implement and enforce a quality assurance program.

Business process re-engineering: Changes made to the various business management systems with the intent of improving both the competitive ability and position of the corporate entity.

Return on investment (ROI): The profit that results from a project or venture, expressed as a percentage of the total value of the resources dedicated to that end.

Risk analysis: The application of analytical techniques to quantify the probability of loss associated with risk.

Risk assessment: An umbrella term that includes all the various activities and methods associated with identifying, quantifying, and alleviating risk.

Run-in: A test designed both to prove the operational capability of a unit under test and to provide baseline data for future operating and maintenance requirements. Run-ins continue until unit operating parameters have been stabilized.

Safety and operating inspection (SOI): An inspection by operating, maintenance, engineering, and safety personnel, conducted prior to the start-up of a new facility or major component, to ensure that the facility or component can be operated safely and is equipped with the required safety items.

Scope of work: A document that details exactly what work is to be accomplished, how the work will be accomplished, when the work will be accomplished, and who shall accomplish the work for a given project.

Second engineering submittal (SES): Following review and comment on the first engineering submittal by the client, the primary supplier issues a second engineering submittal. This document contains revisions and refinements to the process control design, equipment requirements, and configuration, including final software design, final interface design specification, I/O list, database, and start-up strategy. This document also details changes in plant production equipment systems and components, including maintenance requirements, and provides a detailed specification of the scope of supply for the project.

Sequence test schedule: A schedule that lists the proposed preoperational testing dates and types of tests to be performed on all items of plant equipment, including each instrument.

Shop inspection: An inspection conducted by quality assurance personnel in the fabricator's shop to ensure that equipment is being manufactured according to specifications.

Shop performance report: A test, witnessed by quality assurance personnel, conducted in the fabricator's shop to determine if equipment performance meets specifications.

Specification: A document that specifies, in detail or in function, how an industrial facility (or system or equipment within a facility) is to be designed, engineered, and constructed.

Subsystem: A major part of a system which itself has the characteristics of a system, usually consisting of several components.

System: A combination of several pieces of equipment integrated to perform a specific function.

Time costs: The value of the time it takes to bring a product to market.

Time value of money: Currency, as with any medium of exchange, has an inherent ability to appreciate in value over time, and the diversion of capital to any other use interrupts this potential appreciation. Thus, the time value of money in a capital appropriation is a real and actual expense to the venture.

Training needs assessment: A study to determine which classifications of personnel require training in order to operate and maintain equipment, including the specific type and amount of training required.

Value engineering: A critical analysis of a project that divides the project into readily identifiable and understood segments, then analyzes each segment.

Vendor evaluation: A two-part, in-depth analysis to determine a potential vendor's qualifications and certifications for performing a job, as well as an evaluation after job completion to determine not only how well the vendor fulfilled the terms of the contract, but also to determine the quality of the vendor's work.

FORMS

CONTINUATION SHEET

PROJECT NAME:

SITE LOCATION:

PROJECT NO.:   DATE:

CONTINUATION SHEET CAN BE USED WITH ANY OTHER FORM

PBLS Form No. 3.1.1

PUNCH LIST

JOB NO. _____

DATE _____

AREA _____   PAGE _____

COMPLETED BY _____

REV. NO. _____   OF _____

ITEM NUMBER	DESCRIPTION	CORRECTIVE ACTION BY	SCHEDULE DATE COMPLETE	ACTUAL DATE COMPLETE

PBLS Form No. 3.1.2

FINAL COMPLETION LIST

JOB NO. _____

AREA _____

REV. NO. _____

PAGE _____ OF _____

ITEM NUMBER	DESCRIPTION	CORRECTIVE ACTION BY	SCHEDULE DATE COMPLETE	ACTUAL DATE COMPLETE

PBLS Form No. 3.1.3

356

DRAWING CHANGE NOTICE

PROJECT NAME:

SITE LOCATION:

PROJECT NO.:   DATE:

REQUESTED BY _____ D.C.N. NO. _____ REV. NO. _____

AREA _____ COMPONENT _____

SUBJECT _____

DRAWING REFERENCE _____

CORRECTIVE ACTION

_____

_____

_____

_____

_____

_____

_____

_____

_____

_____

_____

_____

_____

_____

_____

_____

REVIEWED BY _____ TITLE _____

APPROVED BY _____ TITLE _____

PBLS Form No. 3.1.4

DRAWING CHANGE NOTICE LOG

SHEET   OF

JOB NO.:   DATE:

REQUEST DATE	REFERENCE	DCN NO.	COMPLETE DATE	SIGNED OFF

PBLS Form No. 3.1.5

FIELD BACKCHARGE NOTIFICATION

PROJECT NAME:

SITE LOCATION:

PROJECT NO.:   DATE:

PURCHASE ORDER _____

COMPANY/EQUIPMENT _____

PROBLEM:

CORRECTIVE ACTION:

ORIGINATOR _____ NOTIFICATION _____
                    (SIGNATURE)   (DATE)

                                    B/C ISSUE _____
                                              (NUMBER)   (DATE)

VENDOR ATTENDANCE _____   _____
                                              (START-UP DIRECTOR)

PBLS Form No. 3.1.6

BACKCHARGE NOTIFICATION LOG

PROJECT NAME:

SITE LOCATION:

PROJECT NO.:   DATE:

REQUEST DATE	VENDOR REPRESENTATIVE NAMES	P.O. NO.	ISSUE DATE	B/C NO.	ORIGINATOR

PBLS Form No. 3.1.7

EXTRA WORK REQUEST

PROJECT NAME:

SITE LOCATION:

PROJECT NO.: DATE:

REQUEST DATE _____ EWO NO. _____

CONTRACTOR _____

LOCATION _____

DATE REQUIRED _____

DETAILED DESCRIPTION OF WORK REQUIRED:

SAFETY CONSIDERATIONS:

ORIGINATOR _____

REVIEWED BY START-UP DIRECTOR _____

APPROVED BY PROJECT MANAGER _____

WORK COMPLETED _____ _____
                    (DATE)   (SIGNATURE)

WORK APPROVED _____ _____
                    (DATE)   (SIGNATURE)

PBLS Form No. 3.1.8

EXTRA WORK ORDER LOG

CLIENT:

LOCATION:

JOB NO.:   DATE:

REQUEST DATE	CONTRACTOR	EWO NO.	START DATE	COMPLETE DATE	SIGNED OFF (✔)

VENDOR DAILY ACTIVITY SUMMARY

PROJECT NAME:

SITE LOCATION:

PROJECT NO.:   DATE:

EQUIPMENT _____ PURCHASE ORDER NO. _____

WORKED FROM _____ TO _____ TOTAL HOURS WORKED _____

	MANHOURS				
SUMMARY OF ACTIVITIES	**VEND.**	**ELECT.**	**M.W.**	**P.F.**	**OTHER**
TOTAL					

S/U ENGINEER _____   VENDOR _____
                        (SIGNATURE)   (SIGNATURE)

DATE _____   TITLE _____

                                                 COMPANY _____

                                                 DATE _____

PBLS **Form 3.1.10**

VENDOR TIME SHEET

CLIENT:

LOCATION:

JOB NO.: _____ DATE: _____

VENDOR _____ P.O. NO. _____

NAME OF REPRESENTATIVE _____

EQUIPMENT _____

DATES (WEEK ENDING SUNDAY) _____

	HOURS TO CLIENT ACCOUNT		HOURS TO VENDOR ACCOUNT		DAILY TOTAL	S.U. OR PROJ. MGR. INITIALS
	STRAIGHT TIME	OVERTIME	STRAIGHT TIME	OVERTIME		
MONDAY						
TUESDAY						
WEDNESDAY						
THURSDAY						
FRIDAY						
SATURDAY						
SUNDAY						
TOTAL						

CLIENT APPROVAL:

VENDOR: _____   _____
           (SIGNATURE)   (SIGNATURE)

TITLE: _____

PBLS Form No. 3.1.11

VENDOR END OF SERVICE REPORT

CLIENT _____

LOCATION _____

JOB NO. _____ DATE _____

COMPANY _____ PURCHASE ORDER NO. _____

NAME OF REPRESENTATIVE _____

EQUIPMENT _____ DATE _____

AS OF THIS DATE ABOVE VENDOR REPRESENTATIVE HAS COMPLETED ALL NECESSARY INSPECTIONS AND TESTS ON THE REFERENCED EQUIPMENT. THE VENDOR REPRESENTATIVE CERTIFIES THAT THIS EQUIPMENT IS INSTALLED CORRECTLY AND IS READY IN ALL RESPECTS FOR PROCESS START-UP AND OPERATION IN ACCORDANCE WITH THE PROJECT SPECIFICATIONS AND OTHER PURCHASE ORDER AND CONTRACTUAL AGREEMENTS. ANY EXCEPTIONS AND/OR ADDITIONAL WORK REQUIRED IS LISTED BELOW:

EXCEPTIONS AND/OR COMMENTS: _____

_____

_____

_____

_____

_____

_____

_____

_____

_____

CERTIFIED _____
           (VENDOR REPRESENTATIVE)

VERIFIED _____ TITLE _____
     (CLIENT REPRESENTATIVE)

PBLS **Form No. 3.1.12**

VENDOR ATTENDANCE LOG

CLIENT

LOCATION

JOB NO.   DATE

REQUEST DATE	VENDOR/REPRESENTATIVE (NAME)	P.O. NO.	ARR. DATE	DEP. DATE	TOTAL MANDAYS

PBLS Form No. 3.1.13

PROBLEM REPORT

PROJECT NAME:

SITE LOCATION:

PROJECT NO.: DATE:

SYSTEM _____ COMPONENT _____

PROBLEM DESCRIPTION

TEST ENGINEER _____

START-UP DIRECTOR _____

CORRECTIVE ACTION TO BE TAKEN

DATE PROBLEM RESOLVED _____

VERIFIED BY _____

PBLS Form No. 3.1.14

PROBLEM REPORT LOG

JOB NO. _____ AREA _____ REV. NO. _____ PAGE _____ OF _____

ITEM NUMBER	DESCRIPTION	DATE REPORTED	SCHEDULE DATE CORRECTED	ACTUAL DATE CORRECTED

PBLS Form No. 3.1.15

REQUEST FOR EQUIPMENT
CLEARANCE PERMIT

CLIENT

LOCATION

JOB NO.   DATE

EQUIPMENT REQUESTED: _____

_____

_____

_____

_____

CLEARANCE POINTS REQUESTED FOR WORK ON ABOVE
EQUIPMENT REQUESTED: _____

_____

_____

_____

_____

SCOPE OF WORK: _____

_____

_____

_____

_____

TIME: FROM __/__/____ A.M. P.M.   TO __/__/_____ A.M. P.M.

REQUESTED BY _____   DATE _____

CLIENT INSP. _____   DATE _____

REQUEST NO. _____   PERMIT NO. _____

START-UP ENGINEER _____
                        (SIGNATURE)

PBLS Form No. 3.1.16

CLEARANCE REMOVAL REQUEST

CLIENT _____

LOCATION _____

JOB NO. _____ DATE _____

PLEASE REMOVE CLEARANCE FROM: _____

_____

_____

_____

_____

WORK IS COMPLETED ON THIS EQUIPMENT AND IT IS READY FOR SERVICE
WITH THE EXCEPTIONS AS STATED: _____

_____

_____

_____

_____

_____

_____

_____

_____

_____

_____

_____

_____

_____

_____

REQUESTED BY _____ DATE _____

CLIENT INSPECTED _____ DATE _____

REF. REQUEST NO. _____ REF. PERMIT NO. _____

START-UP ENGINEER _____

PBLS Form No. 3.1.17

CLEARANCE PERMIT LOG

CLIENT:

JOB NO.:

SHEET ___ OF ___

LOCATION:

DATE:

DATE REQUESTED	REQUEST NO.	PERMIT NO.	EQUIPMENT/SYSTEM	DATE REMOVED

PBLS Form No. 3.1.18

CONSTRUCTION COMPLETION RELEASE
TO PREOPERATIONAL TESTING

PROJECT NAME:

SITE LOCATION:

PROJECT NO.:   DATE:

TRANSFER DOCUMENT NO. _____

1. THE FOLLOWING EQUIPMENT (BY ITEM NUMBER) IS COMPLETE AND IS CONSTRUCTED IN ACCORDANCE WITH APPROVED DRAWINGS (EXCEPT AS NOTED). THE PREOPERATIONAL TESTING GROUP IS CLEARED TO TEST THE LISTED EQUIPMENT FOR ITS LISTED TEST.

ITEM	TEST	ITEM	TEST	ITEM	TEST	ITEM	TEST

2. CONSTRUCTION COMPLETE:

    _____ YES

    _____ NO (REFER TO ATTACHED FIELD ENGINEERING PUNCH LIST, OPEN ORDER REPORT, OR OTHER PERTINENT DATA.)

3. LIST OF ATTACHED QUALITY DOCUMENTS:

4. SIGNATURES:

    FIELD ENGINEER (MECH) _____ DATE _____
    FIELD ENGINEER (ELEC) _____ DATE _____
    FIELD ENGINEER (INSTR) _____ DATE _____
    QUALITY ASSURANCE _____ DATE _____
    OTHER _____ DATE _____
    OTHER _____ DATE _____
    CONSTR. MANAGER _____ DATE _____

PBLS Form No. 3.1.19

FIELD SERVICE REPORT

PROJECT NAME:

SITE LOCATION:

PROJECT NO.:   DATE:

_____
_____
_____
_____
_____
_____
_____
_____
_____
_____
_____
_____
_____
_____
_____
_____
_____
_____
_____
_____
_____
_____
_____
_____
_____
_____
_____
_____
_____

START-UP ENGINEER _____ REVIEWED BY _____

PBLS Form No. 3.1.20

DAILY ACTIVITY SUMMARY

PROJECT NAME:

SITE LOCATION:

PROJECT NO.:   DATE:

TO _____

SUBJECT AREA _____

SUMMARY OF ACTIVITIES	MANHOURS	
	S/U ENGR	**CRAFT**
TOTAL		

SIGNED _____
PROJECT START-UP ENGINEER

DISTRIBUTION

PBLS Form No. 3.1.21

WEEKLY ACTIVITY SUMMARY

CLIENT:

LOCATION:

JOB NO.:   WEEK ENDING:

SUMMARY OF ACTIVITIES	DATE	HOURS
TOTAL		

SIGNED _____

PREOPERATIONAL TESTING ENGINEER
DAILY TIME SHEET

PROJECT NAME:

SITE LOCATION:

PROJECT NO.:   DATE:

TESTING DATA				MANHOURS				COMMENTS
ITEM	TEST	UNITS	OVERRUN	VEND	ELEC	M W	PF	
TOTALS								

TEST ENGINEER _____ REVIEWED BY_____

LETTER OF RELEASE LOG

CLIENT:

LOCATION:

JOB NO.:   DATE:

ISSUE DATE	EQUIPMENT/FACILITY RELEASED	LETTER OF RELEASE NO.	SIGNOFF DATE

PBLS Form No. 3.1.24

RED TAG LOG

PROJECT NAME:

SITE LOCATION:

PROJECT NO.:   DATE:

TAG NO.	DATE PLACED	TAG LOCATION	SYSTEM	PURPOSE OF TAG OUT	STUB HOLDER	DATE REMOVED	LOCK NO.

PBLS Form No. 3.1.25

LETTER OF TRANSMITTAL LOG

PROJECT NAME:

SITE LOCATION:

PROJECT NO.: DATE:

NUMBER	DESCRIPTION	DATE	INITIALS

PBLS Form No. 3.1.26

INSTALLATION CHECK

CLIENT: _____

LOCATION: _____

JOB NO.: _____   DATE: _____

AREA _____

EQUIPMENT NO. _____

COMPONENT _____

SYSTEM _____   VENDOR _____

SERIAL NO. _____   TYPE _____

FABRICATION CHECK: _____
_____

INSTALLATION CHECK: _____
_____

BASE FOUNDATION: _____
_____

CONTRACTOR CLEARANCE: _____
_____

LOCAL METERING INSTRUMENT: _____
_____

LOCAL CONTROLS: _____
_____

FRAME AND SUPPORT: _____
_____

SERVICE EQUIPMENT: _____
_____

COMMENTS:

CHECKED BY: _____

PBLS Form No. 3.2.1

MECHANICAL
PREOPERATIONAL CHECK

CLIENT: _____

LOCATION: _____

JOB NO.: _____ DATE: _____

AREA _____

EQUIPMENT NO. _____

EQUIPMENT ASSEMBLY NO. _____

MOTOR NO. _____ REDUCER NO. ____ EQUIPMENT NO. _____

MFR. _____ MFR. _____ MFR. _____

SER. NO. _____ SER. NO. _____ SER. NO. _____

TYPE _____ TYPE _____ TYPE _____

	<u>MOTOR</u>	<u>REDUCER</u>	<u>EQUIPMENT</u>
LUBRICATION CHECK:			
CPLG. ALIGNMENT CHECK:			
INTERNALS CHECK:			
BASE PLATE ALIGNMENT:			
ANCHOR BOLT TORQUE:			

AS APPLICABLE CHECKS:

PRESSURE TEST _____ TEMPORARY STRAINER _____

FLUSH _____ GUARDS INSTALLED _____

COUPLING INSTALLED _____ SPECIAL TEST INSTRUMENTS _____

FREE RUN _____ SHIPPING STOPS REMOVED _____

DEBRIS CHECK _____ BELT FREE _____

COMMENTS:

_____

_____

_____

_____

CHECKED BY: _____

PBLS Form No. 3.2.2

EQUIPMENT RUN-IN DATA

PROJECT NAME:

SITE LOCATION:

PROJECT NO.:   DATE:

AREA _____

EQUIPMENT NO. _____

EQUIPMENT ASSEMBLY NO. _____ MOTOR NO. _____

REDUCER NO. _____ DRIVE DESCRIPTION _____

PRESTART CHECKS COMPLETE:

                    MECHANICAL INSPECTION _____

                    ELECTRICAL PREOP _____

                    MECHANICAL PREOP _____

                    TAGGING PROCEDURE _____

                    SYSTEM WALKDOWN _____

TIME START _____ TIME STOP _____

PUMP DATA: RATED SPEED _____ ACTUAL SPEED _____

DISCHARGE PRESSURE: FULL FLOW _____ SHUTOFF _____

SUCTION PRESSURE: _____

BEARING TEMP. (INBOARD) _____ °C/°F (OUTBOARD) _____°C/°F

VIBRATION   HORIZ. _____ (MILLS)/(MICRONS) _____ (SEC.)/(MM/SEC.)

               VERT. _____ (MILLS)/(MICRONS) _____ (SEC.)/(MM/SEC.)

               AXL. _____ (MILLS)/(MICRONS) _____ (SEC.)/(MM/SEC.)

VIBRATION   HORIZ. _____ (MILLS)/(MICRONS) _____ (SEC.)/(MM/SEC.)

               VERT. _____ (MILLS)/(MICRONS) _____ (SEC.)/(MM/SEC.)

               AXL. _____ (MILLS)/(MICRONS) _____ (SEC.)/(MM/SEC.)

MOTOR CURRENT READINGS _____ ØA _____ ØB _____ ØC

COMMENTS:

_____

_____

_____

TESTED BY _____

MECHANICAL ALIGNMENT DATA

PROJECT NAME:

SITE LOCATION:

PROJECT NO.: DATE:

AREA _____ COUPLING TYPE _____

EQUIPMENT NO. _____ MFG. & NO. _____

EQUIPMENT _____ LUBRICATION _____

COUPLING ASSEMBLED _____ GUARD INSTALLED _____

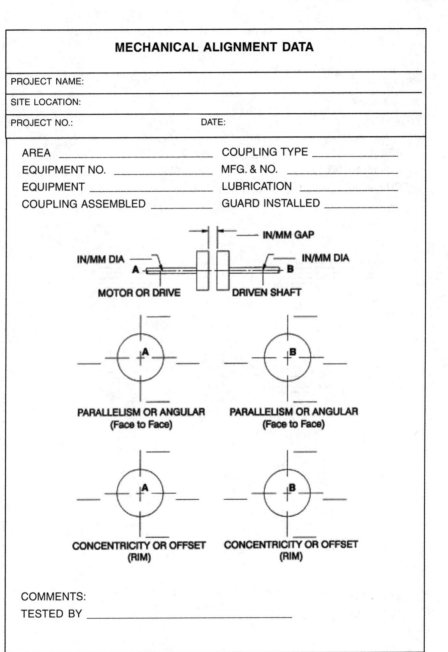

COMMENTS:

TESTED BY _____

V-BELT SHEAVES

PROJECT NAME:

SITE LOCATION:

PROJECT NO.:   DATE:

AREA _____   NO. OF BELTS _____

EQUIPMENT NO. _____   BELT NO. _____

EQUIPMENT _____

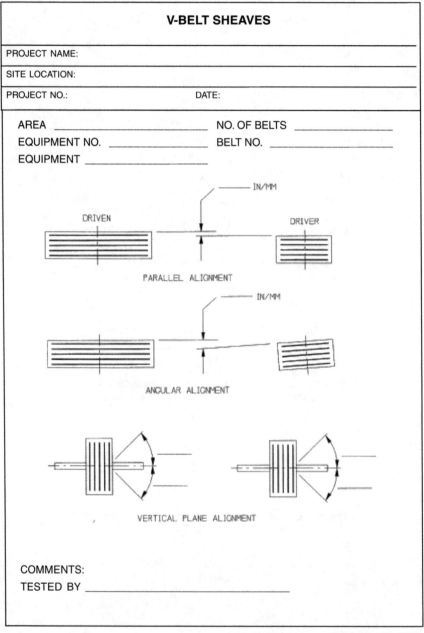

PARALLEL ALIGNMENT

ANGULAR ALIGNMENT

VERTICAL PLANE ALIGNMENT

COMMENTS:

TESTED BY _____

PRESSURE TEST

PROJECT NAME:

SITE LOCATION:

PROJECT NO.:   DATE:

AREA _____

EQUIPMENT NO. _____

SYSTEM _____

TYPE TEST: PNEUMATIC ☐   STATIC ☐   HYDROSTATIC ☐

TEST DESCRIPTION/SPECIFICATION:

_____

_____

_____

_____

_____

OPERATING PRESSURE _____ TEST PRESSURE _____

TIME START _____ TIME FINISH _____

LEAK RATE _____ TEMP. START _____

FINAL TEST PRESSURE _____ TEMP. FINISH _____

COMMENTS:

_____

_____

_____

_____

_____

_____

_____

_____

_____

TESTED BY: _____ APPROVED BY: _____

PBLS Form No. 3.2.6

FLUSHING AND CHEMICAL CLEANING

PROJECT NAME:

SITE LOCATION:

PROJECT NO.:   DATE:

AREA _____ .

EQUIPMENT NO. _____

SYSTEM DESCRIPTION:

_____

_____

_____

_____

_____

FLUSHING MEDIA _____

PRESSURE _____

TEMPERATURE _____ TIME START _____ TIME FINISH _____

SCREEN SIZE _____ FILTER SIZE _____

COMMENTS/SPECIAL CONDITIONS:

_____

_____

_____

_____

_____

_____

_____

_____

_____

_____

TESTED BY _____

APPROVED BY _____

PBLS Form No. 3.2.7

TEMPORARY MODIFICATION LOG

PROJECT: SHEET _____ OF _____

LOG DATE START _____ LOG DATE END _____

MOD. TRACK. NO.	TEMP. MOD. REQUESTED BY	REASON FOR TEMP. MOD.	DATE TEMP. MOD. INSTALLED	MOD. REMOVED		EST. DATE OF REMOVAL
				YES	NO	

PBLS Form No. 3.2.8

LUBRICANT & HYDRAULIC FLUID DATA SHEET

CLIENT:

LOCATION:

AREA:

JOB NO.:

SHEET ___ OF ___

DATE:

EQUIPMENT NO.	POINT OF USE	SPECIFICATION	LUBRICANT TYPE	METHOD OF LUBRICATION	CAPACITY

TEMPORARY MODIFICATION CHECK

CLIENT: _____   TEMP. MOD. TRACK. NO.: _____

LOCATION: _____

JOB NO.: _____   DATE: _____

AREA _____   ASSOCIATED DWG. NO. _____

EQUIPMENT NO. _____   SYSTEM _____

COMPONENT _____   VENDOR _____

SERIAL NO. _____   TYPE _____

TEMPORARY INSTALLATION CHECK:

STRUCTURAL _____ ELECTRICAL _____ MECHANICAL _____ INSTRUMENTATION _____

PRESSURE TEST _____ LEAK RATE _____ FILTER(S) _____ SCREEN(S) _____

JUMPERS INSTALLED: ___ YES ___ NO   LOG NO. _____ (IF APPLICABLE)

SERVICE EQUIPMENT CONNECTED: (Write N/A if Not Applicable)

AIR _____ WATER _____ POWER _____ FUEL _____ DISCHARGE _____ OTHER _____

ALL SAFETY GUARDS IN PLACE _____ AREA SECURED _____

COMMENTS _____

_____

_____

_____

CHECKED BY: _____

_____

ELECTRICAL PREOPERATIONAL CHECK

CLIENT:

LOCATION:

JOB NO.:   DATE:

AREA _____

EQUIPMENT NUMBER _____

MOTOR NAME PLATE DATA : MFR _____ TYPE _____

STYLE _____ SERIAL _____ FRAME _____

HP/KW _____ PHASE _____ HOUSING _____

RPM _____ S.F. _____ HZ _____ VOLTS _____

AMPS _____ CODE _____ DEGREE C RISE _____

STARTER: SIZE _____ LINE FUSE _____ CONTROL FUSE _____

BREAKER SIZE _____ O.L. SIZE _____ O.L. NO. _____

POWER AND CONTROL CIRCUIT CHECK: ROTATION _____ FROM SHAFT END

LOCAL _____ INT'LKS _____ GUARDS _____

REMOTE _____ INDICATION _____ WIRE INDT. _____

MANUAL _____ INSTRU. _____ J.B.'S _____

AUTO _____ LUBRI. _____ _____ _____

RESISTANCE : (A - B) _____ (B - C) _____ (C - A) _____ (A - GND) _____ MEGOHMS

NO LOAD CHECK: TIME START _____ TIME STOP _____

CURRENT PHASE A _____ PHASE B _____ PHASE C _____

COMMENTS: _____

_____

_____

CHECKED BY: _____ APPROVED: _____

PBLS **Form No. 3.3.1**

ELECTRICAL PREOP CHECK

CLIENT:

LOCATION:

JOB NO. :   DATE:

AREA _____

EQUIPMENT NUMBER _____

<u>MOTOR NAME PLATE DATA</u> : MFR _____ TYPE _____

STYLE _____ SERIAL _____ FRAME _____

HP/KW _____ PHASE _____ HOUSING _____

RPM _____ S.F. _____ HZ _____ VOLTS _____

AMPS _____ CODE _____ DEGREE C RISE _____

TEST VOLTAGE 1,000 VDC   MINIMUM ACCEPTABLE RESISTANCE 1 MEGOHM

CABLE RES. (A - B) _____ (B - C) _____ (C - A) _____ (A - GND) _____ MEGOHMS
            (FIELD) _____ (ARMATURE) _____
CABLE+   (A - B) _____ (B - C) _____ (C -A) _____ (A - GND) _____ MEGOHMS
EQUIP.   (FIELD) _____ (ARMATURE) _____

<u>POWER AND CONTROL CIRCUIT CHECK</u>: ROTATION <u>CC CW</u> FROM SHAFT END

LOCAL _____ INT'LKS _____ GUARDS _____

REMOTE _____ INDICATION _____ WIRE INDT. _____

MANUAL _____ INSTRU. _____ J.B.'S _____

AUTO _____ LUBRI. _____ _____ _____

<u>RESISTANCE</u>: (A - B) _____ (B - C) _____ (C - A) _____ (A - GND) _____ MEGOHMS

<u>NO LOAD CHECK</u>: TIME START _____ TIME STOP _____

CURRENT PHASE A _____ PHASE B _____ PHASE C _____ VOLTAGE _____

         FIELD _____ VOLTAGE _____ ARMATURE _____ VOLTAGE _____

COMMENTS: _____
_____
_____

TESTED BY _____ ACCEPTED BY _____

***PBLS* Form No. 3.3.1a**

MOTOR CONTROL CENTERS SWITCHGEAR

CLIENT:

LOCATION:

JOB NO.:   DATE:

AREA _____

EQUIPMENT NUMBER _____

EQUIPMENT DATA :

MANUFACTURER _____   MODEL/TYPE _____

RATED VOLTAGE _____   CURRENT _____

OPERATING VOLTAGE _____   PHASE _____ FREQUENCY _____HZ

CONTROL VOLTAGE _____ VAC/DC MAIN BREAKER FUSE SIZE _____

CALIBRATION/REQUIRED CHECKS:

BASE & FOUNDATION _____   RELAYS _____

GROUNDING _____   METERING/
INSTRUMENTATION _____

SPACE HEATERS _____   CONTROLS _____

CLEANLINESS _____   INTERLOCKS _____

PAINT CONDITION _____   TERMINATIONS _____

NAME TAGS _____   PHASING _____

BREAKER LINE-UP/
ISOLATION _____   FEEDER
MEGGER/HI-POT _____

MEGGER DATA :

AØ - GND _____ MEGOHMS   AØ - BØ _____ MEGOHMS

BØ - GND _____ MEGOHMS   BØ - CØ _____ MEGOHMS

CØ - GND _____ MEGOHMS   CØ - AØ _____ MEGOHMS

TEST VOLTAGE _____ VDC

COMMENTS:

TESTED BY: _____ APPROVED: _____

TRANSFORMER CHECK

CLIENT:

LOCATION:

JOB NO.: DATE:

AREA _____

EQUIPMENT NUMBER _____

TRANSFORMER DATA:

MANUFACTURER _____ RATING _____

PHASE _____ HERTZ _____ SERIAL NO. _____

VOLTAGE HI _____ VOLTAGE LOW _____ TYPE _____

TAPCHANGER SETTING _____

COOLING SYSTEM TYPE _____

OIL TYPE _____ FILL DATE _____

OIL DIELECTRIC TEST _____ KV

CALIBRATION/REQUIRED CHECKS:

  PROTECTIVE RELAYS _____ TURNS RATIO _____

  HIGH POTENTIAL _____ OIL LEVEL _____

  PRESSURE RELAYS _____ EQUIP. GROUNDING _____

  SETTINGS _____ PSIG MOUNTING BOLTS _____

  TEMP. INSTR. _____ PAINT CONDITION _____

  SETTINGS _____ °C/°F BUSHINGS _____

  NITROGEN PRESSURE _____ CHIPPED/CRACKED/DIRTY

COMMENTS:

TESTED BY: _____ APPROVED: _____

PBLS Form No. 3.3.3

POWER DISTRIBUTION PANEL CHECK

CLIENT

LOCATION

JOB NO.   DATE

AREA _____

EQUIPMENT NUMBER _____

EQUIPMENT DATA:

MANUFACTURER _____   MODEL/TYPE _____

RATED VOLTAGE _____   CURRENT _____

OPERATING VOLTAGE _____   PHASE _____ FREQUENCY ____ HZ

MAIN BREAKER/   MAIN BREAKER/
FUSE SIZE _____   FUSE TYPE _____

BRANCH BREAKER/   BRANCH BREAKER/
FUSE SIZE _____   FUSE TYPE _____

REQUIRED CHECKS:

MOUNTING _____   INTERLOCKS _____

GROUNDING _____   TERMINATION _____

SPACE HEATERS _____   PHASING _____

                                    WIRE/CABLE
CIRCUIT DIRECTORY _____   IDENTIFICATION _____

CLEANLINESS _____   TERMINATIONS _____

PAINT CONDITION _____   NAME TAGS _____

BREAKER LINE-UP/
ISOLATION _____   FEEDER MEGGER _____

MEGGER DATA:

AØ - GND _____ MEGOHMS   AØ - BØ _____ MEGOHMS

BØ - GND _____ MEGOHMS   BØ - CØ _____ MEGOHMS

CØ - GND _____ MEGOHMS   CØ - AØ _____ MEGOHMS

COMMENTS:

TESTED BY: _____   APPROVED: _____

GROUNDING SYSTEM RESISTANCE TEST

CLIENT:

LOCATION:

JOB NO.:   DATE:

AREA _____

TYPE SOIL _____ SEASON _____

SOIL CONDITION: DRY ☐ MOIST ☐

ROD DEPTH _____ FT ROD DIAMETER _____ INCHES

TESTS:

SOIL RESISTIVITY

DISTANCE BETWEEN ELECTRODES _____ FT   R = _____ OHMS

MULTIPLIER TIMES R IN OHMS _____

SOIL RESISTIVITY + _____ OHMS PER CUBIC CENTIMETER

MAN-MADE GROUND RESISTANCE

DISTANCE TO AUX. CURRENT ELECTRODE _____ FT

DISTANCE TO AUX. POTENTIAL ELECTRODE _____ FT

TEST POINT RESISTANCE _____

COMMENTS _____
_____
_____
_____
_____

TESTED BY: _____ APPROVED: _____

PBLS Form No. 3.3.7

GROUNDING SYSTEM RESISTANCE TEST DIAGRAM
CLIENT:
LOCATION:
JOB NO.:   DATE:

AREA _____

EQUIPMENT NO. _____

CIRCUIT BREAKER TEST

CLIENT:

LOCATION:

JOB NO.: DATE:

AREA _____

EQUIPMENT NO. _____

MANUFACTURER _____ SERIAL NO. _____

MODEL _____ TYPE _____

TRIP COIL RATING _____ METHOD OF CALIBR. _____

CHECK POINTS:

MECHANICAL OPERATION _____ ELECTRICAL OPERATION _____

ARC CHUTES _____ SLOW CLOSE _____

CLEANLINESS _____ NAME TAGS _____

CALIBRATION:

		LONG TIME	SHORT TIME	INST. TIME	CYCLES	BAND
PHASE A	SPECIFIED					
	AS FOUND					
	AS LEFT					
PHASE B	SPECIFIED					
	AS FOUND					
	AS LEFT					
PHASE C	SPECIFIED					
	AS FOUND					
	AS LEFT					

COMMENTS:

TESTED BY: _____ APPROVED: _____

PBLS Form No. 3.3.9

PROTECTIVE RELAY TEST

CLIENT:

LOCATION:

JOB NO.:   DATE:

AREA _____   FEEDER NAME _____

EQUIPMENT NO. _____   BREAKER TYPE & RATING _____

RELAY TYPE

STYLE NO.

SERIAL NO.

RATING

PT/CT RATING

RELAY SETTINGS	PHASE A			PHASE B			PHASE C		
	AS SPEC.	AS FOUND	AS LEFT	AS SPEC.	AS FOUND	AS LEFT	AS SPEC.	AS FOUND	AS LEFT
TAP									
TIME DIAL									
INSTANTANEOUS									

RELAY CONDITION ___ COVER ___ BEARINGS ___ PIVOTS ___ CONNECTIONS ___

ELECTRICAL TESTS

ZERO ADJUSTMENT			
PICKUP			
V/1 VALVE			
TIME			
INST. PICKUP			
IIT AMPS			
ICS AMPS			

COMMENTS: _____

_____

_____

TESTED BY: _____   APPROVED BY: _____

PBLS Form No. 3.3.10

TRANSFORMER DIFFERENTIAL PROTECTIVE RELAY TEST

CLIENT

LOCATION

JOB NO.   DATE

AREA _____ FEEDER NAME _____

EQUIPMENT NO. _____ BREAKER TYPE & RATING _____

PHASE _____ SERIAL NO. _____

RELAY TYPE _____ RATING _____

MODEL NO. _____ PT/CT RATIO _____

RELAY SETTING	AS SPEC.	AS FOUND	AS LEFT
HIGH TAP			
LOW TAP			
SLOPE			
D.C. VOLTAGE			

ELECTRICAL TESTS

		AS FOUND	AS LEFT
PICKUP	HIGH TAP		
	LOW TAP		
SLOPE	15 %		
	25 %		
	40 %		
HARMONIC RESTRAINT			
INSTANTANEOUS PICKUP			
AUXILIARY RELAY DROPOUT			

COMMENTS: _____

_____

_____

TESTED BY: _____   APPROVED BY: _____

PBLS Form No. 3.3.11

MOTOR OVERLOAD RELAY TEST

CLIENT: _____

LOCATION: _____

JOB NO.: _____   DATE: _____

AREA _____

EQUIPMENT NO. _____

BUILDING _____ PANEL NO. _____

MOTOR IDENTIFICATION _____

RELAY TYPE _____

MANUFACTURER _____

CONDITION _____

TEMPERATURE _____ TEST EQUIPMENT _____

ELEMENT SIZE _____ NUMBER _____

	TEST CURRENT 3X	TRIP TIME	COMMENTS
PHASE A			
PHASE B			
PHASE C			

COMMENTS: _____
_____
_____
_____
_____
_____
_____
_____
_____

TESTED BY: _____   APPROVED BY: _____

PBLS Form No. 3.3.12

TRANSFORMER DIELECTRIC
FIELD SERVICE TEST

CLIENT: _____

LOCATION: _____

JOB NO.: _____ DATE: _____

AREA _____

EQUIPMENT NO. _____

TRANSFORMER NO. _____

TRANSFORMER LOCATION _____

TRANSFORMER RATING: PRIMARY _____ SECONDARY _____

ACCEPTANCE DIELECTRIC BREAKDOWN

   VOLTAGE (PER ASTM D-877): _____

TESTS:

DIELECTRIC BREAKDOWN VOLTAGE (PER ASTM D-877)

   TEST 1: _____

   TEST 2: _____

   TEST 3: _____

   AVERAGE: _____

VISUAL EXAMINATION: _____

_____

_____

_____

COMMENTS: _____

_____

_____

_____

TESTED BY: _____ APPROVED BY: _____

PBLS **Form No. 3.3.13**

JUMPER RECORD

CLIENT: _____ JOB NO.: _____ SHEET _____ OF _____

LOCATION: _____ DATE: _____

DATE	AREA	EQUIPMENT AFFECTED	ELECTRICAL ENCL. NO.	TERM. NO'S FROM	TERM. NO'S TO	DWG. NUMBER	REASON FOR JUMPER	PLACED BY	DATE	REMOVED BY	DATE

PBLS Form No. 3.3.15

402

INSTRUMENT INSTALLATION INSPECTION

CLIENT: _____

LOCATION: _____   DATE:_____

TAG NO.: _____   REF. DRWG'S LOCATION: _____

LOOP NO.: _____   INSTALLATION DETAIL: _____

AREA: _____   P&ID NO.: _____

INSTALLATION SPECIFICATIONS: _____

INSPECTION CHECKLIST: (S) SATISFACTORY (NS) NOT SATISFACTORY

MECHANICAL INSTALLATION, SUPPORTS, MOUNTING	❏ S	❏ NS
FASTENERS, COVERS, TRAY & PIPE OR TUBING SUPPORTS	❏ S	❏ NS
INSTALLATION PER ENGINEERING DRAWINGS	❏ YES	❏ NO
INSTRUMENT TAGGING & IDENTIFICATION	❏ S	❏ NS
INDICATING LAMPS, LENS, GLASS & COVERS COMPLETE	❏ S	❏ NS
TUBING/FITTINGS/PIPING INSTALLED WITH CORRECT SLOPE (IF APPLICABLE)	❏ S	❏ NS
CABLE/CABLE GLANDS/TERMINATIONS/IDENTIFICATION	❏ S	❏ NS
EQUIPMENT GROUNDING FIELD ❏	❏ S	❏ NS
CONTROL ROOM ❏	❏ S	❏ NS
INSTALLATION ASSEMBLY COMPLETION PER MANUFACTURERS' INSTRUCTIONS	❏ S	❏ NS
ALL MARSHALLING OR JUNCTION BOXES TO THIS INSTRUMENT	❏ S	❏ NS
INSTALLATION MAINTAINABILITY AND ACCESSIBILITY	❏ S	❏ NS
INTERFERENCE	❏ S	❏ NS
INSTALLATION OF ENVIRONMENTAL PROTECTION PER N.E.C.	❏ S	❏ NS
CAN CHECKOUT & TESTING COMMENCE?	❏ YES	❏ NO
DO INSTRUMENTS HAVE CALIBRATION STICKER?	❏ YES	❏ NO
ARE SHIPPING BLOCKS & STOPS REMOVED?	❏ YES	❏ NO

DEFICIENCY:

INSPECTED BY: _____

APPROVED BY: _____

_____
TITLE

***PBLS* Form No. 3.4.1**

INSTRUMENT LOOP CHECK

CLIENT:

LOCATION:

JOB NO.: DATE:

AREA _____

EQUIPMENT NO. _____

LOOP NO. _____ DWG. NO. _____

SYSTEM _____ SUBSYSTEM _____

LOOP FUNCTION _____

PRIMARY ELEMENT _____

METHOD _____

LOOP COMPONENTS:

DESIGNATION	TAG NO.	FUNCTIONAL CHECK	CALIBRATION DATA SHEET
_____	_____	_____	_____
_____	_____	_____	_____
_____	_____	_____	_____
_____	_____	_____	_____
_____	_____	_____	_____
_____	_____	_____	_____

COMMENTS: _____

TESTED BY _____ APPROVED _____

PBLS Form No. 3.4.2

INSTRUMENT DATA SHEET

CLIENT: _____

LOCATION: _____

JOB NO.: _____ DATE: _____

AREA _____

EQUIPMENT NO. _____

DRAWING NO. _____ LOOP NO. _____

SYSTEM _____

INSTRUMENT _____

INSTRUMENT DATA:

MANUFACTURER _____ TYPE _____

MODEL NO. _____ SERIAL NO. _____

RANGE _____ ACCURACY _____

APPLICATION _____

METHOD OF CALIBRATION _____

SETPOINT _____

CALIBRATIONS: INPUT   OUTPUT

   0% _____   _____   _____

  25% _____   _____   _____

  50% _____   _____   _____

  75% _____   _____   _____

 100% _____   _____   _____

COMMENTS: _____

_____

_____

_____

_____

TESTED BY _____ APPROVED _____

PBLS Form No. 3.4.3

VENDOR QUALITY CONTROL (QC) SURVEY

Vendor Name: _____

Vendor Address: _____

_____

A. PRODUCT CAPABILITY

Types of Product Presently Manufactured

Customer Design: _____

Commercial Products: _____

The above products are being supplied to the following manufacturers, Government Agencies, Construction Companies and/or Installers buying under 10 CFR 50 (AEC 18-point criteria), ASME Section III, or _____.

Item	Customer
_____	_____
_____	_____
_____	_____

B. ORGANIZATION

Head of Quality Control (QC): _____   Title: _____

Reports to: _____   Title: _____

Number of QC Personnel: _____   Inspection Personnel: _____

Production Personnel (Direct Labor Only): _____

Name(s) of Vendor Personnel Present during Survey: _____

_____

_____

_____

PBLS Form No. QA 4.2.1

C. QUALITY CONTROL SYSTEM AND PROCEDURES

	Yes	No	N/A	Supp. Info. Att'd.
1. Does the facility have a written:				
Quality Control Manual? _____	❑	❑	❑	❑
Inspection Plan? _____	❑	❑	❑	❑
Date: _____	❑	❑	❑	❑
2. Is the AC System derived from a quality specification such as:				
ASME Section III _____	❑	❑	❑	❑
10 CFR 50 (AEC 18 points)				
_____	❑	❑	❑	❑
Other _____	❑	❑	❑	❑
3. Is the manual of QC Procedures undated continually to the latest industry practices, regulatory bodies and code requirements?	❑	❑	❑	❑
4. Is the Quality Control Manual and/or inspection plan approved by Company management?	❑	❑	❑	❑
5. Is responsibility and authority for quality assigned to personnel with sufficient management stature to resolve problems effectively?	❑	❑	❑	❑
6. Are QC & Inspection personnel familiar with instructions and procedures contained in the Quality Control Manual or Inspection plan?	❑	❑	❑	❑

D. PROCUREMENT CONTROL

	Yes	No	N/A	Supp. Info. Att'd.
1. Are adequate, written procedures in use for the quality control of purchased materials and services?	❑	❑	❑	❑
2. Are the quality capabilities of procurement sources, including those furnishing special process service, evaluated prior to procurement?	❑	❑	❑	❑
3. Is a written list of approved sources maintained and periodically updated?	❑	❑	❑	❑
4. Is a supplier performance rating system maintained to ensure continued quality and to assist in the selection of sources?	❑	❑	❑	❑
5. Are applicable drawings and specifications and changes thereto referenced on purchase orders to lower-tier sources?	❑	❑	❑	❑
6. Do Quality Control personnel review purchase orders to assure incorporation of applicable drawings, specifications, and quality requirements?	❑	❑	❑	❑

E. CONTROL OF RAW MATERIALS

	Yes	No	N/A	Supp. Info. Att'd.
1. Are there adequate written procedures in use for the control and issuance of material?	❑	❑	❑	❑
2. Are stock rooms and material storage areas restricted to authorized personnel?	❑	❑	❑	❑
3. Are materials properly handled and stored to prevent damage, contamination, and/or loss?	❑	❑	❑	❑
4. Are original source certified mill test reports or certificates of conformance obtained on purchased material (if applicable)?	❑	❑	❑	❑
5. Are materials traceable to the chemical/physical analysis certifications of compliance, test documents, or purchase orders?	❑	❑	❑	❑
6. When material is issued from stock, is the shop traveler/ stock order, etc., identified with the certification of material or test reports?	❑	❑	❑	❑

F. INCOMING INSPECTION

	Yes	No	N/A	Supp. Info. Att'd.
1. Does Receiving Inspection check incoming shipments to requirements of the Purchase Order, referenced specifications, and applicable drawings?	❑	❑	❑	❑
2. Are copies of applicable purchase orders available to Receiving Inspection?	❑	❑	❑	❑
3. Are incoming materials identified to the applicable Purchase Order or material certification?	❑	❑	❑	❑
4. Do Receiving Inspection records indicate acceptance or rejection of incoming material and reason therefore?	❑	❑	❑	❑
5. Are adequate controls for the handling and protection of received materials in use?	❑	❑	❑	❑
6. Are inspected items properly segregated from material awaiting inspection?	❑	❑	❑	❑
7. Are received items properly segregated from material awaiting inspection?	❑	❑	❑	❑
8. Are controls adequate to prevent entry of uninspected materials into stock or manufacturing?	❑	❑	❑	❑

PBLS Form QA 4.2.1

F. INCOMING INSPECTION (Cont'd.)

	Yes	No	N/A	Supp. Info. Att'd.
9. Is inspected material adequately identified as to acceptance or rejection?	❏	❏	❏	❏
Is rejected material adequately controlled?	❏	❏	❏	❏

G. INSPECTION, MEASURING DEVICES, AND TEST EQUIPMENT

	Yes	No	N/A	Supp. Info. Att'd.
1. Are adequate written procedures in effect to control gauges and test equipment?	❏	❏	❏	❏
2. Does the system adequately provide for mandatory recall of all calibrated/inspection gauges and test equipment?	❏	❏	❏	❏
3. Are controls in effect to prevent production items from being used as a gauge for test equipment?	❏	❏	❏	❏
4. Are employee-owned measuring devices and gauges (if used) subject to the same controls as company owned items?	❏	❏	❏	❏
5. Are there written detailed procedures in use for inspection and calibration of gauges and test equipment?	❏	❏	❏	❏
6. Are gauges and test equipment traceable to the National Bureau of Standards?	❏	❏	❏	❏
7. Do calibration inspection records reflect the essential information?	❏	❏	❏	❏
8. Are gauges and test equipment properly identified? By what means?	❏	❏	❏	❏
9. Do standards currently in calibration have certifications on file that are traceable to the National Bureau of Standards?	❏	❏	❏	❏

H. IN-PROCESS CONTROL & INSPECTION

	Yes	No	N/A	Supp. Info. Att'd.
1. Is sampling covered by adequate written instructions and performed according to statistically correct sampling plans?	❏	❏	❏	❏
2. Are valid statistical QC methods employed for characteristics not 100% inspected?	❏	❏	❏	❏
3. Is periodic training provided for inspection personnel?	❏	❏	❏	❏

H. IN-PROCESS CONTROL & INSPECTION (Cont'd.)

	Yes	No	N/A	Supp. Info. Att'd.
4. Is first article inspection conducted and recorded prior to machining or processing?	❏	❏	❏	❏
5. Are shop travelers, operation sheets and/or inspection logs utilized during manufacturing processes?	❏	❏	❏	❏
6. Do instructions provide for tightened or reduced inspection when results warrant?	❏	❏	❏	❏
7. Do written instructions clearly establish the conditions under which an Inspector can or will issue a stop work order?	❏	❏	❏	❏
8. Are acceptance standards and values documented and available for test and inspection personnel?	❏	❏	❏	❏
9. Are written procedures adequate for the in-process control of fabrication and services?	❏	❏	❏	❏
10. Are in-process inspections pre-planned in such a manner as to be compatible with manufacturing operations?	❏	❏	❏	❏
11. Are written in-process inspection instructions available and adequate?	❏	❏	❏	❏
12. Are in-process inspections documented in such a manner as to provide a positive inspection status of the material?	❏	❏	❏	❏
13. Does QA/QC approve test procedures to assure contractual compliance?	❏	❏	❏	❏
14. Are assembly and inspection operations and tests performed in accordance with approved written instructions?	❏	❏	❏	❏
15. Are assembly and inspection operations and test results documented and validated by inspection on a traveler, work order, or other identifying document?	❏	❏	❏	❏
16. Is material, and/or supporting documentation, identifiable to the manufacturing and inspection personnel responsible for the operation?	❏	❏	❏	❏
17. Is final inspection performed and results recorded?	❏	❏	❏	❏
18. Is product identity maintained throughout the manufacturing operation?	❏	❏	❏	❏

PBLS **Form QA 4.2.1**

I. NONDESTRUCTIVE EXAMINATION METHODS

1. List in-plant nondestructive examination (NDE) capabilities (X-ray, dye penetrant, magnetic particle, etc.)

   NDE Method   **Specification**

   a. _____   _____

   b. _____   _____

   c. _____   _____

2. Are there written non-destructive examination procedures? ❏ ❏ ❏ ❏

3. Are nondestructive examination personnel qualified to SNT-TC-1A requirements? ❏ ❏ ❏ ❏

4. Are personnel resumes and qualification records of NDE personnel on file? ❏ ❏ ❏ ❏

5. Are records of nondestructive examination maintained? ❏ ❏ ❏ ❏

J. NONCONFORMING MATERIAL CONTROL

	Yes	No	N/A	Supp. Info. Att'd.
1. Are written procedures in effect to detect product variations from Buyer or Seller specifications?	❏	❏	❏	❏
2. Is defective and "incomplete" material segregated, identified, and documented as to status?	❏	❏	❏	❏
3. Are nonconforming supplies identified and diverted from normal production channels?	❏	❏	❏	❏
4. Are deviations presented in writing to the customer for approval?	❏	❏	❏	❏
5. Are supplies designated as scrap identified or positively controlled to prevent reissue and use?	❏	❏	❏	❏
6. Is defective or questionable material identified as to its acceptance and the authorizing acceptance documentation?	❏	❏	❏	❏
7. Are management reports on nonconforming products published and acted upon?	❏	❏	❏	❏
8. Are reports of nonconformities analyzed for trends and are corrective actions required?	❏	❏	❏	❏

K. DRAWING AND CHANGE CONTROL

1. Does the company have adequate written procedures governing an Engineering Change Control system? ❏ ❏ ❏ ❏

2. Are applicable engineering drawings and specifications and changes thereto available at time and place of inspection? ❏ ❏ ❏ ❏

3. Is an adequate system in effect to control customer-furnished drawings and specifications? ❏ ❏ ❏ ❏

4. Are records maintained which reflect a history of change incorporation? ❏ ❏ ❏ ❏

5. Is there a written document control procedure in use that will assure shop conformance with drawings and order changes? ❏ ❏ ❏ ❏

6. Are obsolete specifications and drawings systematically recalled from point of use and distribution? ❏ ❏ ❏ ❏

7. Is the responsibility for this recall assigned to a specific person or department? ❏ ❏ ❏ ❏

8. Are recall records maintained? ❏ ❏ ❏ ❏

L. PACKAGING AND SHIPPING

	Yes	No	N/A	Supp. Info. Att'd.
1. Are adequate written instructions covering packaging, packing, marking, and shipping utilized by Shipping and/or Inspection personnel?	❏	❏	❏	❏
2. Are customer P.O. packaging, shipping and marking requirements incorporated by written instructions?	❏	❏	❏	❏
3. Is a check list used to verify shipping requirements and documentation to be enclosed in the shipment?	❏	❏	❏	❏
4. Do packing and shipping records identify the individuals performing and inspecting the shipping operations?	❏	❏	❏	❏
5. Are adequate storage facilities available and in use to safeguard the quality of the product between final acceptance and shipping?	❏	❏	❏	❏

PBLS Form QA 4.2.1

410   APPENDIX A

M. SPECIAL PROCESSES

1. List special process (plating, welding, heat treat, etc.)

Process	Specification
_____	_____
_____	_____
_____	_____

2. Are gauges, instruments, and other devices used in controlling special processes subject to calibration? ❏ ❏ ❏ ❏

3. Are record maintained relative to such calibration? ❏ ❏ ❏ ❏

4. Are personnel and equipment for special process approved or certified when applicable? ❏ ❏ ❏ ❏

N. RECORDS

1. Is there a written system to ensure that sufficient records are maintained to furnish evidence of activities affecting quality? ❏ ❏ ❏ ❏

2. Are procedures adequate to ensure that QA/QC records are accessible, identifiable, and retrievable? ❏ ❏ ❏ ❏

3. Do these procedures specify records retainability, location and classification as well as person(s) responsible for same? ❏ ❏ ❏ ❏

O. AUDITS

	Yes	No	N/A	Supp. Info. Att'd.
1. Are there written provisions for planned and periodic audits of essential functions within own and subcontractor's organizations?	❏	❏	❏	❏
2. Do these procedures provide for:				
Use of Audit Checklists	❏	❏	❏	❏
Training of Auditing Personnel	❏	❏	❏	❏
Written Audit Reports to Management	❏	❏	❏	❏
Follow-up Corrective Action	❏	❏	❏	❏

Company Name _____

Address _____

_____ Zip _____

Telephone (   ) _____

QUESTIONNAIRE PREPARED BY:

_____

PBLS Form QA 4.2.1

Report Number	Page _____ of _____

QUALITY INSPECTION REPORT

P.O. Number _____   Items Inspected _____

Vendor _____   Subcontractor _____

Inspection Location _____   Spec. No. _____

Inspection Procedure Number _____   Inspection Date _____

Drawing Numbers _____

Is Vendor Using Latest Issue of Drawings? _____   Drawing Date _____

TYPE OF INSPECTION:

❑VENDOR SHOP ❑RECEIVING ❑STORAGE ❑INSTALLATION ❑TEST ❑OTHER _____

OBSERVATIONS:

STATUS:

❑SATISFACTORY   ❑NCR ISSUED NO. _____

❑UNSATISFACTORY   ❑RELEASE FOR SHIPMENT ISSUED NO. _____

DISPOSITION:

❑REINSPECT AT SHOP   ❑REINSPECT AT JOBSITE   ❑INSPECTIONS COMPLETE

ADDITIONAL REMARKS: _____

_____

File by: ❑P.O. NUMBER

❑OTHER _____   QA ENGINEER _____   DATE _____

PBLS **Form No. QA 4.3.1**

TESTING AND QUALITY ASSURANCE
NONCONFORMANCE REPORT

P.O. Number _____ Items Inspected _____

Vendor _____

Reference Inspection Report Number _____

Nonconformance Description:

NCR Disposition:

❏ Material Review Board Resolution Required*

❏ Specific Corrective Action

Responsible Assignee _____ QA Engineer _____ Date _____

*Material Review Board Action:

❏ Use "As Is"   ❏ "Scrap"   ❏ Rework to Specification

❏ Other_____

_____

MRB APPROVAL:

Approved _____ **Date** _____

Approved _____ **Date** _____

Approved _____ **Date** _____

NCR Closeout:

Closeout Date _____ Verifying Inspection Report Number_____

QA Engineer _____

File by: ❏ P.O. NUMBER

❏ OTHER _____

PBLS Form No. QA 4.4.1

Report Number   Page _____ of ____

RELEASE FOR SHIPMENT

Vendor_____

P.O. Number _____ Reference Inspection Report _____

The Following Material Is Released for Shipment:

1. _____
2. _____
3. _____
4. _____

Work Items to Be Completed prior to Shipment:

❑ None

❑ NCR Items

❑ Other _____

_____

_____

This inspection was performed by _____ to determine that the material/equipment is ready for shipment. This inspection and release for shipment does not serve to accept the material/equipment and does not release the seller from any obligation of repair or replacement due to defective materials or workmanship found during or after this inspection.

Vendor's Acknowledgment _____ Date _____

QA Engineer _____ Date_____

File by: ❑ P.O. NUMBER

❑ OTHER _____

PBLS Form No. QA 4.5.1

PROCEDURES

GENERAL ADMINISTRATION PROCEDURE NO. GA-002: RELEASE OF EQUIPMENT TO THE OWNER

1.0 PURPOSE

To provide a uniform procedure for the release of equipment to the Owner after construction, preoperational testing and start-up testing are complete.

2.0 SCOPE

This procedure applies to the preoperational testing and start-up testing program, and is administered by the Preoperational Testing and Start-up manager, hereinafter referred to as "Commissioning Manager."

3.0 SPECIAL REQUIREMENTS

3.1 Safety

The Safety Tagging and Clearance Procedure (No. ____) shall be strictly adhered to during the performance of this procedure.

3.2 Documentation Forms

Documents utilized in conjunction with this procedure include but are not limited to the following:

3.2.1 Certificate of Completion (Attachment 1)

3.2.2 Final Completion List (*PBLS* Form No. 3.1.3)

3.2.3 Request for Equipment Clearance Permit (*PBLS* Form No. 3.1.16)

3.2.4 Clearance Removal Request (*PBLS* Form No. 3.1.17)

3.2.5 Clearance Permit Log (*PBLS* Form No. 3.1.18)

3.2.6 Letter of Release Log (*PBLS* Form No. 3.1.24)

3.2.7 Green Tag

3.2.8 Yellow Tag

3.2.9 Red Tag Log (*PBLS* Form No. 3.1.25)

3.2.10 Letter of Transmittal Log (*PBLS* Form No. 3.1.26)

3.2.11 Temporary Modification Record (*PBLS* Form No. 3.2.8)

3.2.12 Jumper Record (*PBLS* Form No. 3.3.15)

3.3 Prerequisites

3.3.1 The construction of the affected equipment/system must be essentially complete in accordance with the drawing, specifications, and intent of the contract with any exceptions documented on the Final Completion List.

3.3.2 The preoperational testing and start-up testing of the affected equipment/system must be complete and all required data entered on the appropriate data forms. Any exceptions to this requirement must be documented on the Final Completion List.

3.3.3 The Commissioning Manager must be satisfied that the equipment/system to be released is safe in respect to both personnel and equipment hazards for operation in a normal manner. Any restrictions to design operation must be documented on the Final Completion List.

3.3.4 The equipment/system released must form, by itself or in conjunction with previously released equipment, an operable system or subsystem (i.e., a pump cannot be released without releasing the tank on which it takes a suction and the vessel to which it discharges).

3.3.5 The Final Completion List must contain the minimum number of items possible at that time. Zero items is the desired goal. The Final Completion List should not contain items for which the design, materials, labor, etc., are available.

3.3.6 All jumpers and temporary modifications must be removed at the time of release, unless specifically waived by the Owner's Project Manager.

4.0 PROCEDURE

4.1 Preparation

When a system or subsystem has been satisfactorily tested and is ready to be operated, the Commissioning Manager shall:

4.1.1   Assemble the equipment test data forms and check them for completeness and legibility. (Where facilities are available these forms should be typed, for clarity).

4.1.2   Update the Construction Punch Lists for the concerned equipment and verify that all work that can be accomplished is complete. If further work is required before the equipment can be turned over, the Commissioning Manager shall notify the Owner's Project Manager. The Owner's Project Manager will pursue the completion of these items or resolution of these items.

4.1.3   By reviewing the jumper and temporary modifications log and visual inspection, ensure that all jumpers and temporary modifications are removed from the system(s) to be released. If jumpers and temporary modifications are required to operate the system because of interlocks to uncompleted equipment, these jumpers and temporary modifications will be reinstalled by the Owner after the equipment is released with the advice of the Commissioning Manager. Every effort will be made to eliminate the need for jumpers and temporary modifications and jumpers and temporary modifications installed in released equipment will be logged by both the Owner's Project Manager and the Preoperational Testing and Start-up Group for follow-up when they are no longer required.

4.1.4   Inform the Owner's Project Manager of the impending release of the system, the anticipated date of the release and the status of the equipment in the weekly meeting with the Owner's Project Manager.

4.2   Release Documents

The Preoperational Testing and Commissioning Manager will prepare the following release documents:

4.2.1   Certificate of Partial Completion

4.2.1.1   This certificate shall be typed in the format shown on Attachment _____.

4.2.1.2   The certificate shall be dated the day of the release.

4.2.1.3   Two copies of this certificate shall be sent to the Owner. The original of the certificate is returned to the Commissioning Manager signed by the Owner's representative.

4.2.1.4   This certificate shall be copied along with Attachments _____ and _____ and distributed as per the distribution list.

4.2.2   List of Equipment Turned Over

4.2.2.1   This list of Equipment Turned Over (PBLS Form 3.1.29) forms Attachment 1 to the Certificate of Partial Completion.

4.2.2.2   The Final Completion List shall contain all known deficiencies on the released equipment at the time of release.

4.2.2.3   Any equipment that might be assumed to be released by the List of Equipment Turned Over but is not to be released must be listed on the Final Completion List.

4.2.2.4   The revision number and the certificate number shall be on the top of the Final Completion List form.

4.2.2.5   The Final Completion List will contain the following information.
   • Date deficiency was identified.
   • Item Number—The item numbers are sequential for any turnover package and do not change.
   • Description of the deficiency.
   • Comments such as Estimated Time of Arrival of needed parts and Estimated Time of Completion.
   • Person responsible for accomplishing the work.
   • Date completed if the work is done.

4.2.2.6   The Preoperational Testing and Commissioning Manager shall periodically update and track the Final Completion List.

4.2.3   Data Package

     4.2.3.1   The data package contains all the test and inspection data collected during construction, preoperation, and start-up testing activities.

     4.2.3.2   This data can form Attachment 3 of the Certificate of Partial Completion or be transmitted under separate cover, at the Preoperational Testing and Commissioning Manager's discretion.

     4.2.3.3   The data package shall normally be issued to the Owner at the same time as the Certificate of Partial Completion.

4.2.4   Drawings

     4.2.4.1   If deemed necessary by the Preoperational Testing and Commissioning Manager to more fully describe the boundaries of the released system, the drawing or drawings shall be marked to illustrate the extent of the system.

     4.2.4.2   These drawings will be Attachment 4 to the Certificate of Partial Completion.

     4.2.4.3   Equipment, piping, systems, etc. that are released will be traced with a yellow highlighter. The boundary components (not released) will be marked in red. Items highlighted in red are hold points.

4.2.5   Interim Certificate of Completion

     4.2.5.1   The Interim Certificate of Completion is issued by the Preoperational Testing and Commissioning Manager when:

- All Certificates of Partial Completion have been issued and accepted.
- All Final Completion List items have been completed or waived by the Owner.
- All tasks have been completed to make the plant ready to commercially produce electricity.

     4.2.5.2   The Interim Certificate of Completion signifies that the entire facility has been transferred to the Owner and is ready for performance or hot start-up (Time of Completion).

4.2.6   Final Certificate of Completion

     4.2.6.1   The Final Certificate of Completion is issued by the Preoperational Testing and Commissioning Manager when:

- Performance or hot start-up is under way and all systems have been verified as operable.
- All systems have been demonstrated as operational (not necessarily demonstrating warranties).
- All known deficiency work has been completed.

4.3   Tagging

   4.3.1   At the time of the release the equipment shall be green tagged in accordance with the provisions of the Safety Tagging and Clearance Procedure (No. ____).

   4.3.2   Tags shall be hung in at least the following locations within the released system.

     4.3.2.1   Starter or controller

     4.3.2.2   Motor

     4.3.2.3   Major valves

     4.3.2.4   Local control stations

     4.3.2.5   Remote control stations

     4.3.2.6   Major instruments

     4.3.2.7   In enough locations around the equipment to clearly identify it as released to the Owner.

   4.3.3   When the released system is within an area where there is a continuing major construction effort or where there is a particular hazard associated with approaching the equipment, the Preoperational Testing and Commissioning Manager may require that barriers or barrier tape be used in conjunction with the green tags.

4.4   Demonstration

    4.4.1   At the time of green tagging or at a time after the issuance of the Certificate of Partial Completion, which is arranged with the Owner, the equipment that is released shall be demonstrated for the purpose of instructing the Owner's operators in the operation of this equipment.

    4.4.2   The demonstration shall be conducted under the guidance of the Preoperational and Start-up Group with Owner's operators performing the hands-on operations in order to obtain familiarity with the equipment.

    4.4.3   Each equipment in the released system shall be demonstrated for at least the following functions:

        4.4.3.1   Stop and start from local and remote stations.

        4.4.3.2   Group starts and stops.

        4.4.3.3   Major interlocks

        4.4.3.4   Mechanical operation.

        4.4.3.5   Indicating devices.

        4.4.3.6   Instrument functions.

    4.4.4   Any valid deficiency items uncovered during the demonstration shall be added to the Final Completion List by the Preoperational Testing and Commissioning Manager.

    4.4.5   Any disputed Final Completion List items that are not readily discernible, as being within the established scope shall be listed separately for resolution later.

    4.4.6   Upon satisfactory completion of the demonstration, the Owner's representative shall confirm the acceptance of the equipment for operation and maintenance by signing the original of the Certificates of Partial Completion and returning them to the Preoperational Testing and Commissioning Manager.

4.5   Completion List Tracking

    4.5.1   The Preoperational Testing and Commissioning Manager shall track the Final Completion List progress, updating the master list daily.

    4.5.2   The Preoperational Testing and Commissioning Manager shall issue a revised Final Completion List at least once a month with distribution as per the distribution list.

    4.5.3   In the event of a dispute on the completeness or validity of any particular item, the Preoperational Testing and Commissioning Manager shall chair special meetings to resolve these differences. The special meeting will be attended by representatives of Construction forces and the Owner's acceptance team.

5.0 PROCEDURE CLOSEOUT

    5.1   Safety

        5.1.1   The green tags shall remain in place until the construction effort is complete.

        5.1.2   If rework is required the applicable requirements of the Safety Tagging and Clearance Procedure (No. ____) shall be followed.

        5.1.3   If rework is required the equipment, system, or sub-system shall be returned to construction forces in accordance with Procedure No. GA-013.

    5.2   Documentation

        5.2.1   The Preoperational Testing and Commissioning Manager shall keep all involved documentation on file and distribute as required.

        5.2.2   The Letter of Release Log and the Letter of Transmittal Log shall be maintained by the Preoperational Testing and Commissioning Manager.

This Procedure Reviewed and Approved by:

_____   _____

Signature   Date

_____

Title

GENERAL ADMINISTRATION PROCEDURE NO. GA-003: TEMPORARY SYSTEM MODIFICATION

1.0 PURPOSE

To provide a uniform procedure for documenting temporary modifications to systems.

2.0 SCOPE

To identify and document any and all temporary changes during construction, preoperational, and start-up testing of plant equipment or systems.

3.0 SPECIAL REQUIREMENTS

    3.1   Safety

        The Safety Tagging and Clearance Procedure (No. ____) will be strictly adhered to during the performance of this procedure.

    3.2   Documentation

        Documents utilized in conjunction with the performance of this procedure include the following:

        3.2.1   Temporary Modification Record (*PBLS* Form No. 3.2.11)

        3.2.2   Temporary Modification Log (*PBLS* Form No. 3.2.8)

        3.2.3   Jumper Record (*PBLS* Form No. 3.3.15)

4.0 PROCEDURE

    4.1   The Preoperational Testing and Start-up Group will be responsible for administration of this procedure during the construction, preoperational testing and start-up testing of plant equipment or systems

    4.2   When the need arises for a temporary equipment or system modification, the forms listed in section 3.2 will be filled out.

        4.2.1   Temporary Modification Record (*PBLS* Form No. 3.2.11) will cover any non-electrical wiring items such as, but not limited to:

            4.2.1.1   Blanks

            4.2.1.2   Blinds

            4.2.1.3   Spool Pieces

            4.2.1.4   Valve Assemblies

            4.2.1.5   Start-up Strainers

        4.2.2   Jumper Record (*PBLS* Form No. 3.3.15) will cover electrical wiring items.

            4.2.2.1   Jumpers

            4.2.2.2   Lifted Leads

5.0 PROCEDURE CLOSEOUT

    5.1   Remove safety tags, if applicable, in accordance with the Safety Tagging and Clearance Procedure (No. ____).

    5.2   Verify the equipment or system has been returned to normal as in designed configuration and sign off the appropriate record.

    5.3   The Preoperational Testing and Commissioning Manager shall check the completeness of the Test Forms listed in section 3.2. The completed forms and any marked-up drawing shall become part of the equipment or system turnover package.

This Procedure Reviewed and Approved by:

_____   _____

Signature   Date

_____

Title

GENERAL ADMINISTRATION PROCEDURE NO. GA-004: START-UP DRAWING CHANGE NOTICE

1.0 PURPOSE

To provide a uniform procedure for documenting and distributing a notice of a change to or discrepancy between actual installation configurations and drawing configurations.

2.0 SCOPE

Start-up change drawing notifications shall be completed in all instances of change and/or discrepancy for all items contained in the engineering and construction drawings and documents.

3.0 SPECIAL REQUIREMENTS

3.1 Safety

3.1.1 The Safety Tagging and Clearance Procedure (No. ____) will be strictly adhered to as required for the completion of this procedure.

3.2 Documentation

3.2.1 Documents utilized in conjunction with the performance of this procedure include the following:

3.2.1.1 Start-up Drawing Change Notice (*PBLS* Form No. 3.1.4)

3.2.1.2 Drawing Change Notice Log (*PBLS* Form No. 3.1.5)

4.0 PROCEDURE

4.1 The Start-up Drawing Change Notice procedure shall utilize the information contained in the following documents.

4.1.1 Reference Drawings

4.1.2 Vendor Drawings

4.1.3 As-built Drawings

Prior to filing a Start-up Drawing Change Notice, the Preoperational Testing and Start-up Group will ensure that they have access to the most recent revision of the drawing(s) in question.

4.2 When the Preoperational Testing and Start-up Group discovers a discrepancy between actual installation configuration and drawing configuration, the following actions will be taken:

4.2.1 The discovering individual will immediately complete a Start-up Drawing Change Notice (*PBLS* Form No. 3.1.4), providing a detailed description of the discrepancy.

4.2.2 The discovering individual will then mark in red on the relevant drawing the exact details of the discrepancy.

4.2.3 The discovering individual will check to see if the same discrepancy exists on overlapping or related drawings. If so, Start-up Drawing Change Notice procedures will be applied to those drawings also.

4.2.4 The Start-up Drawing Change Notice and the drawing will be given to the Commissioning Manager, who will verify the information contained in the Notice and on the drawing, and sign the "Review" block on the Notice.

4.2.5 The Commissioning Manager will enter the notification of the Start-up Drawing Change on the Start-up Drawing Change Notice Log (*PBLS* Form No. 3.1.5).

4.2.6 The Owner's Project Manager will then approve/disapprove the documentation.

4.2.7 The Commissioning Manager will ensure that copies of the Notice and the marked drawing are distributed per the distribution list.

5.0 PROCEDURE CLOSEOUT

5.1 Remove safety tags, if applicable, in accordance with The Safety Tagging and Clearance Procedure (No. ____).

5.2   The Commissioning Manager shall check the completeness of the Start-up
      Drawing Change Notice and the Start-up Drawing Change Notice Log. The
      Start-up Drawing Change Notice and the marked-up drawing shall become part
      of the equipment turnover package.

                                This Procedure Reviewed and Approved by:

                          _____   _____
                                   Signature   Date

                          _____
                                         Title

GENERAL ADMINISTRATION PROCEDURE NO. GA-005: EXTRA WORK REQUEST

1.0 PURPOSE

To provide a uniform procedure for initiating, processing, and tracking requests for extra work.

2.0 SCOPE

2.1   This procedure applies to requests for work related to preoperational and start-up testing activities that, for any reason, cannot be performed by the test engineers or personnel assigned to them.

2.2   An example of this type of work would be the erection of a scaffold required by the test engineer in order to conduct a test or inspection.

2.3   In general, this procedure is concerned with work that the Preoperational Testing and Start-up Group would request of the Owner's Project Manager, i.e., work that must be done so that test personnel can carry out their testing and inspection function.

3.0 SPECIAL REQUIREMENTS

3.1   Safety

        3.1.1   The Safety Tagging and Clearance Procedure (No. ____) shall be strictly adhered to during the performance of this procedure.

        3.1.2   Personnel performing work requested are required to request the appropriate tags to perform the work safely.

3.2   Documentation

        Documents utilized in conjunction with this procedure include but are not limited to the following:

        3.2.1   Extra Work Request (*PBLS* Form No. 3.1.8)

        3.2.2   Extra Work Order Log (*PBLS* Form No. 3.1.9)

4.0 PROCEDURE

When a situation arises requiring extra work, the following actions will be taken:

4.1   The Preoperational Testing and Start-up Group will complete an Extra Work Request (*PBLS* Form No. 3.1.8). The Extra Work Request will be addressed to the attention of the Owner's Project Manager.

4.2   Under the heading "Extra Work Request," the initiating person will explain, in detail, the nature of the work required, and where the work is to be done. In addition, a completion date should be given, allowing Owner's operation and maintenance personnel (or Owner's contracted personnel) a reasonable amount of time to accomplish the work.

4.3   Under the heading "Reason for Work," the initiating person will explain, in detail, why the extra work is required.

4.4   The initiating Test Engineer or Technician shall sign in the "Originated" block of the form and submit the Extra Work Request to the Commissioning Manager.

4.5   The initiating test engineer shall review the request to determine if any safety problems are posed either by the nature of the work or by other preoperational and start-up activities taking place in the area. Any safety considerations or recommendations shall be detailed on the Extra Work Request Form.

4.6   The Preoperational Testing and Start-up Group Manager (hereinafter referred to as "Commissioning Manager") will review the Extra Work Request for completeness, safety, legibility and record the request on the Extra Work Order Log (*PBLS* Form No. 3.1.9). On some projects the Extra Work Request will be typed. The Extra Work Request will be reviewed to verify the validity of the required work, and when satisfied with the content of the request, the Commissioning Manager shall sign in the "Reviewed" block of the form.

4.7   The Commissioning Manager shall then forward the work request to the Owner's Project Manager, maintaining a copy of the request in the project file.

4.8   It is the responsibility of the Owner's Project Manager to approve/disapprove the Extra Work Request. If the Owner's Project Manager approves, he must sign the original in the "Approved By" block, assign the extra work order number (EWO), then return the original to the Commissioning Manager.

4.9 The Owner's Project Manager shall review the work from a safety aspect and ensure that the people performing the work follow the necessary procedures and precautions.

4.10 If the Project Manager does not approve the Extra Work Request, he should so signify in writing. The Commissioning Manager must then attempt to resolve the problem with his own resources.

4.11 If the Extra Work Request is approved, the Owner's Project Manager will direct the appropriate field forces to accomplish the work under the coordination of the Commissioning Manager.

4.12 When an approved Extra Work Request is returned, the cognizant Preoperational Testing and Start-up Group technician shall enter the appropriate information in the Extra Work Order Log. When the work is finished, the Preoperational Testing and Start-up Group technician shall so signify by initialing in the appropriate "Sign Off" block on the Extra Work Order Log.

5.0 PROCEDURE CLOSEOUT

5.1 Safety

Remove safety tags, if applicable, in accordance with the Safety Tagging and Clearance Procedure (No. _____).

5.2 Documentation

The Commissioning Manager shall ensure that the Extra Work Order Log is completed. The Extra Work Request and the Extra Work Order Log shall become part of the turnover package.

This Procedure Reviewed and Approved by:

_____   _____
Signature   Date

_____
Title

GENERAL ADMINISTRATION PROCEDURE NO. GA-006: VENDOR ADMINISTRATION

1.0 PURPOSE

To provide a uniform procedure for supervising, reporting, and administrating the activities of vendors involved in Preoperational Testing and Start-up testing activities.

2.0 SCOPE

This procedure applies to any vendor working in areas or on equipment under the control of the Preoperational Testing and Start-up Group.

3.0 SPECIAL REQUIREMENTS

3.1 Safety

The Safety Tagging and Clearance Procedure (No. ____) shall be strictly adhered to during the performance of this procedure.

3.2 Documentation

Documents utilized in conjunction with this procedure include but are not limited to the following:

3.2.1 Vendor Daily Activity Summary (*PBLS* Form No. 3.1.10)

3.2.2 Vendor Time Sheet (*PBLS* Form No. 3.1.11)

3.2.3 Vendor End of Service Report (*PBLS* Form No. 3.1.12)

3.2.4 Vendor Attendance Log (*PBLS* Form No. 3.1.13)

4.0 PROCEDURE

4.1 Because vendor organizations are an integral part of the preoperational testing and start-up process, it is imperative that their activities be closely administered and coordinated by the Preoperational Testing and Start-up Group.

4.1.1 The Preoperational Testing and Start-up Group shall cooperate with vendor engineering and technical personnel to resolve field start-up problems.

4.1.2 The Preoperational Testing and Start-up group shall communicate directly with vendor engineering organizations on start-up equipment and process related problems.

4.1.3 The Preoperational Testing and Start-up Group shall maintain a thorough record of field changes made by vendor organizations during the preoperational and start-up testing period.

4.2 Vendor Schedule

4.2.1 The Preoperational Testing and Start-up Group Manager (hereinafter referred to as the "Commissioning Manager") shall maintain a list of vendors whose on-site activities are required during the preoperational testing and start-up period.

4.2.2 This list is based upon:

4.2.2.1 Client-furnished list of existing prepaid service agreements

4.2.2.2 Equipment complexity/replacement cost

4.2.2.3 Vendor recommendations

4.2.2.4 Vendor availability

4.2.2.5 Testing experience

4.2.2.6 Commissioning Spares

4.2.3 Using the Master Schedule as a guide, the Commissioning Manager shall compile a vendor schedule designating the dates and duration of vendor assistance which will be required in support of the schedule.

4.2.4 This vendor schedule will be computerized and cross-referenced to applicable scheduled items so that changes in the schedule can be easily reflected in the vendor schedule.

4.3 Vendor Initial Contact

4.3.1 Depending upon equipment complexity, the initial contact with the vendor may be through the Preoperational Testing and Start-up Group, the Owner's Project Manager, or someone in the Construction/Engineering Organization (such as a purchasing agent or administrator.)

4.3.2 The initial contact should include at least the following:

4.3.2.1 Activation of a clause in the equipment purchase order or issue of a purchase order for services

4.3.2.2 Clear description of the equipment to be serviced

4.3.2.3 Clear description of the service required from the manufacturer's representative

4.3.2.4 Any special qualifications required

4.3.2.5 Any special conditions which must exist on site before the representative can begin his work

4.3.2.6 A contact name and number, preferably the vendor who will perform the work

4.3.2.7 An estimated date when the service will be required

4.3.3 The vendor will be informed that the Preoperational Testing and Start-up Group Manager (Commissioning Manager) will confirm the service date one or two weeks prior to the actual needed date.

4.4 Vendor Schedule Confirming Contact

One or two weeks prior to the date when the vendor is required on site, the Commissioning Manager will call and confirm that date. This conversation will include at least the following:

4.4.1 Date and time service required

4.4.2 Directions to the jobsite and who to see upon arrival

4.4.3 Confirmation of work that will be required

4.4.4 Confirmation that vendor is qualified to do the work

4.4.5 Update on equipment status and required work prior to vendor arrival

4.4.6 Confirmation of any required equipment the vendor needs to bring

4.4.7 Recommendations for area hotels, etc.

4.5 Vendor Arrival Conference

4.5.1 When the vendor first arrives at the jobsite, a meeting will be held for orientation. The attendees may vary depending on the vendor and the jobsite organization, but must include the Test Engineer who will be supervising the work and may include as applicable:

4.5.1.1 Commissioning Manager

4.5.1.2 Owner's Project Manager

4.5.1.3 Operators

4.5.1.4 Maintenance Personnel

4.5.2 This meeting will include at least the following:

4.5.2.1 Jobsite rules

4.5.2.2 Jobsite working hours

4.5.2.3 Jobsite Safety Requirements

4.5.2.4 Contacts in the site organization

4.5.2.5 Vendor requirements for craft assistance

4.5.2.6 Paper work requirements

4.5.2.7 Backcharge procedures

4.5.2.8 Specifics of the work to be accomplished

4.5.3 After this meeting, the cognizant Test Engineer will show the vendor the location of the equipment and the required facilities and obtain for the vendor the necessary craft and equipment support.

4.5.4 Depending on the nature of the services, the responsible Test Engineer may stay with the vendor or regularly check on the progress of the work.

4.6 Vendor activities shall be supervised and recorded, using the vendor-related forms, by the cognizant Test Engineer. Completed vendor forms shall be submitted to the Commissioning Manager and maintained in the project file.

4.6.1 Vendor Daily Activity Summary (*PBLS* Form No. 3.1.10)

4.6.1.1 This form shall be completed daily by the vendor and reviewed and signed by the responsible Testing Engineer.

4.6.1.2 This form is also used to describe and account for the activities and manhours of the vendor and craft personnel assigned to assist the vendor.

4.6.2 Vendor Time Sheet (*PBLS* Form No. 3.1.11)

4.6.2.1 This form shall be completed by the vendor weekly, or for the total number of days the vendor is on-site, if less than a week. The form shall be reviewed and signed by the responsible Testing Engineer.

4.6.2.2 The form is used to consolidate the vendor hours recorded on the Vendor Daily Activity Summary (Form No. 3.1.10). This form is used for vendor hours only, and shall not include craft hours.

4.6.2.3 Vendor shall record all straight time and overtime hours accountable for each day in two categories:
- Hours to Account—hours chargeable to client.
- Hours to Vendor Account—hours chargeable to vendor.

4.6.2.4 Responsible Test Engineer shall initial the totals for each day, ensuring that the accounting is correct and accurate.

4.6.2.5 Vendor and Testing Engineer shall verify the accuracy of this form by signing in the appropriate blocks.

4.6.2.6 This form may be supplied to the Owner's Project Manager upon request in order to ensure proper billing.

4.6.3 Vendor End of Service Report (*PBLS* Form No. 3.1.12)

4.6.3.1 This form certifies that the vendor has completed all required services. Vendor shall list all exceptions and comments in the space provided.

4.6.3.2 Vendor and Test Engineer shall sign-off in the spaces provided.

4.6.3.3 This form shall become a part of the appropriate equipment turnover package.

4.6.4 Vendor Attendance Log

4.6.4.1 This form shall be maintained by the Commissioning Manager.

4.6.4.2 The purpose of this form is to maintain a record of vendors, their arrival and departure dates, and the total number of man-days spent on-site by each vendor.

4.7 Vendor Exit Interview

4.7.1 When the work by the vendor is completed and/or the vendor is leaving the site, an exit meeting will be held. This meeting will cover at least the following:

4.7.1.1 Test Documentation
4.7.1.2 Vendor Time Sheets
4.7.1.3 Vendor End of Service Report
4.7.1.4 Deficiencies and Corrective Action
4.7.1.5 Backcharge Documentation and Resolution
4.7.1.6 Equipment Status
4.7.1.7 Special Operating Requirements
4.7.1.8 Special Maintenance Requirements
4.7.1.9 Any additional requirements for this vendor's attendance on site.

5.0 PROCEDURE CLOSEOUT

5.1 Safety

Remove safety tags, if applicable, in accordance with the Safety Tagging and Clearance Procedure (No. ____).

5.2 Documentation

5.2.1 The responsible test engineers shall check the completeness of all vendor-related forms.

5.2.2 The Commissioning Manager shall ensure that the Vendor end of service reports are included as a part of the appropriate turnover packages.

5.2.3 All other vendor documentation shall be maintained in the project file.

This Procedure Reviewed and Approved by:

_____   _____
Signature   Date

_____
Title

GENERAL ADMINISTRATION PROCEDURE NO. GA-007: DAILY ACTIVITY REPORTING

1.0 PURPOSE

To provide a uniform procedure for reporting the daily activities of preoperational testing and start-up engineers and technicians, vendor personnel working under the supervision of test engineers, and craft personnel working under test engineer supervision.

2.0 SCOPE

This procedure applies to all preoperational testing and start-up activities conducted or supervised by that group.

3.0 SPECIAL REQUIREMENTS

Documents utilized in conjunction with this procedure include but are not limited to the following:

  3.1   Continuation Sheet (*PBLS* Form No. 3.1.1)

  3.2   Field Service Report (*PBLS* Form No. 3.1.20)

  3.3   Daily Activity Summary (*PBLS* Form No. 3.1.21)

  3.4   Preoperational Testing Engineers Daily Time Sheet (*PBLS* Form No. 3.1.23)

4.0 PROCEDURE

All Preoperational Testing and Start-up Group personnel shall document their daily activities using the Field Service Report (*PBLS* Form No. 3.1.20), the Daily Activity Summary (*PBLS* Form No. 3.1.21), or the Preoperational Testing Engineers Daily Time Sheet (*PBLS* Form No. 3.1.23)

  4.1   Field Service Report (*PBLS* Form No. 3.1.20)

      4.1.1   Test Engineers shall fill out the Field Service Report, when necessary.

      4.1.2   Test Engineers shall sign the completed form and pass it to the Commissioning Manager for review and signature.

  4.2   Daily Activity Summary (*PBLS* Form No. 3.1.21)

      4.2.1   Test Engineers shall list each of their major activities under the heading "Summary of Activities." The description should be concise but explanatory.

      4.2.2   Under the "Manhours" heading, Test Engineers shall list manhours expended on each summary item. Manhours shall be recorded for the Test Engineer, vendor, and associated craft workers as required.

      4.2.3   It is important that all manhours be recorded by category. Recorded vendor hours, along with the activity summary, will form the basis for preparing Backcharge Notifications. See Backcharge Notification Procedure No. GA-008 and Field Backcharge Notification (*PBLS* Form No. 3.1.6).

      4.2.4   Test Engineers shall sign the Daily Activity Summary in the "Project Start-up Engineer" block.

      4.2.5   Test Engineers shall submit the completed and signed form to the Commissioning Manager at the close of each working day.

      4.2.6   The Commissioning Manager shall review the Daily Activity Summaries for accuracy and completeness.

  4.3   Preoperational Testing Engineers Daily Time Sheet (*PBLS* Form No. 3.1.23)

      4.3.1   Preoperational Testing Engineers Daily Time Sheet shall be filled out by all Preoperational and Start-up Group personnel. The Test Engineer shall list the required information under "Test Data."

          4.3.1.1   Item

          4.3.1.2   Test

          4.3.1.3   Units

          4.3.1.4   Over run

      4.3.2   The Test Engineer shall list the vendor and craft manhours under "Manhours."

      4.3.3   The Test Engineer shall make any related comments in the "Comments" block.

      4.3.4   The Test Engineer shall total the information and state it in the "Totals" block.

4.3.5   The Test Engineer shall sign the Preoperational Testing Engineers Daily Time Sheet in the "Start-up Engineer" block.

4.3.6   The Test Engineer shall submit the completed and signed form to the Commissioning Manager.

4.3.7   The Commissioning Manager shall review the Preoperational Testing Engineers Daily Time Sheet for accuracy and completeness. He shall then sign the form in the "Reviewed By" block and pass it on to the Owner's Project Manager, when requested.

5.0 PROCEDURE CLOSEOUT

5.1   Documentation

The Commissioning Manager shall maintain all Field Service Reports, Daily Activity Summaries, and Preoperational Testing Engineers Daily Time Sheet in the project file.

This Procedure Reviewed and Approved by:

_____   _____

Signature   Date

_____

Title

GENERAL ADMINISTRATION PROCEDURE NO. GA-008: BACKCHARGE NOTIFICATION

1.0 PURPOSE

To provide a uniform procedure for processing and logging field backcharge notifications.

2.0 SCOPE

The procedure applies to work completed by Test Engineers, Vendors, or craft personnel under Test Engineer supervision.

3.0 SPECIAL REQUIREMENTS

   3.1   Documentation

      Documents utilized in conjunction with this procedure include but are not limited to:

      3.1.1   Continuation Sheet (*PBLS* Form No 3.1.1)

      3.1.2   Construction Punch List (*PBLS* Form No. 3.1.2)

      3.1.3   Field Backcharge Notification (*PBLS* Form No. 3.1.6)

      3.1.4   Backcharge Notification Log (*PBLS* Form No. 3.1.7)

      3.1.5   Daily Activity Summary (*PBLS* Form No. 3.1.21)

4.0 PROCEDURE

   4.1   A Field Backcharge Notification must be prepared whenever test engineers or test engineer–supervised craft personnel perform work on equipment or discover the need for work for which a vendor organization is financially or contractually liable.

   4.2   If possible, the work should be accomplished with a vendor representative present. If a vendor representative is not present, test engineers must consult with the vendor and thoroughly document all work in order to properly support Field Backcharges.

   4.3   Field Backcharge Notification supporting documents are:

      4.3.1   Construction Punch List (*PBLS* Form No. 3.1.2)

         4.3.1.1   Whenever a test engineer discovers an equipment problem, it must be immediately recorded on the construction punch list.

         4.3.1.2   When a problem is the responsibility of the vendor, the punch list item becomes the first document proof in support of a subsequent backcharge.

         4.3.1.3   The Construction Punch List not only helps establish vendor liability, but also identifies the organization that took, or will take, corrective action.

      4.3.2   Daily Activity Summary (*PBLS* Form No. 3.1.21)

         4.3.2.1   The Daily Activity Summaries provide a record of any work that may require backcharge notification to vendor organizations. Not only do these summaries provide a written description of the work, but they also provide a record of the manhours expended by test engineers, vendors, and craft personnel in completing the work.

         4.3.2.2   The Daily Activity Summaries comprise the base documentation for the preparation of Field Backcharge Notifications. For additional information, see Daily Activity Reporting Procedure (No. GA-007).

   4.4   Field Backcharge Notification (*PBLS* Form No. 3.1.6)

      4.4.1   Ensure that correct purchase order number is entered and that vendor and equipment are identified.

      4.4.2   Under the heading "Problem," the responsible test engineer shall provide a detailed explanation of why the vendor equipment required work, and the exact nature of the work required. A continuation sheet (*PBLS* Form No 3.1.1) should be used if necessary.

      4.4.3   Under the heading "Corrective Action," the responsible test engineer shall explain in detail the actual work that was, or is, necessary.

4.4.4   If necessary, the test engineer may attach a copy of the applicable Daily Activity Summary (*PBLS* Form No. 3.1.21) to the Field Backcharge Notification as further documentation for the backcharge.

4.4.5   The responsible test engineer shall sign the Field Backcharge Notification in the "Originator" block.

4.4.6   If the vendor representative was present during the work, the vendor representative shall sign in the "Vendor Attendance" block. The responsible test engineer shall then submit the Field Backcharge Notification to the Commissioning Manager.

4.4.7   The Commissioning Manager shall ensure that the Backcharge Notification is complete and that the backcharge is warranted and justifiable in accordance with supporting documentation. The Commissioning Manager shall sign in the "Commissioning Manager" block.

4.4.8   The Commissioning Manager shall enter the notification information on the Backcharge Notification Log (*PBLS* Form 3.1.7), enter the date in the "Notification" block of the Field Backcharge Notification, and forward a copy of the notification to the Owner's Project Manager.

4.4.9   When the backcharge number is issued, the *PBLS* Commissioning Manager shall enter the issue number and date in the "B/C Issue" block. This date shall also be entered, along with the backcharge number, on the Backcharge Notification Log.

4.4.10   Preoperational Testing and Start-up Group personnel shall monitor closely all work under their supervision which is related to the backcharge and report all work by Test Engineers, Vendors, Crafts, or others which are required due to the deficiency documented by the backcharge.

4.4.11   All of this data shall be submitted to the organization responsible for accumulating the backcharge information.

5.0 PROCEDURE CLOSEOUT

5.1   Documentation

5.1.1   All Field Backcharge Notifications will be maintained in the project file and shall become a part of the systems turnover packages.

5.1.2   The Backcharge Notification Log will be maintained in the project file.

This Procedure Reviewed and Approved by:

_____   _____

Signature   Date

_____

Title

GENERAL ADMINISTRATION PROCEDURE NO. GA-009: CONSTRUCTION PUNCH LIST

1.0 PURPOSE
To provide a uniform procedure for the documentation of discovered discrepancies and any subsequent corrective action taken during preoperational testing, inspections, and start-up.

2.0 SCOPE
This procedure applies to all preoperational and start-up tests and inspections.

3.0 SPECIAL REQUIREMENTS
  3.1 Safety
  The Safety Tagging and Clearance Procedure (No. ____) shall be strictly adhered to in the performance of this procedure.
  3.2 Documentation
  Documents utilized in conjunction with this procedure include but are not limited to the following:
    3.2.1 Construction Punch List (*PBLS* Form No. 3.1.2)
    3.2.2 Final Completion List (*PBLS* Form No. 3.1.3)

4.0 PROCEDURE
  4.1 Proper use of the Construction Punch List will allow precise control of remaining work for construction forces, and will ensure that all construction items possible have been completed prior to equipment or system start-up and turnover to the Owner.
  4.2 Construction Punch Lists shall be prepared and filed by the Preoperational Testing and Start-up Group, listing the project number, system, subsystems, and equipment.
  4.3 Test engineers shall use the Construction Punch List to note deficiencies discovered during any test sequence, inspection, or walk-down.
    4.3.1 The Test Engineer shall fill out the heading information for each Construction Punch List form used, including the Job No. (Contract No.), the Area (System No. and Title), page numbers, and revision number.
    4.3.2 An "Item Number" shall be listed for each discrepancy noted.
      4.3.2.1 The "Item Number" shall be the first two segments of the sequence number as listed in the project's test sequence schedule.
      4.3.2.2 For clarity or convenience, sub-numbers may be added for all discrepancies bearing the same "Item Number."
    4.3.3 In the "Description" column, the Test Engineer shall give a concise explanation of the discrepancy, providing enough detail so that anyone concerned will have a clear understanding of the problem.
      4.3.3.1 The description should include specific references to engineering drawings, vendor manuals and instructions, or other applicable installation or regulatory materials.
      4.3.3.2 Normally punch list items will be listed as imperative action statements beginning with the action verb, such as:
        • Install seal water hose connection
        • Remove debris in tank
  4.4 The Commissioning Manager shall collect Construction Punch Lists from the Test Engineers at the close of each working day, review the construction punch list for completeness and accuracy, compile all punch lists into a master file, and provide copies of all punch lists to the Owner's Project Manager. These functions must be performed on a daily basis.
  4.5 The agency responsible for taking corrective action on each discrepancy, and a schedule date for completion, shall be decided in consultations between the Commissioning Manager and Owner's Project Manager. Once these decisions have been made, the Commissioning Manager shall complete the "Corrective

Action By" and "Schedule Date Complete" columns on the appropriate Construction Punch Lists.

4.6 If a computerized punch list is used, its structure may vary according to project requirements, but normally shall contain the following fields:

    4.6.1　Item No.
    4.6.2　Date Discovered
    4.6.3　Turnover Package No.
    4.6.4　Equipment No.
    4.6.5　Sequence No.
    4.6.6　Description
    4.6.7　Scheduled Completion Date
    4.6.8　Actual Completion Date
    4.6.9　Originator's Initials
    4.6.10　Verified Completed (Y/N)
    4.6.11　Disposition Category
    4.6.12　Discipline Code
    4.6.13　Owner Representative Initials
    4.6.14　Current Status Memo
    4.6.15　Estimated Cost
    4.6.16　EWO Number
    4.6.17　Change Number
    4.6.18　Backcharge Number
    4.6.19　Source

4.7 When the discrepancy has been corrected, the responsible Test Engineer shall verify the work by inspection or testing, and enter his/her initials and the date in the "Actual Date Complete" column of the Construction Punch List.

5.0 PROCEDURE CLOSEOUT

5.1 Safety

Remove safety tags, if applicable, in accordance with the Safety Tagging and Clearance Procedure (No. ____).

5.2 Documentation

All Construction Punch Lists shall be filed with their corresponding system file.

5.3 Incomplete Items

Any incomplete Construction Punch List items that remain at the end of the pre-operational testing and start-up test and inspection period shall be recorded on the Final Completion List (see Procedure GA-010 and *PBLS* Form No. 3.1.3).

This Procedure Reviewed and Approved by:

_____   _____

Signature   Date

_____

Title

GENERAL ADMINISTRATION PROCEDURE NO. GA-010: FINAL COMPLETION LIST TRACKING AND REPORTING

1.0 PURPOSE

Developed both prior to and during equipment demonstration, the final completion list is the primary vehicle for interfacing among the Owner's Maintenance and Operations Forces, Owner's Project Manager, and the Preoperational and Start-up Group prior to system turnover to the Owner. The purpose of this interface is to assure completion of as many open items and test deficiencies as possible prior to turnover, and to provide a uniform procedure for tracking and reporting incomplete punch list items and equipment demonstration deficiencies both prior to and after system turnover.

2.0 SCOPE

This procedure applies to all preoperational and start-up tests, inspections, and demonstrations.

3.0 SPECIAL REQUIREMENTS

  3.1 Safety

  The Safety Tagging and Clearance Procedure (No. _____) shall be strictly adhered to in the performance of this procedure.

  3.2 Documentation

  Documents utilized in conjunction with this procedure include but are not limited to the following:

  3.2.1 Construction Punch List (*PBLS* Form No. 3.1.2)

  3.2.2 Final Completion List (*PBLS* Form No. 3.1.3)

4.0 PROCEDURE

  4.1 The primary resource documents for the Final Completion List are the System Construction Punch List and the computerized punch list, if used. Also, any discrepancies discovered during equipment demonstrations shall be added to the Final Completion List.

  4.2 The Commissioning Manager is responsible for the preparation, consolidation and distribution of the Final Completion List(s).

  4.2.1 At the time a system is turned over, the Commissioning Manager will transfer all incomplete construction punch list items for that system to the Final Completion List. Also included in the Final Completion List will be any discrepancies discovered during system/equipment demonstration.

  4.2.2 The above procedure will be repeated for each system of the project.

  4.2.3 Subsequently, the Commissioning Manager shall distribute copies of the Final Completion List each week until project testing and start-up activities terminate.

  4.2.4 Copies of the weekly Final Completion List shall be distributed per the distribution list.

  4.3 If a computerized Final Completion List is used, its structure may vary according to project requirements, but normally shall contain the following fields:

  4.3.1 Item No.

  4.3.2 Date Discovered

  4.3.3 Turnover Package No.

  4.3.4 Equipment No.

  4.3.5 Sequence No.

  4.3.6 Description

  4.3.7 Scheduled Completion Date

  4.3.8 Actual Completion Date

  4.3.9 Originator's Initials

  4.3.10 Verified Completed (Y/N)

  4.3.11 Disposition Category

  4.3.12 Discipline Code

  4.3.13 Owner Representative Initials

  4.3.14 Current Status Memo

  4.3.15 Estimated Cost

4.3.16   EWO Number

4.3.17   Change Number

4.3.18   Backcharge Number

4.3.19   Source

4.5   When a Final Completion List item is reported complete (by Construction or Test Engineers), the Commissioning Manager shall delete the item from the Final Completion List, and mark the item as complete on the appropriate Construction Punch List.

5.0 PROCEDURE CLOSEOUT

5.1   Safety

Remove safety tags, if applicable, in accordance with the Safety Tagging and Clearance Procedure (No. ____).

5.2   Documentation

5.2.1   Normally, all items on the Final Completion List should be completed prior to departure from site of the Preoperational Testing and Start-up Group. However, if items remain on the Final Completion List, the Commissioning Manager shall provide copies of the Final Completion List to the Owner's Project Manager for final resolution.

5.2.2   A copy of the Final Completion List shall be stored in the project files.

This Procedure Reviewed and Approved by:

_____   _____

Signature   Date

_____

Title

GENERAL ADMINISTRATION PROCEDURE NO. GA-011:
ACCEPTING EQUIPMENT AND SYSTEMS FROM CONSTRUCTION

1.0 PURPOSE

To provide a uniform procedure for accepting equipment and systems from construction.

2.0 SCOPE

This procedure applies to the preoperational testing and start-up testing program. The Preoperational Testing and Start-up Group's Manager, hereinafter referred to as "Commissioning Manager," will administer this procedure.

3.0 SPECIAL REQUIREMENTS

3.1 Safety

The applicable Safety Tagging and Clearance Procedure (No. ____) shall be strictly adhered to during the performance of this procedure.

3.2 Documentation Forms

Documents utilized in conjunction with this procedure include but are not limited to the following:

3.2.1 Punch List (*PBLS* Form 3.1.2)

3.2.2 Construction Completion Release to Preoperational Testing (*PBLS* Form No. 3.1.19)

3.2.3 Letter of Release Log (*PBLS* Form No. 3.1.25)

3.2.4 Red Tag

3.2.5 Yellow Tag

3.2.6 Red Tag Log (*PBLS* Form No. 3.1.26)

3.2.7 Letter of Transmittal Log (*PBLS* Form No. 3.1.28)

3.3 Prerequisites

3.3.1 The construction of the affected equipment or system must be essentially complete in accordance with the drawing, specifications and intent of the contract with any exceptions documented on the Construction Punch List.

3.3.2 The Preoperational Testing and Start-up Group must be satisfied that the equipment or system to be accepted is safe in respect to both personnel and equipment hazards for operation in a normal manner. Any restrictions to design operation must be documented on the Construction Punch List.

3.3.3 The Construction Punch List must contain the minimum number of items possible at that time. (Zero items is the desired goal.) The Construction Punch List should not contain items for which the design, materials, labor, etc., is available.

4.0 PROCEDURE

4.1 Preparation

4.1.1 When equipment, system, or operable portion thereof has been satisfactorily completed and is ready to be tested, the Owner's Project Manager shall inform the Preoperational Testing and Start-up Group's Commissioning Manager. (On some projects, notification will come from the Construction Manager, with copy to the Owner's Project Manager.)

4.1.2 The Commissioning Manager shall review the Construction Punch Lists related to the concerned equipment and verify that all work that can be accomplished is complete. If further work is required before the equipment can be turned over, the Commissioning Manager shall notify the Owner's (and/or Construction's) Project Manager. The applicable Manager will pursue the completion of these items or resolution of these items.

4.2 Release Documents

The Construction Manager will prepare the following release documents.

4.2.1 List of Equipment—"Construction Completion Release to Preoperational Testing" (*PBLS* Form No. 3.1.19).

The list of equipment or systems can be itemized on this form, or Construction may use their own form.

4.2.2   Any equipment that might be assumed to be released by the List of Equipment—"Construction Completion Release to Preoperational Testing" but is not actually released must be listed on a separate sheet.

4.2.3   Data Package

The data package shall contain all the test and inspection data that was collected during construction, quality control or construction testing activities, as well as the Construction Punch List of incomplete or deficient items.

4.2.4   Drawings

If deemed necessary by the cognizant managers to more fully describe the boundaries of the released system, the drawing or drawings shall be marked to illustrate the extent of the system. Equipment, piping, systems, etc. that are released will be traced with a yellow highlighter. The boundary components (not released) will be marked in red.

4.3   Tagging

4.3.1   Prior to accepting the equipment or system, anything that is a potential hazard shall be de-energized and isolated. Red tags shall be placed in accordance with the applicable safety tagging and clearance procedure (No. ____).

4.3.2   At the time of accepting the equipment or system, all items shall be yellow tagged (Caution—Testing in Progress) in accordance with the provisions of the applicable Safety Tagging and Clearance Procedure (No.____).

4.3.3   Tags shall be hung in at least the following locations within the released system:

     4.3.3.1   Starter or controller

     4.3.3.2   Motor

     4.3.3.3   Major valves

     4.3.3.4   Local control stations

     4.3.3.5   Remote control stations

     4.3.3.6   Major instruments

     4.3.3.7   In enough locations around the equipment to clearly identify it as released to the Preoperational Testing and Start-up Group.

4.3.4   When the released system is within an area where there is a continuing major construction effort or where there is a particular hazard associated with approaching the equipment, the Commissioning Manager may require that barriers or barrier tape be used in conjunction with the yellow tags.

5.0   PROCEDURE CLOSEOUT

5.1   Safety

5.1.1   The yellow "Caution" tags shall remain in place until the preoperational testing and start-up effort is complete; then all such tags will be removed.

5.1.2   If rework is required the requirements of the applicable Safety Tagging and Clearance Procedure (No. ____) shall be followed.

5.2   Documentation

5.2.1   The Commissioning Manager shall keep all involved documentation on file and distribute as required.

5.2.2   The Letter of Release Log and the Letter of Transmittal Log shall be maintained by the Commissioning Manager.

This Procedure Reviewed and Approved by:

_____   _____

Signature   Date

_____

Title

GENERAL ADMINISTRATION PROCEDURE NO. GA-012: RETURN OF FAULTY EQUIPMENT AND SYSTEMS TO CONSTRUCTION FOR CORRECTION

1.0 PURPOSE

To provide a uniform procedure for the return of equipment and/or systems to construction for correction of deficiencies or for further work after preoperational testing and start-up has started.

2.0 SCOPE

This procedure applies to the preoperational testing and start-up program, and is administered by the Preoperational Testing and Start-up Group Manager, hereinafter referred to as "Commissioning Manager."

3.0 SPECIAL REQUIREMENTS

3.1 Safety

3.1.1 The applicable Safety Tagging and Clearance Procedure (No. ____) shall be strictly adhered to during the performance of this procedure.

3.1.2 All jumpers must be removed at the time of return.

3.1.3 The Commissioning Manager and Construction Manager must be satisfied that the equipment or system to be returned is safe in respect to both personnel and equipment hazards.

3.2 Documentation

Documents utilized in conjunction with this procedure include but are not limited to the following:

3.2.1 Punch List (*PBLS* Form No. 3.1.2)

3.2.2 Problem Report (*PBLS* Form No. 3.1.14)

3.2.3 Problem Report Log (*PBLS* Form No. 3.1.15)

3.2.4 Letter of Release Log (*PBLS* Form No. 3.1.24)

3.2.5 Red Tag

3.2.6 Red Tag Log (*PBLS* Form No. 3.1.25)

3.2.7 Letter of Transmittal Log (*PBLS* Form No. 3.1.26)

3.2.8 Equipment Turned Over (*PBLS* Form No. 3.1.28)

4.0 PROCEDURE

4.1 The preoperational testing and start-up of the affected equipment or system must be an uncorrectable failure and all required information entered on the appropriate data forms.

4.2 Describe the uncorrectable failure and complete in detail a problem report using the Problem Reporting Procedure (No. GA-014). Attach the problem report to the List of Equipment Turned Over. Typical problems can be, but are not limited to, the following:

4.2.1 Equipment fabrication that is not in accordance with the requirements of the purchase order, specification and/or drawings. This could include materials used, welding, dimensions, painting, etc.

4.2.2 Equipment installation that is not in accordance with the purchase order, specification and/or drawings.

4.2.3 Contaminated piping systems that need to be dismantled for cleaning because they are too dirty to be flushed.

4.2.4 Equipment or systems that are revised by a drawing change and the amount of work warrants returning it to construction's control.

4.2.5 Equipment or systems that fail their designed preoperational testing and start-up parameters and correction is best accomplished by returning it to construction's control.

4.2.6 An equipment or system that is damaged after construction has turned it over and correction is best accomplished by returning it to construction's control.

4.3 List of Equipment Turned Over (*PBLS* Form No. 3.1.28)

The list of equipment or systems returned to construction can be itemized on this form.

4.4   Tagging

       4.4.1   Prior to returning the equipment or system, anything that is a potential hazard shall be de-energized and isolated. Red tags shall be placed in accordance with the applicable Safety Tagging and Clearance Procedure (No. ____).

       4.4.2   At the time the equipment or system is returned, all yellow tags shall be removed in accordance with the provisions of the applicable Safety Tagging and Clearance Procedure (No. ____).

5.0 PROCEDURE CLOSEOUT

    5.1   Safety

       5.1.1   The red tags shall remain in place until construction has accepted the returned equipment or system.

       5.1.2   In the case of red tag removal, all requirements of the applicable Safety Tagging and Clearance Procedure (No. ____) shall be followed.

    5.2   Documentation

    The Commissioning Manager shall keep all involved documentation on file and make distribution as required.

This Procedure Reviewed and Approved by:

_____   _____

Signature   Date

_____

Title

GENERAL ADMINISTRATION PROCEDURE NO. GA-013: PROBLEM REPORTING

1.0 PURPOSE

To provide a uniform procedure for reporting and correcting problems related to the performance of Preoperational Testing and Start-up Group testing and inspection procedures or functions.

2.0 SCOPE

This procedure applies to any problem, regardless of type or nature, that could impact or affect the timely completion of the preoperational testing and start-up testing and inspection program.

3.0 SPECIAL REQUIREMENTS

3.1 Safety

The applicable Safety Tagging and Clearance Procedure (No. ____) shall be strictly adhered to during the performance of this procedure.

3.2 Documentation

Documents utilized in conjunction with this procedure include but are not limited to the following:

3.2.1 Punch List (*PBLS* Form No. 3.1.2)

3.2.2 Problem Report (*PBLS* Form No. 3.1.14)

3.2.3 Problem Report Log (*PBLS* Form No. 3.1.15)

4.0 PROCEDURE

4.1 When a problem that falls within the scope of this procedure is brought to the attention of, or discovered by, the Preoperational Testing and Start-up Group, the following actions will be taken:

4.1.1 A Problem Report (*PBLS* Form No. 3.1.14) will be initiated and completed by the cognizant Preoperational and Start-up Group technician or Engineer.

4.1.2 A complete and detailed description of the problem will be provided, including reference to drawings, manuals, or other cogent material. The Preoperational Testing and Start-up Engineer or technician initiating the Problem Report will sign the report in the "Start-up Engineer" block (*PBLS* Form 3.1.14).

4.1.3 The cognizant Test Engineer or technician will verify the accuracy and completeness of the information contained in the Problem Report, and enter a notation of the Problem Report on the Construction Punch List (*PBLS* Form No. 3.1.2), and the Problem Report Log (*PBLS* Form No. 3.1.15).

4.1.4 After careful review and investigation of the contents of the report, the Commissioning Manager will sign the Problem Report in the "Start-up Director" block.

4.1.5 The Commissioning Manager will initiate action to have the problem corrected by ensuring that the problem is on the agenda of the Weekly Schedule Meeting and by providing coordination and liaison with the Construction Manager and/or the Owner's Project Manager.

4.1.6 The Problem Report will be distributed, as required, by the distribution list.

4.1.7 Once the problem has been resolved, the "Corrective Action" portion of the Problem Report will be completed by the cognizant Test Engineer or technician.

4.1.8 When the Commissioning Manager is satisfied that the problem has been completely and correctly resolved, he will signify such by signing the "Verified by" block of the Problem Report.

5.0 PROCEDURE CLOSEOUT

5.1 Safety

Remove safety tags, if applicable, in accordance with The Safety Tagging and Clearance Procedure (No. ____).

5.2 Documentation

  5.2.1 The Commissioning Manager or the responsible Preoperational Testing and Start-up Test Engineer or technician will verify that the Problem Report is complete and the report with any accompanying documentation shall become part of the equipment turnover package.

This Procedure Reviewed and Approved by:

_____ _____

Signature   Date

_____

Title

GENERAL ADMINISTRATION PROCEDURE NO. GA-014: OPERATOR RESPONSIBILITIES AND INTERFACING WITH THE PREOPERATIONAL TESTING AND START-UP GROUP PRIOR TO OWNER ACCEPTANCE

1.0 PURPOSE

To provide a uniform procedure regarding Owner's Operator responsibilities and interfacing with the Preoperational Testing and Start-up Group prior to Owner acceptance.

2.0 SCOPE

This procedure applies to the preoperational testing and start-up testing program. This procedure is administered by the Preoperational Testing and Start-up Group Manager, hereinafter referred to as "Commissioning Manager."

3.0 SPECIAL REQUIREMENTS

3.1 Safety

The applicable Safety Tagging and Clearance Procedure (No. _____) shall be strictly adhered to during the performance of this procedure.

3.2 Documentation

Documents utilized in conjunction with this procedure include but are not limited to the following:

3.2.1 Continuation Sheet (*PBLS* Form No. 3.1.1)

3.2.2 Field Service Report (*PBLS* Form No. 3.1.20)

4.0 PROCEDURE

4.1 When equipment or system is ready to be preoperationally or start-up tested, the Preoperational Testing and Start-up Group cognizant Engineer or technician shall instruct the Owner's operating personnel in the operation of that equipment or system. The Operators will be instructed as follows:

4.1.1 The test engineer shall inform the operator as to proper start-up and/or operational steps, including emergency shutdown procedure(s).

4.1.2 The operator shall repeat the instructional steps back to the test engineer.

4.1.3 The test engineer, insofar as possible, shall "show" the operator the required steps.

4.1.4 The operator shall demonstrate to the test engineer what he has been shown.

4.1.5 A written test may be required.

4.1.6 Operator's qualification records may be signed, if requested.

4.2 The instruction shall be conducted under the guidance of the Preoperational Testing and Start-up Group, including, as necessary, instruction from equipment supplier representatives. Owner personnel will be encouraged to perform the hands-on operations in order to obtain familiarity with the equipment.

4.3 Each equipment or system shall be demonstrated for at least the following functions:

4.3.1 Stop and start from local and remote stations.

4.3.2 Group starts and stops.

4.3.3 Major interlocks

4.3.4 Mechanical operation without product.

4.3.5 Indicating devices.

4.3.6 Instrument functions.

4.3.7 Unusual or abnormal operating characteristics.

4.4 Any valid deficiency items uncovered during the demonstration shall be added to the Punch List by the Preoperational Testing and Start-up Group.

5.0 PROCEDURE CLOSEOUT

5.1 Safety

If applicable, remove safety tags in accordance with the applicable Safety Tagging and Clearance Procedure (No. _____).

5.2   Documentation
The Commissioning Manager shall keep all involved documentation on file and distribute as required.

This Procedure Reviewed and Approved by:

_____   _____
Signature   Date

_____
Title

TEST PROCEDURE NO. TP-001: INSTALLATION INSPECTION

1.0 PURPOSE

To provide a uniform procedure for the reporting and performance of installation inspections.

2.0 SCOPE

2.1 The inspection shall cover the installation of equipment systems, such as piping (i.e., hanger settings, orifice plates, strainers, and component stresses), supporting equipment, and equipment cleanliness that could affect the operability of the equipment or system being inspected.

2.2 Electrical equipment to be inspected and tested in accordance with this procedure shall include, but is not limited to, motors, motor starters, motor control centers, switchgear, transformers, batteries, breakers, associated circuits and cables.

2.3 Mechanical equipment to be inspected and tested in accordance with this procedure shall include, but is not limited to, line terminal equipment, furnaces, valves, pumps, cranes, hoists, fans, blowers, grouting, pot equipment, and any internal inspection or test.

2.4 Instrumentation to be inspected and tested in accordance with this procedure shall include, but is not limited to, tubing, gauges, transmitters, recorders or indicating devices, controllers, alarms, PLCs, DCS, I/Os, differential pressure cells, relays, solenoid valves, and thermocouples.

2.5 Tests that are included in a subcontractors scope of work shall be documented by the subcontractor. The responsible Test Engineer shall audit that documentation and spot witness the tests. This test sequence is not completed until all the tests are documented properly.

3.0 SPECIAL REQUIREMENTS

3.1 Safety

The Safety Tagging and Clearance Procedure (No. _____) will be strictly adhered to during the performance of this test procedure.

3.2 Documentation

Documents utilized in conjunction with the performance of this procedure and which become part of the turnover package include, but are not limited to, the following:

3.2.1 Punch List (*PBLS* Form No. 3.1.2)

3.2.2 Problem Report (*PBLS* Form No. 3.1.14)

3.2.3 Safety Analysis Report (*PBLS* Form No. 3.1.30)

3.2.4 Safety Analysis Log (*PBLS* Form No. 3.1.31)

3.2.5 Mechanical Installation Check (*PBLS* Form No. 3.2.1)

3.2.6 Instrument Installation Inspection (*PBLS* Form No. 3.4.1)

3.3 Prerequisites

The equipment or system to be inspected must, at a minimum, meet the following conditions:

3.3.1 Mounted and fastened in its permanent designated position.

3.3.2 Associated piping or ductwork connected.

3.3.3 Electrical connections to the equipment terminated.

3.3.4 Instrumentation hardware installed and associated electrical connections terminated.

4.0 PROCEDURE

4.1 Reference

The installation inspection shall utilize the information contained in the following documents:

4.1.1 Equipment Specification

4.1.2 Equipment Purchase Order

4.1.3 Reference Drawings (Mechanical, Electrical, Piping, and Civil)

4.1.4 Vendor Manuals and Drawings

4.1.5 Applicable Preoperational Testing Procedures

4.1.6   Reference documents used for the installation inspection shall be recorded on the Installation Inspection form.

4.1.7   The Test Engineer shall verify that reference documents are the latest revision issued per the Engineering Drawing Schedule.

4.2   Safety Analysis

4.2.1   The Test Engineer shall examine the equipment and reference documents to determine if the testing and operation of the equipment poses any special hazards to personnel. The Test Engineer shall also determine if special precautions must be taken to safely lock out the equipment for construction rework. The Test Engineer's findings shall be published as a Safety Analysis Report.

4.2.2   This analysis shall include, but not be limited to:

4.2.2.1   Potential Energy Sources (i.e., suspended loads, compressed springs, etc.).

4.2.2.2   Pinch Points.

4.2.2.3   Pressure or Vacuum.

4.2.2.4   Temperature (high or low).

4.2.2.5   Multiple Power Sources.

4.2.2.6   Special component checks required prior to initial testing.

4.2.2.7   Periodic checks required by site or governmental regulations or vendor recommendation.

4.2.3   The analysis shall be approved by the Commissioning Manager and routed to all concerned Test Engineers. Copies shall be distributed as required by the distribution list.

4.2.4   A file of all Safety Analyses shall be kept in the Preoperation and Start-up Group office and be available to all personnel.

4.2.5   A log of Safety Analyses that have been issued shall be maintained by the Commissioning Manager.

4.2.6   Test Engineers shall ensure that they have knowledge of any applicable safety analyses prior to testing or administering a lockout on the equipment.

4.3   Installation Inspection

4.3.1   The intent of the inspection is to ensure that the equipment is completely installed in accordance with the reference documents and standard practice, and that any deficiencies will not affect the safety or the validity of further testing.

4.3.2   Equipment serial numbers, proper identification, and other pertinent information required by the Installation Inspection form shall be recorded.

4.3.3   The Test Engineer shall inspect and verify the completeness of the equipment installation based on the information contained in the reference documents.

4.3.4   Mechanical

4.3.4.1   Write in dimensions and measurements to identify accuracy of drawings or as-built units.

4.3.4.2   Verify that stock used for fabrication meets the drawing and specification requirements.

4.3.4.3   Verify high strength steel used in conjunction with other materials is identified and per specifications and drawings.

4.3.4.4   Verify dimensions of fabricated sections are per specifications and drawings.

4.3.4.5   Verify that specified straightness or camber of structural members are within specified tolerances per specifications and drawings.

4.3.4.6   Verify that welding materials are of the proper size and type per specifications and drawings.

4.3.4.7   Verify that alignment, orientation, squareness and dimensions of welded or bolted mating surfaces and assemblies are per specifications and drawings.

4.3.4.8   Verify weldout is complete per specifications and drawings.

4.3.4.9 Verify weld burrs, ferrule, remnants, etc. are removed per specifications and drawings.

4.3.4.10 Verify that welded assemblies are stress relieved by heat as required by specifications and drawings.

4.3.4.11 Verify that welds are dimensionally correct and of suitable quality per specifications and drawings prior to painting (if any).

4.3.4.12 Verify section match marks are per specifications and drawings and easily visible.

4.3.4.13 Verify bolt or rivet patterns match per specifications and drawings.

4.3.4.14 Verify bolts and rivets are of required size and type per specifications and drawings.

4.3.4.15 Verify proper torque application to bolted assemblies per specifications and drawings.

4.3.4.16 Verify flooring, walkways, handrails and stairways are installed per specifications and drawings.

4.3.4.17 Verify that rotation directional arrow, if any, is correct per specifications and drawings.

4.3.4.18 Verify freedom of movement and rotation of shafts.

4.3.4.19 Verify that bearings (i.e., greaseless, roller, sleeve, etc.) are per specifications and drawings.

4.3.4.20 Verify proper lubrication of bearings per specification and drawings.

4.3.4.21 Verify that motor is *never* used as a ground path for welding.

4.3.4.22 Piping, valves, pumps, vessels, furnaces, panels, transformers, drives, pulpits, and cubicles should have a cover over all openings. The covers should remain in place until final fit-up to the system.

4.3.4.23 Lubricants used for threading and cutting should be removed with solvent prior to applying thread compound.

4.3.4.24 All exposed machine surfaces should be coated with rust inhibitor and covered to prevent damage. Verify cleaning and applied protective coatings are per specifications and drawings.

4.3.4.25 Verify that all rust inhibitor or paint applied to mating surfaces as protection during storage and shipment is removed before final fit-up per specifications and drawings.

4.3.4.26 When performing any work inside of installed equipment or piping where tools, parts, etc. could fall into inaccessible internals, care must be exercised to prevent loss (a tool log is recommended).

4.3.4.27 Tank internals shall be inspected for cleanliness. Verify they are clean prior to final closure.

4.3.4.28 Verify anchor bolts and foundations are of required size and type per specifications and drawings.

4.3.4.29 Verify temporary erection techniques are not detrimental to the equipment or system being installed and that they are completely removed after erection.

4.3.5 Piping

4.3.5.1 Verify that piping and tubing are per specifications and drawings.

4.3.5.2 Verify that the routing of piping and tubing are per specifications and drawings.

4.3.5.3 Verify that proper identification of piping and tubing has been affixed per specifications and drawings.

4.3.5.4 Verify that hangers and supports are per specifications and drawings.

4.3.5.5 Verify that valves are per specifications and drawings.

4.3.5.6 Verify that mechanical joints are made up per specifications and drawings.

4.3.5.7 During installation of components and piping, all openings, access opening, and open-ended pipe should have covers installed whenever actual work is not in progress. These covers can be made from plywood, sheet metal, or tape. Rubber sheeting or rags are not considered acceptable.

4.3.5.8 All component suction or inlet piping should be inspected prior to making final fit-up.

4.3.6 Electrical

4.3.6.1 Verify proper identification of wiring and terminations has been affixed per specifications and drawings.

4.3.6.2 Verify that the routing and termination of wires are per specifications and drawings.

4.3.6.3 Verify that grounding is installed per specifications and drawings.

4.3.6.4 Verify that the size, type, and rating of wire and cables, heaters, switches, push buttons, transformers, fuses, motors, circuit breakers, overloads, motor control centers, switchgear, conduit, cable trays, panels, junction boxes, grounding, lugs, bus bars, insulators, contacts, and relays are per specifications and drawings.

4.3.6.5 Verify that the NEMA rating of the housing, panels, and enclosures are per specifications and drawings.

4.3.6.6 Verify that the positions of mounted electrical hardware (push button, lights, controllers, alarms, etc.) are per specifications and drawings.

4.3.6.7 Verify terminations are tight and properly identified.

4.3.6.8 Verify that conduit and conductor routing is neat, strain free, and secure per specifications and drawings.

4.3.6.9 Verify that gaskets on motor terminal box and frame are installed per specifications and drawings.

4.3.6.10 Verify that motor service duty (i.e., mill and chemical type) are per specifications and drawings.

4.3.6.11 Switchgear panels, control boards, cubicles, and consoles must be covered as required to prevent the entry of dirt, dust, moisture, or any other foreign material. Verify internals and externals are clean.

4.3.7 Instrumentation

4.3.7.1 Verify that motor RTD connections and other thermal protection are installed and wired per specifications and drawings.

4.3.7.2 Verify that any bearing-mounted instrumentation, such as vibration or temperature probes, are properly positioned per specifications and drawings.

4.3.7.3 Verify indicating instrumentation is correct size and rating per specifications and drawings.

4.3.7.4 Verify gauges and thermometers are per specifications and drawings.

4.3.8 Painting

4.3.8.1 Verify that sand blasting to the required finish prior to painting is performed per specifications and drawings.

4.3.8.2 Verify the paint thickness by gauge, if required.

4.3.8.3 Verify proper interior and exterior finish(es) (including field painting) are per specifications and drawings.

4.3.9 Cleanliness

4.3.9.1 All personnel should be advised to the importance of keeping foreign material out of the systems and system components. All systems and components must be cleaned prior to being placed in regular operation.

4.3.9.2 An area free of dust, sand, and debris should be provided for stockpiling material.

4.3.9.3 All equipment assembled in the field and all vendor assembled equipment opened in the field should be inspected for cleanliness and, if necessary, cleaned prior to closing.

4.3.9.4   Any plug resulting from cutting an inlet into a piping system will be retrieved and debris removed before installing the pipe, nipple, or boss into the outlet.

4.3.9.5   All gauge connections and thermometer bosses will remain covered until the final connection is made.

4.3.9.6   Field mounted instruments should be protected by polyethylene bags.

4.3.9.7   All work areas should be maintained in a neat and orderly manner allowing no scrap and rubbish to accumulate.

4.3.9.8   All sumps and troughs will be cleaned and free of foreign material before any testing commences.

4.3.10   The Test Engineer shall record on the Punch List or Problem Report any nonconforming condition and incomplete items encountered during the inspection.

4.3.11   The Test Engineer shall determine during the inspection if potential equipment operational problems or personnel safety hazards exist. The Test Engineer shall record these conditions on the Safety Analysis Report.

4.3.12   Shipping

Verify that item(s) positioning in crate, shipping container, and/or carrier is such that excessive handling for placement/ erection is avoided.

4.3.13   Receiving

4.3.13.1   Verify that the equipment has not been damaged in shipment.

4.3.13.2   Verify that the item(s) and quantities are as listed on the bill of lading.

4.3.13.3   Verify that required documentation is present, complete, and accurate.

4.3.14   Storage

4.3.14.1   Designate proper storage and retrieval areas for received items per specifications and drawings.

4.3.14.2   Verify that dunnage is adequate for warp sensitive items.

4.3.14.3   Verify proper storage and maintenance of environmentally sensitive items.

4.3.14.4   Verify that established maintenance procedures are being implemented.

5.0 PROCEDURE CLOSEOUT

5.1   Safety

5.1.1   Remove safety tags, if applicable, in accordance with The Safety Tagging & Clearance Procedure (No. ____).

5.1.2   Ensure any enclosure that was opened, or covering that was removed to facilitate the installation inspection, is replaced.

5.2   Documentation

5.2.1   The responsible Test Engineer shall check the completeness of the Installation Inspection form and sign off if complete. The completed Installation Inspection form shall become part of the equipment turnover package.

5.2.2   The applicable Punch List, Problem Report and Safety Analysis Report shall be reviewed, signed off, and distributed by the Commissioning Manager, as required.

This Procedure Reviewed and Approved by:

_____   _____

Signature   Date

_____

Title

TEST PROCEDURE NO. TP-002: MECHANICAL PREOPERATIONAL CHECK

1.0 PURPOSE

To provide a uniform direction for the performance and documentation of the mechanical preoperational check in order to assure in writing that the requirements of the purchase order, specification, and associated drawings have been met, and that the equipment is mechanically complete and can be operated without danger to equipment or personnel.

2.0 SCOPE

2.1   To include and categorize the areas of concern during mechanical preoperational testing and start-up testing and inspection.

2.2   Mechanical equipment to be inspected and tested in accordance with this procedure shall include, but is not limited to, line terminal equipment, furnace, valves, pumps, cranes, hoists, fans, blowers, grouting, pot equipment, and any internal inspection or test.

2.3   The subcontractor shall document tests that are included in a subcontractor's scope of work. The responsible Test Engineer shall audit that documentation and spot witness the tests. This test sequence is not completed until all the tests are documented properly.

2.4   This is a general procedure covering the common mechanical testing requirements for many types of equipment. It generally represents the minimum testing that must be done. The mechanical preoperational testing and start-up testing requirements may be further amplified by the following resources:

2.4.1   Specific Equipment Testing Procedures

2.4.2   Vendor Procedures and Manuals

2.4.3   Industry or Owner Standards

2.4.4   Test Engineer Experience

2.5   It is the intent of this test sequence to accomplish all of the mechanical testing required prior to safely running or energizing the equipment.

3.0 SPECIAL REQUIREMENTS

3.1   Safety

3.1.1   The Safety Tagging and Clearance Procedure (No. ____) will be strictly adhered to during the performance of this test sequence.

3.1.2   Any Safety Analysis requirements shall be observed.

3.2   Documentation

Documents utilized in conjunction with the performance of this procedure and which become part of the turnover package include, but are not limited to, the following:

3.2.1   Punch List (*PBLS* Form No. 3.1.2)

3.2.2   Problem Report (*PBLS* Form No. 3.1.14)

3.2.3   Mechanical Preoperational Check (*PBLS* Form No. 3.2.2)

3.2.4   Mechanical Alignment Data (*PBLS* Form No. 3.2.4)

3.2.5   Lubricant and Hydraulic Fluid Data Sheet (*PBLS* Form No. 3.2.9)

3.2.6   Pressure Test (*PBLS* Form No. 3.2.6)

3.3   Test Equipment

Equipment normally necessary to satisfactorily complete the equipment run-in shall consist of, but is not limited to, the following:

3.3.1   Torque Wrench

3.3.2   Dial Indicator

3.3.3   Strap Wrench

3.4   Prerequisites

3.4.1   The equipment to be tested shall meet the following conditions:

3.4.1.1   Equipment must be clean and free from debris.

3.4.1.2   Lubrication of the equipment must be completed.

3.4.1.3   Equipment alignment must be completed.

3.4.1.4   Any pressure testing must be completed.

3.4.1.5 Any special flushing, except for service flush, must be completed.

3.4.1.6 All shipping stops and temporary bracing shall be removed (except as required for safety).

3.4.2 The Test Engineer has reviewed the Safety Analysis Report for the equipment (if applicable) and has determined if any special precautions must be observed.

4.0 PROCEDURE

4.1 Reference

4.1.1 The mechanical preoperational check shall utilize the information contained in the following documents:

4.1.1.1 Equipment Specification

4.1.1.2 Equipment Manuals and Drawings

4.1.1.3 Lubrication Schedule

4.1.1.4 Mechanical Drawings

4.1.1.5 Applicable Preoperational Testing Procedures

4.1.2 The Test Engineer shall verify that reference documents to be used are the latest revisions issued.

4.1.3 The Test Engineer shall record on the Construction Punch List any nonconforming condition or incomplete item encountered during the inspection and test.

4.1.4 The Test Engineer shall determine during the inspection and test if potential equipment operational problems or personnel safety hazards exist. These conditions shall be recorded on the Problem Report form.

4.2 General

4.2.1 Verify that equipment is lubricated as specified in the lubrication schedule and manufacturer's manual. Lubrication type, quantity, and location shall be verified.

4.2.2 Verify that equipment is aligned as specified.
NOTE: *Completeness of applicable mechanical alignment report shall be verified.*

4.2.3 Verify that specified equipment clearances and levels are correct.

4.2.4 Verify that coupling or drive belts are installed.

4.4.5 Verify that safety guards are installed.

4.2.6 Verify that shipping stops are removed.

4.2.7 Verify that equipment rotates freely by hand.

4.2.8 Verify that equipment is free of debris, internally and externally.

4.2.9 Verify that applicable pressure tests have been accomplished.
NOTE: *Completeness of applicable pressure test report shall be verified.*

4.2.10 Verify that applicable flushing or chemical cleaning has been accomplished.
NOTE: *Completeness of applicable flush/chemical cleaning report shall be verified.*

4.2.11 Verify that applicable temporary strainers are installed.

4.2.12 Test Engineer shall record necessary data on the Mechanical Preoperational Check form.

4.3 The intent of this test sequence is to ensure that all the equipment in the mechanical systems and components are ready in all respects for the run-in of the equipment. To that end, the Test Engineer may recommend and the Commissioning Manager may approve additional testing of the equipment beyond the requirements of the procedure.

5.0 PROCEDURE CLOSEOUT

5.1 Safety

5.1.1 Remove safety tags, if applicable, in accordance with the Safety Tagging and Clearance Procedure (No. ____).

5.1.2 If new information requires that the Safety Analysis Report be updated, a revision shall be issued through the Commissioning Manager.

5.2   Documentation

    5.2.1   The responsible Test Engineer shall check the completeness of the Mechanical Preoperational Check report and sign off if complete. The completed form shall become part of the equipment turnover package.

    5.2.2   The applicable Construction Punch List and Problem Report forms shall be reviewed, signed off, and distributed by the Commissioning Manager.

This Procedure Reviewed and Approved by:

_____   _____

Signature   Date

_____

Title

TEST PROCEDURE NO. TP-003: ELECTRICAL PREOPERATIONAL CHECK

1.0 PURPOSE

To provide a uniform direction for the performance and documentation of the electrical preoperational check in order to assure in writing that the requirements of the purchase order, specification, and associated drawings have been met, and that the equipment is electrically complete and can be operated without danger to equipment or personnel.

2.0 SCOPE

2.1 To include and categorize the areas of concern during electrical preoperational testing and start-up testing and inspection.

2.2 Electrical equipment to be inspected and tested in accordance with this procedure shall include, but is not limited to, motors, motor starters, motor control centers, switchgear transformers, batteries, breakers, and associated circuits and cables.

2.3 The subcontractor shall document tests that are included in a subcontractor's scope of work. The responsible Test Engineer shall audit that documentation and spot witness the tests. This test sequence is not completed until all the tests are documented properly.

2.4 This is a general procedure covering the common electrical testing requirements for many types of equipment. It generally represents the minimum testing that must be done. The electrical preoperational testing and start-up testing require-ments may be further amplified by the following resources:

2.4.1 Specific Equipment Testing Procedures

2.4.2 Vendor Procedures and Manuals

2.4.3 Industry or Owner Standards

2.4.4 Test Engineer Experience

2.5 It is the intent of this sequence to accomplish all the electrical testing required prior to safely running or energizing the equipment.

3.0 SPECIAL REQUIREMENTS

3.1 Safety

3.1.1 The Safety Tagging and Clearance Procedure (No. ____) will be strictly adhered to during the performance of this procedure.

3.1.2 Any Safety Analysis requirements shall be observed.

3.2 Documentation Forms

Documents utilized in conjunction with the performance of this procedure and which become part of the turnover package include, but are not limited to, the following:

3.2.1 Punch List (*PBLS* Form No. 3.1.2)

3.2.2 Problem Report (*PBLS* Form No. 3.1.14)

3.2.3 Electrical Preoperational Check (*PBLS* Form No. 3.3.1)

3.3 Test Equipment

Equipment normally necessary to satisfactorily complete the equipment run-in shall consist of, but is not limited to, the following:

3.3.1 Volt-Ohm Multimeter (Simpson 260 or equal)

3.3.2 Ammeter

3.3.3 Megger-Resistance Tester

3.4 Prerequisites

3.4.1 The equipment to be tested shall meet the following conditions:

3.4.1.1 Motor, starter, and associated wiring must be installed and fas-tened to its permanent location.

3.4.1.2 Motor must be uncoupled with motor coupling half positioned to allow running.

3.4.1.3 Equipment must be clean and free of debris.

3.4.1.4 Electrical power must be available.

3.4.1.5 Motor must be properly grounded (if applicable).

3.4.1.6 Required testing of associated circuit breakers, protective relays, and other safety devices is complete and satisfactory. (See associated procedures.)

452

3.4.1.7   Concerned PLC equipment must be energized and loaded with software. Preliminary testing of the PLC system must have been accomplished.

3.4.1.8   Lubrication, if any, must be completed.

3.4.1.9   All shipping stops and temporary bracing shall be removed (except as required for safety).

3.4.2   The Test Engineer has reviewed the Safety Analysis Report for the equipment (if applicable) and has determined if any special precautions must be observed.

4.0   PROCEDURE

4.1   Reference

4.1.1   The electrical preoperational check shall utilize the information contained in the following documents:

4.1.1.1   Equipment Specifications

4.1.1.2   Equipment Manuals and Drawings

4.1.1.3   Lubrication Schedule

4.1.1.4   Electrical Drawings

4.1.1.5   Applicable Preoperational Testing Procedures

4.1.2   The Test Engineer shall verify that reference documents to be used are the latest revisions issued.

4.1.3   The Test Engineer shall record on the Construction Punch List form any nonconforming condition or incomplete item encountered during the inspection and test.

4.1.4   The Test Engineer shall determine during the inspection and test if potential equipment operational problems or personnel safety hazards exist. These conditions shall be recorded on the Problem Report form.

4.2   Motor Inspection

4.2.1   Verify that the motor nameplate data is as specified in the reference documents. This data shall be recorded on the Electrical Preoperational Check form.

4.2.2   Verify that proper identification has been affixed per drawing.

4.2.3   Verify that motor supports are as specified.

4.2.4   Verify that motor has freedom of rotation. Verify removal of shipping stops, if applicable.

4.2.5   Verify that motor is lubricated as specified by the manufacturer's recommendation.

4.2.6   Verify that motor grounding is as specified.

4.2.7   Verify that electrical connections (as applicable) to motor windings, space heater, thermal switches, etc. are correct. Tightness of connection, proper insulation, cable size and identification shall be verified.

4.3   Starter Inspection

4.3.1   Verify size of starter is correct as required.

4.3.2   Verify size of circuit breaker, if applicable, is as specified and that the breaker trip settings are adjusted as specified.

4.3.3   Verify size and type of control and line fusing are as specified.

4.3.4   Verify wire terminations are as specified by drawing. Tightness of termination, cable size, and identification shall be verified.

4.3.5   Verify that shipping stops, if applicable, have been removed.

4.3.6   Verify rating of motor overloads is as required.

4.3.7   Verify that starter cabinet is clean and free of debris.

4.3.8   Verify that starter grounding is as specified.

4.3.9   Verify size and rating of starter control transformer.

4.4   Control Circuit Inspection

4.4.1   Verify that wire terminations are as specified. Tightness of connection, cable size, and identification shall be verified.

4.4.2   Verify that associated hardware such as push buttons, lights, switches, relays, and timers are installed as required by drawing. Identification of hardware shall be verified.

4.4.3   Verify that all junction boxes, conduits, push buttons, etc. are closed to prevent contamination from dirt and water.

4.5   Testing

    4.5.1   Verify by test that motor winding insulation quality is in accordance with manufacturer's recommendations. Motor shall be meggered phase-to-ground.

    4.5.2   Verify by test that motor winding resistance is in accordance with manufacturer's ratings and is equal between all phases.

    4.5.3   Verify by test that motor power feed cable's insulation quality is above minimum specified values. Cables shall be meggered phase-to-phase and phase-to-ground.

    4.5.4   Verify by test that all control circuit interlocks, safety devices, push buttons, indicating lights, etc. function as required by drawing. Functional tests shall be conducted using control power and/or PLC equipment.

    4.5.5   Verify by test the correct operation of motor starter. Operation of contactor, disconnect switch, and/or circuit breaker shall be verified.

    4.5.6   Verify by test the correct rotation of motor.

    4.5.7   Verify by test that motor running current, vibration, speed, and bearing temperatures are within manufacturer's ratings.

    4.5.8   Test Engineer shall record necessary data on the Electrical Preoperational Check form.

4.6   Upon satisfactory completion of the electrical preoperational check, the Test Engineer shall notify responsible personnel to couple or belt the motor to driven equipment.

4.7   Test Engineer shall verify that any jumpers used during this procedure are removed and that the electrical circuits are in the "ready" condition.

4.8   The intent of this test sequence is to ensure that all the equipment in the electrical systems and components are ready in all respects for the run-in of the equipment. To that end, the Test Engineer may recommend and the Commissioning Manager may approve additional testing of the equipment beyond the requirements of this procedure.

5.0   PROCEDURE CLOSEOUT

5.1   Safety

    5.1.1   Remove safety tags, if applicable, in accordance with the Safety Tagging and Clearance Procedure (No. ____).

    5.1.2   If new information requires that the Safety Analysis Report be updated, a revision shall be issued through the Commissioning Manager.

5.2   Documentation

    5.2.1   The responsible Test Engineer shall check the completeness of the Electrical Preoperational Check report and sign off if complete. The completed form shall become part of the equipment turnover package.

    5.2.2   The applicable Construction Punch List and Problem Report forms shall be reviewed, signed off, and distributed by the Commissioning Manager.

This Procedure Reviewed and Approved by:

_____   _____
Signature   Date

_____
Title

TEST PROCEDURE NO. TP-004: INSTRUMENTATION PREOPERATIONAL CHECK

1.0 PURPOSE

To provide a uniform direction for the performance of the instrumentation preoperational check in order to assure in writing that the requirements of the purchase order, specification, and associated drawings have been met, and that the equipment is instrumentally complete and can be operated without danger to equipment or personnel.

2.0 SCOPE

2.1   To include and categorize the areas of concern during instrumentation preoperational testing and start-up testing and inspection.

2.2   Instrumentation to be inspected and tested in accordance with this procedure shall include, but is not limited to, tubing, gauges, transmitters, recorders or indicating devices, controllers, alarms, PLCs, DCS, I/Os, differential pressure cells, relays, solenoid valves and thermocouples.

2.3   Tests that are included in a subcontractor's scope of work shall be documented by the subcontractor. The responsible Test Engineer shall audit that documentation and spot witness the tests. This test sequence is not completed until all the tests are documented properly.

2.4   This is a general procedure covering the common instrument testing requirements for many types of equipment. It generally represents the minimum testing that must be done. The preoperational testing and start-up testing requirements may be further amplified by the following resources:

2.4.1   Specific Equipment Testing Procedures

2.4.2   Vendor Procedures and Manuals

2.4.3   Industry or Owner Standards

2.4.4   Test Engineer Experience

2.5   It is the intent of this sequence to accomplish all the instrumentation testing required prior to safely running or energizing the equipment.

3.0 SPECIAL REQUIREMENTS

3.1   Safety

3.1.1   The Safety Tagging and Clearance Procedure (No. ____) will be strictly adhered to during the performance of this procedure.

3.1.2   Any Safety Analysis requirements shall be observed.

3.2   Documentation Forms

Documents utilized in conjunction with the performance of this procedure and which become part of the turnover package include, but are not limited to, the following:

3.2.1   Punch List (*PBLS* Form No. 3.1.2)

3.2.2   Problem Report (*PBLS* Form No. 3.1.14)

3.2.3   Instrument Installation Inspection (*PBLS* Form No. 3.4.1)

3.2.4   Loop Check (*PBLS* Form No. 3.4.2)

3.2.5   Instrument Data Sheet (*PBLS* Form No. 3.4.3)

3.2.6   Calibration Record Gauges (*PBLS* Form No. 3.4.4)

3.2.7   Calibration Record Transmitters (*PBLS* Form No. 3.4.5)

3.2.8   Recorder or Indicating Device Inspection and Calibration (*PBLS* Form No. 3.4.6)

3.2.9   Calibration Record Converter/I/O/ Computing Relay (*PBLS* Form 3.4.7)

3.2.10   Instrument Switch Device (*PBLS* Form No. 3.4.8)

3.2.11   Controller (*PBLS* Form No. 3.4.9)

3.2.12   Control Valve (*PBLS* Form No. 3.4.10)

3.2.13   Calibration Record Alarms & Switches (*PBLS* Form No. 3.4.11)

3.2.14   Differential Pressure Transmitter (*PBLS* Form No. 3.4.12)

3.3   Test Equipment

Equipment normally necessary to satisfactorily complete the equipment run-in shall consist of, but is not limited to, the following:

3.3.1   Volt-Ohm Multimeter (Simpson 260 or equal)

           3.3.2   Ammeter

           3.3.3   Megger-Resistance Tester

           3.3.4   Torque Wrench

           3.3.5   Wire Seals

           3.3.6   Calibration Gauges

3.4   Prerequisites

           3.4.1   The equipment to be tested shall meet the following conditions:

                  3.4.1.1   Equipment must be clean and free of debris.

                  3.4.1.2   Power must be available.

                  3.4.1.3   Required testing of associated circuit breakers, protective relays, and other safety devices is complete and satisfactory. (See associated procedures.)

                  3.4.1.4   Concerned PLC and DCS equipment must be loaded with software.

                  3.4.1.5   Lubrication, if any, must be completed.

                  3.4.1.6   All shipping stops and temporary bracing shall be removed (except as required for safety).

                  3.4.1.7   Flushing, if any, must be completed.

           3.4.2   The Test Engineer has reviewed the Safety Analysis Report for the equipment (if applicable) and has determined if any special precautions must be observed.

4.0 PROCEDURE

4.1   Reference

           4.1.1   The instrumentation preoperational check shall utilize the information contained in the following documents:

                  4.1.1.1   Equipment Specifications

                  4.1.1.2   Equipment Manuals and Drawings

                  4.1.1.3   Lubrication Schedule

                  4.1.1.4   Instrument Drawings

                  4.1.1.5   Applicable Preoperational Testing Procedures

                  4.1.1.6   The Test Engineer shall verify that reference documents to be used are the latest revisions issued.

                  4.1.1.7   The Test Engineer shall record on the Construction Punch List form any nonconforming condition or incomplete item encountered during the inspection and test.

                  4.1.1.8   The Test Engineer shall determine during the inspection and test if potential equipment operational problems or personnel safety hazards exist. These conditions shall be recorded on the Problem Report form.

4.2   Control Circuit Inspection

           4.2.1   Verify that wire terminations are as specified. Tightness of connection, cable size, and identification shall be verified.

           4.2.2   Verify that associated hardware, such as push buttons, lights, switches, relays, and timers are installed as required by drawing. Identification of hardware shall be verified.

           4.2.3   Verify that all junction boxes, conduits, push buttons, etc. are closed to prevent contamination from dirt and water.

4.3   Testing

           4.3.1   Verify by test that all control circuit interlocks, safety devices, push buttons, indicating lights, etc. function as required by drawing. Functional tests shall be conducted using control power and/or PLC equipment.

           4.3.2   Verify by test the correct operation of the instrument. Operation of contactor, disconnect switch, and/or circuit breaker shall be verified.

           4.3.3   Test Engineer shall record necessary data on the Applicable Instrumentation form.

4.4   Test Engineer shall verify that any jumpers used during this procedure are removed and that the electrical circuits are in the "ready" condition.

4.5   The intent of this test sequence is to ensure that all the equipment in the instrument systems and components are ready in all respects for the run-in of the equipment. To that end, the Test Engineer may recommend and the Commissioning Manager may approve additional testing of the equipment beyond the requirements of this procedure.

5.0 PROCEDURE CLOSEOUT

5.1 Safety

5.1.1   Remove safety tags, if applicable, in accordance with the Safety Tagging and Clearance Procedure (No. ____).

5.1.2   If new information requires that the Safety Analysis Report be updated, a revision shall be issued through the Commissioning Manager.

5.2 Documentation

5.2.1   The responsible Test Engineer shall check the completeness of the Instrumentation Preoperational Check report and sign off if complete. The completed form shall become part of the equipment turnover package.

5.2.2   The applicable Construction Punch List and Problem Report forms shall be reviewed, signed off and distributed by the Commissioning Manager.

This Procedure Reviewed and Approved by:

_____   _____

Signature   Date

_____

Title

TEST PROCEDURE NO. TP-005: EQUIPMENT RUN-IN PREOPERATIONAL CHECK

1.0 PURPOSE
   To provide a uniform direction for the performance and documentation of equipment run-in testing in order to assure in writing that the requirements of the purchase order, specification, and associated drawings have been met and that the equipment is operational.

2.0 SCOPE
   2.1 To include and categorize the areas of concern during equipment run-in testing.
   2.2 Equipment to be inspected and tested in accordance with this procedure shall be driven equipment.
   2.3 The subcontractor shall document tests that are included in a subcontractor's scope of work. The responsible Test Engineer shall audit that documentation and spot witness the tests. This test sequence is not completed until all the tests are documented properly.
   2.4 This is a general procedure covering the common testing requirements for many types of driven equipment. It generally represents the minimum testing that must be done. The equipment run-in preoperational testing and start-up testing requirements may be further amplified by the following resources:
      2.4.1 Specific Equipment Testing Procedures
      2.4.2 Vendor Procedures and Manuals
      2.4.3 Industry or Owner Standards
      2.4.4 Test Engineer Experience
   2.5 It is the intent of this test sequence to accomplish all of the equipment run-in testing requirements while safely running or energizing the driven equipment.

3.0 SPECIAL REQUIREMENTS
   3.1 Safety
      3.1.1 The Safety Tagging and Clearance Procedure (No. ____) will be strictly adhered to during the performance of this test sequence.
      3.1.2 Any Safety Analysis requirements shall be observed.
      3.1.3 Prior to equipment run-in, the system to be tested shall be walked down and given a final visual inspection.
      3.1.4 If necessary, equipment to be tested shall be roped off to prevent possible injury to personnel not involved in actual testing.
   3.2 Documentation
      Documents utilized in conjunction with the performance of this procedure and which become part of the turnover package include, but are not limited to, the following:
      3.2.1 Punch List (*PBLS* Form No. 3.1.2)
      3.2.2 Problem Report (*PBLS* Form No. 3.1.14)
      3.2.3 Equipment Run-In Data (*PBLS* Form No. 3.2.3)
   3.3 Test Equipment
      Equipment normally necessary to satisfactorily complete the equipment run-in shall consist of, but is not limited to, the following:
      3.3.1 Volt-Ohm multimeter
      3.3.2 Ammeter
      3.3.3 Tachometer
      3.3.4 Vibration/Sound Level Meter
      3.3.5 Surface Contact Thermometer
   3.4 Prerequisites
      3.4.1 Equipment that is to be run-in and tested must meet the following conditions:
         3.4.1.1 Preliminary inspections and tests have been performed and are complete. This includes installation inspections, mechanical, electrical, and instrumentation preoperational check.
         3.4.1.2 Deficient items listed on the Construction Punch List from previous inspections and tests are verified as complete. If open items remain, the Test Engineer must verify that the remaining

Punch List items will not in any way endanger personnel and equipment or affect the validity of the data collected.

3.4.2 The Test Engineer has reviewed the Safety Analysis Report for the equipment and has determined if any special precautions must be observed.

4.0 PROCEDURE

4.1 Reference

The equipment run-in and testing shall utilize the information contained in the following documents:

4.1.1 Equipment Specification

4.1.2 Equipment Manuals and Drawings

4.1.3 Lubrication Schedule

4.1.4 Electrical, Instrumentation, and Mechanical Drawings

4.1.5 Applicable Preoperational Test Procedures

4.2 Test Duration

Length of run-in will depend upon the size and complexity of equipment and manufacturer's recommendation. In any event, the run-in will continue until operating parameters have stabilized and meaningful baseline data can be recorded.

4.3 Test Condition

4.3.1 In most cases, the run-in will be accomplished "no load" so that the baseline data can be compared with later "full load" data taken during operations start-up.

4.3.2 Equipment shall be tested at all operating levels (i.e., 0–100% speed, 0–100% valve opening). The test condition at which baseline data is taken shall be described on the Equipment Run-In Data form by the Test Engineer.

4.4 The Test Engineer shall record any deficiencies encountered during the test on the Construction Punch List form, unless those deficiencies are corrected at the time of run-in.

4.5 The Test Engineer shall determine during the test if potential equipment operational problems or personnel safety hazards exist. These conditions shall be recorded on the Problem Report form.

4.6 General

4.6.1 Verify by test that all equipment modes are functional (i.e., auto, manual, load, unload, high fire, low fire, opened/ closed).

4.6.2 Verify by test that associated instrumentation is operating as specified.

4.6.3 Verify by test (where possible) that operating parameters are as specified (i.e., speed, flow rate, pressure, temperature).

NOTE: *Measured versus design operating parameters shall be recorded on the run-in report.*

4.6.4 Verify by test that equipment bearings are functioning as specified.

4.6.4.1 Bearing temperatures shall be monitored and recorded.

4.6.4.2 Bearing vibration shall be monitored and recorded.

4.6.4.3 A sketch of the equipment and bearing location shall be marked and attached to the Equipment Run-in Data Report by the Test Engineer.

4.6.5 Verify by test that motor running currents are below full load rating. Run current shall be recorded on Run-in Report.

4.6.6 Verify by test that equipment moving parts are not rubbing and have sufficient clearance for continued operation.

4.7 The intent of this test sequence is to ensure that the equipment is ready in all respects for operation at "full load" and that baseline information is collected on the equipment's operating characteristics. To that end, the Test Engineer may recommend and the Commissioning Manager may approve additional testing of the equipment beyond the requirements of this procedure.

5.0 PROCEDURE CLOSEOUT

5.1 Safety

5.1.1 Remove safety tags, if applicable, in accordance with the Safety Tagging and Clearance Procedure (No. ____).

5.1.2   If new information requires that the Safety Analysis Report be updated, a revision shall be issued through the Commissioning Manager.

5.2   Documentation

5.2.1   The responsible Test Engineer shall check the completeness of the Equipment Run-In form and sign off if complete. The completed form shall become part of the equipment or system turnover package.

5.2.2   The applicable Construction Punch List and Problem Report forms shall be reviewed, signed off, and distributed by the Commissioning Manager.

This Procedure Reviewed and Approved by:

_____   _____

Signature   Date

_____

Title

TEST PROCEDURE NO. TP-006: CLEANING AND FLUSHING

1.0 PURPOSE

To provide a uniform direction for the performance and documentation of necessary cleaning and flushing of piping systems in order to assure that the requirements of the specification and associated drawings have been met and that the system can be operated without damage to components due to foreign material in the lines.

2.0 SCOPE

2.1   To include and categorize the areas of concern during cleaning and flushing by fluids necessary to ensure piping systems are free of foreign material detrimental to operation.

2.2   Equipment and systems to be inspected and tested in accordance with this procedure shall be any fluid system.

2.3   The subcontractor shall document tests that are included in a subcontractor's scope of work. The responsible test engineer shall audit that documentation and spot witness the tests. This test sequence is not completed until all the tests are documented properly.

2.4   This is a general procedure covering the common testing requirements for many types of fluid systems. It generally represents the minimum cleaning and flushing requirements that must be done. The preoperational testing and start-up testing requirements may be further amplified by the following resources:

    2.4.1   Specific Equipment or System Testing Procedures

    2.4.2   Vendor Procedures and Manuals

    2.4.3   Industry or Owner Standards

    2.4.4   Test Engineer Experience

2.5   It is the intent of this test sequence to accomplish all of the cleaning and flushing requirements while safely running or energizing the equipment or system.

3.0 SPECIAL REQUIREMENTS

3.1   Safety

    3.1.1   The Safety Tagging and Clearance Procedure (No. ____) will be strictly adhered to during the performance of cleaning and flushing testing sequence.

    3.1.2   Any safety analysis requirements shall be observed.

    3.1.3   Prior to cleaning and flushing, the equipment or system shall be walked down and given a final visual inspection.

    3.1.4   If considered necessary by the Test Engineer, the areas of the flush will be roped off with barrier tape to restrict access.

3.2   Documentation

Documents utilized in conjunction with the performance of this procedure and which become a part of the turnover package include, but are not limited to, the following:

    3.2.1   Mechanical Installation Check (*PBLS* Form No. 3.2.1)

    3.2.2   Flushing Chemical Cleaning (*PBLS* Form No. 3.2.7)

    3.2.3   Punch List (*PBLS* Form No. 3.1.2)

    3.2.4   Temporary Modification Record (*PBLS* Form No. 3.2.10)

    3.2.5   Temporary Modification Log (*PBLS* Form No. 3.2.8)

3.3   Test Equipment

Equipment normally necessary to satisfactorily complete the equipment run-in shall consist of, but is not limited to, the following:

    3.3.1   Test Gauges (Range ± 10% of test pressure)

    3.3.2   Flushing Test Rig (Flush sample pot consisting of valves and strainers or steam target holder)

    3.3.3   Sample Cloth

    3.3.4   Blank and Blind Flanges

    3.3.5   Jumpers (Hoses and Spool Pieces)

    3.3.6   Black Light

    3.3.7   Silencers

    3.3.8   Flow Meters

3.4 Prerequisites
    3.4.1 Equipment and systems that are to be cleaned and flushed must meet the following conditions:
        3.4.1.1 Preliminary inspections and tests have been performed and are complete. This includes installation inspections, mechanical preoperational check, electrical preoperational check, and instrumentation preoperational check.
        3.4.1.2 Deficient items listed on the construction punch list from previous inspections and tests are verified as complete. If open items remain, the Test Engineer must verify that the remaining punch list items will not in any way endanger personnel and equipment or affect the validity of the data collected.
    3.4.2 The Test Engineer has reviewed the Safety Analysis report for the equipment or system and has determined if any special precautions must be observed.

4.0 PROCEDURE
    4.1 Reference
    The cleaning and flushing of the involved piping systems shall be performed in accordance with the specific requirement of this procedure and those contained in the following test procedures and recommendations.
        4.1.1 Equipment and System Specification
        4.1.2 Mechanical and Instrumentation Drawings
        4.1.3 Equipment and System Manuals and Drawings
        4.1.4 Manufacturer's Cleaning and Flushing Recommendations
        4.1.5 Applicable Preoperational Test Procedures
    4.2 General
        4.2.1 Verify that the Installation Inspection has been completed.
        4.2.2 Verify Construction Punch List items which would affect the validity of this procedure have been corrected.
        4.2.3 Verify temporary strainers and filters have been installed where necessary and are of correct size.
        4.2.4 Verify orifice plates have been removed and marked as to location and direction of flow to ensure they are reinstalled in the correct position.
        4.2.5 Verify instrumentation in the system has been valved off or removed and a plug installed in its place before beginning the flush.
        4.2.6 Verify complex equipment (heat exchangers, condensers, filters, and pumps) have been temporarily bypassed.
        4.2.7 Verify lines with control valves are valved to flush through the bypass line initially where possible.
        4.2.8 Open vents to displace air during system filling, and then close the vents when filled.
        Caution: Contaminated fluids (i.e., oils, sewer, and radioactive liquids) must be controlled and disposed of in compliance with the applicable Clean Water Acts.
        4.2.9 Verify the hoses and temporary piping used to direct flushing media to a waste drain or a suitable container.
        4.2.10 Flush the main header initially with branch lines isolated, except as required to obtain a flushing path.
        4.2.11 Position the valves properly to allow for an effective and complete flush.
        4.2.12 Flush branch lines separately to obtain maximum flow and cleaning effectiveness.
        4.2.13 Flush at one and one-half times design velocity where possible, but at a minimum use design velocity.
        4.2.14 Blow air lines clear by pressurizing main header with clean, dry air. Blow main header first, then alternate opening and closing branch header valves until proven free of foreign matter.
        4.2.15 Verify cleaning and flushing has been successful by checking temporary strainers for cleanliness, holding targets at blow-out points, checking for

foreign matter on sample cloths, performing internal visual inspection and/or laboratory analysis of final flushing media.

4.2.16 Owner's representative must witness and approve Cleaning and Flushing Test as performed.

4.2.17 Verify vents and drains are opened to facilitate complete draining of lines and drain slowly to guard against collapse.

4.2.18 Verify that all temporary piping, hoses, and strainers have been removed and systems are returned to an operating configuration.

4.2.19 List test results on the Flushing Chemical Cleaning Report (*PBLS* Form No. 3.2.7)

5.0 PROCEDURE CLOSEOUT

5.1 Safety

5.1.1 Remove safety tags, if applicable, in accordance with the Safety Tagging & Clearance Procedure (No. ____).

5.1.2 If new information requires the Safety Analysis report to be updated, a revision shall be issued through the Commissioning Manager.

5.1.3 Verify the system has been returned to a normal design configuration and is properly protected against corrosion and the entry of foreign material. Close out *PBLS* Form No. 3.2.10 (Temporary Modification Record), if applicable, and record the closeout in *PBLS* Form No. 3.2.8 (Temporary Modification Log).

5.2 Documentation

5.2.1 The responsible Test Engineer shall check the completeness of test forms listed in Section 3.2 of this procedure and sign off if complete. The completed forms shall become part of the equipment turnover package.

5.2.2 The applicable Construction Punch List and Problem Report forms shall be reviewed, signed off, and distributed by the Commissioning Manager.

This Procedure Reviewed and Approved by:

_____   _____

Signature   Date

_____

Title

TEST PROCEDURE NO. TP-007: PRESSURE TESTING

1.0 PURPOSE

To provide a uniform direction for the performance and documentation of the pressure testing of piping systems in order to assure in writing that the requirements of the purchase order, specification, and associated drawings have been met and that the system is operational.

2.0 SCOPE

2.1 To include and categorize the areas of concern during pressure tests, the testing shall include applicable hydrostatic, pneumatic, or static test methods to prove integrity of piping systems prior to operation.

2.2 Equipment and systems to be inspected and tested in accordance with this procedure shall be any fluid system.

2.3 The subcontractor shall document tests that are included in a subcontractor's scope of work. The responsible Test Engineer shall audit that documentation and spot witness the tests. This test sequence is not completed until all the tests are documented properly.

2.4 This is a general procedure covering the common testing requirements for many types of fluid systems. It generally represents the minimum leak testing that must be done. The preoperational testing and start-up testing requirements may be further augmented by the following resources:

2.4.1 Specific Equipment or System Testing Procedures

2.4.2 Vendor Procedures and Manuals

2.4.3 Industry or Owner Standards

2.4.4 Test Engineer Experience

2.5 It is the intent of this test sequence to accomplish all of the pressure testing requirements while safely pressurizing the equipment or system.

3.0 SPECIAL REQUIREMENTS

3.1 Safety

3.1.1 The Safety Tagging and Clearance Procedure (No. ____) will be strictly adhered to during the performance of the pressure testing sequence.

3.1.2 Any Safety Analysis requirements shall be observed.

3.1.3 Prior to pressure testing, the equipment or system shall be walked down and given a final visual inspection.

3.1.4 Area of systems to be tested should be roped off and identified as a test area. All personnel not involved in testing should be kept clear of the test area.

3.2 Documentation

Documents utilized in conjunction with the performance of this procedure and which become a part of the turnover package include, but are not limited to, the following:

3.2.1 Mechanical Installation Check (*PBLS* Form No. 3.2.1)

3.2.2 Pressure Test (*PBLS* Form No 3.2.6)

3.2.3 Punch List (*PBLS* Form No. 3.1.2)

3.2.4 Temporary Modification Record (*PBLS* Form No. 3.2.10)

3.2.5 Temporary Modification Log (*PBLS* Form No. 3.2.8)

3.3 Test Equipment

Equipment normally necessary to satisfactorily complete the equipment run-in shall consist of, but is not limited to, the following:

3.3.1 Test Gauges (Range ≤ 10% of Test Pressure)

3.3.2 Pressure Test Rig (Pump, Valves, and Relief Valves)

3.3.3 Snoop (Liquid Soap)

3.3.4 Blank and Blind Flanges

3.3.5 Jumpers (Hoses and Spool Pieces)

3.4 Prerequisites

3.4.1 Equipment and systems that are to be pressure tested must meet the following conditions:

3.4.1.1 Preliminary inspections and tests have been performed and are complete. This includes installation inspections, mechanical preoperational check, electrical preoperational check, and instrumentation preoperational check.

3.4.1.2 Deficient items listed on the Construction Punch List from previous inspections and tests are verified as complete. If open items remain, the Test Engineer must verify that the remaining punch list items will not in any way endanger personnel and equipment or affect the validity of the data collected.

3.4.2 The Test Engineer has reviewed the Safety Analysis Report for the equipment or system and has determined if any special precautions must be observed.

4.0 PROCEDURE

4.1 Reference

The pressure testing of the involved piping systems shall be performed in accordance with the specific requirement of this procedure, and those contained in the following test procedures and recommendations.

4.1.1 Equipment and System Specification

4.1.2 Mechanical and Instrumentation Drawings

4.1.3 Equipment and System Manuals and Drawings

4.1.4 Manufacturer's Hydrostatic Testing Recommendations

4.1.5 Applicable Preoperational Test Procedures

4.2 General

4.2.1 Verify the Installation Inspection has been completed.

4.2.2 Verify Construction Punch List items which would affect the validity of this test have been completed.

4.2.3 Verify components subject to damage by overpressure or test medium such as control valve, gauges, switches, instruments, hose, etc. have been removed or bypassed prior to testing. (Complete applicable Temporary Modification Forms.)

4.2.4 Verify piping bypassed has been completed in such a way to provide as complete a system as possible for testing.

4.2.5 Verify cleaning and flushing has been completed prior to testing.

4.2.6 Verify insulation has not been installed prior to testing.

4.2.7 Verify gauge used to monitor test pressure is of correct range and has been recently calibrated.

4.2.8 Vent adjacent systems to atmosphere to prevent unintentional pressurization.

4.2.9 Open vents to displace air during system fill for hydrostatic test. Close vents when filled and pressure will then be increased slowly.

4.2.10 Hold specified pressures for the designated length of time before releasing (reference piping specifications).

4.2.10.1 For balance of plant piping, when the length of time is not stated, hold for ten (10) minutes before inspecting for leaks. Release when inspection is completed.

4.2.10.2 For fire protection piping, when the length of time is not stated, hold for two (2) hours before inspecting for leaks. Release when inspection is completed.

4.2.11 Owner's representative must witness and approve test as performed.

4.2.12 Verify vents and drains are opened to facilitate complete draining of lines, and drain slowly to guard against collapse.

4.2.13 Verify that all temporary piping has been removed and systems are returned to an operating configuration. (Complete and/or close out applicable Temporary Modification Forms.)

4.2.14 List test results on Pressure Test Report (*PBLS* Form No. 3.2.6).

5.0 PROCEDURE CLOSEOUT

5.1 Safety

5.1.1 Remove safety tags, if applicable, in accordance with the Safety Tagging and Clearance Procedure (No. ____).

5.1.2 If new information requires the Safety Analysis Report be updated, a revision shall be issued through the Commissioning Manager.

5.2   Documentation

    5.2.1   The responsible Test Engineer shall check the completeness of test forms listed in Section 3.2 of this procedure and sign off if complete. The completed forms shall become part of the equipment or system turnover package.

    5.2.2   The applicable Construction Punch List and Problem Report forms shall be reviewed, signed off, and distributed by the Commissioning Manager.

This Procedure Reviewed and Approved by:

_____   _____

Signature   Date

_____

Title

TEST PROCEDURE NO. TP-008: MECHANICAL ALIGNMENT CHECK

1.0 PURPOSE

To provide a uniform direction for the performance and documentation of necessary inspections of mechanical alignment of coupled equipment in order to assure in writing that the requirements of the specification and associated drawings have been met and that the equipment can be operated without damage to itself or personnel.

2.0 SCOPE

2.1 To thoroughly check and document the areas of alignment concern during preoperational inspection and testing of equipment and systems, performing full alignment rechecks when deemed necessary to assure integrity of equipment alignment.

2.2 Equipment and systems to be inspected and tested in accordance with this procedure shall include, but are not limited to, fans, blowers, pumps, bridles, rolls, shafts, motors, cranes and hoists. The alignment inspection shall be for the input and output shafts of the "driven" equipment and the "driver" respectively.

2.3 The subcontractor shall document tests that are included in a subcontractor's scope of work. The responsible Test Engineer shall audit that documentation and "spot witness" the testing program, calling for retest when deemed necessary. This test sequence is not completed until all tests are properly documented.

2.4 This is a general procedure covering the alignment testing requirements for many types of equipment. It generally represents the minimum testing that must be done. The alignment preoperational and start-up inspection and testing requirements may be further augmented by the following resources:

2.4.1 Specific Equipment Testing Procedures

2.4.2 Vendor Procedures and Manuals

2.4.3 Industry or Owner Standards

2.4.4 Test Engineer Experience

2.5 It is the intent of this test sequence to accomplish all of the alignment testing required prior to safely running or energizing the "driven" equipment and the "driver" respectively.

3.0 SPECIAL REQUIREMENTS

3.1 Safety

3.1.1 The Safety Tagging and Clearance Procedure (No. ____) will be strictly adhered to during the performance of this test sequence.

3.1.2 Any Safety Analysis requirements shall be observed.

3.2 Documentation

Documents utilized in conjunction with the performance of this procedure and which become part of the turnover package include, but are not limited to, the following:

3.2.1 Punch List (*PBLS* Form No. 3.1.2)

3.2.2 Problem Report (*PBLS* Form No. 3.1.14)

3.2.3 Couplings (*PBLS* Form No. 3.2.4)

3.2.4 Lubricant and Hydraulic Fluid Data Sheet (*PBLS* Form No. 3.2.9)

3.3 Test Equipment

Equipment normally necessary to satisfactorily complete the equipment run-in shall consist of, but is not limited to, the following:

3.3.1 Hand Wrenches

3.3.2 Dial Indicator (See diagram below)

3.3.3 Feeler Stock and Gauges

3.3.4 Spacer Bars

3.3.5 Micrometer

3.4 Prerequisites

3.4.1 The equipment or system to be tested shall meet the following conditions:

3.4.1.1 Preliminary inspections and tests have been performed and are complete. This includes installation inspections, mechanical preoperational check, electrical preoperational check and instrumentation preoperational check.

3.4.1.2   Deficient items listed on the Construction Punch List from previous inspections and tests are verified as complete. If open items remain, the Test Engineer must verify that the remaining Punch List items will not in any way endanger personnel and equipment or affect the validity of the data collected.

3.4.1.3   All supports and grouting for the equipment must be complete.

3.4.2   The Test Engineer has reviewed the Safety Analysis Report for the equipment or system and has determined if any special precautions must be observed.

4.0   PROCEDURE

4.1   Reference

Alignment inspections shall utilize the information contained in the following documents:

4.1.1   Equipment Specifications

4.1.2   Equipment Manuals and Drawings

4.1.3   Lubrication Schedule

4.1.4   Mechanical Drawings

4.1.5   Applicable Preoperational Testing Procedures

4.1.6   Vendor equipment instructions covering tolerances and alignment methods

4.2   General

4.2.1   Verify that all supporting equipment, piping, foundations, etc. that affect the operability of the machinery are installed before performing the alignment inspection.

4.2.2   Verify all coupling parts are clean. If necessary, use solvent to remove all foreign matter. To ensure smooth surfaces are obtained, sand surfaces with emery cloth and file burrs smooth.

4.2.3   Verify motor shaft is set at magnetic center before performing alignment measurements. If magnetic center is not established, divide end play evenly in both directions. Magnetic center is usually identified by a manufacturer's scribe line on the motor shaft. This line should be set flush with the leading edge of the motor housing, or to the manufacturer's instruction.

4.2.4   Verify shaft gap is within the tolerances specified in the reference documents. To verify shaft gap, measure four (4) equally spaced positions around the coupling at the 12, 3, 6, and 9 o'clock positions. All measurements should be taken from these positions. Record gap dimensions on Couplings Data Sheet (*PBLS Form No. 3.2.4*).

NOTE: *Use of a spacer bar equal in thickness to the nominal gap clearance, as specified by the coupling manufacturer, may be required to adjust the gap to proper dimension. Also, moving the motor until the faces are square with each other and the gap measurement is the same may be required.*

4.2.5   Verify shaft diameters are as specified. Obtain measurement of driven and driver shafts using a suitable outside machinist micrometer. Record shaft dimensions on Couplings Data Sheet (*PBLS Form No. 3.2.4*).

4.2.6   Verify shaft parallelism or angular misalignment (face-to-face) and concentricity or offset misalignment (rim) is within the tolerances specified in the reference documents. The parallelism or angular misalignment (face-to-face) and concentricity or offset misalignment (rim) of the coupling hubs is determined by measuring the clearance both angular and offset between the coupling hubs. This clearance measurement shall be obtained by using a spacer bar and feeler gauges, or by a dial indicator if the gap space between the hubs will permit.

NOTE: *The dial indicator's position should return to zero after the shaft has been rotated 360° from beginning point to ending point (i.e., the same point). A typical acceptable coupling reading may look like this:*

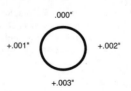

The above reading, when corrected, indicates the coupling hubs are out of alignment by .0015" on the vertical plane and .0005" on the horizontal plane. The correction formula between any two (2) readings at 180 degrees is to subtract one (1) reading from the other reading and divide the difference by two (2).

4.2.7   Mount a dial indicator on the motor shaft with a suitable clamping device and with the dial indicator touching the driven shaft's coupling hub, zero the angular reading at the 12 o'clock position and the offset reading at the 3 or 9 o'clock position. Rotate around the driven shaft, taking angular and offset readings at the 12, 3, 6, and 9 o'clock positions. Record the results as "A" on Couplings Data Sheet (*PBLS* Form No. 3.2.4).

NOTE: *If adjustment is required, change the elevation and horizontal or angular offset of the motor to make the gap measurements at all four places differ by less than the manufacturer's specified tolerance or three thousandths of an inch (.003") corrected value when checked at each position with a dial indicator.*

4.2.8   If the coupling surface is warped, verify pins were inserted into coupling bolt holes and both hubs were rotated together. Rotated together, the warping does not affect the measured values of the angular readings. Then use the total indicator runout or offset readings taken before.

4.2.9   When conditions permit, mount the dial indicator on the driven shaft with a suitable clamping device with the dial indicator touching the motor's shaft coupling hub, zero the angular reading at the 12 o'clock position and the offset reading at the 3 or 9 o'clock position. Rotate around the stationary hub of the motor shaft's coupling hub taking angular and offset readings at the 12, 3, 6, and 9 o'clock positions. Record results as "B" on the Couplings Data Sheet (*PBLS* Form No. 3.2.4).

4.3   At completion of satisfactory alignment inspection, verify that coupling is assembled according to manufacturer's procedure, including lubrication, and that the coupling guard is installed.

4.4   The Test Engineer shall record on the Construction Punch List form any nonconforming condition and incomplete items encountered during the inspection.

4.5   The Test Engineer shall determine during the inspection if potential equipment operational problems or personnel safety hazards exist. The Test Engineer shall record these conditions on the Problem Report form.

5.0   PROCEDURE CLOSEOUT

5.1   Safety

5.1.1   Remove safety tags, if applicable, in accordance with the Safety Tagging and Clearance Procedure (No. ____).

5.1.2   If new information requires the Safety Analysis Report be updated, a revision shall be issued through the Commissioning Manager.

5.2   Documentation

5.2.1   The responsible Test Engineer shall check the completeness of test forms listed in Section 3.2 of this procedure and sign off if complete. The completed forms shall become part of the equipment turnover package.

5.2.2   The applicable Construction Punch List and Problem Report forms shall be reviewed, signed off, and distributed by the Commissioning Manager.

This Procedure Reviewed and Approved by:

_____   _____
Signature   Date

_____
Title

TEST PROCEDURE NO. TP-009: FANS AND BLOWERS

1.0 PURPOSE

To provide a uniform direction for the performance and documentation of inspections and testing of fans and blowers in order to assure in writing that the requirements of the purchase order, specifications, and associated drawings have been met and that the fan is operational.

2.0 SCOPE

    2.1   To thoroughly check and document the areas of inspection and testing concern in fan or blower testing.

    2.2   Fans or blowers to be inspected and tested in accordance with this procedure shall include fan casing, fan wheel assembly, fan lubrication system, bearing cooling system, fan damper, and fan motor.

    2.3   The subcontractor shall document tests that are included in a subcontractor's scope of work. The responsible Test Engineer shall audit that documentation and spot witness the tests. This test sequence is not complete until all the tests are documented properly.

    2.4   This is a general procedure covering the common testing requirements for many types of fans or blowers. It generally represents the minimum testing that must be done. The fan operation and start-up testing requirements may be further amplified by the following resources:

        2.4.1   Specific Fan or Blower Testing Procedures

        2.4.2   Vendor Procedures and Manuals

        2.4.3   Industry or Owner Standards

        2.4.4   Test Engineer Experience

    2.5   It is the intent of this test sequence to accomplish all of the fan's testing requirements while safely running or operating the fan.

3.0 SPECIAL REQUIREMENTS

    3.1   Safety

        3.1.1   The Safety Tagging and Clearance Procedure (No. ____) will be strictly adhered to during the performance of this procedure.

        3.1.2   Any Safety Analysis requirements shall be observed.

        3.1.3   Prior to fan testing, the system shall be walked down and given a final visual inspection.

        3.1.4   If necessary, fans to be tested shall be roped off to prevent possible injury to personnel not involved in actual testing.

    3.2   Documentation Forms

Documents utilized in conjunction with the performance of this procedure and which become a part of the turnover package include, but are not limited to, the following:

        3.2.1   Installation Check (*PBLS* Form No. 3.2.1)

        3.2.2   Punch List (*PBLS* Form No. 3.1.2)

        3.2.3   Problem Report (*PBLS* Form No. 3.1.14)

        3.2.4   Mechanical Preoperational Check (*PBLS* Form No. 3.2.2)

        3.2.5   Electrical Preoperational Check (*PBLS* Form No. 3.3.1)

        3.2.6   Equipment Run-In Data (*PBLS* Form No. 3.2.3)

    3.3   Test Equipment

Equipment normally necessary to satisfactorily complete the turbine tests shall consist of, but is not limited to, the following:

        3.3.1   Volt-Ohm Ammeter

        3.3.2   Contact Pyrometer

        3.3.3   Wallace and Tiernan Pressure Calibrator

        3.3.4   Sand Bath

        3.3.5   Pressure Calibrator with Test Gauges

        3.3.6   Strob-tac

        3.3.7   Vibration/Sound Level Meter

    3.4   Prerequisites

        3.4.1   Fans that are to be inspected and tested must meet the following conditions:

3.4.1.1 Preliminary inspections and tests have been performed and are complete. This includes installation inspections, mechanical, electrical and instrumentation preoperational checks, cleaning and flushing, and pressure tests.

3.4.1.2 Deficient items listed on the Construction Punch List from previous inspections and tests are verified as complete. If open items remain, the Test Engineer must verify that the remaining punch list items will not in any way endanger personnel and equipment, or affect the validity of the data collected.

3.4.2 The Test Engineer has reviewed the Safety Analysis Report for the fan and has determined if any special precautions must be observed.

4.0 PROCEDURE

4.1 References

Fan inspection and testing shall utilize the information contained in the following documents.

4.1.1 Vendor Instructions, Procedures, Drawings, and Specifications

4.1.2 Mechanical, Electrical, and Instrument Data Sheets, Drawings and Specifications

4.1.3 Lubrication Schedule

4.1.4 QA Inspection Report(s)

4.1.5 Operation Procedures

4.2 Inspection

4.2.1 Verify that inlet, outlet, and mounting flanges are assembled per the drawing.

4.2.2 Verify that bolted assemblies are dimensionally correct, assembled, and properly torqued, where required, per drawings.

4.2.3 Verify alignment and clearance of damper assemblies are per drawing.

4.2.4 Verify proper finish(es) per specification as applicable.

4.2.5 Verify that the proper identification has been affixed per specification.

4.2.6 Verify that lubrication system (if applicable) is per drawing.

4.2.7 Verify that bearing and lube system internals are clean of contaminants.

4.2.8 Verify that bearing cooling system (if applicable) is per drawing.

4.2.9 Verify that lubrication is complete according to specification.

4.2.10 Verify associated instrumentation is properly installed and not damaged.

4.2.11 Verify that the fan wheel assembly has been statically and dynamically balanced according to specification.

4.2.12 Verify freedom and correct operation of fan damper(s).

4.2.13 Verify that specified gasketing and shims (as required) are installed per drawings.

4.2.14 Verify that fan assemblies are dimensionally aligned, torqued to specified limits (where required), and otherwise assembled per drawings and specifications.

4.2.15 Verify coupling alignment between motor and fan has been accomplished.

4.2.16 Verify coupling has been properly packed with grease.

4.2.17 Verify freedom of rotation of the fan and motor assembly.

4.3 Testing

4.3.1 Verify by test the proper operation of the following components prior to fan operation:

4.3.1.1 Fan control circuit from all controlling locations

4.3.1.2 Damper Control

4.3.1.3 All Associated Instrumentation

4.3.1.4 Fan Lubrication System

4.3.1.5 Cooling System

4.3.1.6 All Interlocking or Safety Devices

4.3.1.7 Correct Rotation of the Fan Motor

4.3.2 Start the fan against a closed damper and make the following checks:

4.3.2.1 Check for unusual noise or vibration.

4.3.2.2 If possible, time the acceleration of the fan from start to running speed and record.

4.3.2.3   Check the actual running speed of the fan and record.

4.3.2.4   Check bearing gland temperatures at 15-minute intervals and record until readings are stabilized.

4.3.2.5   Take vibration readings on the inboard and outboard fan and motor bearings.

4.3.2.6   Take amperage readings on all phases of the motor.

4.3.3   Open damper to full open or to the nameplate full current rating of the motor, whichever comes first.

4.3.3.1   Record damper position.

4.3.3.2   Record again all readings that were taken under paragraph 4.3.2. Ensure that temperatures are stabilized.

4.3.4   Close damper to a position between the closed position and the position recorded in paragraph 4.3.3. Attempt to obtain a position where the motor current is halfway between the currents recorded in paragraphs 4.3.2 and 4.3.3.

4.3.4.1   Record damper position.

4.3.4.2   Record again all readings that were taken under paragraph 4.3.2. Ensure temperatures are stabilized.

4.3.5   Allow the fan to run at least four (4) hours after the temperatures have stabilized. Check running conditions and system parameters regularly.

4.3.6   Compare the recorded data against fan and system design parameters.

4.3.7   Shut down the fan and any auxiliary equipment, and return to a safe and normal configuration.

4.4   The Test Engineer shall record any deficiencies encountered during the test on the Construction Punch List form, unless those deficiencies are corrected at the time of testing.

4.5   The Test Engineer shall determine during the test if potential equipment operational problems or personnel safety hazards exist. These conditions shall be recorded on the Problem Report form.

5.0 PROCEDURE CLOSEOUT

5.1   Safety

5.1.1   Remove safety tags, if applicable, in accordance with the Safety Tagging and Clearance Procedure (No. ____).

5.1.2   If new information requires that the Safety Analysis Report be updated, a revision shall be issued through the Commissioning Manager.

5.1.3   Ensure that any enclosure that was opened, or covering that was removed to facilitate testing, is replaced.

5.2   Documentation

5.2.1   The responsible Test Engineer shall check the completeness of the inspection and testing reports and sign off if complete. The complete forms shall become part of the equipment turnover package.

5.2.2   The applicable Construction Punch List and Problem Report forms shall be reviewed, signed off, and distributed by the Commissioning Manager.

This Procedure Reviewed and Approved by:

_____   _____

Signature   Date

_____

Title

TEST PROCEDURE NO. TP-010: INSPECTION AND TESTING OF PUMPS

1.0 PURPOSE

To provide a uniform direction for the performance and documentation of the preoperational inspection and testing of pumps in order to assure in writing that the requirements of the purchase order, specifications, and drawings have been met and that the pump is operational.

2.0 SCOPE

2.1   To thoroughly check and document the areas of inspection and testing concern in the testing of pumps.

2.2   Pumps to be inspected and tested in accordance with this procedure shall include centrifugal, positive displacement, propeller, and educator. Also included are all moving assemblies, supporting structures, driver motor, and alignment of pumps.

2.3   The subcontractor shall document tests that are included in a subcontractor's scope of work. The responsible Test Engineer shall audit that documentation and "spot witness" the tests. This test sequence is not complete until all the tests are documented properly.

2.4   This is a general procedure covering the common testing requirements for many types of pumps. It generally represents the minimum testing that must be done. The pump operation and start-up testing requirements may be further amplified by the following resources:

    2.4.1   Specific Pump Testing Procedures

    2.4.2   Vendor Procedures and Manuals

    2.4.3   Industry or Owner Standards

    2.4.4   Test Engineer Experience

2.5   It is the intent of this test sequence to accomplish all of the pump's testing requirements while safely running or operating the pump.

3.0 SPECIAL REQUIREMENTS

3.1   Safety

    3.1.1   The Safety Tagging and Clearance Procedure (No. ____) will be strictly adhered to during the performance of this test sequence.

    3.1.2   Any Safety Analysis requirements shall be observed.

    3.1.3   Prior to pump testing, the system to be tested shall be given a "walk down" and a final visual inspection.

    3.1.4   If necessary, pumps to be tested shall be roped off to prevent possible injury to personnel not involved in actual testing.

3.2   Documentation Forms

Documents utilized in conjunction with the performance of this procedure include the following:

    3.2.1   Installation Check (*PBLS* Form No. 3.2.1)

    3.2.2   Punch List (*PBLS* Form No. 3.1.2)

    3.2.3   Problem Report (*PBLS* Form No. 3.1.14)

    3.2.4   Mechanical Preoperational Check (*PBLS* Form No. 3.2.2)

    3.2.5   Electrical Preoperational Check (*PBLS* Form No. 3.3.1)

    3.2.6   Equipment Run-In Data (*PBLS* Form No. 3.2.3)

    3.2.7   Pressure Test (*PBLS* Form No. 3.2.6)

    3.2.8   Flushing Chemical Cleaning (*PBLS* Form No. 3.2.7)

3.3   Test Equipment

Equipment normally necessary to satisfactorily complete the pump tests shall consist of, but is not limited to, the following:

    3.3.1   Volt-Ohm Ammeter

    3.3.2   Contact Pyrometer

    3.3.3   Wallace and Tiernan Pressure Calibrator

    3.3.4   Sand Bath

    3.3.5   Pressure Calibrator with Test Gauges

    3.3.6   Strob-tac

    3.3.7   Vibration/Sound Level Meter

3.4   Prerequisites

    3.4.1   Pumps that are to be inspected and tested must meet the following conditions:

        3.4.1.1   Preliminary inspections and tests have been performed and are complete. This includes installation inspections, mechanical, electrical and instrumentation preoperational checks, cleaning and flushing, and pressure tests.

        3.4.1.2   Deficient items listed on the Construction Punch List from previous inspections and tests are verified as complete. If open items remain, the Test Engineer must verify that the remaining punch list items will not in any way endanger personnel and equipment or affect the validity of the data collected.

    3.4.2   The Test Engineer has reviewed the Safety Analysis Report for the pump and has determined if any special precautions must be observed.

4.0 PROCEDURE

4.1   Reference

Pump inspection and testing shall utilize the information contained in the following documents:

    4.1.1   Vendors Instructions, Procedures, Drawings, and Specifications

    4.1.2   Mechanical, Electrical, and Instrument Data Sheets, Drawings and Specifications

    4.1.3   Lubrication Schedule

    4.1.4   QA Inspection Report(s)

    4.1.5   Operation Procedures

4.2   Inspection

    4.2.1   Verify all associated equipment and piping is permanently installed and properly secured.

    4.2.2   Verify all shipping stops have been removed.

    4.2.3   Verify freedom of rotation of the pump motor assembly.

    4.2.4   Verify that suction piping is clear of foreign material by visual inspection between the impeller and suction strainer.

    4.2.5   Verify electrical preoperational tests have been performed.

    4.2.6   Verify the pump-to-motor coupling or belt alignment has been properly completed.

    4.2.7   Verify the concerned tanks have been cleaned.

    4.2.8   Verify installation of suction strainer.

    4.2.9   Verify coupling guards are in place.

    4.2.10   Verify auxiliary systems such as seal water and instrument air are available to support pump testing.

    4.2.11   Verify the valve lineup.

4.3   Testing

    4.3.1   Prime the pump by opening the suction valve. Vent the pump as required.

    4.3.2   Apply the proper seal water pressure, as required, and adjust to manufacturer's recommendation.

        Caution: Do not overtighten packing and packing gland.

    4.3.3   Verify packing glands are loose and tighten them in accordance with pump manufacturer's instructions.

        NOTE: *If no manufacturer instructions are available, allow one (1) drop to form and fall away per one (1) minute during initial start-up and until packing is properly lubricated. At end of initial start-up, packing should not drip less than one (1) drop forming and falling away per five (5) minutes. One (1) drop per hour is normal tightness during operation.*

    4.3.4   Start the pump against a closed discharge valve.

        NOTE: *On large pumps, valve may be off its seat.*

    4.3.5   Slowly open the discharge valve to start flow.

    4.3.6   Check gland water flow rates as applicable.

    4.3.7   Allow pump to obtain steady-state conditions (i.e., temperature).

4.3.8   With the discharge valve(s) fully open, take the following readings:
    4.3.8.1   Suction Pressure
    4.3.8.2   Discharge Pressure
    4.3.8.3   Pump Flow (where possible)
    4.3.8.4   Gland Flow (where possible)
    4.3.8.5   Motor Current
    4.3.8.6   Bearing Temperatures
    4.3.8.7   Gland Temperatures

4.3.9   With the discharge valve fully closed, take the following readings:
    4.3.9.1   Suction Pressure
    4.3.9.2   Discharge Pressure
    4.3.9.3   Motor Current

4.3.10   Allow pump to test run at least two hours (where possible).

4.3.11   Compare recorded readings with pump/system design parameters.

4.4   The Test Engineer shall record any deficiencies encountered during the test on the Construction Punch List form, unless those deficiencies are corrected at the time of testing.

4.5   The Test Engineer shall determine during the test if potential equipment operational problems or personnel safety hazards exist. These conditions shall be recorded on the Problem Report form.

5.0   PROCEDURE CLOSEOUT

5.1   Safety

    5.1.1   Remove safety tags, if applicable, in accordance with the Safety Tagging and Clearance Procedure (No. ____).

    5.1.2   If new information requires that the Safety Analysis Report be updated, a revision shall be issued through the Commissioning Manager.

5.2   Documentation

    5.2.1   The responsible Test Engineer shall check the completeness of the inspection and testing reports and sign off if complete. The completed forms shall become part of the equipment turnover package.

    5.2.2   The applicable Construction Punch List and Problem Report shall be reviewed, signed off, and distributed by the Commissioning Manager.

This Procedure Reviewed and Approved by:

_____   _____
Signature   Date

_____
Title

TEST PROCEDURE NO. TP-011: RELAY CALIBRATION

1.0 PURPOSE

To provide a uniform direction for the performance and documentation of relay calibration in order to assure in writing that the requirements of the purchase order, specification, and associated drawings have been met, and that the equipment is electrically complete and can be operated without danger to equipment or personnel.

2.0 SCOPE

To thoroughly check and document the areas of inspection and testing concern in protective relay calibration.

3.0 SPECIAL REQUIREMENTS

  3.1   Safety

      3.1.1   The Safety Tagging and Clearance Procedure (No. ____) will be strictly adhered to during the performance of this test sequence.

      3.1.2   All safety precautions associated with current transformers will be observed. Current transformers can develop dangerous voltages when open circuited.

  3.2   Documentation Forms

Documents utilized in conjunction with the performance of this procedure include the following:

      3.2.1   Protective Relay Inspection and Test Record (*PBLS* Form No. 3.3.10)

      3.2.2   Punch List (*PBLS* Form No. 3.1.2)

      3.2.3   Problem Report (*PBLS* Form No. 3.1.14)

  3.3   Test Equipment

      3.3.1   Relay Tester-Calibrator (Multi-Amp Model SR-196-51 or equivalent)

      3.3.2   Volt-Ohm Multimeter (Simpson 260 or equal)

  3.4   Prerequisites

      3.4.1   Relays which are to be calibrated must meet the following conditions:

          3.4.1.1   Relay and case must be installed in their permanent location.

          3.4.1.2   Wiring to relay case, both power and trip circuits, must be complete.

      3.4.2   A bench setup or test area must be available.

4.0 PROCEDURE

  4.1   Reference

      4.1.1   The following references will be used in conjunction with this procedure as applicable:

          4.1.1.1   Equipment Specifications

          4.1.1.2   Relay Calibration Data Sheets

          4.1.1.3   Equipment Purchase Order

          4.1.1.4   Relay Manufacturer's Instruction Leaflet

          4.1.1.5   Test Equipment Operating Instructions

          4.1.1.6   Protective Relay Coordination Study

      4.1.2   The Test Engineer shall verify that reference documents to be used are the latest revisions issued.

  4.2   Relay Inspection

      4.2.1   Inspect relay case cover gasket for fit.

      4.2.2   Inspect glass for tightness in frame, cracks, etc.

      4.2.3   Verify relay case is cleaned and free of dust, metal particles, etc.

      4.2.4   Inspect relay for physical damage, loose connectors, dirt, or moisture.

  4.3   Relay Calibration

      4.3.1   Remove relay, following manufacturer's instructions, in order to perform the secondary injection tests. Remove any shipping stops.

      4.3.2   Check mechanical parts for freedom of movement, especially rotating discs. Make sure disc does not rub and has good clearance between magnet poles.

4.3.3 Verify mechanical operation of targets by lifting the armature and observing showing of target(s).

4.3.4 Verify relay calibration by test. Each specific relay shall be tested in accordance with manufacturer's recommendations and the test equipment operating instructions; results to be recorded on the Protective Relay Test Report (*PBLS* Form No. 3.3.10). Tests for specific relays shall include, but are not limited to, the following:

    4.3.4.1 Under/Overvoltage Relays
        4.3.4.1.1 Zero Check
        4.3.4.1.2 Induction Disk Pickup and Drop-out
        4.3.4.1.3 Time Characteristics
        4.3.4.1.4 DC Target and Seal-in
        4.3.4.1.5 Instantaneous Pickup

    4.3.4.2 Overcurrent Relay
        4.3.4.2.1 Zero Check
        4.3.4.2.2 Induction Disk Pickup and Drop-out
        4.3.4.2.3 Time/Current Characteristics
        4.3.4.2.4 DC Target and Seal-in
        4.3.4.2.5 Instantaneous Pickup

    4.3.4.3 Instantaneous Overcurrent Relays and Elements
        4.3.4.3.1 Pickup
        4.3.4.3.2 Time Characteristics
        4.3.4.3.3 DC Target and Seal-in

    4.3.4.4 Differential Relays
        4.3.4.4.1 Pickup
        4.3.4.4.2 Time Characteristics
        4.3.4.4.3 DC Target and Seal-in

    4.3.4.5 Directional Rays
        4.3.4.5.1 Overcurrent Pickup
        4.3.4.5.2 Pickup Directional Unit (Voltage or Current)
        4.3.4.5.3 DC Target and Seal-in

4.3.5 Verify settings on relay (tap setting, tire dial, etc.) are correct.

4.3.6 Verify calibration sticker has been placed on relay.

4.3.7 Replace relay in proper location, again following manufacturer's procedure.

4.3.8 Inspect the primary detectors (CTs, PTs, etc.) for installation, proper rating, condition, and interconnecting wiring.

4.3.9 Prove wiring between the primary detectors and the relays by ringing the circuits or by injecting current or voltage.

4.3.10 Prove proper polarity of polarity sensitive relays.

4.3.11 Prove the integrity of the trip circuit by tripping each concerned breaker from each of its protective relays.

4.3.12 Verify all shorting devices are removed.

4.3.13 Primary injection tests shall be performed at the discretion of the Test Engineer or if called for in the specifications.

4.3.14 Results of relay calibration tests performed by others may be used provided proper documentation is furnished. These test results shall be included in the equipment turnover package.

4.4 The Test Engineer shall record any nonconforming condition or incomplete item encountered during the inspection and calibration on the Construction Punch List form.

4.5 The Test Engineer shall determine during the inspection and calibration if potential equipment operational problems or personnel safety hazards exist. The conditions shall be recorded on the Problem Report form.

5.0 PROCEDURE CLOSEOUT

5.1 Safety
Remove safety tags, if applicable, in accordance with the Safety Tagging and Clearance Procedure. (No. ____)

5.2.1   The responsible Test Engineer shall check the completeness of the Relay Calibration Test form and sign off if complete. The completed forms shall become part of the equipment turnover package.

5.2.2   The applicable Construction Punch List and Problem Report forms shall be reviewed, signed off, and distributed by the Commissioning Manager.

This Procedure Reviewed and Approved by:

_____   _____
Signature   Date

_____
Title

TEST PROCEDURE NO. TP-013: ELECTRICAL POWER TRANSFORMERS

1.0 PURPOSE

To provide a uniform direction for the performance and documentation of necessary inspection and testing of electrical power transformers in order to assure in writing that the requirements of the purchase order, specifications, and drawings have been met.

2.0 SCOPE

To thoroughly check and document the areas of inspection and testing concern of electrical power transformers, components, and supporting equipment that affect the operability of the transformer.

3.0 SPECIAL REQUIREMENTS

3.1   Safety

The Safety Tagging and Clearance Procedure (No. _____) will be strictly adhered to during the performance of this test sequence.

3.2   Documentation Forms

Documents utilized in conjunction with the performance of this procedure and which become a part of the turnover package include, but are not limited to, the following:

3.2.1   Installation Checkoff (*PBLS* Form No. 3.2.1)

3.2.2   Electrical Preoperational Check (*PBLS* Form No. 3.3.1)

3.2.3   Transformer (*PBLS* Form No. 3.3.3)

3.2.4   Punch List (*PBLS* Form No. 3.1.2)

3.2.5   Final Completion List (*PBLS* Form No. 3.1.3)

3.2.6   Problem Report (*PBLS* Form No. 3.1.14)

3.3   Prerequisite

Equipment which is to be inspected and tested must meet the following conditions:

3.3.1   Transformer must be permanently and securely mounted.

3.3.2   Transformer must be properly grounded.

3.3.3   Primary and secondary power connections must be complete.

3.3.4   Protective relaying and associated control circuits must be installed and ready for testing.

3.3.5   Primary and secondary feeder breakers, disconnect switches, and fuses must be complete and ready for energization.

4.0 PROCEDURE

4.1   Reference

4.1.1   The inspection and testing shall utilize the information contained in the following documents:

4.1.1.1   Equipment Specification

4.1.1.2   Equipment Purchase Order

4.1.1.3   Reference Drawings

4.1.1.4   Vendor Specifications and Drawings

4.1.2   The Test Engineer shall verify that reference documents are the latest revision issued per the engineering drawing schedule.

4.2   Transformer Inspection

4.2.1   Inspect transformer for chipped, cracked, or dirty bushings.

4.2.2   Inspect exterior of transformer for damage to cooling fins, cooling fans, chipped paint, or rust spots.

4.2.3   Verify that transformer contains correct amount and type of insulating oil.

4.2.4   Verify that transformer is correctly pressurized with proper medium.

4.2.5   Inspect grounding resistors for damage and verify they are of correct resistance and rating.

4.2.6   Verify that primary and secondary power connections are made up properly, bus is aligned and properly spaced, and all bolts are torqued to manufacturer's specification.

4.3   Transformer Testing

4.3.1   Perform a dielectric breakdown test on insulating oil. Previous test results may be used provided they have been properly documented and the oil sample was taken directly from the transformer while located at the jobsite. These test results must be included in the turnover package.

4.3.2   Perform a megger test on the transformer windings. The test voltage will be determined by the transformer winding, operating voltage, and the manufacturer's recommendations. Test voltage should not exceed twice the operating voltage; however, it may be limited by the capacity of the test equipment. Test the windings as follows:

     4.3.2.1   Primary windings to ground, secondary windings and case grounded.

     4.3.2.2   Secondary windings to ground, primary windings and case grounding.

     4.3.2.3   Primary windings to secondary windings, case grounding.

4.3.3   High-potential testing of the transformer windings will be performed only if so stated in the specifications or deemed necessary by the Project Test Engineer. Manufacturer's testing procedures will be strictly adhered to.

4.3.4   Check operation of tap changer and set on correct tap.

4.3.5   Perform full preoperational check on cooling fans where applicable, including a functional check of the control circuit.

4.3.6   Check resistance of grounding resistance.

4.3.7   Verify phasing is correct, incoming feeder through secondary feeder.

4.3.8   Verify that transformer CTs and PTs are wired for correct polarity.

4.3.9   Verify that internal protective devices are properly connected and have been tested by the transformer manufacturer.

4.3.10   Verify that external protective relaying and control circuits have been tested and calibrated and are operational prior to transformer energization.

4.3.11   Additional testing may be required by specifications or where deemed appropriate by Project Test Engineer. To this end, job and vendor specifications must be thoroughly researched.

5.0   PROCEDURE CLOSEOUT

   5.1   Safety

     5.1.1   Remove safety tags, if applicable, in accordance with the Safety Tagging and Clearance Procedure (No. ____).

     5.1.2   Ensure any enclosure which was opened, or covering which was removed to facilitate testing, is replaced.

   5.2   Documentation

     5.2.1   The responsible Test Engineer shall check the completeness of the appropriate documents and sign off if complete. These documents shall become part of the equipment turnover package.

     5.2.2   The applicable Construction Punch List (*PBLS* Form No. 3.1.2) and Problem Report (*PBLS* Form No. 3.1.14) forms shall be reviewed, signed off, and distributed by the Commissioning Manager.

This Procedure Reviewed and Approved by:

_____   _____

Signature   Date

_____

Title

TEST PROCEDURE NO. TP-014: ELECTRICAL SWITCHGEAR

1.0 PURPOSE
To provide a uniform direction for the performance and documentation of necessary inspection and testing of electrical switchgear in order to assure in writing that the requirements of the purchase order, specifications, and drawings have been met.

2.0 SCOPE
Inspection and testing of electrical switchgear and components that affect the operability of the switchgear.

3.0 SPECIAL REQUIREMENTS
   3.1   Safety
      The Safety Tagging and Clearance Procedure (No. ____) will be strictly adhered to during the performance of this test sequence.
   3.2   Documentation Forms
      Documents utilized in conjunction with the performance of this procedure and which become a part of the turnover package include, but are not limited to, the following:
      3.2.1   Installation Check (*PBLS* Form No. 3.2.1)
      3.2.2   Electrical Preoperational Check (*PBLS* Form No. 3.3.1)
      3.2.3   Mechanical Preoperational Check (*PBLS* Form No. 3.2.2)
      3.2.4   Drawing Change Notice Log (*PBLS* Form No. 3.1.5)
      3.2.5   Circuit Breaker (*PBLS* Form No. 3.3.9)
      3.2.6   High Potential Test (*PBLS* Form No. 3.3.6)
      3.2.7   Problem Report (*PBLS* Form No. 3.1.14)
      3.2.8   Punch List (*PBLS* Form No. 3.1.2)
      3.2.9   Final Completion List (*PBLS* Form No. 3.1.3)
   3.3   Prerequisite
      Equipment that is to be inspected and tested must meet the following conditions:
      3.3.1   Switchgear must be securely and permanently mounted.
      3.3.2   All interconnecting wiring must be complete.
      3.3.3   Switchgear must be properly grounded.
      3.3.4   All bus work must be installed, aligned, and tightened.
      3.3.5   Instrumentation and protective relays must be installed and correctly wired to CTs or PTs.

4.0 PROCEDURE
   4.1   References
      4.1.1   The inspection and testing shall utilize the information contained in the following documents:
         4.1.1.1   Equipment Specification
         4.1.1.2   Equipment Purchase Order
         4.1.1.3   Reference Drawings
         4.1.1.4   Vendor Specifications and Drawings
   4.2   Switchgear Inspection
      4.2.1   Bus
         4.2.1.1   Verify that all bus connections are tight and torqued to manufacturer's specification.
         4.2.1.2   Check all insulators for chips, cracks, or dirt.
         4.2.1.3   Verify bus is properly insulated and protected.
         4.2.1.4   Verify that phasing is correct throughout switchgear.
      4.2.2   Circuit Breakers
         4.2.2.1   Inspect breaker for physical damage and loose parts.
         4.2.2.2   Inspect arc chutes for chips, cracks, and dirt.
         4.2.2.3   Verify breaker is properly identified.
      4.2.3   Relays and Metering
         4.2.3.1   Verify that all relays and meters have been calibrated and have proper calibration stickers.
         4.2.3.2   Verify relays and meters are installed in their proper location.

4.2.3.3 Verify meters have the correct scales.

4.2.3.4 Verify that all internal wiring is complete.

4.2.4 Verify that all devices and cubicles are correctly labeled.

4.2.5 Verify that switchgear is properly grounded.

4.2.6 Verify that all cubicle doors and sub-panels operate and fit properly.

4.2.7 Verify that switchgear is clean and free of debris.

4.3 Switchgear Testing

4.3.1 Bus

4.3.1.1 Disconnect any equipment from the bus that may be damaged by the test.

4.3.1.2 Megger each phase to ground with the other two phases grounded. If suspicious readings are encountered, phase-to-phase meggering may be required.

4.3.1.3 480-V switchgear will be meggered at 1000 V with a hold time of at least 2 minutes.

4.3.1.4 Switchgear with an operating voltage above 480 V will be meggered at operating voltage where possible, before and after the high potential test, with a hold time of at least 2 minutes.

4.3.1.5 Minimum acceptable megohm reading for energization will be the operating kV in megohms plus 1 megohm. (Example: For a 480-V system, the minimum acceptable value would be 0.48 megohms +1 megohm or approximately 1.5 megohms.) However, for new installations, readings far in excess of the minimums would be expected. Therefore, any values found close to a minimum should be suspect and causes for the low readings to be investigated.

4.3.1.6 Perform high-potential test on bus with operating voltage above 480 V.

4.3.1.6.1 All safety, tagging, and operating procedures and precautions as outlined in Cable High Potential Testing Procedure No. 3.4.2 must be followed.

4.3.1.6.2 Test voltage will be 1.5 times operating voltage.

4.3.1.6.3 Hold at test voltage for 2 minutes or until leakage current stabilizes.

4.3.1.6.4 Record all test data on appropriate forms.

4.3.1.6.5 Reconnect equipment that was disconnected for testing purposes.

4.3.2 Circuit Breakers

4.3.2.1 Check alignment of contact blades.

4.3.2.2 Check for proper lubrication or contact grease on contact blades.

4.3.2.3 Check operation of racking mechanism.

4.3.2.4 Check operation of manual trip and close devices.

4.3.2.5 Check mechanical interlocks.

4.3.2.6 Check control wiring for completion and correct terminations.

4.3.2.7 Solid-state trip units will be tested in accordance with manufacturer's test practice to verify trip value calibration.

4.3.2.8 Energize control circuit and perform circuit checks on all protective trip devices and electrical close and trip switches.

4.3.3 Relays and Metering

4.3.3.1 Check wiring of current and potential transformers to ensure correct polarities.

4.3.3.2 Primary inspection testing will be performed to check C.T. ratios and wiring if so stated in the specifications or at the discretion of the Test Engineer.

4.3.3.3 Check continuity and polarity of CT loops.

4.3.3.4 Verify correct termination of shielding on applicable cables. Shield termination to ground should not be made through the ground fault detection CT.

5.0 PROCEDURE CLOSEOUT

    5.1   Safety

        5.1.1   Remove safety tags in accordance with the Safety Tagging and Clearance Procedure (No. ____).

        5.1.2   Ensure any enclosure which was opened, or covering which was removed to facilitate testing, is replaced.

    5.2   Documentation

        5.2.1   The responsible Test Engineer shall check the completeness of the appropriate documents and sign off if complete. These documents shall become part of the equipment turnover package.

        5.2.2   The applicable Construction Punch List (Form No. 3.1.2) and Problem Report (3.1.14) forms shall be reviewed, signed off, and distributed by the Commissioning Manager.

This Procedure Reviewed and Approved by:

_____   _____

Signature   Date

_____

Title

TEST PROCEDURE NO. TP-016: ELECTRICAL DISTRIBUTION PANELS

1.0 PURPOSE

To provide a uniform direction for the performance and documentation of electrical distribution panel inspection and testing in order to assure in writing that the requirements of the purchase order, specifications, and associated drawings have been met, and that the equipment is electrically complete and can be operated without danger to equipment or personnel.

2.0 SCOPE

To thoroughly check and document the areas of inspection and testing concern during the inspection and testing of electrical distribution panels.

3.0 SPECIAL REQUIREMENTS

    3.1   Safety

          The Safety Tagging and Clearance Procedure (No. ____) will be strictly adhered to during the performance of this procedure.

    3.2   Documentation Forms

          3.2.1   Documents utilized in conjunction with the performance of this procedure include, but are not limited to, the following:

                    3.2.1.1   Electrical Preoperational Check (*PBLS* Form No. 3.3.1)

                    3.2.1.2   Power Distribution Panel (*PBLS* Form No. 3.3.4)

                    3.2.1.3   Punch List (*PBLS* Form No. 3.1.2)

                    3.2.1.4   Problem Report (*PBLS* Form No. 3.1.14)

    3.3   Test Equipment

          Equipment necessary to complete the electrical distribution panel testing satisfactorily shall consist of the following:

          3.3.1   Volt-Ohm Multimeter (Simpson 260 or equal).

          3.3.2   Megger Resistance Tester

    3.4   Prerequisites

          Electrical distribution panels which are to be inspected and tested must meet the following conditions:

          3.4.1   Panel must be installed and fastened to its permanent location.

          3.4.2   Panel must be properly grounded.

          3.4.3   Panel must be free and clean of debris.

4.0 PROCEDURES

    4.1   References

          4.1.1   Electrical distribution panel inspection and testing shall utilize the information contained in the following documents:

                    4.1.1.1   Equipment Specifications

                    4.1.1.2   Electrical and Mechanical Drawings

                    4.1.1.3   Vendor Manuals and Drawings

                    4.1.1.4   Equipment Purchase Order

          4.1.2   The Test Engineer shall verify that reference documents to be used are the latest revisions issued.

    4.2   Inspection

          4.2.1   Verify that panel is mounted properly.

          4.2.2   Verify that panel is rated as specified in reference documents. Record this data on Electrical Distribution Panel Test Report.

          4.2.3   Verify that proper identification has been affixed as per drawing.

          4.2.4   Verify that panel is grounded properly.

          4.2.5   Verify that circuit directory is filled out as per drawings.

          4.2.6   Verify that individual circuit breakers are installed properly, labeled correctly, and rated as specified on the drawings.

          4.2.7   Check operation of any mechanical interlocks.

          4.2.8   Verify that enclosure doors operate and fit properly.

          4.2.9   Verify that electrical terminations are correct. Tightness of connection, proper insulation, cable size, and identification shall be verified.

4.2.10   Verify correct installation, wiring, size, and insulation of space heaters where applicable.

4.2.11   Verify phasing of internal buswork.

4.3   Testing

4.3.1   Verify by test that phases are isolated from each other and ground.

4.3.2   Verify mechanical operation of each breaker.

4.3.3   Verify by test the condition of insulators. Panel bus shall be meggered phase-to-ground and phase-to-phase.

4.3.4   Energize panel and verify correct phasing and operating voltage.

4.4   The Test Engineer shall record any nonconforming condition or incomplete item encountered during the inspection and test on the Construction Punch List form.

4.5   The Test Engineer shall determine during the inspection and test if potential equipment operational problems or personnel safety hazards exist. These conditions shall be recorded on the Problem Report form.

5.0   PROCEDURE CLOSEOUT

5.1   Safety

5.1.1   Remove safety tags, if applicable, in accordance with the Safety Tagging and Clearance Procedure (No. ____).

5.2   Documentation

5.2.1   The responsible Test Engineer shall check the completeness of the Electrical Distribution Panel Test Report and sign off if complete. The completed form shall become part of the equipment turnover package.

5.2.2   The applicable Construction Punch List and Problem Report forms shall be reviewed, signed off, and distributed by the Commissioning Manager.

This Procedure Reviewed and Approved by:

_____   _____

Signature   Date

_____

Title

INDEX

ABOUT THE AUTHOR

William J. Pinkerton of Pittsburgh, Pennsylvania, has more than 30 years' experience working on many of the world's most challenging projects. This includes assignments ranging from the original Apollo moonshot series and a breeder-reactor in Washington state to a billion-dollar nickel mine and refinery in Indonesia, iron-ore pelletizing plants in the United States, Canada, Brazil, and Australia, and many more in the minerals and metals fields.

His project management workshops, conducted throughout the United States, Canada, Southeast Asia, and Europe, have indoctrinated, to date, literally thousands of project managers, engineers, contractors, equipment suppliers, and other project stakeholders in the precepts and principles of *Project Bottom-Line Success!*